VIRGIL IN THE RENAISSANCE

The disciplines of classical scholarship were established in their modern form between 1300 and 1600, and Virgil was a test case for many of them. This book is concerned with what became of Virgil in this period, how he was understood, and how his poems were recycled. What did readers assume about Virgil in the long decades between Dante and Sidney, Petrarch and Spenser, Boccaccio and Ariosto? Which commentators had the most influence? What story, if any, was Virgil's *Eclogues* supposed to tell? What was the status of his *Georgics*? Which parts of his epic attracted the most imitators? Building on specialized scholarship of the last hundred years, this book provides a panoramic synthesis of what scholars and poets from across Europe believed they could know about Virgil's life and poetry.

DAVID SCOTT WILSON-OKAMURA received his Ph.D. from the University of Chicago. He is an Associate Professor of English at East Carolina University.

VIRGIL IN THE RENAISSANCE

DAVID SCOTT WILSON-OKAMURA

East Carolina University

CAMBRIDGE UNIVERSITY PRESS
Cambridge, New York, Melbourne, Madrid, Cape Town, Singapore,
São Paulo, Delhi, Dubai, Tokyo, Mexico City

Cambridge University Press
The Edinburgh Building, Cambridge CB2 8RU, UK

Published in the United States of America by Cambridge University Press, New York

www.cambridge.org
Information on this title: www.cambridge.org/9780521198127

© David Scott Wilson-Okamura 2010

This publication is in copyright. Subject to statutory exception
and to the provisions of relevant collective licensing agreements,
no reproduction of any part may take place without the written
permission of Cambridge University Press.

First published 2010

Printed in the United Kingdom at the University Press, Cambridge

A catalogue record for this publication is available from the British Library

Library of Congress Cataloguing in Publication data
Wilson-Okamura, David Scott, 1970–
Virgil in the Renaissance / David Scott Wilson-Okamura.
p.   cm.
ISBN 978-0-521-19812-7 (hardback)
1. Virgil – Appreciation – Europe.   2. Virgil – Influence.   3. European literature – Renaissance,
1450–1600 – Classical influences.   4. Literature, Medieval – Classical influences.   5. Authors and
readers – Europe – History – To 1500.   6. Authors and readers – Europe – History –
16th century.   I. Title.
PA6825.W537   2010
873′.01–dc22
2010000070

ISBN 978-0-521-19812-7 Hardback

Cambridge University Press has no responsibility for the persistence or
accuracy of URLs for external or third-party internet websites referred to
in this publication, and does not guarantee that any content on such
websites is, or will remain, accurate or appropriate.

Multa renascentur quae iam cecidere, cadentque quae nunc sunt in honore . . .

Contents

Illustrations	*page* x
Acknowledgements	xi
Texts and abbreviations	xii
Introduction	1
Method	3
Lacunae	6
Models	8
Plan	10
PART I PUBLICATION	13
1 Virgil with an *i*	15
Poliziano's proof	15
How they reacted to Poliziano's bombshell	18
The market for Virgil editions and commentaries	20
The state of publishing in England; or Did the Reformation make any difference?	27
Servius and Donatus: the authority of antiquity	31
Landino vs. Badius: originality vs. utility	35
Valeriano: the scholarly argument for *i*	37
Innovation vs. influence	40
Latin: dead language or living?	42
PART II REPUTATION	45
2 Patronage and the *Eclogues*	47
The idea of Virgil and its ancient sources	47
How Virgil got rich	50
Virgil as counselor to the prince	54
Eclogues as encomia	56

	Was Virgil a flatterer?	59
	Maecenas as the model patron	60
	Darkness invisible	64
	Imitating Theocritus: the bookishness of Virgilian pastoral	66
	Love among the shepherds	69
	Christian prophecy and Epicureanism	70
	Variety and the low style	73
3	Variety and the *Georgics*	77
	The ancient tradition of Virgil's erudition	78
	Science or poetry?	81
	Labor and the plow	82
	Looking for the *Georgics* in Renaissance poetry	83
	"Ille ego qui quondam"	85
	Generic substitution	87
	A spectrum of styles	89
	The myth of Virgil's Wheel	90
	Style and genre	91
	Style and variety	93
	Listing variety	95
	Virgil as second Nature	96
4	Morals and minimalism	101
	Virgil the reviser	101
	Style and character	103
	Virgil's chastity	106
	Rumors about Virgil's sex life	108
	Nisus and Euryalus	109
	Virgil's gay eclogue	113
	Defense by forgery	115
	Perfect poetry	119
	Virgil and Ennius	120
	Virgil as imitator of Homer	124
	Refining Homer	128
	Brevity as chastity	129
	Defenders of Homer against Virgil	132
	Why brevity is better	134
	Style: Virgil's last stand	138

PART III INTERPRETATION   143

5	Virgil's Odyssey	145
	Prioritizing episodes	145
	Troy in the Odyssey	146

The weight of the underworld	149
The Gates of Sleep	153
Descent by murder	157
Character by example	163
Pluto's daughter: hell as riches	166
Mourir, c'est facile: hell as habit	170
Life in hell	172
Purgatory	173
"Sinfull mire": the moral status of matter	178
Resurrection	181
Imitation: competition or assimilation?	185
Dynastic prophecy	187

6 Virgil's Iliad   191
   Turnus as tragic hero   191
   Modern relativism   194
   Defining *pietas*   196
   Weighing anger   199
   Organizing interpretation I: classroom techniques   203
   Organizing interpretation II: the ideal man theory   208
   Organizing interpretation III: repetition and rereading   212
   Six-book readers vs. twelve-book readers   215
   The renaissance of Virgil's Iliad   220
   Camilla   227
   The modernity of romance   230
   Dido and Lavinia: the importance of *Eneas*   233
   Vegio's sequel: the missing link with the Middle Ages   237
   Vegio's influence   247

   Epilogue   248

Appendix A   *Virgil commentaries in Latin editions, 1469–1599*   252
Appendix B   *Virgil commentaries ranked by number of printings*   267
Index   282

Illustrations

1 Virgil and Ovid: Latin texts and commentaries published in France, 1469–1599   *page* 22
2 Geography of printed editions   34
3 Geography of new commentaries   34
4 Prompted by Venus (viz., beauty), Aeneas woos Lavinia   244
5 Lavinia's wooing and wedding feast   246

Acknowledgements

My cup is full. This book was written with the aid of several institutions: the University of Chicago, the Mellon Foundation, the Newberry Library, Macalester College, the Bibliothèque Nationale de France (through its Gallica collection), the Rare Book Library of Duke University, the Rare Book Collection of the University of North Carolina at Chapel Hill, and the Thomas Harriott College of Arts and Sciences at East Carolina University. Special thanks are due to Sarah Stanton, Sarah Roberts, and Rebecca Jones of Cambridge University Press; my copy-editor Caroline Howlett; and two anonymous readers. I am grateful to the many friends, classmates, colleagues, and teachers who answered questions, commented on drafts, made gifts of their books, and offered fellowship: Joel Baer, David Bevington, Garth Bond, April Brewer, Jean R. Brink, Colin Burrow, Nina E. Cannizzaro, Alan Cottrell, Raymond J. Cormier, my research assistant LeAnna Cox, Jeff Dolven, Charles Fantazzi, Robert Fehrenbach, Julia Haig Gaisser, Mario Geymonat, John Given, Timothy C. Graham, Peter Green, Andrew Hadfield, A. C. Hamilton, Richard F. Hardin, Peter C. Herman, Thomas Herron, Leofranc Holford-Strevens, Craig Kallendorf, Carol V. Kaske, Arthur Kinney, Christopher Kleinhenz, Roger Kuin, Elisabeth Leedham-Green, Allen Mandelbaum, Stuart McDougal, Scott McGill, David Lee Miller, Jerry Leath Mills, Janel Mueller, James Nohrnberg, Jim O'Hara, Wendy Olmsted, William Oram, Anthony Papalas, Adrian Pay, Lee Piepho, Joshua Phillips, Tanya Pollard, Anne Lake Prescott, Michael C. J. Putnam, Thomas P. Roche, Jr., Frank Romer, Charles Ross, Sarah Skwire, Andrew Smyth, John Stevens, Richard Strier, Sandra Tawake, Bart van Es, Matteo Venier, and Jan M. Ziolkowski. In particular I wish to thank W. R. Johnson, Joshua Scodel, my classmate Greg Kneidel, and Michael Murrin, *il mar di tutto 'l senno*. I am especially grateful to my in-laws, Arnold and Patricia Okamura, and my learned wife, Tricia Wilson-Okamura, who labored with me on the index. This book is dedicated to my parents, Ralph and Jean Wilson.

Texts and abbreviations

Virgil's works are cited from *P. Virgilii Maronis Opera* ... (Venice: Heirs of Luca Antonio Giunta, 1544), facsimile repr., The Renaissance and the Gods, 2 vols. (New York: Garland, 1976), as are the *Supplementum* of Maffeo Vegio; the life of Virgil by Aelius Donatus; and the Virgil commentaries of Marius Servius Honoratus, Tiberius Claudius Donatus, Pierio Valeriano, Agostino Dati, Antonio Mancinelli, and Jodocus Badius Ascensius; in the notes, this edition is cited as "Giunta 1544." The Bible is cited from *The Geneva Bible: A Facsimile of the 1560 Edition* (Madison: University of Wisconsin Press, 1969). Except in the appendices, where Latin names are used throughout, the names of Renaissance authors are given in whatever form seems familiar now: hence "Jodocus Badius Ascensius" for "Josse Bade van Asche," but "Cristoforo Landino" instead of "Christophorus Landinus." Abbreviations, with the exception of *&*, have been silently expanded. Translations are mine except where otherwise noted.

Aen.	*Aeneid.*
Ecl.	*Eclogues.*
ECE	*Elizabethan Critical Essays*, ed. G. Gregory Smith, 2 vols. (London: Oxford University Press, 1904). Repr. 1937.
FQ	Edmund Spenser, *The Faerie Queene*, ed. A. C. Hamilton, 2nd edn. (Harlow: Pearson, Longman, 2001).
Geo.	*Georgics.*
Giunta 1544	*P. Virgilii Maronis Opera* ... (Venice: Heirs of Luca Antonio Giunta, 1544), facsimile repr., The Renaissance and the Gods, 2 vols. (New York: Garland, 1976).
GL	Torquato Tasso, *Gerusalemme liberata* (1582), ed. Lanfranco Caretti (1971; repr. Turin: Einaudi, 1993).
OF	Ludovico Ariosto, *Orlando furioso* (1532), ed. Cesare Segre, I Meridiani (Vicenza: Mondadori, 1976).

OI	Matteo Maria Boiardo, *Orlando innamorato* (1482, 1494), ed. Giuseppe Anceschi, I Grandi Libri, 2 vols. (Milan: Garzanti, 1978).
SC	Edmund Spenser, *The Shepheardes Calender*, in *The Shorter Poems*, ed. Richard A. McCabe (London: Penguin, 1999).
STC	A. W. Pollard and G. R. Redgrave, *A Short-Title Catalogue of Books printed in England, Scotland, & Ireland and of English Books Printed Abroad, 1475–1640*, 2nd edn., rev. W. A. Jackson, F. S. Ferguson, and Katharine F. Pantzer, 3 vols. (London: Bibliographical Society, 1986–91), supplemented by *English Short Title Catalogue* [database], Online, British Library and North American Center for ESTC, 1997.
Supp.	Maphaeus Vegius, *Libri XII Aeneidos supplementum* (1428), in Giunta 1544.
VT	Jan M. Ziolkowski and Michael C. J. Putnam (eds.), *The Virgilian Tradition: The First Fifteen Hundred Years* (New Haven: Yale University Press, 2008). Where two page numbers are provided (e.g., "279/280"), the first number indicates a Latin original, the second an English translation.

Introduction

> Do not let me hear
> Of the wisdom of old men, but rather of their folly.
> T. S. Eliot, *East Coker*

What did poets in the Renaissance know – or think they knew – about Virgil, and how did they interpret his major poems? It is an important question: for students of Spenser, Tasso, Ronsard, and Ariosto, because Virgil was the poet they all imitated; and for classicists, because this period was a pivotal one in the history of their field. The disciplines as we know them today, of archaeology, paleography, epigraphy, numismatics, and textual criticism, all date from the Renaissance, and Virgil was a test case for most of them. Piety aside, and scholarship too, what became of Virgil in the Renaissance – how he was received and how his poems were recycled – is an instance of something that occurs to every classic when it outlives its original context: when the institutions of religious and civil life from which it drew inspiration, and to which it gave substance in return, recede from it like the waters of a dying sea. The text becomes stranded. The words remain, but in the absence of institutions their meaning becomes unsponsored – until they are buoyed up once more on new tides, of new ideas and new institutions.

It is a rich tale and strange, even for one poet, and when that poet is Virgil, a central author in the European tradition, the interest – and the intricacy – are both magnified. The goal of this book is to chart the big picture: to construct a map of the whole field, which students can use and scholars can argue with. For the Middle Ages, this was done more than a hundred years ago by Domenico Comparetti. His *Virgilio nel medio evo* was the first major work of scholarship on Virgil's post-classical, pre-Enlightenment reception and, when non-specialists want to gesture at the subject, it is still the one book that everyone has heard of. Published in 1872 and translated in 1895, its errors have been chastened, its omissions supplied, but it has never been replaced.¹ There are better books, but none with the same breadth.²

There ought to have been a sequel, *Virgil in the Renaissance*. Vladimiro Zabughin came close, with *Vergilio nel Rinascimento italiano da Dante a Torquato Tasso: fortuna, studi, imitazioni, traduzioni e parodie, iconografia* (1921, 1923). Zabughin is more reliable than Comparetti, and there is still much in his two volumes that is not available elsewhere. Zabughin did not succeed, however, in writing the companion to Comparetti. He restricted himself to figures in Italy and he was never translated. Since Zabughin there have been many specialized studies, of which the most important are Craig Kallendorf's books on reception and epideictic rhetoric, book production in Venice, readership in Venice and, most recently, pessimistic readings of the *Aeneid* in the Renaissance which seem to anticipate the Harvard school.³ Kallendorf's basic tool is the case study, in the tradition of Arnaldo Momigliano and Anthony Grafton.

This book has different aims and, where appropriate, different methods. Without skimping on particulars, it is meant to be panoramic: a survey, in the best sense, of what readers across Europe thought about Virgil and the meaning of his poems. For Virgil in painting and sculpture, there is already an excellent overview,⁴ but on the literary side there is still room, even need, for synthesis: not just for summary, but for stepping back, taking stock, seeing trends. What did poets in the Renaissance believe about Virgil, and when they wrote poems modeled on his, what did they think they were imitating?

These are big questions. The answers proposed here, even if they find acceptance, are sure to be debated, modified, and (in some cases) abandoned. That is how scholarship progresses. In what follows, I have done my best to be accurate. But accuracy, by itself, is not enough: of embroidery and elaboration there is no end. What's required at this stage is structure.

---

¹ See Jan M. Ziolkowski, "The Making of Domenico Comparetti's *Vergil in the Middle Ages*," in *Vergil in the Middle Ages*, trans. E. F. M. Benecke (repr. Princeton: Princeton University Press, 1997), pp. vii–xxxvii.

² Cf. W. P. Ker, *Epic and Romance: Essays on Medieval Literature* (London, 1896); the scholarship is very dated, but for coverage it still has no equal.

³ See my review of Craig Kallendorf, *Virgil and the Myth of Venice: Books and Readers in the Italian Renaissance* (Oxford: Clarendon Press, 1999) in *Modern Philology* 100 (2002), 75–79. Kallendorf's *The Other Virgil: "Pessimistic" Readings of the* Aeneid *in Early Modern Culture* (Oxford: Clarendon Press, 2007) is a sequel.

⁴ Bernadette Pasquier, *Virgile illustré de la renaissance à nos jours en France et en Italie* (Paris: Touzot, 1992); see also Werner Suerbaum, *Handbuch der illustrierten Vergil-Ausgaben, 1502–1840* (Hildesheim: Olms, 2008).

METHOD

There have been scores if not centuries of books on Renaissance epic, most of which begin with a chapter on what the classical poets, Virgil especially, really meant. There is no such chapter here, not to be coy or disguise any bias, but because, for our purpose, it doesn't matter what Virgil actually meant, much less what this reader thinks about him. Too many books on the reception of classical authors have been spoilt by tracing the scholar's preferred explanation of the text through the ages, until it becomes revealed in its full glory by the scholar himself, his teacher, or his school. A sure symptom is when scholars praise authors in the Renaissance for being ahead of their time. It is usually better, though, not to worry overmuch about separating the wheat from the tares, the progressive ideas about Virgil from the dead ends of literary scholarship. Once we start, it is too easy to dismiss an idea, simply because it doesn't appeal to us or conform with our expectations. Poets, moreover, have been known to use those dead ends, while the correct notions that we cherish in our bosom were gathering dust in disregard, spending their sweetness on the desert air. The important thing, for understanding poetry based on Virgil, is the idea of Virgil in the mind of the poet imitating him: not what Virgil wrote, necessarily, but what Virgil seemed to intend, to that poet.

In the twentieth century, the concept of authorial intention became suspect to many critics. Fortunately for us, the death of the author did not occur until after the great Renaissance poets had already written their masterpieces. The scholars they read discuss intention directly and without embarrassment.[5] Renaissance readers did not always agree about what Virgil's intention was, but they assumed he had one, and they recorded it in writing: through letters, marginalia, printed commentaries, treatises on literary theory, and lectures on literary criticism. To some degree, the poetry that they wrote in imitation of Virgil is also a record of interpretation,[6] but that kind of evidence is hard to use, because imitations were supposed to overgo or even correct their sources. For example, how can we tell when Tasso is interpreting Virgil, and when he is trying to supersede him? We can read Tasso's prose, but some critics do not trust even that. In what follows,

---

[5] Examples will follow. For the history of *intentio* as a category in literary criticism, see A. J. Minnis, *Medieval Theory of Authorship: Scholastic Literary Attitudes in the Later Middle Ages* (London: Scolar, 1984), chs. 1 and 3.
[6] See Charles Martindale, *Redeeming the Text: Latin Poetry and the Hermeneutics of Reception* (Cambridge University Press, 1993), chs. 2–3.

then, imitations are restricted to illustrating how an interpretation could be used, not invoked as evidence for its existence.

When I first began writing about this subject, my primary aim was to avoid anachronism. For example, when quoting a classical text, I made a point of using a Renaissance edition whenever possible. The Loeb of Virgil is not a bad translation or even a bad text, but when Spenser composed *The Faerie Queene*, the Loeb Classical Library did not exist. For classicists, OCT and Teubner editions are more respectable, but they didn't exist either. In practice, it matters less for Virgil's text, which has been relatively stable over the centuries, than for authors who were lost during the Middle Ages and whose texts were retrieved, often in corrupt or mutilated form, during the lifetimes of Petrarch and Poggio. Catullus is now a well-known example,[7] and Quintilian should be. Reading them in Renaissance editions, one admires the tenacity of those early scholars who must have struggled through them, and raises at the same time a prayer of thanks for the editors who came afterward and made the texts readable again for mortals such as ourselves. If we want to read the same classics that our poets read, and especially if we want to make arguments about word choice or even verb tense, we need to read them in the bad, old, beautifully printed, sometimes horribly corrupt editions that Ariosto and Ronsard would have owned and studied. This is even more true for authors whose texts have been reduced in size by recent scholarship. I shall say more on this in Chapter 2, when we consider Aelius Donatus, whose *Life of Virgil* was longer in the Renaissance, more corrupt, and more colorful.

Most of the time, in practice, it makes no difference. Still, we have to check. Even when the authors are ancient, we can never be sure what they "said" in the Renaissance unless we consult them in a Renaissance edition or, for Greek authors such as Aristotle, a Latin translation from the Renaissance (since that would be the form that most readers absorbed him in).

As a rule, printers gave more care to proofreading classical texts than commentaries. Since the prose of commentaries is usually straightforward, a sentence that is unintelligible is often a sign of corruption. The problem can frequently be solved by comparing another edition (preferably an independent one) of the same commentary. Sometimes, though, the corruption is not obvious; or the printer has shortened the commentary, and a later edition is not complete. The best practice, therefore, is to compare several editions, preferably with a range of dates, for every quotation. That is

---

[7] See Julia Haig Gaisser, *Catullus and His Renaissance Readers* (Oxford: Clarendon Press, 1993), ch. 1.

getting easier now that libraries are digitizing their old books and putting them online; we must do what we can with the tools that are available.

Textual anachronism (i.e., quoting classical texts from an edition that didn't exist yet) is something that can and should be avoided. But what about interpretations: can they be anachronistic as well and, if so, should they be eliminated? There are many articles and books on Renaissance epic which assume that the meaning of Virgil's text is self-evident and stable through time: that of course Ariosto, because he is intelligent, would have understood Virgil in the same, intelligent way that we do. Formulated that way, the assumption is patently ridiculous. If we read Ovid or Virgil in the editions and with the commentaries that Ariosto would probably have used, we will quickly find that some interpretations which we take for granted have not, in fact, always been obvious.[8]

However, just because it wasn't part of the scholarly tradition yet doesn't mean an interpretation was "unthinkable" by Ariosto. As Richard Strier argues, "We must strive to see traditional works against the backdrop of their traditions, not as merging indistinguishably into them."[9] Kallendorf's most recent book, *The Other Virgil*, gives numerous examples of scholars and especially poets who broke ranks with their contemporaries and read Virgil in ways that are similar to our own.[10]

What use, then, is researching the traditional interpretations if they weren't binding on poets? There is some value, first, in reminding ourselves that what seems, in our own limited circles (whether of conversation, colleagues, scholarship, or merely century) obvious, permanent, and unarguable is actually contingent, temporary, and hypothetical. By loosening our grip on the obvious, we become receptive to, capable of alternatives.

What the old commentaries are really good for, I have concluded, is not excluding "unthinkable" readings – what Rosemond Tuve called "'illegal' critical practices ... and 'illegitimate' readings"[11] – but for uncovering what I think of as the "unguessables." There are some interpretations so perverse they would never have occurred to most of us in a hundred years of concentrated cerebration: for example, the bizarre notion discussed in Chapter 5 that Aeneas actually murdered one of his shipmates in order to propitiate demons. If we were separating the wheat from the tares, that would be one of the tares, surely. Yet this particular tare seems to have

---

[8] See Daniel Javitch, "Rescuing Ovid from the Allegorizers," *Comparative Literature* 30 (1978), 97–107; and Javitch, "The *Orlando Furioso* and Ovid's Revision of the *Aeneid*," *MLN* 99 (1984), 1023–36.
[9] Richard Strier, *Resistant Structures: Particularity, Radicalism, and Renaissance Texts* (Berkeley and Los Angeles: University of California Press, 1995), p. 25.
[10] Kallendorf, *The Other Virgil*. [11] Qtd. in Strier, *Resistant Structures*, p. 17.

rooted itself in the receptive soil of Petrarch's brain; ergo, it is useful to know about, even if we ourselves don't make bread with it.

Finding out what people did not think – proving a negative – is often impossible. As we shall see in Chapter 1, the amount of commentary that Virgil's text generated in the Renaissance was and is genuinely overwhelming, even if we ignore materials in manuscript. Even after years of study, the most one can usually say about an opinion is, "It wasn't *widely* held" or "It wasn't mentioned by any of the more *popular* commentators." Usually, though, we don't start that way, looking for a negative. Ordinarily the only way we notice what the commentators *don't* talk about is by actively looking for something and not finding it. It's a frustrating experience, but if we can let go of what we "know" about Virgil – of what we think the commentators ought to have said – it can also be an opportunity. When absence acquires an outline, when darkness becomes visible, the vacua stand out, like black holes in a sea of stars. We can regard them as opacities, obstacles to a desired conclusion; or, if we have grace to use them so, as information, clues. Sometimes it is the voids that reveal most dramatically what is different. A couple of examples are the category of Hellenistic poetry, which did not exist in the Renaissance (and which I touch on in Chapter 1), and the anger of Aeneas, about which there is less to say in Chapter 6 than one might wish. We can complain about the thickheadedness of our ancestors or (what is worse) we can leverage some little scrap of evidence to mean something we approve of. But that is partisanship, not scholarship. Better to ask, when we don't find what we were looking for, what there is instead, and resolve to become interested in that.

LACUNAE

In my account there will be some absences as well. A few of these are more apparent than real. Dido, for example, does not have her own chapter. She could have: in just the last fifteen years, there have been at least three major books on Dido all by herself.[12] What I have to say original about Dido has already been published elsewhere, and this allows me to be briefer here.[13] Also, Dido has a way of taking books over. With poems as rich as Virgil's, it

---

[12] Marilynn Desmond, *Reading Dido: Gender, Textuality, and the Medieval* Aeneid (Minneapolis: University of Minnesota Press, 1994); John Watkins, *The Specter of Dido: Spenser and Virgilian Epic* (New Haven: Yale University Press, 1995); Paola Bono and M. Vittoria Tessitore, *Il mito di Didone: avventure di una regina tra secoli e culture* (Milan: Mondadori, 1998).

[13] David Scott Wilson-Okamura, "Virgilian Models of Colonization in Shakespeare's *Tempest*," *ELH* 70 (2003), 709–37.

is impossible to talk about all of the episodes in a meaningful way. Instead, the discussion here is organized around problems, with episodes indexed at the back. This is why, for example, there are many pages on the underworld (in Chapter 5) and only several on Turnus (in Chapter 6). In the Renaissance, Turnus was a problem, but the underworld was an even bigger problem. With some episodes, such as Carthage, the discussion is spread over several chapters. In Chapter 1, I assess Landino's theory that Dido represents political ambition; in Chapter 5, her role as obstacle or temptation; and in Chapter 6, her role as foil for Lavinia.

Some terms are missing as well. I am grateful to Gérard Genette for coining the term *paratext*; nothing has done more to popularize the study of prefaces, woodcuts, marginalia, and commentary than giving them a collective existence and an exotic new name.[14] With the vocabulary, though, comes a theory of reading which I can subscribe to only half-heartedly, that the paratext is a kind of frame or threshold (*seuil*) which mediates between reader and text. As a teacher I've observed that readers frequently bypass the frame, by skipping introductions, ignoring footnotes, in extreme cases even by crossing out what they disagree with. I myself, for example, almost never read Spenser's dedicatory sonnets en route to *The Faerie Queene*. (It was different, I imagine, for the original dedicatees.) Sometimes the paratext is a threshold, and sometimes it is just extra paper. Here is another reason not to be doctrinaire about what kinds of interpretations were "thinkable" in the Renaissance: for someone who doesn't read what he's supposed to, almost anything is thinkable.

Another omission in this book is reception theory, or at least the theory most scholars are familiar with. The project of the Konstanz School, as represented by Wolfgang Iser and Hans Robert Jauss, is to validate reading as a form of co-authorship. This is something, as Jauss points out, that critics have been doing for many centuries.[15] I am not trying, though, to rehabilitate the old readings, so much as argue for their importance in understanding old poetry. Idiotic or insightful does not matter: if an idea about Virgil had currency in the Renaissance, then we want to know about it, not so we can honor it (necessarily), but to interpret the poems, such as *Orlando furioso* and *The Faerie Queene*, that were formed under its influence. It is hard when writing reception history not to congratulate the old

---

[14] The word first appears in Genette's *Palimpsestes: la littérature au second degré* (Paris: Seuil, 1982), p. 93; *Seuils* (Paris: Seuil, 1987) develops the concept and gives examples.
[15] Hans Robert Jauss, "The Theory of Reception: A Retrospective of its Unrecognized Prehistory," in *Literary Theory Today*, ed. Peter Collier and Helga Geyer-Ryan (Ithaca: Cornell University Press, 1990), pp. 53–73.

commentators when they agree with us or, when they miss a seemingly obvious point, to curse their blind spots. But I have not tried to adjudicate between what I called a moment ago dead ends and what, looking back, seems progressive in Renaissance scholarship. This book is meant to be a survey of what poets in the Renaissance knew about Virgil, not a scorecard.

The last outleaving is *early modern*. This is handy, in place of *Renaissance*, when the rhythm of a sentence calls for an extra syllable, but in this book I have decided to avoid the term for three reasons. First, for our subject, the term *Renaissance* is more precise. Admittedly not everything that happened during the Renaissance was part of the Renaissance. Whatever it became, though, the Renaissance began as a movement in classical scholarship, and this book is about that movement. Second, *rinascimento*, "rebirth," is a term that was actually used in the Renaissance, whereas no one in any period has ever called him- or herself "early modern." If we want to understand an earlier period, it is helpful to employ at least some of the period's own vocabulary. Finally, I want to save the word *modern* for what seemed *modernus*, "timely," in the Renaissance itself. At one level, nothing had really changed: as we shall see, the idea of Virgil that was current in the sixteenth century is largely the same one as was current in the fourth and fourteenth centuries. This continuity – of classical, medieval, and Renaissance scholarship – is one of the book's two main theses. The second, not quite incompatible thesis is that some things at least seemed new. There were new manuscripts, new technologies, and, in poetry, a new ethos. Love, no less than war, was a subject that readers in the sixteenth century demanded from an epic, and this was felt to be modern, even though the taste for it had been developing since the High Middle Ages; I shall say more on this in Chapter 6.

MODELS

If classical scholarship is a dry subject sometimes, the history of classical scholarship can be positively arid. Following the example of Anthony Grafton, I have done what I can, especially in Chapter 1, to flesh out its actors. It is not necessary, for example, to know that Pierio Valeriano, a key figure in our story, also composed – in addition to works on iconography and textual criticism – a *Declamation in Favor of Bearded Priests* (1531). But these learned people, some of them, were also quite lively. Following Grafton again, I have not refrained from retelling some of the old stories that seemingly everyone has heard. A book that did refrain would be shorter, more knowing, and have a narrower audience. I do assume, on the part of my readers, a knowledge of the *Aeneid* and an interest in Renaissance poetry. For the Renaissance epics, I do not give plot summaries, but most of what I say will be intelligible even to someone who has not read them yet; at least, it would be strange if someone finished this book and did not absorb something of their substance. Here my model was C. S. Lewis, who by writing about *The Faerie Queene* made me want to read it.

This is an academic book, with footnotes. I have tried, nevertheless, to imitate certain popular historians, Barbara Tuchman, Norman Cantor, and Jacques Barzun. They did not deliver the last words in any of their respective fields, but they did not neglect, either, the scholar's task of striving, in spite of difficulty and without dismissing details, to grasp their subjects as a whole. They were not satisfied, as we say now, merely to "complicate" the discussion. They did not say everything they knew, or cite everything they had read, merely to show they had read it.

In choosing examples, I have cast a wide net. It would, I recognize, be possible and even desirable to compose a book about Virgil in the Renaissance by writing a chapter on each of the major poets who imitated him; that would have the advantage of specificity. But it would still leave many gaps. The alternative is to read as much and as widely as one can, and to identify what seems normal, central, common: "following," as Descartes says in his third *Discourse on Method*, "the most temperate opinions and the ones most distant from excess which are commonly received." Findings collected on this basis ought to be usable, not just for a handful of major poets, but for many minor poets as well. A byproduct of this procedure is that national differences are going to seem less evident than international trends. There was not, so far as I have found, an English Virgil distinct from an Italian or French Virgil. The underworld, for example, has the same range of meanings in Spenser as it does in Petrarch, Boiardo, Ronsard, and Ariosto. As we shall see in Chapter 1, poets in England used the same editions and the same commentators as poets in France and Italy. This is not to say that no one will ever discover national as well as international trends in Virgil's influence and reputation: under the microscope, even the smoothest plain will be seen to have ridges. The important thing is to view everything in perspective, and not to mistake ripples for tides.

To some, the focus on what was normal will seem boring, if not actually misbegotten. The history of classical scholarship, as an academic discipline, goes back to the eighteenth century, since when it has always been told in the form of highlights, as a series of turning points. That is both economical and dramatic. But most readers of Virgil, even most poets, have not been great or even good classical scholars. They knew Latin, but their libraries were small. We are daunted sometimes by their learning, but their canon, even of classical texts, was not the same as ours. There was more Mantuan, less Homer, and (in England) almost no Dante. The plays of Sophocles and Aeschylus were available in print, but there were no early translations and only very advanced scholars could penetrate their still formidable language. Your first-year university student, with no Latin and less Greek, probably knows more about what is in *Oedipus Rex* than Spenser, Christopher Marlowe, Ben Jonson, and Shakespeare combined.

The task of this book is to discover what was widely known about Virgil, not just what could be known by specialists. In order to learn what commentaries were available and how frequently they appeared, I have relied on library catalogues and printed bibliographies. The best of these, as it happens, do not extend beyond 1599: this provides us with a *terminus ad quem* and precludes, unfortunately, any serious treatment of Dryden or Milton. As I shall show in Chapter 5, there is so much continuity with the ancient and medieval idea of Virgil that fixing a *terminus a quo* is less important.

PLAN

This book has three parts. Part I, Publication, uses the controversy over how to spell Virgil's name in order to survey the conditions of both classical scholarship and academic publishing. In its own way, it makes a small contribution to the history of the book, by tabulating (for one, canonical author) production over time and space. But the main purpose of the chapter is to establish which commentaries on Virgil were printed most often, and which commentaries were printed over the longest period. Without this knowledge, we could spend the rest of this book, and maybe the rest of our lives, reading randomly in rare, beautiful, and expensive books that had almost no impact. Along the way, we shall make a distinction between innovation in classical scholarship and actual influence.

Part II, Reputation, has three chapters: patronage, variety, and refinement. What was Virgil's image as a poet? What were his specialties? Where was he vulnerable to criticism? What was his relationship with Augustus? To which school of philosophy did he subscribe? How did he compare with previous Latin poets? With Homer? Was Virgil homosexual? While we are answering these questions, we shall also establish the parameters of interpretation for Virgil's *Eclogues* (in Chapter 2) and his *Georgics* (in Chapter 3).

Part III, Interpretation, has two chapters, one for each half of the *Aeneid*. The challenge here is to place episodes in perspective. For the first half, this is easy: everything leads to the underworld. For the second half, there is heated discussion about the death of Turnus, but no one episode that dominates interpretation. This raises a question about the history of reading: how organized was classroom instruction, and did students come away from the *Aeneid* with anything more than a jumble of episodes? We shall also address what is still the major problem in Renaissance epic as a genre: how did married love become central, when in Virgil it seems peripheral? To answer the question, we will go back to twelfth-century France and then forward again to Italy in the fifteenth century, when a young drop-out from law school, Maffeo Vegio, composed a sequel to the *Aeneid* which became an international bestseller for the next two hundred years.

I conclude with an epilogue about style.

PART I

Publication

CHAPTER I

Virgil with an i

> And how the same inexorable price must still be paid for the same great purchase.
> Walt Whitman, "Beginners"

Vergil or Virgil? The correct answer, as any Latinist can tell, is that the poet spelled his own name with an *e*: Vergilius. Where did the *i* come in? A scribe, taking dictation, hears the word *Vergilius* (which he has never seen before), and writes down the word *Virgilius*, which sounds right and starts in a familiar way, with the Latin word for *man*. Or perhaps he thinks of *virgo*, "virgin," because Virgil was nicknamed *Parthenias*, "the virgin"; or of *virga laurea*, because according to legend Virgil's mother dreamt that she gave birth to a laurel branch; or of *virga populea*, because Virgil's mother is said to have planted a poplar branch to mark his birth-place.[1] There were other stories as well. What concerns us here, though, is not how the confusion began, but why it has persisted.

POLIZIANO'S PROOF

In fact, the question was settled long ago, by a man who is universally recognized as the greatest classical scholar of the fifteenth century. His parents named him Angelo Ambrogini (1454–94), but his readers knew him by his Latin surname, Politianus, on account of his birthplace, Montepulciano. Poliziano, as he is known to us, entered the University of Florence at the age of ten, where he took up the study of Greek. At fifteen, he began to publish a Latin translation of the *Iliad*, which he dedicated to Lorenzo de' Medici (1449–92). Seven years later, he entered the service of Lorenzo as a tutor to his children and began a long poem

---

[1] Aelius Donatus, "P. Virgilii Maronis vita," in Giunta 1544, sig. *ii^r.

on Lorenzo's brother, the famous *Stanze per la giostra* (1475). This was followed in 1479 by *La favola d'Orfeo*, the first pastoral drama in Italian literature and a precursor of the modern opera. So much for his hobbies. What set Poliziano apart from his learned contemporaries was his detailed knowledge, unprecedented and unparalleled, of Latin literature, its Greek models, and the ancient scholia; his sustained interest, not only in Greek literature from the classical period but also from the Hellenistic period (as we now call it); and, most important, his methodical approach to textual criticism: not only collating the extant manuscripts, but organizing them into families.[2] He has been called "the first Italian of the Renaissance who did work of permanent value on a Greek text, so that his name can still be found in the apparatus criticus of a modern edition."[3]

Where possible, Poliziano also used non-literary texts to corroborate the readings of his literary manuscripts, and this was how he arrived at the correct spelling of Virgil's name. "On the question," he begins his little essay on the subject, "of whether we ought to say 'Vergilius' or 'Virgilius,' I observe that the learned are still walking around in circles (*ambigi*)." This is a small point, he admits, but he begs his readers not to get impatient if, like a man wandering on the beach, he sometimes picks up a random shell for his own amusement. "Virgilius," he knows, is the spelling that most people use, but "certain records, of great antiquity" have convinced him that "Vergilius" is preferable. The first of these is not a document but an inscription: "In Bolsena," he says,

> you will find inside the chapel of Christina the Virgin a certain marble table which is in front of St. Peter [of Prague]'s altar; here, in old letters that have almost rubbed off, the word VERGILI is legible. In Sutri you will also find the name "Vergilius" written in the same way on a stone table … Both of these we have inspected closely, and not without several people present. For in the examination of these ancient things we did not wish to be ear-witnesses only, but eye-witnesses as well. The name is also written with an *e* in the original of Justinian's Digest that is preserved in the official archives of Florence. It is the same in the Vergil that is displayed in the inner chambers of the Vatican library, a volume of astonishing antiquity and written out in large characters.[4] There is moreover a commentary by

---

[2] See Anthony Grafton, "Quattrocento Humanism and Classical Scholarship," in *Renaissance Humanism: Foundations, Forms, and Legacy*, ed. Albert Rabil, Jr., 3 vols. (Philadelphia: University of Pennsylvania Press, 1988), vol. III, pp. 23–66.

[3] L. D. Reynolds and N. G. Wilson, *Scribes and Scholars: A Guide to the Transmission of Greek and Latin Literature*, 2nd edn. (Oxford: Clarendon Press, 1974), p. 137.

[4] I.e., what are now called "rustic capitals."

Tiberius Donatus that is now in the hands of Landino, a man of both eloquence and erudition who has been popular in Florence for some time now as a professor of literature. A great deal of the basic material (*rudimenta*) that I picked up in my youth is due to this teacher – I was tempted to say, to this professional colleague, for now his reputation is so firmly and securely established that he befriends even those who labor to compete with him in this race; whatever we ourselves have acquired of praise, he seems to embrace and recognize as his own. Now then, as I was saying, Landino has in his hands a commentary by Tiberius Donatus and this commentary is written in a very large and very old script; in this respect its authority leaves no room for doubt. [The same spelling] is also found in a codex of St. Augustine's *City of God* in the Medici public library and in a codex of Columella from the same family's private library, both of which codices are written out in *literæ langobardæ*. Then there is a very old book of Seneca's letters, access to which was provided to me by Nicolaus Micheloctius, a man of discriminating intellect, from the private things of Lorenzo de' Medici, along with many other volumes of venerable antiquity. On several occasions we have shown either what these things contain, or what they leave out, sometimes to Jacobus Pratensis, our sober companion and research assistant, and sometimes to others who would listen. [Fra Giovanni] Giocondo is a man alone above other mortals, not only for his extreme diligence but also for his undisputed expertise, and in his collection of ancient inscriptions and records that was only just now dedicated to Lorenzo de' Medici, I also come upon the report of two epitaphs which are found among the marbles of Rome, just as Giocondo indicates: TI. VERGILIUS DONATVS and again C. PAPIRIVS CESTVS VERGILIAE OPTATAE VXORI SVAE BENE MERENTI DE SE. And yet, although it is confirmed by records of age-long antiquity (a sufficient defense, I should think), yet reason and the thing itself also bear witness. The term *Vergiliae* ["Pleiades"] is said to come from *verae stellæ* ["true stars"]; the poet's name is correctly derived in the same way, from these very stars, or even from *ver* [spring] – not from *virga laurea*, which is just an old wives' tale found in a not very respectable author, and therefore false. Indeed, many people were named "Vergilius" before the poet was even published. To sum up, where there is either no weightier evidence or no stronger reason, the question is obviously to be settled on the basis of ancient usage (*uetusta ... consuetudine*) rather than recent ignorance (*noua inscitia*), which is where we get this hodgepodge element coming into our languages. Indeed, we most of us in recent times suffer from a clouded vision of the truth (*caligamus ad ueri conspectum*). But to follow up on what's left, the name *Verginius* is also closely allied to this one, and when we recently looked at the carved marble basin in front of the chapel of Santa Maria Maior in Rome, we did not find *Virginius*.[5]

The chapter ends there, with a seeming afterthought. The tone, though, is clipped and haughty: "we" did not find *Virginius*, because the basin was carved when men knew how to spell. But the issue here is more than just

---

[5] *Miscellanea* 1.77, in *Omnia opera* (Venice: Aldo Manuzio, 1498), sig. H^r–Hii^r. Poliziano also discusses the question in his January 1, 1493 letter to Bartolomeo della Scala.

orthography: for Poliziano, misspelling is a form of mental blindness, a vapor or fog (*caligo*). That fog can be dispelled through dedicated research and a willingness to look for evidence in unlikely places: not just in manuscripts, or even monuments, but also on church altars and even a stone basin. Poliziano has a keen eye for romantic details (the "old letters that have almost rubbed off"), and he never misses an opportunity to flaunt his famous connections. Hence the invocations of Lorenzo de' Medici and his family's private book collection; the off-hand allusion to the *intima* of the Vatican library; the emphasis on eyewitness testimony; and the mention of his famous teacher, which is a combination of bragging about his own background (I was instructed by the great Landino) and of putting the older scholar in his place (Landino was learned enough . . . to teach me the preliminaries).[6] In point of fact, though, the boastful, fawning, ungrateful name-dropper was right: Virgil did spell his name with an *e*, and Poliziano had proven it.

HOW THEY REACTED TO POLIZIANO'S BOMBSHELL

Europe yawned – and went on spelling the name as it had always done, with an *i*. Indeed, it is unusual to find it spelled otherwise until the latter half of the nineteenth century; and it is still spelled with an *i* in most of the European vernaculars. What happened? We dwell on this trifle – what Poliziano calls his seashell – because it illustrates some larger points about the peregrinations of information, the publication of classical texts, and the general character of Virgil scholarship in the fifteenth and sixteenth centuries.

Poliziano was, by all accounts, a prodigy and he was not the sort to hide his light under a bushel. Yet in this one thing, Europe closed its ears to him. In trying to understand why, we should not underestimate the force of inertia, combined with sloth and compounded with reverence. Literate men, teachers and students alike, had been spelling *Virgil* with an *i* since the fourth century AD; by the time Poliziano tried to break it, the habit was more than a thousand years old.

But there were more reasons than just habit. One of them was Poliziano's novel method of getting the word out. In previous generations, the normal format for academic publishing was the commentary, which proceeded through a text line by line and often word by word. The most basic commentary was linguistic and simply provided vocabulary; syntax was also explained where necessary, along with references to history, geography,

---

[6] On Poliziano's ambition to outstrip (and outearn) his former teacher, see Anthony Grafton and Lisa Jardine, *From Humanism to the Humanities: Education and the Liberal Arts in Fifteenth- and Sixteenth-Century Europe* (London: Duckworth, 1986), pp. 94–97.

classical religion, and whatever else the commentator happened to know about the subject at hand: etymology, allegory of all kinds, critical reception, manuscript variants, and figures of speech. For the most part, this was also the format of the classroom lecture and, indeed, it was not uncommon for a book to begin as a series of lectures: many of the printed commentaries from this period were actually assembled from the lecture notes of anonymous students.[7] If the dictation service was sometimes unreliable, at least it was free.[8]

The disadvantages of the commentary format were real, though they have been exaggerated.[9] Except for Tiberius Claudius Donatus, the most important commentators on Virgil were all what the ancients called *grammatici*. Marius Servius Honoratus (4th century AD), the most famous of the ancient Virgil commentators, was a *grammaticus*, as was his predecessor Aelius Donatus (4th century AD). Charged with the task of teaching young men how to parse, interpret, and emend classical texts, the *grammaticus* was, by training and tradition, a polymath; his knowledge was sometimes immense, but it was always miscellaneous.[10] Today much of what he knew and was paid to teach could be found in a good college dictionary. But books, even in the age of print, were still relatively expensive. Much of the *grammaticus*'s energy, therefore, was expended on what Poliziano calls, in his left-handed compliment to Landino, the *rudimenta* of education: giving synonyms for hard words, parsing unfamiliar syntax, and explaining that *Tygris* is "a river in Armenia that empties into the Persian gulf" (Servius on *Ecl.* 1.62).

Poliziano shunned such drudgery and determined to apply his talents selectively.[11] Although he gave lecture courses on several classical authors

---

[7] Prior to the invention of movable type, students would sometimes record a lecture in the margins of a hand-written text that had been purchased beforehand from a university stationer; see Craig Kallendorf, *Virgil and the Myth of Venice: Books and Readers in the Italian Renaissance* (Oxford: Clarendon Press, 1999), pp. 44–49.

[8] See Paul F. Grendler, *Schooling in Renaissance Italy: Literacy and Learning, 1300–1600* (Baltimore: Johns Hopkins University Press, 1989), ch. 9; Anthony Grafton, "Renaissance Readers and Ancient Texts: Comments on Some Commentaries," *Renaissance Quarterly* 38 (1985), 615–49; and Grafton and Jardine, *Humanism to the Humanities*, chs. 3 and 4.

[9] See Chapter 6.

[10] See Robert Andrew Kaster, *Guardians of Language: The Grammarian and Society in Late Antiquity* (Berkeley and Los Angeles: University of California Press, 1988); Martin Irvine, *The Making of Textual Culture: Grammatica and Literary Theory 350–1100* (Cambridge University Press, 1994); Gerald Snare, "The Practice of Glossing in Late Antiquity and the Renaissance," *Studies in Philology* 92 (1995), 439–59.

[11] Poliziano did not disdain the title of grammarian, but insisted that a *grammaticus* is more than a mere *grammatista*: a scholar-critic in the tradition of Aristarchus and Zenodotus, not the poor slave who actually teaches boys their vocabulary and morphology. See Aldo Scaglione, "The Humanist as Scholar and Politian's Conception of the *Grammaticus*," *Studies in the Renaissance* 8 (1961), 49–70.

(including Virgil), he never published a commentary.[12] Instead, he adopted the procedure of Aulus Gellius (fl. AD 180) and composed a series of short chapters on one hundred of the most challenging problems in classical philology; Chapter 77 was the brief essay on Virgil's name that we quoted earlier. He called the work *Liber miscellaneorum*. It was, as Anthony Grafton describes it, "a brilliantly original work, which fully deserved to exert widespread influence."[13] And it did exert widespread influence, especially on the methods for editing of classical texts. But it had almost no impact on the way that educated people spell the name of Rome's most honored poet.

THE MARKET FOR VIRGIL EDITIONS AND COMMENTARIES

By abandoning the commentary format, Poliziano freed himself to concentrate on problems that were worthy of his abilities. In the long run, though, he also limited his own influence. He should have published a commentary.

The market for academic odds and ends, even when authored by the prince of classical scholarship himself, was limited. After its initial publication in 1489, *Liber miscellaneorum* was reprinted in 1496, 1508, 1522, and 1550 (with his letters). It also appeared in editions and reprints of his complete *opera* (1498, 1499, 1502, 1512, 1519, 1528, 1533, 1546, 1553). Those are respectable numbers for any book, but the dates are telling: after 1553, the market dries up. In the second half of the sixteenth century, there is still an interest in Poliziano's writings, but what publishers think will sell is not his scholarly work, in Latin, but his poetry, in Italian: his *Stanze* and *Orfeo*.[14]

Writing commentaries may have been, as Grafton says, "donkey-work,"[15] but there was always a market for them. Precisely how many commentaries on Virgil were printed in this period is a question that will be settled only when the *Catalogus translationum et commentarium* publishes its entry for

---

[12] The problem was lack of time, not material. Poliziano lectured extensively and the books that survive from his personal library are often densely annotated in his distinctive handwriting. Some of these annotations have now been edited; see especially *Commento inedito alle* Georgiche *di Virgilio*, ed. Livia Castano Musicò (Florence: Olschki, 1990) and Julia Haig Gaisser, *Catullus and His Renaissance Readers* (Oxford: Clarendon Press, 1993), pp. 42–47, on his Catullus annotations. Virgil is also the subject of seven chapters (37, 39, 59, 71, 77, 89, and 100) in the *Liber miscellaneorum* described below. Additional material on Virgil remains in manuscript; see Alessandro Perosa, *Mostra del Poliziano nella Biblioteca medicea laurenziana* (Florence: Sansoni, 1955), index, s.v. *Virgilio* and *Appendix Vergiliana*.
[13] Grafton, "Quattrocento Humanism," p. 32.
[14] See Giuseppe Sergio Martini, *Catalogo della mostra bibliografica onoranze a Agnolo Poliziano nel v centenario della nascita* (Florence: Giunta, 1954).
[15] Grafton, "Quattrocento Humanism," p. 28.

Virgil.[16] Craig Kallendorf is also working on an exhaustive bibliography, to be issued in two volumes. In the meantime, we can compile some rough statistics by collating the Virgil entries in standard bibliographies and library catalogues, some of which enumerate all of the commentaries printed in a given edition,[17] and some of which do not.[18] Latin, of course, was still the language of scholarship in this period, so our tallies will not include translations.[19] When the numbers have been tabulated, two facts stand out.

First is the priority which early printers assigned to Virgil's works. The chart in Figure 1 shows that from *c.* 1500 onward, French printers consistently produced more Ovid editions than Virgil editions. The same was also true in Italy: in this period Ovid was printed more frequently than any other Roman poet; Virgil was next, followed by Terence and Horace, "in that order."[20] But Figure 1 also shows that, when French printers were deciding which Roman poet to print first, they did not choose Ovid (the popular poet), but Virgil, the so-called prince of poets.[21] This was typical. In 1465, two Germans, Conrad Sweynheym and Arnold Pannartz, crossed the Alps to establish the first printing press in Italy. Four years later, they announced that they were going to publish the classical poets of antiquity, none of

---

[16] *Catalogus translationum et commentarium: Medieval and Renaissance Latin Translations and Commentaries, Annotated Lists and Guides* (Washington: Catholic University of America Press, 1960–). The Virgil entry will represent the combined efforts of six scholars led by Professor Virginia Brown; at last report (in 1993), Brown's team had "identified over 130 different commentaries"; see Kallendorf, "Recent Trends in the Study of Vergilian Influences," in *Vergil*, ed. Kallendorf (New York: Garland, 1993), pp. 1–20, at 4 n. 7; and Mario A. Di Cesare, "Seeking the Renaissance Vergil," in *Bibliography and the Study of 15th-Century Civilisation*, ed. Lotte Hellinga and John Goldfinch (London: British Library, 1987), pp. 185–96.

[17] Kallendorf, *A Bibliography of Venetian Editions of Virgil, 1470–1599* (Florence: Olschki, 1991); Martin Davies and John Goldfinch, *Vergil: A Census of Printed Editions 1469–1500* (London: The Bibliographical Society, 1992).

[18] Christian Gottlob Heyne *et al.*, "Recensus editionum P. Virgilii Maronis" (1775), augmented and corrected in *P. Virgilii Maronis Opera omnia ex editione Heyniana*, 9 vols. (London: A. J. Valpy, 1819), vol. IX, pp. 4401–73 and *Publius Virgilius Mario varietate lectionis et perpetua adnotatione illustratus a Christ. Gottl. Heyne*, 4th edn. rev. Georg P. E. Wagner, 5 vols. (Leipzig: Libraria Hahniana, 1830–41), vol. IV, pp. 635–722; the British Museum short-title catalogues for books printed in France, Germany, Italy, the Netherlands, and Spain before 1600; Giuliano Mambelli, *Gli annali delle edizioni vergiliane* (Florence: Olschki, 1954); A. W. Pollard and G. R. Redgrave, *A Short-Title Catalogue of Books printed in England, Scotland, & Ireland and of English Books Printed Abroad, 1475–1640*, 2nd edn., rev. W. A. Jackson, F. S. Ferguson, and Katharine F. Pantzer, 3 vols. (London: Bibliographical Society, 1986–91); H. M. Adams, *Catalogue of Books Printed on the Continent of Europe, 1501–1600, in Cambridge Libraries*, 2 vols. (Cambridge University Press, 1967); and WorldCat [database], Online Computer Library Center (OCLC), accessed July 30, 1997, search terms: "au:virgil" and "limit years 1450–1600."

[19] See, however, Craig Kallendorf, *A Bibliography of Renaissance Italian Translations of Virgil* (Florence: Olschki, 1994).

[20] A. F. Johnson, "Italian Sixteenth-Century Books," *The Library* 5th ser. 13 (1958), 161–74, at 165.

[21] For a description, see Charles Mortet, *La première édition de Virgile imprimée à Paris, 1470–1472* (Besançon: Jacquin, 1906).

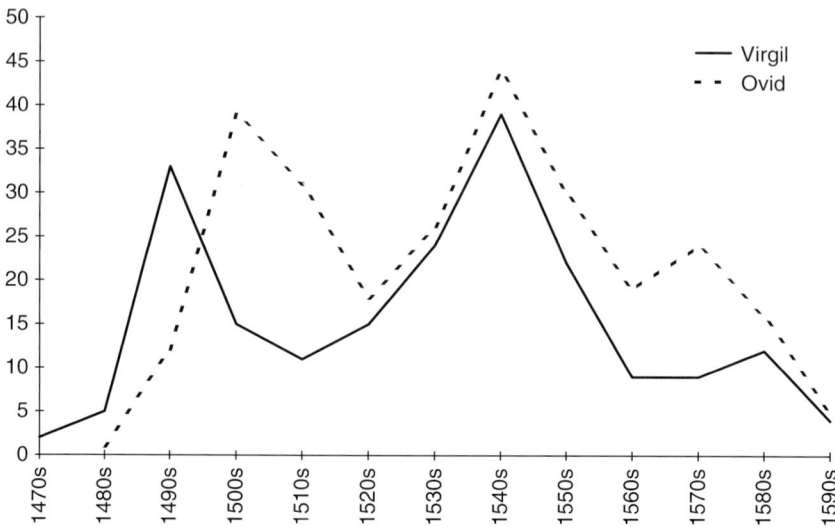

Figure 1. Virgil and Ovid: Latin texts and commentaries published in France, 1469–1599. Statistics for Ovid are derived from Ann Moss, *Ovid in Renaissance France: A Survey of the Latin Editions of Ovid and Commentaries Printed in France before 1600* (London: Warburg Institute, 1982), pp. 63–79.

whom was in print yet. The first volume in the series was an edition of Virgil (Rome, 1469).[22] The commentaries of Servius appeared soon after, perhaps within as little as a year.[23] The works of Ovid, on the other hand, remained in manuscript until 1472. In Brescia, Virgil was not only the first classical poet, he was also the first author to come from the city's presses.[24] Thirty years later, it was hard to find a Latin classic that someone had *not* committed to print,[25] but the principle of "Virgil first" was still operative.

---

[22] See Matteo Venier, *Per una storia del testo di Virgilio nella prima età del libro a stampa (1469–1519)* (Udine: Forum, 2001), pp. 27–38. Six copies are now extant.

[23] *Mauri Seruii grammatici in tria Virgilii Opera expositio* (Rome: Ulrich Han, *c.* 1470). See Davies and Goldfinch, *Census*, p. 121 and Mambelli, *Annali* §4. The longer version of Servius known as Servius Danielis or, more recently, Servius auctus was not widely known, although fragments of it were quoted in the Middle Ages; see Christopher Baswell, *Virgil in Medieval England: Figuring the Aeneid from the Twelfth Century to Chaucer* (Cambridge University Press, 1995), p. 142. With the exception of some notes on Varro that Joseph Scaliger published in 1573, the longer text did not begin to circulate broadly until after 1600, when it was published by the French jurist Pierre Daniel (1530–1603), on whom see Louis Jarry, *Une correspondance littéraire au XVIe siècle: Pierre Daniel ... et les érudits de son temps* (Orléans: Herluison, 1876) and Hermann Hagen, *Étude littéraire & historique sur Pierre Daniel d'Orléans*, trans. Paul de Félice (Orléans: Herluison, 1876).

[24] Davies and Goldfinch, *Census* §13.

[25] The best account is now Howard Jones, *Printing the Classical Text* (Utrecht: Hes & De Graaf, 2004).

In 1501, Aldo Manuzio started a new series of classical authors, printed in the octavo format. Once again, the first volume in the series (which was also the first book printed in Manuzio's new italic typeface, designed by Francesco Griffo) was an edition of Virgil's *opera*. Forty years after that, in 1542, Sébastien Gryphe announced that he was going to publish yet another series of classic poets, in the even more convenient format of sextodecimo (16°); the idea was that perambulating young persons would slip the poets into their pockets. Gryphe said he was starting with Virgil, "just as Aratus, when speaking of the gods, began with Jupiter."[26]

Ovid may have been the most popular poet of the Renaissance, but Virgil was consistently the first poet of the Renaissance. He seems also to have been taught more often and illustrated with more frequency.[27]

The second point that stands out in this preliminary census is the sheer number of books that were in circulation. In the 130-year period between 1469 (when the *editio princeps* of Virgil's works was printed at Rome) and 1599 (when our survey ends), there were approximately 750 print runs of Virgil and Virgil commentaries. This figure includes reprints, which were numerous – and probably some pseudo-reprints that were really just unsold sheets, freshened up with a new title-page. Still, the shape of the data echoes what we already know about the publication of Ovid (graphed in Figure 1). Even if the Virgil figures are not exact, they conform with a known pattern.

What's striking about the pattern is the consistency of its scale. Production of Virgil texts and commentaries increases in some periods, but it never dips below the level it reached in the 1470s (44 editions) until the last decade of the 1500s (when there were "only" 37 editions). Production sometimes exceeded this level, by as much as a factor of two, but even in the off-years the baseline market for Virgil's works was apparently such that it could absorb 4 to 5 new printings every year for more than

---

[26] Qtd. in Alice Hulubei, "Virgile en France au XVIᵉ siècle: Éditions, traductions, imitations," *Revue du seizième siècle* 18 (1931–32), 1–77, at 17.

[27] "It seems that the percentage of Renaissance edns. of Virgil in Latin that contained illustrations was higher than for other classical authors" (Kallendorf, *Virgil and the Myth of Venice*, p. 158 n. 40). Steven W. May, introduction, *Elizabethan Poetry: A Bibliography and First-line Index of English Verse, 1559–1603*, 3 vols. (New York: Thoemmes Continuum, 2004), vol. 1, p. xvi finds 483 translations from Virgil and "more than 470" from Ovid. On Virgil's status in the classroom, see Margaret Tudeau-Clayton, *Jonson, Shakespeare and Early Modern Virgil* (Cambridge University Press, 1998), chs. 1–2; and Grendler, *Schooling in Renaissance Italy*, pp. 240–55. According to Grendler, Virgil was taught by 94 Venetian teachers in 1587–88, Terence by 46, Horace by 36, and Ovid by 13 (p. 206). Elizabeth Nitchie gives more modest figures, from the day-book of John Dorne, an Oxford book-seller: "In the year 1520, for which the record was kept, [Dorne] sold twenty-nine copies of Vergil, this number being greater than that of the works of any other classic writer except Cicero, Terence, . . . and Aristotle." Nitchie, *Vergil and the English Poets* (New York: Columbia University Press, 1919), p. 75.

a hundred years. In 1990, when William J. Kennedy wrote the "Virgil" article for the *Spenser Encyclopedia*, he was able to find 275 editions of the "collected works in Latin and many more of the individual works in Latin or in translation."[28] This figure should now be revised upward, by about 30 percent, to around 390 printings of the collected works in Latin, not including translations or solo commentaries, and not counting printings of just one work, such as the *Aeneid* or *Eclogues*.

How many Virgils were actually produced? Estimating the size of editions is notoriously difficult, but between *c*. 1490 and *c*. 1800, print runs of 1,000 to 1,500 copies per edition seem to have been the norm.[29] For Virgil editions, this translates into as many as 14,000 copies per year when production was at its height in the 1490s, and around 5,000 per annum when production was "slow."[30]

The market for Virgil's text was apparently inexhaustible; it was matched, moreover, by an overwhelming appetite for commentaries on the text. Excluding prefatory letters, dedicatory verses, and book summaries,[31] a preliminary census of Latin editions from 1469 to 1599 finds at least 150 separate commentaries on Virgil and identifies at least 125 commentators.[32] These are listed in Appendix A.

Again, the numbers are overwhelming, and they testify to the importance of Virgilian poetry in Renaissance culture. "The early editions of Virgil's *Opera* are the most profusely annotated classical texts the world has ever seen. Each ten lines of the *Aeneid* is surrounded by hundreds of lines of

---

[28] William J. Kennedy, "Virgil," in *The Spenser Encyclopedia*, gen. ed. A. C. Hamilton (Toronto: University of Toronto Press, 1990), p. 719. Kennedy based his totals on Mambelli.

[29] See Lucien Febvre and Henri-Jean Martin, *The Coming of the Book: The Impact of Printing, 1450–1800* (1958), trans. David Gerard (London: Verso, 1984), pp. 216–19; and Philip Gaskell, *A New Introduction to Bibliography* (Oxford: Oxford University Press, 1972), pp. 160–63. Rudolf Hirsch gives higher estimates based on maximum capacity rather than normal practice; see *Printing, Selling and Reading, 1450–1550* (Wiesbaden: Harrassowitz, 1967), p. 72. On variations in edition size, even at the same press, see D. F. McKenzie, "Printers of the Mind," *Studies in Bibliography* 22 (1969), 1–75.

[30] These figures do not include stand-alone commentaries, which were usually published in smaller print runs; see Julia Haig Gaisser, "Teaching Classics in the Renaissance: Two Case Histories," *Transactions of the American Philological Association* 131 (2001), 1–21, at 10–11 n. 30.

[31] On the utility of such documents, see J. W. Binns, *Intellectual Culture in Elizabethan and Jacobean England: The Latin Writings of the Age* (Leeds: Francis Cairns, 1990), pp. 160–71. Unfortunately, their presence is not uniformly recorded in catalogues and bibliographies.

[32] I say "at least" because my sources do not always distinguish between commentaries when the author is unknown. For instance, the sixteen items described in the Appendix A as "Unknown, [Marginal commentary on *Eclogues*, *Georgics*, and *Aeneid*]" may represent a single set of scholia reprinted sixteen times, sixteen individual sets of scholia each reprinted once, or something in between. The total number of commentaries given here represents therefore a minimum.

exposition."³³ This wealth is both a challenge and a burden. There are so very many books on Virgil that survive from this period, and only so much time to read. Where to begin?

For some authors, the answer is direct. Petrarch's Virgil has survived and is annotated in his own hand, largely with excerpts from Servius and Macrobius.³⁴ Also extant is a printed Virgil owned by Tasso. The edition, which had an index and commentary, was by the Venetian legal scholar Nicolaus Erythraeus.³⁵ In Italian, he would have been Niccolò Rossi; in English, Nick the Red: a name that seems wasted, somehow, on expertise merely juridical. His commentary on Virgil, first published in 1538/9, was reprinted at least nine times before century's end, mostly in Venice, then in Germany. Eventually the index outsold the commentary: more than a concordance, it was a learned study of Virgil's word choice; and like a dinner guest who will not go home, it refused to go out of print almost until the reign of Queen Victoria. Tasso's copy, which included both, was dated 1582, but he must have owned at least one additional Virgil because, by this time, Tasso had already been studying Virgil for more than two decades. Montaigne used the same edition, but an earlier printing, which he purchased as a teenager and which is still preserved, with his notes and underlining, in the Bibliothèque Nationale.³⁶ Ben Jonson's Virgil, including Jonson's marginalia, is also available for study. It is an expensive folio edition, with lengthy scholia by the Jesuit scholar Jacobus Pontanus (1542–1626), as he was known in print, Jakob Spanmueller, as he was called on the street in Heidelberg.³⁷ Both names suggest a bridge-maker somewhere in the family tree. The same edition was also used by Queen Elizabeth's godson Sir John Harington (1539/40–1613).³⁸

---

³³ Don Cameron Allen, *Mysteriously Meant: The Rediscovery of Pagan Symbolism and Allegorical Interpretation in the Renaissance* (Baltimore: Johns Hopkins University Press, 1970), pp. 140–41. This format, known as *modus modernus*, was actually developed in the 1100s; see Konrad Haebler, *The Study of Incunabula*, trans. Lucy Eugenia Osborne (New York: Grolier, 1933), p. 91 and C. F. R. De Hamel, *Glossed Books of the Bible and the Origins of the Paris Booktrade* (Cambridge: Brewer, 1984), ch. 2.

³⁴ A facsimile is available: *Francisci Petrarcæ Vergilianus codex . . .*, ed. Giovanni Galbiati and Achille Ratti (Milan: Hoepli, 1930). On the annotations, see Pierre de Nolhac, *Pétrarque et l'humanisme*, 2nd edn., 2 vols. (Paris: Champion, 1907), vol. I, pp. 139–61.

³⁵ Angelo Solerti, ed., *Appendice alle opere in prosa di Torquato Tasso* (Florence: Monnier, 1892), p. 450. For the contents, see Kallendorf, *Venetian Editions*, §112.

³⁶ Dorothy Gabe Coleman, "L'exemplaire de Virgile de 1539 que possédait Montaigne," *Bulletin de la société internationale des amis de Montaigne*, 6th series, 1/2 (1980), 61–66.

³⁷ Jacobus Pontanus, *Symbolarum libri XVIJ Virgilij* (Augsburg: J. Prætorius, 1599). The edition was reprinted at Lyon, by Pillohette, in 1604; there is also a modern facsimile (3 vols.; New York: Garland, 1976). For Jonson's ownership of and borrowings from this edition, see David McPherson, "Ben Jonson's Library and Marginalia: An Annotated Catalogue," *Studies in Philology* 71 (1974), 3–110, at 96, and Tudeau-Clayton, *Early Modern Virgil*, pp. 120–22.

³⁸ Simon Cauchi, ed., *The Sixth Book of Virgil's* Aeneid, *Translated and Commented on by Sir John Harington* (Oxford: Clarendon Press, 1991), pp. xxiv–xxvi.

What if the poet's copy has not survived, or not been identified? The case of Edmund Spenser will illustrate. A volume that Spenser must have owned but has never been found is the *Canterbury Tales*. Nevertheless, we can establish which edition he used on the basis of readings and spellings that occur in Spenser's own poetry.[39] A similar method has been applied to the text of Virgil, but with uncertain results. In the early 1930s, Henry G. Lotspeich collated multiple editions of the pseudo-Virgilian "Culex" with Spenser's English translation, which he titled "Virgils Gnat." Lotspeich found only one edition that could explain all of Spenser's seeming errors.[40] This edition was printed in 1542, a decade before Spenser was born, and included the commentaries of Philip Melanchthon and Eobanus Hessus. Unfortunately, Lotspeich was able to collate only about half of the more than eighty different printings that Spenser could have worked from. To date, no one has collated the other forty: they are scattered across too many libraries in too many different countries.

The best we can probably manage, for Spenser and authors like him, is to calculate probabilities. Which commentaries were most popular? Library inventories from this period do survive,[41] but seldom indicate more than the author's name, sometimes accompanied by a short title (e.g., "Virgill" or "Virgilius. Opera").[42]

---

[39] *The Workes of Geffrey Chaucer*, ed. William Thynne (STC 5075, 5076; London: John Kyngston, 1561). See Alice S. Miskimin, *The Renaissance Chaucer* (New Haven: Yale University Press, 1975), ch. 8; and A. Kent Hieatt, "Room of One's Own for Decisions: Chaucer and *The Faerie Queene*," in *Refiguring Chaucer in the Renaissance*, ed. Theresa M. Krier (Gainesville: University Press of Florida, 1998), pp. 147–64, at pp. 161–63 n. 5.

[40] "Spenser's *Virgils Gnat* and Its Latin Original," *ELH* 2 (1935), 235–41.

[41] R. J. Fehrenbach and E. S. Leedham-Green, eds., *Private Libraries in Renaissance England: A Collection and Catalogue of Tudor and Early Stuart Book-Lists*, 4 vols. (Binghamton, NY: MRTS, 1992–95) records the existence of several Virgils in private libraries, but not specific editions. We do have a partial inventory of the 1599 holdings at the Merchant Taylors' School library, which Spenser attended in the 1560s (R. T. D. Sayles, "Annals of the Merchant Taylors' School Library," *The Library* 4th ser. 15 [1934–35], 459, 464–67, at 459), but an edition of Virgil does not appear there. On the Cambridge University Library during Spenser's time there, see J. C. T. Oates, *Cambridge University Library: A History, From the Beginnings to the Copyright Act of Queen Anne* (Cambridge University Press, 1986), chs. 3 and 4. The University Library inventories from this period do not record a specific Virgil edition, either, but Spenser may not have used it anyway: the library was off-limits to undergraduates, and Spenser may not have been in residence while he completed his MA; see Mark H. Curtis, *Oxford and Cambridge in Transition, 1558–1642* (Oxford: Oxford University Press, 1959), pp. 97, 125.

[42] There are exceptions; see E. S. Leedham-Green, *Books in Cambridge Inventories: Book-Lists from Vice-Chancellor's Court Probate Inventories in the Tudor and Stuart Periods*, 2 vols. (Cambridge University Press, 1986), vol. II, pp. 777–80. Servius is named once, in a Geneva edition from 1620. Eobanus Hessus's catalogue (first printed in 1529) of Virgil's borrowings in the *Eclogues* and *Georgics* also appears once, as do "{Gr} collationes in virgiliun [sic]" in a 1589 octavo. If this is the Heidelberg text that was printed that year by Hieronymus Commelinus (see Heyne [1819], vol. IX, p. 4470), it would have contained Fulvius Orsinus's "Notæ ad Servium in Bucolica et Georgica" (1543), and may also therefore have included the same author's "Virgilius collatione scriptorum græcorum illustratus"

THE STATE OF PUBLISHING IN ENGLAND; OR DID THE
REFORMATION MAKE ANY DIFFERENCE?

Since Spenser was English, it would make sense to begin with commentaries printed in England. How many were there? The answer, for the *Aeneid*, is disappointing: exactly three. The most popular of these, a set of scholia by Paulo Manuzio (1511–74), was originally printed at Venice in 1558; a London edition appeared for the first time in 1570, and was reprinted seven more times.[43] Beginning in 1576, the Manuzio annotations were supplemented by English printers with some not-very-recent remarks on the state of Virgil's text, *Observationes virgilianae lectionis* (1557) by Georgius Fabricius (1516–71). Born Georg Goldschmidt, Fabricius came from Chemnitz and was schooled at Leipzig, then Italy. His masterpiece was a two-volume treatise on Roman archaeology, matching buildings and artifacts with written descriptions in classical literature. He also conducted experiments in chemistry; among other things, he found that silver chloride goes black when exposed to sunlight, a discovery that later generations would recognize as a turning point in the history of photography. As for Manuzio, he was the youngest son of the renowned scholar-printer Aldo Manuzio (1449/1450–1515). Already a respected scholar at the age of twenty-two, Paolo won fame for himself by translating the speeches of Demosthenes and correcting the text of Cicero's letters. Like Fabricius, he wrote a book on Roman antiquities. Unlike Fabricius, whose works were placed on the Index of Prohibited Books in 1559, Manuzio was a solid Catholic, and in 1561 he moved to Rome and opened a new printing press for the promulgation of Catholic doctrine. His business partner in this venture was the pope.[44]

It was an unlikely pairing: one man, a servant of the Church; the other, a heretic from upper Saxony. As a rule, though, printers used whatever they had on hand. There were several reasons. The invention of movable type had sharply lowered the amount of labor involved in reproducing a text, but

(1567). The one commentator who does stand out is Peter Ramus, whose *Prælectiones* on the *Eclogues* (1555) and the *Georgics* (1556) are mentioned six times in the Cambridge inventories. On this commentary, see ch. 2 below.

[43] *Pub. Virgilii Maronis opera. De integro collatis probatissimæ fidei exemplaribusque diligentissimè restituta, ac doctissimis scholijs & annotationibus Pauli Manutij in margine ascriptis, illustrata.* (STC 24788; [London]: Henry Bynneman, 1570); reprinted 1572 (STC 24788a), 1576 (STC 24788a.5), 1580 (STC 24789), 1583 (STC 24790), 1597 (STC 24791), 1616 (STC 24792), and 1632 (STC 24793). For the *Eclogues*, there was also a "Commentum familiare," perhaps that of Hermannus Torrentinus; this commentary was printed five times by Wynander de Worde (1512: STC 24813, 1514: STC 2814, 1516: [no STC], 1522: STC 24814.5, and 1533: [no STC]). On Torrentinus, see p. 31, below.

[44] The story ends badly for Manuzio, but is well told by Martin Lowry in *Facing the Responsibility of Paulus Manutius* (Los Angeles: Dept. of Special Collections, University Research Library, University of California, 1995).

the medium of reproduction – paper – was still costly and would remain so until wood pulp replaced linen rag as the raw material; then the price of paper plunged, along with its longevity. But that did not occur until the end of the eighteenth century. In our period, the price of paper made printers cautious. One way to minimize risk was to reprint a text that was already selling well in another market. Manuzio's commentary had already proven itself in Europe and, to English printers, he must have seemed like a safe bet. True, Manuzio was a papist. But this does not seem to have hurt him: Harvey spoke well of him,[45] and his commentary was a bestseller.

This was not for lack of Protestant alternatives. In 1593, the widow of Thomas Orwin decided to publish a new commentary on Virgil, by Henri Estienne (1528–98). Actually, the commentary was almost twenty years old, having debuted in Geneva *c.* 1576. Like Manuzio, Estienne came from a family of scholar-printers. His grandfather was Badius Ascensius (1462–1535), a key figure in our story. His father, Robert Estienne (1503–59), was the editor of a Greek New Testament (the first to be divided into verses) and the author of a monumental work of classical scholarship, the *Thesaurus linguæ latinæ* (1532; rev. 1536, 1543); it was the best Latin dictionary of its time, and was not superseded until the late eighteenth century. The son, though, was even more learned and prolific than his father. Henri's Greek dictionary, the five-volume *Thesaurus græcæ linguæ* (1572), was far and away the best of its kind, and was still the basis for the big Greek dictionaries of the nineteenth century. In addition to his lexical compilations, Henri published "seventy-four Greek texts of which no fewer than eighteen were first editions ... At his peak he managed to produce about 4,000 pages of Greek texts in a year. His discovery and publication of the *Anacreontea* (1554) was a sensation of the first class and the starting-point for a new branch of modern literature ... His Plato (1578) became the standard edition, and we still quote the numbers of its pages."[46] At one point, he and Manuzio were collaborators. Compared with Estienne, though, Manuzio was an intellectual pigmy.[47] Will it surprise you if I say this made almost no difference in sales?

---

[45] Gabriel Harvey, *Gabriel Harvey's Ciceronianus*, ed. Harold S. Wilson and trans. Clarence A. Forbes (Lincoln: University of Nebraska Press, 1945), pp. 40, 44, 68, 94.
[46] Rudolf Pfeiffer, *History of Classical Scholarship from 1300 to 1850* (Oxford: Clarendon Press, 1976), p. 109.
[47] According to Estienne, the notes in Manuzio "would with more justice carry the name of Servius than of their author" (Hulubei, "Virgile en France," 19). Heyne (1830), vol. IV, p. 706, confirms this judgment: "other things were added to the mix, but nothing of great importance." But Estienne was not much better: according to Heyne, his marginal notes are mostly drawn from Servius, though his preface is thoughtful; on the state of Virgil's text, his off-hand remarks contain "many good things, but not new things" (vol. IV, p. 714).

Again, religion seems not to have been a factor. Though he fell afoul of the Geneva consistory, Estienne was a staunch Protestant. Still Estienne's commentary did not sell. The title-page of the English printing advertises it as a second edition,[48] but a first edition has not been identified, and there was no third. Manuzio was a papist, and he never achieved Estienne's level of scholarly eminence; by this time, he was also dead. And yet, death and popery notwithstanding, English publishers kept Manuzio's Virgil commentary in print until 1632.

It probably helped that the commentary itself was short. Manuzio made his reputation, as we said before, by working on the writings of Demosthenes and Cicero; the commentary on Virgil was a side-project, and consisted mainly of extracts from Servius and cross-references to passages in Homer. The purpose of the cross-references was to facilitate the study of imitation; however, he did not translate Virgil's sources, but merely provided page numbers.[49] This lightened the burden on the annotator, and restored the visual balance on the page of text and commentary. Manuzio intended his edition for publication in the small, octavo format popularized by his father's press in the first decade of the 1500s. Books in this format had little space for commentary, but they were cheap. Whereas the English translations of Virgil usually appeared in the mid-sized quarto (4°) format, the Latin Virgils that come from English presses in this period are all printed in octavo (8°) or even sextodecimo (16°). Two generalizations are possible. Not only did English printers restrict themselves to small-format books with minimal annotation; they also relied exclusively on a very small stable of commentators, all of whom worked and published on the Continent.

Apparently, they had no choice. Apart from a Latin prose paraphrase of the *Georgics*,[50] there were no English contributions to Virgil scholarship until 1634.[51] None. Again, this is typical. Peter Ramus, who was working in Paris, claimed not to be able to name even one English scholar.[52] According

---

[48] *Publii Virgilii Maronis poemata. Novis scholiis illustrata, quæ H. Stephanus partim domi nata, partim è virorum doctissimorum libris excerpta dedit. Secunda editio* (STC 24790.7; London: Widow of T. Orwin, 1593).

[49] E.g., for the death of Turnus: "Homerus in Ili. 226. 245." Is the reference to a Greek text, or a Latin translation?

[50] *Nicolai Grimoaldi Vergilii in quatuor libros Georgicorum paraphrasis* (STC 24822; London: George Bishop and Radulph Newbery, 1591). Even this was stale, the author of it having died in or before 1562.

[51] *P. Virgilii Maronis Opera notis ad margines illustrata a Th. Farnabio* (STC 24794; London: Felix Kyngston, 1634). Reprinted 1642, 1646, 1650, 1652, 1677 (Mambelli, *Annali* §304).

[52] Qtd. in J.A. Van Dorsten, *The Radical Arts: First Decade of an Elizabethan Renaissance* (Leiden University Press, 1970), p. 12.

to J. W. Binns, the sixteenth century was "not a great age" in England for classical scholarship of any kind.[53] The printers may have been partly to blame. By 1600, London had become an important printing center, ranking as high as third behind Paris and Venice. Yet English scholars complained that English printers were not interested in publishing learned books.[54] It is hard to imagine, but the Cambridge University Press did not begin full-scale operations until 1584, and with the exception of a five-year interval in the late teens and early twenties, there was no press at Oxford until 1586. English printers apparently believed that they could not compete with foreign presses on price, and therefore specialized in works for domestic consumption.[55] There is even some evidence to suggest that England lacked compositors with the requisite language skills to set up Greek and Latin manuscripts in type.[56]

The result was that, with the exception of basic textbooks, England imported most of her classical texts from the Continent,[57] including the works of the all-important Cicero.[58] Badius Ascensius, one of the great printer-scholars of this age, seems to have intended "a significant proportion" of at least one edition for the English market.[59] He did this, in part, because the tradition of the great printer-scholar did not yet exist in England. This situation "lasted well into the seventeenth century."[60]

Chances are, then, that Spenser's Virgil was printed overseas (as we know that Jonson's and Harington's were).

---

[53] Binns, *Intellectual Culture*, p. 194.   [54] Binns, *Intellectual Culture*, pp. 402–3.
[55] David Shaw, "The First English Editions of Horace, Juvenal, and Persius," *The Library*, 5th ser., 25 (1970), 219–25, at 223; see also Julian Roberts, "The Latin Trade," in *The Cambridge History of the Book in Britain: Volume IV, 1558–1695*, ed. John Barnard and D. F. McKenzie (Cambridge University Press, 2002), pp. 141–73, at pp. 141–42.
[56] See Binns, *Intellectual Culture*, Appendix A, items 1a, 1b, 2, 3, 5, 6, 7, 14, 30, and 45.
[57] Binns, *Intellectual Culture*, p. 194. See also David McKitterick, *Printing and the Book Trade in Cambridge, 1534–1698*, vol. 1 of *A History of Cambridge University Press*, 3 vols. (Cambridge University Press, 1992–), p. 42; and Lotte Hellinga, "Importation of Books Printed on the Continent into England and Scotland before c. 1520," in *Printing and the Written Word: The Social History of Books*, circa *1450–1520*, ed. Sandra Hindman (Ithaca: Cornell University Press, 1991), pp. 205–24.
[58] Howard Jones, *Master Tully: Cicero in Tudor England* (Nieuwkoop: De Graaf, 1998), ch. 5.
[59] Elizabeth Armstrong, "English Purchases of Printed Books from the Continent 1465–1526," *English Historical Review* 94 (1979), 268–90, at 289.
[60] Hellinga, "Importation of Books," p. 209. See also Graham Pollard, "The English Market for Printed Books: The Rise of the Wholesale Trade," *Publishing History* 4 (1978), 9–17; Margaret Lane Ford, "Importation of Printed Books into England and Scotland," in *The Cambridge History of the Book in Britain: Volume III, 1400–1557*, ed. Lotte Hellinga and J. B. Trapp (Cambridge University Press, 1999), pp. 179–201; McKitterick, *Printing and the Book Trade*, pp. 22–37; and Marjorie Plant, *The English Book Trade: An Economic History of the Making and Sale of Books*, 3rd edn. (London: Allen & Unwin, 1974), esp. pp. 259–60.

SERVIUS AND DONATUS: THE AUTHORITY OF ANTIQUITY

As we have seen, the number of editions and commentaries that issued from European presses is simply staggering. What we need – not just for Spenser but for any poet whose copy of Virgil does not happen to be preserved – is a way of determining which commentaries made the biggest impact on contemporary readers. Appendix B is a ranked list of commentaries on Virgil that were circulating in print between 1469 and 1599, grouped according to *Eclogues*, *Georgics*, and *Aeneid*. For each poem, the "Total" figure in the left-hand column indicates the number of times that a given commentary was printed: this number may be taken to represent the availability of a commentary, and therefore to approximate its influence.

It will be seen that some commentaries, such as Jodocus Willichius's recondite little treatise on the chronology of the *Aeneid* (1551), made one appearance and then disappeared. Others, such as Hermannus Torrentinus's commentary on the *Eclogues* (1492), were reprinted again and again over the course of eighty years or more.[61] Had we but world enough and time, we could read Willichius as well as Torrentinus, and all the commentators in between. But where time and access to old books are finite, the scholar must choose to read some now and put off reading others. Appendix B, therefore, is offered as a guide, not only to the commentaries that were available for a given work, but also to their relative importance.

Consider, for example, commentaries on the *Aeneid*. Table 1 shows which ones appeared in thirty or more editions.[62] Apart from quantity, what distinguishes them from the rest of the herd? The most obvious factor is antiquity, since both of the most popular commentaries were composed in the waning decades of the Roman Empire. Servius was writing in the latter half of the fourth century AD and the early part of the fifth; Tiberius Claudius Donatus, who was his junior by several decades, was flourishing in the 430s. Together, they are a good example of how classical scholarship actually operated in the age of humanism and the printing press.

On the one hand, there was Servius, whose text was copied out and excerpted for the entire duration of the Middle Ages.[63] He stands, if you

---

[61] This is a conservative figure. On the difficulty of assessing Torrentinus's popularity, see M. E. Kronenberg, *Campbell's* Annales de la typographie néerlandaise au XV. siècle: *Contributions to a New Edition* (The Hague: Nijhoff, 1956), §1737.

[62] The cut-off is not arbitrary: whereas Landino was reprinted thirty-three times and Valeriano thirty-two, the next three commentators in the ranking (Franciscus Campanus, Agostino Dati, and Ludovicus Rhodiginus) were printed only seventeen times. See Appendix B.

[63] See Baswell, *Virgil in Medieval England*, p. 49 *et passim*.

Table 1 Aeneid *commentaries that appeared in thirty or more editions, 1470–1599*

Printings	Author	*Editio princeps*
125	Servius Maurus Honoratus	*c.* 1470
55	Tiberius Claudius Donatus	1488
38	Filippo Beroaldo	1482
37	Jodocus Badius Ascensius	1501/2
35	Philip Melanchthon	1530
34	Paulo Manuzio	1558
33	Cristoforo Landino	1488
32	Giovanni Pierio Valeriano	1521

like, for the residual medievalism of Renaissance scholarship. Donatus, on the other hand, was a genuine discovery, a text of the Renaissance, properly so called. With the exception of one rare sighting in the mid-thirteenth century, Donatus' commentary on the *Aeneid* disappeared in the eleventh century and was not seen again until 1415–17, when Poggio Bracciolini found eight of the twelve books at a monastery in Constance, where he was attending a council on heresy and schism. This manuscript does not survive. Then, in 1438, a young abbot from eastern France found five books in his abbey library and carried them to Italy. Again, he was traveling on church business. This manuscript, known subsequently as Laur. 45.15, was acquired by Pietro de' Medici, who deposited the manuscript in his private library and made it available to Cristoforo Landino; this is the same codex that Poliziano mentioned (in a passage cited earlier) as evidence for the *e* spelling of Virgil. The rest of the commentary was discovered in the 1460s, under circumstances which are now obscure. In 1488, Landino published a digest of the complete text, after which Donatus and his commentary soared rapidly to the top of the charts.[64]

This is a pity since, unlike Servius, Donatus is dull. But he was ancient, and that insured his success. The same is true for commentaries on the *Eclogues* and *Georgics*: three of the top four *Eclogues* commentaries (Servius, Aelius Donatus, and Probus) were written in late

---

[64] On the history of the manuscripts, see Remigio Sabbadini, *Storia e critica di testi latini*, 2nd edn., rev. Eugenio and Myriam Billanovich (Padua: Antenore, 1971), pp. 147–51; R. H. Rouse, "Ti. Claudius Donatus," in *Texts and Transmission: A Survey of the Latin Classics*, ed. L. D. Reynolds (Oxford: Clarendon Press, 1983; rev. 1986), pp. 157–58; and Peter K. Marshall, *Servius and Commentary on Virgil* (Asheville, NC: Pegasus, 1997), pp. 7–12.

antiquity, as were two of the top four *Georgics* commentaries (Servius and Probus).

Servius, in particular, was so popular that he was sometimes published solo, without the text of Virgil. Full of lore about the history, religion, and customs of the ancient world,[65] he was even the subject of his own commentary. This is the third item on our list, *Annotations on the Commentaries of Servius*, by Filippo Beroaldo the Elder (1453–1505). Beroaldo was an extremely successful teacher; students flocked to his lectures, because he was learned and also because it was funny to hear what he said about other scholars.[66] What he said about Servius was mostly negative: in some copies, the work is actually titled *Annotations against the Commentaries of Servius*. This was not entirely new: for more than a hundred years, scholars had been noticing that Servius is frequently unreliable or even irrelevant.[67] Beroaldo's innovation was to sustain the attack into a separate book.[68] But Servius was (and still is) irreplaceable. So Servius stayed in print. As, for a time, did Beroaldo: sometimes alone, and sometimes collated with Servius, like a parasite on his victim.[69]

The text of Servius was first printed in 1482. This illustrates another feature of the most popular commentaries on Virgil: they were all published early. Five of the eight commentaries on this list were already in print by 1490; a sixth (by Badius Ascensius) came out in 1501. The same thing happened with commentaries on Catullus: as Julia Gaisser explains, "the first explanation, whatever its merits, tends to survive and to form the core of subsequent explanations, even when it is explicitly rejected."[70] The text of Virgil was subject to the same law. The first edition was printed in 1469 and edited by Giovanni Andrea Bussi. Unfortunately, Bussi relied on recent copies of Virgil, rather than seeking out older, more reliable manuscripts. Better manuscripts surfaced quickly, but Bussi was used by other editors as a base text for the rest of the fifteenth century.[71]

---

[65] On Servius as a classical text, see also Marshall, *Servius*, pp. 14–17. *Inter alia*, Marshall has identified "seven fifteenth-century Italian manuscripts of pure Servius (i.e., with no text of Virgil)," each of which is also annotated with additional commentary on the commentary.

[66] See Gaisser, "Teaching Classics," 2–12.

[67] An example of the new, more critical approach to Servius is Benvenuto da Imola (d. 1387/8); see Mary Louise Lord, "The Use of Macrobius and Boethius in Some Fourteenth-Century Commentaries on Virgil," *International Journal of the Classical Tradition* 3.1 (1996), 3–22. Several chapters of Poliziano's *Miscellanea* – 1.37, 89, 100, and 2.8 – are also corrections of Servius.

[68] The commentary on a commentary was a popular genre in the late fifteenth century; see Grafton, "Quattrocento Humanism," pp. 28–30.

[69] For the latter, see Kallendorf, *Venetian Editions*, §38 and §39.   [70] Gaisser, *Catullus*, p. 108.

[71] Venier, *Storia del testo*, esp. ch. 2.1 and the *stemma delle edizioni* on pp. 136–37.

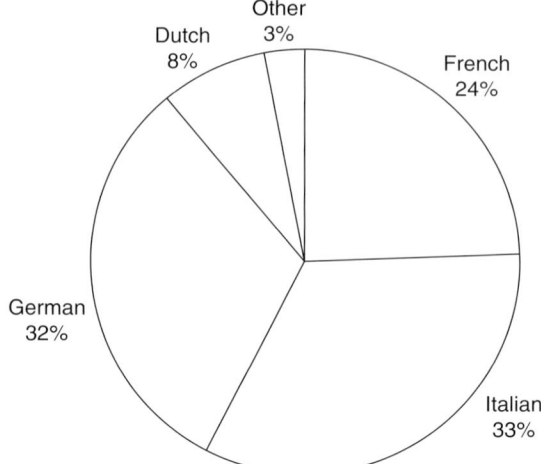

Figure 2. Two-thirds of all Virgil editions printed between 1469 and 1599 were issued from Italian- or German-speaking towns, with French-speaking towns (including Geneva) making up the bulk of the remainder.

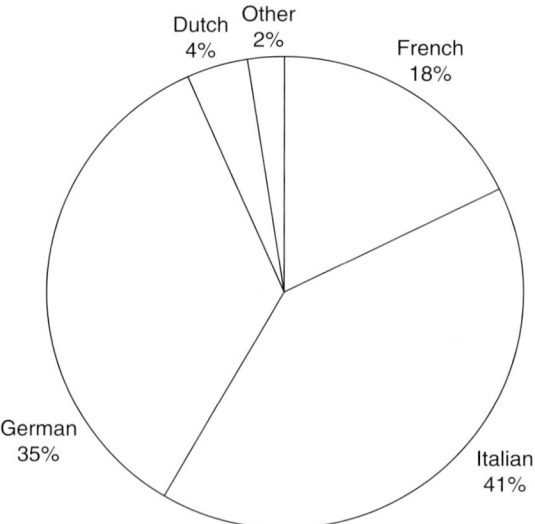

Figure 3. First editions of new commentaries. Italian printing towns outproduced their German counterparts by just 1 percent (see Figure 2), but introduced more new material. French printers were more conservative, and preferred to reprint proven bestsellers; Lyon, in particular, was notorious for counterfeiting Aldine editions of classical authors.

The other common feature of the most popular commentators was location. It helped if you worked in Italy. Not only did Italian printers contribute more Virgil editions than anyone else (Figure 2), they also seem to have been more willing (or to have had more opportunities) to bring out new commentaries that had never before been printed (Figure 3). It is not surprising, therefore, that of the six "moderns" on our short list of top *Aeneid* commentators, four were Italians. (Badius Ascensius and Philip Melanchthon were Flemish and German, respectively, though Badius spent most of his working life in Paris and was educated at Louvain and Bologna.)

LANDINO VS. BADIUS: ORIGINALITY VS. UTILITY

The Italian commentator whom most scholars are familiar with is Cristoforo Landino (1424–1504).[72] We have already encountered his name in connection with Poliziano and Donatus, and his works on Virgil are justly famous. Merritt Y. Hughes called him once "[t]he prince of Virgilian allegorists,"[73] and the publication figures given in Table 1 confirm that he was at least of the blood royal. Hughes, like most scholars today, was primarily interested in Landino's *Camaldolensian Dialogues* (c. 1473), a four-book treatise on the active and contemplative lives; the conclusions arrived at in the first half of the dialogue are illustrated in the second half of the dialogue by an allegorical interpretation of *Aeneid* 1–6.[74] This is an important document in the history of Florentine Neo-Platonism, but its influence was limited

---

[72] There are several good introductions: in English, see Allen, *Mysteriously Meant*, 142–54; Michael Murrin, *The Allegorical Epic: Essays in Its Rise and Decline* (Chicago: University of Chicago Press, 1980), ch. 2 and appendix; and Craig Kallendorf, *In Praise of Aeneas: Virgil and Epideictic Rhetoric in the Early Italian Renaissance* (Hanover, NH: University Press of New England, 1989), ch. 6. These works focus on Landino's Virgil scholarship, but he was also the author of important commentaries on Horace (1482) and Dante (1481). Frank J. Fata gives a sketch of Landino's career, with sidenotes on his poetry, in "Landino on Dante," diss., Johns Hopkins University (1966), ch. 1. According to Deborah Parker, "Landino's work dominated expositions of the *Comedy* for roughly 120 years" (*Commentary and Ideology: Dante in the Renaissance* [Durham, NC: Duke University Press, 1993], p. 136). For Landino and Spenser, see Jon A. Quitslund, *Spenser's Supreme Fiction: Platonic Natural Philosophy and* The Faerie Queene (Toronto: University of Toronto Press, 2001), ch. 4. But cf. Graham Hough, *A Preface to* The Faerie Queene (New York: Norton, 1962), p. 122: "I can see no sign that Spenser had read Landino at all."

[73] M. Y. Hughes, "Virgilian Allegory and *The Faerie Queene*," *PMLA* 44 (1929), 696–705, at 700.

[74] Cristoforo Landino, *Disputationes camaldulenses*, ed. Peter Lohe (Florence: Sansoni, 1980). The discussion of Virgil occurs in books three and four, which are translated in Thomas H. Stahel, "Cristoforo Landino's Allegorization of the *Aeneid*: Books III and IV of the *Camaldolese Disputations*," diss., Johns Hopkins University (1968).

by the infrequency of republication: after the *editio princeps* (*c.* 1480), the *Dialogues* was reprinted five times and then dropped out of sight for sixty-five years. There was a miniature revival in 1577, when a Swiss printer repackaged the second half of the book and appended it to an edition of Virgil's poetry; it was reprinted in this form two more times, in 1596 and 1606, both times in Switzerland.[75] More influential, though, at least in raw numbers, was the line-by-line commentary on Virgil that Landino published in 1488: unlike the *Dialogues*, this commentary did not stop at Book 6 of the *Aeneid*, but went on to cover Books 7 through 12, as well as the *Eclogues* and *Georgics*. Not only was the line-by-line commentary more complete than the *Dialogues*, it also enjoyed a much wider circulation: approximately thirty-three editions in sixty years.

These are big numbers, and we shall have more to say about this commentary later. But total output can be deceiving: a decade-by-decade breakdown of the publication statistics (provided below in Appendix B) shows that demand for Landino's commentary was at its peak in the 1490s; from there, it tapered off until 1539, after which there were no new copies.[76] Out of print is not always out of mind: our predecessors, like ourselves, relied on books that could only be obtained in libraries and used-book stores. But there are other signs that Landino was falling out of favor. In the Renaissance it was not uncommon for students to record their lecture notes in the margins of a printed text. Many of these notes can be traced to printed commentaries, especially Servius and Badius Ascensius, but there are few such notes from Landino.[77]

There is also the puzzling fact that Landino's most distinctive contribution to Virgilian allegory seems to have had no influence on poets or subsequent commentators. For the broad outlines of his interpretation, there was already ample precedent in the medieval tradition of Fulgentius and Bernardus Silvestris: the journey of the hero represents the journey of the soul; the descent to the underworld is the climax of the story, and represents the achievement of wisdom; Dido is a distraction from that goal, and represents the temptations of the flesh. But Landino's Dido is more complicated. Considered in herself, she is an example of sexual

---

[75] Lohe, ed., *Disputationes camaldulenses*, pp. xvi, xxiv–xxv. In his commentary on *Inf.* 1.63, Landino refers to an Italian translation of the *Dialogues* by Andrea Cambini, "nostro discepolo," which to date has not been found.

[76] Landino's prefaces were sometimes reprinted after this date, but apparently without the line-by-line commentary; see Kallendorf, *Venetian Editions*, §83 and §87.

[77] Kallendorf, *Virgil and the Myth of Venice*, pp. 66–67.

intemperance. Aeneas, though, is enticed less by sex than by politics. According to Landino, Dido represents the allure of rulership, the active life *qua* temptation. On this point, Landino was completely original – and completely alone: he had no predecessors, and no disciples. Giraldi Cinzio, writing in the 1550s, confirms our sense that Landino's influence was short-lived. Landino, he explains, wanted to do for Virgil what the Greeks had already done for Homer, "imposing (*inducendo*) meanings on his poem which [Homer] perhaps never imagined." But the outcome, says Cinzio, was disappointing (*ma poco felicemente gli successe*): not because Landino wasn't learned or clever, but because the field of scholarship was too crowded.[78]

Badius Ascensius was pedestrian compared with Landino, but probably had more influence: his commentary stayed in print clear up to the end of the sixteenth century. It was long: not until 1599, when Jacobus Pontanus published his great variorum commentary, would there be another commentary on Virgil so loquacious. It was not that Badius had more to say than other commentators, but he was very generous with syntax and vocabulary; he also gave liberal quotations from other scholars and commentators. As he explains in a dedication, Badius intended his commentaries for students who have no teacher.[79] His Virgil, though, was a large book, and therefore expensive; its success, therefore, is all the more remarkable. Addressed to students, its real audience was probably their instructor: not the scholar or lecturer, but the grammar-school teacher who needed help staying ahead.

VALERIANO: THE SCHOLARLY ARGUMENT FOR *I*

It remains to say something of the last name on our short list, Giovanni Pierio Valeriano (1477–1558). Born and educated in the Veneto, Valeriano is well known to art historians as the author of *Hieroglyphica* (1556), a 58-book commentary on the symbolic vocabulary of pagan antiquities. A love poet, satirist, and translator, Valeriano also wrote a dialogue, *The Misfortune of Educated Men* (pub. 1620), which documents the culture of a Renaissance court and the personalities of classical scholarship. His lectures on Catullus were ground-breaking and "constitute the first intelligent commentary" on this author.[80] But his first great success was a book on Virgil, *Castigationes et*

---

[78] Giraldi Cinzio, *Discorso dei romanzi* (1554), in *Scritti critici*, ed. Camillo Guerrieri Crocetti (Milan: Marzorati, 1973), p. 71.
[79] Hulubei, "Virgile en France," p. 10.
[80] Julia Haig Gaisser, ed. and trans., *Pierio Valeriano on the Ill Fortune of Learned Men: A Renaissance Humanist and His World* (Ann Arbor: University of Michigan Press, 1999), p. viii. For biography and bibliography, see Gaisser's introduction, pp. 1–78, and Gaisser, *Catullus*, ch. 3.

variantes Virgilianæ lectionis (1521). Unlike the grammarians, who dabbled in a bit of everything, Valeriano devoted his book almost entirely to textual criticism: not "What does Virgil mean?" but "What did Virgil write?" He called the book *Chastenings and Variants*; it was an attempt to chasten (i.e., correct) the text of Virgil by recording and collating the variant readings in old, sometimes ancient, manuscripts. It was the biggest undertaking of its kind, and it was still in use as late as 1827.

Valeriano's editorial method has been described elsewhere, as has the history of Virgil's text in this period.[81] For our purpose, it is sufficient to note two things. First, Valeriano is the single most important source for questions about the state of Virgil's text in the sixteenth century. (The other source, Eobanus Hessus, will be discussed in the next chapter; but he recorded fewer variants and was reprinted less frequently.) Second, it was Valeriano who gave Europe scholarly permission to ignore Poliziano and spell Virgil's name with an *i*.

The subject comes up, for a textual critic, in the closing verses of the *Georgics*, which function as a kind of colophon:

> Illo Virgilium me tempore dulcis alebat
> Parthenope studiis florentem ignobilis oci:

---

[81] On the state of Virgil's text prior to Valeriano, see Venier, *Storia del testo*, esp. ch. 1. On Valeriano's editorial method, see Vladimiro Zabughin, *Vergilio nel rinascimento italiano da Dante a Torquato Tasso*, 2 vols. (Bologna: Zanichelli, 1921–23), vol. II, pp. 72–75, with important notes on pp. 96–100; Alessandra Malaman, "Le 'Castigationes virgilianae lectionis' di Pierio Valeriano e il codice romano vaticano di Virgilio," *Atti del Reale istituto veneto di scienze, lettere ed arti* 100 (1940–41), 81–91; Ettore Bolisani, "Vergilius o Virgilius? L'opinione di un dotto umanista," *Atti dell'Istituto veneto di scienze, lettere ed arti* 117 (1958–59), 131–41; Anthony Grafton, *Joseph Scaliger: A Study in the History of Classical Scholarship*, 2 vols. (Oxford: Clarendon Press, 1983–93), vol. I, pp. 47–51; and Vincenzo Fera, "Dai *Miscellanea* alle *Castigationes virgilianae*," in *Umanisti bellunesi fra quattro e cinquecento*, ed. Paolo Pellegrini (Florence: Olschki, 2001), pp. 119–36. Most editors in this period make only vague references to the *antiqui codices* they have consulted. Valeriano, however, describes his manuscripts in some detail. Though he makes frequent use of a "codex Oblongus" and a "codex Longobardus," his main authorities are a "codex Romanus" and a "codex Mediceus." Zabughin identified these manuscripts as Vat. Lat. 1574, Vat. Lat. 1573, Laurentian 39.23, and Vat. Lat. 3867, respectively. The most important of these, as Valeriano recognized, was the codex Romanus: along with the codex Palatinus (Vatican, Pal. lat. 1631) and a different codex Mediceus (Laurentian Lib. 39.1 and Vatican lat. 3225 sig. 76), the Romanus is the "mainstay" of the modern editor (L. D. Reynolds, "Virgil," in *Texts and Transmission*, ed. Reynolds, pp. 433–34). Poliziano also used the Romanus in his *Miscellanea*, as did Antonio Mancinelli in his commentary on the *Eclogues* and *Georgics*; see Zabughin, *Vergilio nel rinascimento*, vol. I, pp. 112–22, 204. The codex Mediceus was consulted by Pomponio Leto (what may be his corrections are listed under "M⁷" in Mario Geymonat, ed., *P. Vergili Maronis opera* [Rome: Edizioni di Storia e letteratura, 2008]) and may have been used by Bussi, as well (Venier, *Storia del testo*, ch. 2.5). The codex Palatinus takes its name, not from Roman geography, but from the title of its most prominent owners, the electors palatine. The manuscript was at Lorsch until 1565, when it was moved to nearby Heidelberg. In 1623, Heidelberg surrendered to imperial troops and in 1625 the palatine library was given to the Vatican; until then, the manuscript had little or no influence on Italian scholarship.

>   Carmina qui lusi pastorum: audaxque iuuenta
>   Tityre te patule cecini sub tegmine phagi.   (*Geo.* 4.563–66)

[At that time, sweet Naples nourished me, Virgil, while I flourished in the pursuits of honorless otium: I, who composed songs about shepherds and sang, in the boldness of my youth, of you, O Tityrus, under the shelter of a spreading beech tree.]

This is the first and only time that Virgil's name occurs in the text of his poetry; here, if nowhere else, an editor must decide: is it to be *Vergilium*, with an *e*, or *Virgilium*, with an *i*? Valeriano devoted a miniature essay to the question, and came down in favor of *i*.[82] He acknowledged the manuscripts and monuments that Poliziano adduced in favor of *e*, and even added a few that Poliziano had missed. He insisted, though, that the witnesses in favor of *i* outnumber those in favor of *e*. Those that do favor *e* he tried to explain in terms of linguistic history. The codex Romanus, for instance, is Valeriano's oldest manuscript of Virgil's text – and it spells the poet's name with an *e*. This was a setback, but not a fatal one, for Valeriano noted that the codex Romanus does the same thing to a number of other words: for *sublimis* it reads *sublimes*; for *alitis*, *alites*; for *Phyllidis*, *Phyllides*; and for *rigidas*, *regidas*. In each case, the word that is spelt with an *e* in the manuscript was originally spelt with an *i*. According to Valeriano, this is related to long-term trends in Latin orthography: "some eras," he writes, "seem to have hunted down the letter *i* with a kind of hatred; instead of an *i*, they preferred to substitute an *e*." This sounds vague, but Valeriano can cite a classical precedent: according to the ancient linguist Varro (116–27 BC), the Roman god Mercurius was originally worshiped under the name of *Mircurius*. The same mutation that Valeriano detected in his treacherous manuscript was also observed by a native speaker in antiquity.

Valeriano's learning was impressive by any standard, even when it was marshaled on the wrong side. Like Poliziano, he understood the importance of inscriptions, even non-literary ones;[83] unlike Poliziano, he also acknowledged that sometimes inscriptions disagree with each another. Valeriano dealt with this problem by looking for an inscription that could be directly linked to the poet. He found one in Trajan's Forum: "In one man,

---

[82] Valeriano on *Geo.* 4.563 (Giunta 1544, fol. 143ᵛ).
[83] Cf. Richard Pace, *De fructu qui ex doctrina percipitur* (1517), "God knows I put more faith in [ancient marbles] than I do in all our new grammarians … For it was an inscription that taught Angelus Politianus to write *Vergil* and not *Virgil*, which was the way it was usually spelled for five hundred years before. God only knows what we owe to inscriptions." Trans. Frank Manley and Richard S. Sylvester, *De fructu qui ex doctrina percipitur* (*The Benefit of a Liberal Education*) (New York: Ungar, for the Renaissance Society of America, 1967), p. 69.

Claudianus, Rome and the kings placed the judgment (*noon*) of Virgil and the inspiration (*mousan*) of Homer."[84] Claudianus was a court poet in the late Empire; these verses, inscribed on a pedestal, were all that remained of his statue. He was not, in fact, the ideal blend of Homeric invention and Virgilian discretion (although, as we shall see in Chapter 4, that was a durable formula). What mattered, though, for Valeriano, was not Claudianus' station in the firmament of fame and letters, but the orthography of Virgil's name: in the Greek inscription, it was BIRGILIOIO, with B pronounced as V and I in the first syllable.

Poliziano, though he read Greek fluently, had missed this one somehow. And yet it was Poliziano, not Valeriano, who pioneered the methods that both critics employed; and scholarship today has vindicated his conclusion: the poet did spell his own name with an *e*. Nevertheless, Valeriano carried the day and most writers continued to use the *i* spelling. Why?

Chastenings was dedicated to Cardinal Giulio de' Medici (1478–1534); like Poliziano, Valeriano was a protégé of the Florentine banking family and tutored some of their children. But the House of the Golden Balls was no longer just the most important family in Florence; now, if only for a brief hour, it was also the most important family in Rome, perhaps in all of Italy. Within two years, the cardinal would become a pope; in the meantime, that seat was already occupied by Giulio's cousin, Giovanni de' Medici (1476–1521). Leo X, as he is known to the faithful, was a great patron of learning, and favored the family tutor with a preface. In that preface, he not only praised Valeriano for his erudition, but threatened would-be plagiarists with excommunication. Enforcement, however, was lax, and before the decade was over the *Corrections* had been picked up by pirates in Lyon and Paris; it quickly became a standard commentary and was reprinted with Virgil's text on a regular basis until 1586.

INNOVATION VS. INFLUENCE

The best accounts of classical scholarship have usually focused on the pioneers, and with good reason: because that is usually where the action is, and because we recognize the pioneers as forerunners of ourselves.[85] This

---

[84] For the text and history of the inscription, see Bolisani, "Vergilius o Virgilius," 134–35. The inscription was unearthed in Rome, where Valeriano lived, but it was owned by a Neapolitan. Valeriano would have learned of it through the published transcription by Battista Spagnoli (a.k.a. "Mantuan").

[85] "[I]t is obvious," says Rudolf Pfeiffer, "that we do not want to know what is obsolete and passed forever, but what is still enduring; we want to explore the continuity of knowledge, the *philologia*

is natural, and it is pharisaical to sermonize on the perils of teleology. But innovation is not the same as influence. To find out what the poets knew, it is not enough to ask "What was known?" We also have to ask, "How widely was it known, and by whom?"

There is a lag, often long, between the publication of advanced research and its acceptance by the educated public. But much of the scholarship on Virgil that was published in the Renaissance was not innovative anyway. Servius was behind most of it: what little he did not anticipate usually concerned religion, and that mattered less than one might think (as we saw from Manuzio's success in Reformation England). As we shall see in subsequent chapters, the Renaissance approach to Virgil was usually the same as the medieval approach, and that was usually the same as the ancient. There were new sources (such as Donatus), but few breakthroughs. From our point of view, the real shift is quite recent, and has come about through exploration of Virgil's non-Homeric sources: Hellenistic, neoteric, and dramatic. This body of work was available in the Renaissance, but not widely known, or even conceptualized. No one, for example, called Apollonius of Rhodes a Hellenistic poet, or spoke of him as part of a movement. Poliziano had some notion of Callimachus and used his knowledge to correct the text of Catullus 66.[86] But even the advances he did make were not always retained by the next generation. The spelling of Virgil's name is a case in point.

The academic community absorbed Poliziano's methods, but it did not always remember his examples or adopt his conclusions. His status was high, but his role was different. For us, Poliziano is a poet and a scholar, but in the century after his death he seems to have been remembered primarily as a poet and letter-writer. For every reprint of his *Miscellanea*, there are at least two or three reprints of his collected Latin epistles, of which there are twelve volumes.[87] Poliziano had the good fortune to be a great scholar, and the bad fortune also to be a successful poet and letter-writer, so that for many decades his poetry and his letter-writing overshadowed his scholarship. Valeriano had the bad fortune to be less original than Poliziano, and the good fortune to be pirated. His conclusions were wrong, but he published them in the right format: a commentary on Virgil.

---

perennis." *History of Classical Scholarship from the Beginnings to the End of the Hellenistic Age* (Oxford: Clarendon Press, 1968), p. vii. Grafton's method is similar; see *Joseph Scaliger*, vol. I, p. I and "The Origins of Scholarship," *American Scholar* 48 (1979), 236–46, 256–61, at 256: "What we do need, first of all, is a body of accurate descriptions of those scholarly works that achieved new results or – sometimes for unsavory reasons – enjoyed large reputations for doing so."

[86] See Gaisser, *Catullus*, pp. 73–74.
[87] See Georg Wolfgang Panzer, *Annales typographici ab artis inventae origine ... ad annum MDVI continuati*, 11 vols. (Nuremberg: Eberhard, 1793–1803), vol. XI, pp. 56, 592 and Martini, *Catalogo*.

LATIN: DEAD LANGUAGE OR LIVING?

That is not quite the end of the story, though. Poliziano was too busy to write an actual commentary on Virgil, but his findings did get quoted in a commentary. Of all the modern commentators, Badius was the one who had the most influence, and, in his preface to Virgil, Badius gives a lengthy excerpt from Poliziano on the spelling of Virgil's name. This is typical, not just of commentaries but of scholarship in general: a lot of it is just repeating what other scholars have already said. In this case, the simple act of reprinting Poliziano's argument probably doubled or even tripled the number of readers who knew about it. Why, then, weren't more writers persuaded to adopt the *e* spelling?

One reason was probably Badius himself. He listened to Poliziano, and by reprinting his evidence he made sure that other people would listen too. But in his own publications (he was a printer as well as a scholar) Badius used the *i* spelling of Virgil's name, not the *e*.

Another reason was Valeriano. When Badius composed his preface *c.* 1500, Valeriano's textual criticism did not yet exist. However, after 1521, when Valeriano published his *Corrections and Variants*, it was not uncommon for printers to combine both commentaries in one volume. An example is the Giunta edition of 1544, which also includes commentaries by Landino, Mancinelli, and the ancient commentaries of Probus, Servius, and Tiberius Claudius Donatus. Badius's preface to Virgil appears in the front matter and includes the excerpt from Poliziano, but now there is a note in the margin (author unidentified), which says that Valeriano uses more robust sources (*validioribus auctoritatibus*) and directs us to *Geo.* 4.563, where he discusses the poet's name. This tends to neutralize Poliziano and promote the *i* spelling of Virgil, which is in fact used throughout the volume.[88]

But the best explanation comes, fittingly, from Poliziano's letters; or rather, from a commentary on them written by one of his younger contemporaries. There were two commentaries, actually: one by our old friend Badius Ascensius and one by François Dubois, an Amiens native who taught literature at the Collège de Tournay in Paris.[89] Writing *c.* 1520, Dubois offers an assessment of Poliziano's legacy: "Many who were keen on the new fashion (*novitatis*) wanted to imitate Poliziano, and wrote 'adgredi, adloquor' [for post-classical *aggredi, alloquor*] and all the other

---

[88] Giunta 1544, sig. *ix^v.
[89] His Latin name, Franciscus Sylvius, was also used by the German anatomist Franz De Le Boë (1614–72).

affectations, 'Vergilius, adulescens, intellego' [for *Virgilius, adolescens, intelligo*]. But usage has now triumphed over novelty (*Sed novitatem vicit consuetudo*)."⁹⁰

What occasions Dubois's remark is a debate in the letters between Poliziano and the historian Bartolomeo della Scala, about what kind of words are permissible in Latin prose. The story is well told now by Martin McLaughlin.⁹¹ Scala starts the fight (which is what it turned into) by saying that Poliziano uses words that are so rare, even in classical texts, that no one is sure what they mean anymore. Poliziano is mild at first, but eventually he makes a counter-charge: Scala's Latin is blemished by *dehonestamenta*, an unusual word that means "deformities" and is an example of the rare (but technically classical) diction that prompted Scala to complain in the first place. What Poliziano objects to in Scala's writing is the use of Latin words that do not appear in classical authors. This is hard to avoid, since Scala is writing about events in post-classical history, and therefore has to describe things and ideas (such as the Florentine office of gonfaloniere, *vexilliferatum* in medieval Latin) that did not exist in the classical world. But the real issue is whether Latin should be considered a dead language or a living.⁹² For Poliziano, Latin stopped improving at the end of the classical period and can now only decay; Poliziano has a very broad notion of what qualifies as "classical" Latin, but he draws the line at medieval Latin: that is *dehonesta*. For Scala, though, Latin is alive and still growing; the world is changing, and language must change with it.

We can now understand better what Dubois means when he says "*consuetudo* has now triumphed over *novitas*," to explain why Poliziano's *e*-spelling of Virgil failed to take root. Insofar as it is custom that trumps novelty, it sounds like a conservative argument. And so it is. But it is not a "preservative" argument; that is, Dubois doesn't want to preserve the classical form of Latin or fix its development. For him, Latin is still one of the modern languages, with new words and even new forms, which custom licenses. What defines Latin is not, for Dubois, a period in its history, but the consensus of those who use it. (To use the technical terms: solecism is worse than barbarism.) Poliziano's error was to ignore usage, and to oppose something that cannot be stopped.

---

⁹⁰ Trans. Martin L. McLaughlin, *Literary Imitation in the Italian Renaissance* (Oxford: Clarendon Press, 1995), p. 216 n. 75.
⁹¹ McLaughlin, *Literary Imitation*, pp. 206–9.
⁹² This debate would not end with Poliziano's death; see also G. W. Pigman III, "Imitation and the Renaissance Sense of the Past: The Reception of Erasmus' *Ciceronianus*," *Journal of Medieval and Renaissance Studies* 9 (1979), 155–77.

But, of course, Latin did stop and has even regressed now to its classical form. That event had far-reaching consequences which are still coming into focus.[93] Yes, every year the Vatican issues a list of new Latin words and there is now a Latin news broadcast on the internet, but those are fringe activities. In their own day, Dubois and Scala were not on the fringe – they were not even "alternative." Both were swimmers in the central current of European culture. That current was still Latin and the *i* in Virgil is a reminder, frozen now, of its once-flowing stream. The *i* itself was not invented by the Renaissance, only preserved and passed on – preserved, paradoxically, by insisting that Latin must evolve. That period in Latin's history is over and today the *i* in Virgil is no more than a fossil: not just of something that used to be alive, but of Latin's very aliveness, its *vitalitas*.

---

[93] See now Ann Moss, *Renaissance Truth and the Latin Language Turn* (Oxford: Oxford University Press, 2003).

PART II

Reputation

CHAPTER 2

Patronage and the Eclogues

> Once out of nature I shall never take
> My bodily form from any natural thing,
> But such a form as Grecian goldsmiths make
> Of hammered gold and gold enameling
> To keep a drowsy Emperor awake.
> W. B. Yeats, "Sailing to Byzantium"

THE IDEA OF VIRGIL AND ITS ANCIENT SOURCES

As we saw in the previous chapter, Virgil was printed first, even before Ovid, who was more popular. For St. Augustine, Virgil was "the greatest poet, and of all poets the most splendid and best." For Lactantius, he was "the first of the Latin poets." For Velleius Paterculus, "the prince of poets." For Julius Caesar Scaliger, "the king of poets," "the father of poesy," even "the god of poets."[1] What was the basis for these broad claims? We know that most of the epics and pastorals written in the sixteenth century were modeled at least in part on Virgil's *Aeneid* and *Eclogues*. But what made those poems worthy of imitation? And what was the idea of Virgil that poets carried in their heads, the image to which they aspired?

The history of classical scholarship has, as I said before, usually been told as a roll-call of great originals, of pioneers and pathfinders. Again, though,

---

[1] These quotations are from "Testimonials of Emperors, Orators, and Historians" and "Testimonials of Certain Learned Men," in Jacobus Pontanus, *Symbolarum libri xvij Virgilij* (Augsburg: J. Prætorius, 1599), facsimile repr., 3 vols. (New York: Garland, 1976), vol. 1, pp. 15–17, 22–25. Additional testimonials are gathered in John Penkethman, *The Epigrams of P. Virgilius Maro, and Others. With The Praises of him and his Workes* (STC 24825; London: George Purslowe, 1624), sigs. C8^r–D2^v. Virgil's so-called epigrams (e.g., "Of Wine and Women," "The Letter Y," "A River Frozen") are no longer assigned to him, but in the Renaissance they were known collectively as "Virgil's exercises" (*experientiae virgilianae*) and printed with other of his *opuscula* ("minor works"), on which see below, p. 68.

we need to distinguish between innovation and influence. To study influence, what we need to recover are the clichés: the chitchat about Virgil that could be exchanged over cocktails without fear of contradiction, because educated people had all learned more or less the same things in the course of their schooling, and could be expected to hold compatible views. These truisms, to give them no better name, are a better indication of what most readers – including most poets – knew or thought they knew about Virgil than the esoteric lucubrations of an Angelo Poliziano or a Joseph Scaliger.

In this chapter and the two that follow, the conventional wisdom about Virgil is collected under five headings: patronage, erudition, versatility, refinement, and style. Two of these, patronage and versatility, are of special importance in understanding the reception of Virgil's *Eclogues* and *Georgics*, and will be used here to structure an account of those two poems. It is notable – and entirely typical of the whole process of reception in the fifteenth and sixteenth centuries – that each of the five commonplaces we examine was already current in the ancient world,[2] and can be traced to one of six classical sources: the *Institutes* of Quintilian (fl. AD 85), the *Epigrams* of Martial (fl. AD 100), the *Attic Nights* of Aulus Gellius (fl. AD 180), the *Saturnalia* of Macrobius (fl. AD 385), the commentaries of Servius (fl. AD 400), and the biography of Virgil by Aelius Donatus (fl. AD 350). Martial, a contemporary of Statius, was not (like Statius) a disciple of Virgil; but he wrote about Virgil in some of his epigrams, and these influenced Virgil's reputation. Quintilian was, like Martial, born in Spain. Martial mocked him for trying to make young people old before their time (*Epigrams* 2.90.1–4), but in the Renaissance, Quintilian probably had more readers, including young ones; at Cambridge in the sixteenth century, he was frequently assigned in the first year of undergraduate study.[3] Servius has been mentioned before and the *Attic Nights* we have already met, as the model for Poliziano's *Miscellanea*. It preserves anecdotes about scores of classical authors, their critics, and especially their style; Virgil, though, is quoted by Gellius "over twice as often as any of his Latin predecessors."[4]

Macrobius was, if possible, even more influential, because his works did not go out of circulation during the Middle Ages (as Quintilian and Gellius had done). Spenser's friend Gabriel Harvey spoke of reading the *Saturnalia*

---

[2] For general treatments of Virgil's early reception, see R. J. Tarrant, "Aspects of Virgil's Reception in Antiquity," in *The Cambridge Companion to Virgil*, ed. Charles Martindale (Cambridge University Press, 1997), pp. 56–72; Nicholas Horsfall, *A Companion to the Study of Virgil* (Leiden: Brill, 1995), ch. 6; and Richard F. Thomas, *Virgil and the Augustan Reception* (Cambridge University Press, 2001), chs. 1–3.
[3] See Peter Mack, *Elizabethan Rhetoric: Theory and Practice* (Cambridge University Press, 2002), p. 51.
[4] Leofranc Holford-Strevens, *Aulus Gellius* (Chapel Hill: University of North Carolina Press, 1988), p. 153.

for a whole week and began writing a commentary on it in the mid-1570s.[5] His interest was neither unusual nor unwarranted. Modeled on Cicero, the *Saturnalia* is a fictional dialogue that purports to record the dinner conversation at a holiday banquet in AD 383. Servius is one of the speakers in the dialogue, and the primary topic of conversation is Virgil: his learning, his wisdom, and (again, as in Gellius) his style. In the Renaissance, Macrobius was sometimes attacked because, although ancient, he is not always classical – at least in his diction. But as a guide to Virgil, he was regarded as authoritative and indispensable. Thus Antonio da Rho, a professor of rhetoric at Milan in the 1430s: "Not knowing Macrobius, one cannot know Virgil either."[6] Like Servius, the *Saturnalia* was published early: the *editio princeps* appeared in 1472, and never went out of print.

The last figure, but possibly the most important, is Aelius Donatus, who is easily confused with a character from our previous chapter, Tiberius Claudius Donatus (fl. AD 430). Both Donati were regarded as classics, both wrote commentaries on Virgil, and in the Renaissance it was common for printers to misattribute the Tiberius commentary to Aelius, because (unlike Tiberius) Aelius was already famous: for writing a grammar, for being the teacher of St. Jerome, and as the author of a commentary on Terence. Terence was almost universal in Renaissance schoolrooms and Donatus' commentary on Terence was a primary source for scholarship on the origins of comedy.[7] Donatus also wrote a commentary on Virgil, but except for some fragments preserved in Servius, his *Life of Virgil* is all that survives.[8]

The importance of the *Life* has been underestimated.[9] Much of what, today, we attribute to Servius and later commentators was, in fact, original to Donatus; and, in the period we are concerned with, Donatus was probably known to more readers (including, presumably, more poets)

---

[5] See *Gabriel Harvey's Ciceronianus*, ed. Harold S. Wilson and trans. Clarence A. Forbes (Lincoln: University of Nebraska Press, 1945), p. 56.
[6] Qtd. in Martin L. McLaughlin, *Literary Imitation in the Italian Renaissance* (Oxford: Clarendon Press, 1995), p. 112.
[7] See Marvin T. Herrick, *Comic Theory in the Sixteenth Century* (Urbana: University of Illinois Press, 1950).
[8] This work formed the basis of most biographies that circulated in the Middle Ages and Renaissance, including Servius'; see Hollis Ritchie Upson, "Medieval Lives of Virgil," *Classical Philology* 38 (1943), 103–11; Giorgio Brugnoli and Heinrich Naumann, "Vitae Vergilianae," in *Enciclopedia virgiliana*, ed. Francesco Della Corte, 5 vols. in 6 (Rome: Istituto della Enciclopedia Italiana, 1984–91), vol. V, pt. 1, pp. 570–88; and Virginia Brown, "Vitae Vergilianae in Virgilian Commentaries (Saec. XV and XVI)," in *Style and Tradition: Studies in Honor of Wendell Clausen*, ed. Peter Knox and Clive Foss (Stuttgart: Teubner, 1998), pp. 174–98.
[9] But see M. L. Donnelly, "The Life of Vergil and the Aspirations of the 'New Poet,'" *Spenser Studies* 17 (2003), 1–35.

than Servius himself. The census of commentators summarized in Appendix A shows that Donatus' *vita* appeared in at least 112 printed editions before 1600, compared with 125 for Servius. But the real total is probably higher, since the *vita*'s presence often goes unrecorded in library catalogues. In Venetian editions, for which we have complete records,[10] Donatus appears more than 60 percent of the time, compared with exactly 50 percent for Servius.

What made Donatus so popular? Unlike Servius, he was short; this made him cheap to print and, in consequence, cheap to buy. Also, because he was short, Donatus was easy to read in a single sitting. Finally, his is the one document of Virgil criticism that was available from an early date in English translation.[11]

HOW VIRGIL GOT RICH

Virgil's life, as told by Donatus, is a tale of patronage: the story of a middle-class boy who, because of his talent, makes friends with wealthy, influential statesmen and becomes, with their help, wealthy himself. Before he died, Virgil was said to have almost ten million sesterces (when a legionary's annual pay was nine hundred), a house in the exclusive Esquiline district of Rome (next to the famous Gardens of Maecenas), and the use of vacation homes in Campania and Sicily. "Every year, he supported his parents with gold in abundance."[12] The money, says Donatus, came from Virgil's friends (which was the polite way, in ancient society, of saying *patrons*). With friendship came political influence, in addition to wealth, so that in the Renaissance Virgil was remembered, not just as a successful poet – one who could spin verses into gold – but an important poet, a confidant of great men, a counselor to princes, even (what Shelley thought could never be) an acknowledged legislator. The resulting image was one of great power and persistence. For commentators in the Renaissance, the plot of Virgil's eclogues – insofar as they had one – was the story of Virgil's quest for patronage. It suggested that poetry was a way of achieving not only glory after death, but comfort in this world and political influence.

Part of what made the story appealing was that its hero did not begin life as a member of the ruling class. Virgil was born in the provinces, to what

---

[10] See Craig Kallendorf, *A Bibliography of Venetian Editions of Virgil, 1470–1599* (Florence: Olschki, 1991).
[11] Thomas Phaer and Thomas Twyne, trans., *The Whole .xii. Bookes of the Æneidos of Virgill* (STC 24801; London: William How, 1573), sig. aiii^r–bii^v; repr. 1584, 1596, 1600, and 1620.
[12] Donatus auctus 24–25 (Giunta 1544, sig. *ii^r).

Donatus terms "parents of the middling sort." What property they did have was lost when Virgil was in his late twenties, in the aftermath of yet another civil war: this time between the young Octavian and the assassins of Julius Caesar. The assassins were decisively defeated at Philippi and, in order to reward his veterans, Octavian confiscated lands from towns that had sponsored his enemies; the farmers of Virgil's region, Mantua, were loyal to Octavian, but their lands were swallowed up nevertheless, in the confiscations of neighboring Cremona. What saved Virgil was talent. Through poetry, Virgil came to the attention, first of the local administrators; then of Octavian's inner circle; and finally of Octavian himself. More than the so-called *rota Virgilii* of eclogues, georgics, and epic (a sequence which, as we shall see in the next chapter, has been poorly understood), this was the career pattern that poets in the Renaissance tried to imitate from Virgil: not a cycle of genres, but a *cursus honorum*, climaxing in royal patronage. In the formula of one commentator, Jacobus Pontanus, "Talent (*ingenium*) gave birth to friendships, and friendships gave birth to riches."[13]

The most colorful of Virgil's early friendships was that with Cornelius Gallus (70/69–27/6 BC), who was appointed by Octavian to supervise the confiscation of lands and, after Actium, to be the first prefect of Egypt. Once established in the East, however, Gallus was seen to put on airs; and Augustus, scenting another Antony, compelled him through the senate to commit suicide. The story of Gallus and his fall was transmitted to Renaissance scholars by Servius in his commentary on the *Georgics*, for which Virgil was said to have composed two conclusions: the original ending, praising Gallus; and the inset tale of Orpheus and Eurydice, which Virgil inserted "after Gallus was cut down by a wrathful Augustus."[14] In the *Eclogues*, however, Gallus appears as a love poet (the originator, in fact, of Latin elegy), whose faithless girlfriend, identified by Donatus as the courtesan Volumnia Cytheris, abandoned Gallus to follow a soldier, identified in the commentaries as none other than Mark Antony.[15]

Antony, as it happens, did conduct an affair with the celebrated courtesan (also a famous actress). Still, it is surprising how often his name appears in commentaries on the *Eclogues*, since the poems were published in the early thirties, *before* Antony and Augustus had their big dust-up. Servius, however, was muddled about chronology, and conflated the defeat of Brutus and Cassius (at Philippi in 42 BC) with that of Antony and Cleopatra

---

[13] Pontanus (1599) on *Ecl.* 3.85 (col. 79).   [14] Servius on *Geo.* 4.1 (Giunta 1544, fol. 124^r).
[15] Servius, Mancinelli, and Badius on *Ecl.* 10.1 (Giunta 1544, fols. 48^v–49^r), Badius on *Ecl.* 10.31 (fol. 50^r).

(at Actium nine years later).[16] For Servius, then, the political background of the *Eclogues* was not (as we sometimes read) the end of Republican liberty, but the contest for universal empire, between Antony and Octavian. This mistake, made by someone writing more than four centuries after the events in question, cascaded through a thousand years of biographies and commentaries, was not corrected until the sixteenth century, and gave rise to otherwise inexplicable absurdities. The ancient commentator known as Probus made the same error. As late as the fifteenth century, one reads repeatedly that Virgil's lands were confiscated in the aftermath of a war with Mark Antony or his brother Lucius.[17] In some medieval lives of the ninth and tenth centuries, it is even said that Virgil went with Antony to Egypt, and served him there as poet and counselor![18] Renaissance scholars did not make this particular blunder, but they did sometimes continue to give Actium as a context for the *Eclogues*.[19]

According to Servius, the poet who did accompany Antony was named Anser ("Goose") and, like Virgil, he was rewarded for his literary service with lands.[20] Virgil was thought to allude, scornfully, to Anser in Eclogues 7 and 9, and to two other rivals, Bavius and Maevius, in Eclogue 3. Whatever their real talents may have been, Bavius and Maevius were known for being the worst poets of the Augustan age, and for smelling like goats.[21] As for lands, Donatus tells that Virgil got his by making friends with two of Gallus' colleagues, Asinius Pollio (76 BC–AD 4) and Gaius Maecenas (70–8 BC). Maecenas does not appear in the *Eclogues*, but the *Georgics* is addressed to him; and his name (as we shall see) became a byword for patronage as such. Pollio is mentioned a couple of times in Virgil's pastoral, most notably in Eclogue 4, which was later known by his name, as "the Pollio." But even in this poem, Pollio was edged out in the commentaries by the most powerful and famous of all Virgil's patrons, the emperor Augustus. While conceding that the poem is addressed to Pollio, probably on the occasion of his son's birth, Servius refers all of the

---

[16] James E. G. Zetzel, "Servius and Triumviral History in the *Eclogues*," *Classical Philology* 79 (1984), 139–42.
[17] *VT*, pp. 203/205, 253/255, 257/258, 260/262, 271/273, 276/277, 282, 290/292, 295/300, 325/336, 326–27/338–39, 374/388, 376–77/389–90, 399/402, 713.
[18] *VT*, pp. 251/252, 260/262, 264/266, 279/280.
[19] E.g., Mancinelli (1490) on *Ecl*. 4.14 (fol. 25ʳ); Paulo Manuzio (1558) on *Ecl*. 9.109 in *Opera P. Virgilii Maronis* (STC 24789; London: Henry Middleton, 1580), p. 63. The problem of ancient chronology would bedevil scholars well into the next century; see Anthony Grafton, *Joseph Scaliger: A Study in the History of Classical Scholarship*, 2 vols. (Oxford: Clarendon Press, 1983–93), vol. II, pp. 489–743.
[20] Servius on *Ecl*. 9.36 (Giunta 1544, fol. 47ʳ); see also Pontanus (1599), col. 197.
[21] Michael W. Herren, "Bavius and Maevius: 'Duo Pessimi Poetae Sui Temporis,'" in *Anglo-Latin and Its Heritage*, ed. Siân Echard and Gernot R. Wieland (Turnhout: Brepols, 2001), pp. 3–15. The Renaissance text of Donatus has numerous anecdotes about Virgil and his rivals; but while their existence was probably surmised from references in the *Eclogues*, rivalry is (at most) a submotif in the major commentaries.

poem's prophecies to Augustus.[22] For Servius, and even more so for his modern disciples, Virgil's relationship with his patron Augustus was the central theme, not just of Eclogue 4, but of the whole collection.

Servius, though, did not invent this image, or even its application to the *Eclogues*. In his *Life of Virgil*, Donatus tells how Virgil was introduced into the emperor's inner circle, where he succeeded in gaining, not only his farm, but the friendship of Augustus. In the *Life*, Augustus demonstrates his appreciation for fine literature, both by lavishing estates and gold on the poet, and by saving the manuscript of his unfinished epic. Ever the perfectionist, Virgil had consigned it to the flames in his will. (This speaks to his refinement, the subject of Chapter 4.) Augustus, however, recognized the value of the work and countermanded the poet's instructions. True or false, the intervention of the emperor became part of the lore of the *Aeneid*'s history. The Elizabethan critic George Puttenham (1529–1590/91) tells the story as an illustration of poetry's high regard in the ancient world and quotes from a Latin poem, attributed to Augustus, that gave texture to the legend.[23] Another poem on the same theme was attributed to the teacher of Aulus Gellius, C. Sulpicius Apollinaris (2nd century AD). Both poems were printed frequently in Renaissance editions of Virgil.[24]

Octavian's sister, Octavia, was also remembered as a friend to Virgil and poetry. In *Palladis Tamia* (1598), Francis Meres tells how she rewarded Virgil for some lines (*Aen.* 6.860–86) on the untimely death of her only son, Marcellus, and proposes her as a model for modern female patrons:

Octauia, sister vnto Augustus the Emperour, was exceeding bountifull vnto Virgil, who gave him for making 26 verses, 1,137 pounds, to wit, tenne *sestertiæ* for euerie verse (which amounted to about 43 pounds for euery verse): so learned Mary, the honourable Countesse of Pembrook, the noble sister of immortall Sir Philip Sidney, is very liberall vnto Poets.[25]

The story of Octavia and Virgil is also found in Donatus (where Meres found it), but not until the fifteenth century.

---

[22] See also *Ecl.* 8.6–11: where today scholars see an allusion to Pollio's military campaign in Parthia, Servius and the modern commentators Mancinelli and Badius found a reference to Augustus (Giunta 1544, fol. 41ʳ). Commenting on *Ecl.* 6.9, Badius characterizes the whole book as a command performance, in which Virgil pauses occasionally to acknowledge a friend of lower rank (fol. 32ᵛ).
[23] George Puttenham, *The Arte of English Poesie* (1589), 1.8, ed. Gladys Doidge Willcock and Alice Walker (Cambridge University Press, 1936), p. 22.
[24] See Kallendorf, *Venetian Editions*; Martin Davies and John Goldfinch, *Vergil: A Census of Printed Editions 1469–1500* (London: The Bibliographical Society, 1992).
[25] *ECE*, vol. II, pp. 321–22. "Tenne *sestertiae*" is an error for "ten thousand sesterces"; cf. Donatus auctus 39 (Giunta 1544, sig. *iiᵛ).

54   *Patronage and the* Eclogues

VIRGIL AS COUNSELOR TO THE PRINCE

This brings us to an important distinction. The text of Donatus exists in two versions: the *vita* proper, and a work that is variously known as *Donatus auctus*, the interpolated *vita*, the vulgate *vita*, and the humanistic *vita* (because it first appears in humanistic manuscripts of the fifteenth century).[26] In the printed editions that I have handled myself, it is always the longer, humanistic version of the *Life* that appears. The additions consist of anecdotes such as the following. According to Donatus, Virgil's *Eclogues* met with immediate success and were even recited on stage. This was high praise, but it still lacked one thing: the authority of Cicero. That was supplied in the humanistic version by an anecdote from Servius:

> As for Cicero, when he had heard some of the verses, his piercing (*acri*) judgment immediately perceived that these were productions of uncommon genius, and ordered the whole eclogue to be recited from the beginning. Having familiarized himself with its every nuance (*accurate pernotasset*), he declared it "the second great hope of Rome," as if he himself were the first hope of the Latin language and Maro the second. These words Virgil later inserted in the *Aeneid* [at 12.168].[27]

Cicero had a big ego and the remarks are in character. There was only one problem: Cicero died in 43 BC, but Virgil's *Eclogues* did not begin to appear in Roman bookstalls until *c.* 39 BC. As we have seen, confusion about the chronology of Virgil's writings was widespread and long-lasting. The discrepancy was pointed out in 1555, by Sebastiano Corrado and, in the same year, by Peter Ramus,[28] but to no effect. Readers did not care, or did not care to know, that their favorite episodes were bogus. In 1600, Pierre Daniel issued a corrected text of the *vita* which omitted the interpolations, and again the book-buying public looked the other way. As Fabio Stok has shown, "the *Donatus auctus* was

---

[26] Fabio Stok now dates the humanistic *vita* to between 1426 and 1437; see *Prolegomeni a una nuova edizione della Vita Vergilii di Svetonio-Donato* (Rome: Accademia nazionale dei Lincei, 1991), pp. 197–200. On the history of the text, its sources and afterlife, see Vladimiro Zabughin, *Vergilio nel rinascimento italiano da Dante a Torquato Tasso*, 2 vols. (Bologna: Zanichelli, 1921–23), vol. I, ch. 2; and Stok, "Il rinascimento della biografia virgiliana," *Res publica litterarum* 14 (1991), 229–39. A critical edition is available; see Giorgio Brugnoli and Fabio Stok, eds., *Vitae vergilianae antiquae* (Rome: Istituto polygraphico, 1997), pp. 71–135 (cited here as "Donatus auctus"). My translation, available online at virgil.org, indicates the post-classical insertions with angle brackets.

[27] Donatus auctus 41 (Giunta 1544, sig. *ii^v). Cf. Servius on *Ecl.* 6.11.

[28] For Corrado, see Zabughin, *Vergilio nel rinascimento*, vol. II, p. 83 and Duane Reed Stuart, "Biographical Criticism of Vergil since the Renaissance," *Studies in Philology* 19 (1922), 1–30, at 12–14; for Ramus, see Alice Hulubei, "Virgile en France au XVIe siècle: éditions, traductions, imitations," *Revue du seizième siècle* 18 (1931–32), 1–77, at 17. The problem was noticed a century earlier by Sicco Polenton (1375/6–1447), who reasoned that, if Cicero knew the *Eclogues*, it was evidence that Virgil composed them at an earlier date than was usually thought (*VT*, pp. 326–27/338–39, 376–77/389–90).

the current biography of Virgil (the 'Vulgata') right up to the beginning of the nineteenth century."[29]

The two versions differ primarily in that the vulgate *Life* includes more anecdotes relating to the poet's learning (discussed in the next chapter) and the patronage of Augustus, which is our subject here. In one anecdote, Augustus asks Agrippa and Maecenas whether or not he should abdicate and restore the Republic. Agrippa urges the emperor to abdicate, but Maecenas counsels against it.[30] Virgil is called upon to cast the deciding vote, and the rest is history. Actually, it was fiction. The source for the episode is the Roman historian Cassius Dio (*c*. AD 164–after 229), who records that a debate between Maecenas and Agrippa did take place in the year 29 BC. Dio invents a series of long speeches for both of Caesar's interlocutors, and clearly favors the side of monarchy.[31] But Virgil's role he does not mention; that was an invention of the fifteenth century.

At least, the form of it was; the idea that a poet can offer political advice to his patron was older and had a parallel (or perhaps even its roots) in the medieval tradition that Virgil was a magician.[32] This tradition was still vital

---

[29] Fabio Stok, "Virgil between the Middle Ages and the Renaissance," *International Journal of the Classical Tradition* 1.2 (1994), 15–22, at 21–22. Corrado's strictures on the humanistic *vita* appeared in *Sebastiani Corradi Commentarius, in quo P. Virgilii Maronis liber primus Aeneidos explicatur* (Florence: Laurentius Torrentinus, 1555). The book was small (16°) but stout (390 numbered pages), and covered only the first book of Virgil's epic; to my knowledge, it was never reprinted, though excerpts on the life of Virgil – "Alia ad Virgilii vitam pertinentia, ex Sebastiano Corrado" – were included in a Parisian edition by Henri Estienne in 1583. Errors in the life were also noticed by Lorenzo Valla, who in 1449 suggested that perhaps the famous grammarian was not the author of the life after all (Stuart, "Biographical Criticism," 10–11). Consequently the life was titled in some editions "The Life of P. Virgilius Maro which is said to have been authored by Donatus" (*Opera* [Paris: Thielman Kerver, 1500], no sig.) or even "The Life of P. Virgilius Maro which is said to have been authored by Donatus even though it hardly sounds like him" (*cum tamen minime eius phrasim redoleat*; Giunta 1544, sig. *ii^r). Badius Ascensius welcomed the suggestion that Donatus was not the author of the life because it did away with the main evidence for assigning to Virgil the pornographic epigrams mentioned below; see his preface to Virgil's *Opera* in Giunta 1544, sig. *ix^v. Scholars today assign most of the life to Suetonius, but treat even this material with skepticism; see Horsfall, *Companion*, ch. 2.

[30] Donatus auctus 78–79 (Giunta 1544, sig. *ii^r, printer's error for *iii^r). See also *ibid.* 72: "When Augustus asked, under what constitution a state might be governed most productively, Virgil said, 'If the wiser sort (*prudentiores*) should steer, and were good men appointed over evil men, then would the aristocrats (*optimi*) have the honors that were due to them, while the rest would suffer no injustice.'" In today's editions of the *vita*, both passages are omitted.

[31] L. Cassius Dio, *The Roman History*, bk. 52.

[32] Many of these stories were first collected by Domenico Comparetti in *Virgilio mago e innamorato* (n.p.: Nuova Antologia, 1867); a larger collection was made by John Webster Spargo, *Virgil the Necromancer: Studies in Virgilian Legends* (Cambridge, MA: Harvard University Press, 1934). S. J. Tunison, *Master Virgil, The Author of the Æneid as He Seemed in the Middle Ages: A Series of Studies*, 2nd edn. (Cincinnati: Clark, 1890), traces the legends to the eighteenth century. According to Comparetti, the *magus* was a folk tradition and originated in Virgil's adopted hometown of Naples. Tunison showed that, in fact, the legends were already in written form when they arrived in Naples, having originated in France and Germany.

56   *Patronage and the* Eclogues

in the sixteenth century, and even gained currency through the medium of print. The formula of these legends is unvarying: in Rome or Naples there was such-and-such a crisis, and "the Emperour asked counsayl of Virgilius" what to do.³³ Virgil's solution is often some piece of new technology: an iron robot to hunt down criminals, or mechanical statues that point to Rome's enemies. None of these stories has any classical documentation, so in the Renaissance scholars tend to ignore them. But the message which they encoded – the prince of poets is one who counsels princes – was carried over into the commentaries by way of woodcuts. One image, repeated by several artists, has Virgil posed by Augustus' throne, as if he is one of his counselors.³⁴ For imitators of Virgil, this was what success looked like. It was a fantasy, perhaps, but not an absurdity. According to George Puttenham, King Francis I (1494–1547) "made *Sangelais, Salmonius Macrinus*, and *Clement Marot* of his priuy Chamber for their excellent skill in vulgare and Latine Poesie."³⁵ Ariosto was an ambassador and Boiardo an administrator.

ECLOGUES AS ENCOMIA

In the humanistic *vita*, Virgil gains the friendship of Augustus through wit and cleverness. Three ancient writers – Macrobius, Aelius Donatus, and Tacitus – mention letters as passing between them,³⁶ and as late as the fifteenth century one sometimes reads that the two men were classmates in the rhetoric school of Epidius.³⁷ But in commentaries on the *Eclogues*, Virgil is presented as courting the emperor's favor by praising him allegorically (especially in Eclogues 1, 4, 8.6–11, and 9); or by lauding his adoptive father, Julius Caesar (throughout Eclogue 5 and fleetingly in 9.46–48); or by complimenting a male favorite (in Eclogue 2).³⁸ As Appendix B shows, there were numerous commentaries on the *Eclogues*, but in what follows we shall be looking primarily at the five who were printed most frequently: the ancient commentators Servius, Aelius Donatus (who ended his *Life of Virgil* with an introduction to the *Eclogues*), and Marcus Valerius Probus (who probably did not write the commentary that was printed under his name);

---

³³ Anonymous, *Virgilius* (STC 24828; Antwerp: Iohan Doesborcke, 1518?), sig. C4ʳ.
³⁴ See Donnelly, "Aspirations of the 'New Poet,'" 10–18.
³⁵ Puttenham, *Arte of English Poesie* 1.8 (ed. Willcock and Walker, p. 16).   ³⁶ *VT*, pp. 4–5, 60.
³⁷ *VT*, pp. 250, 271/273, 281/282, 397/400.
³⁸ Such were the views of the most popular ancient commentator, Servius, and the most popular modern commentators, Mancinelli and Badius. In each case, Servius proposes the interpretation and the moderns elaborate; the exception, Eclogue 2, is discussed in Chapter 4.

and the modern commentators Antonio Mancinelli (1452–c. 1505) and Jodocus Badius Ascensius (whom we have met already and shall encounter again many times in the chapters to come).

One thing that the five agreed on was that Virgil's *Eclogues* praise the emperor. When, in *Ecl.* 8.10, Virgil promises to sing someone's deeds (today we think Pollio's) in the tragic manner of Sophocles, Mancinelli says that these are the achievements of Augustus, which Virgil publicized (*celebrauit*) in the *Eclogues*, the *Georgics*, and the *Aeneid*. Badius agrees, and makes a further generalization: "Virgilian poetry has for its goal (*definit ad*) the praise of Augustus, as is well known."[39]

How well known? Since at least the fourth century AD. According to Donatus, and after him Servius, the aim (*intentio*) of the *Eclogues* was two-fold: to imitate Theocritus and "to praise Caesar and the other leading men who helped him to regain his home and all his belongings."[40] For Servius, the goal of the *Aeneid* was similar: "to imitate Homer and praise Augustus through his ancestors."[41] What this meant for imitators of Virgil is shown by Ariosto's Elizabethan translator, Sir John Harington (1539/40–1613). "*Virgill*," he writes, "extolled *Æneas* to please *Augustus*, of whose race he was thought to come; *Ariosto* prayseth *Rogero* to the honour of the house of *Este*." For Harington, the panegyrical material in Ariosto is part of what makes him a Virgilian poet, and therefore an acceptable poet for high-minded audiences: "there is nothing of any speciall obseruation in *Virgill* but my author hath with great felicitie imitated it, so as whosoeuer will allow *Virgil* must *ipso facto* (as they say) admit *Ariosto*."[42]

As we shall see, Ariosto was critical of Virgil, because he saw Virgil's praise as propaganda. But there was a theory, widespread in the ancient world and well nigh universal in the Renaissance, that all poetry, no matter what genre, can be classified as praise or blame.[43] We shall say more on this in Chapter 6; here our subject is praise of patrons. What is the proper relationship

---

[39] Giunta 1544, fol. 41r.
[40] Donatus 64 (Giunta 1544, sig. *iiv, printer's error for *iiiv). Servius, in his introduction to the *Eclogues*, uses almost the same language (sig. *xr).
[41] Giunta 1544, fol. 146r.   [42] *ECE*, vol. II, pp. 211–12.
[43] For the ancient world, see Gregory Nagy, "Early Greek Views of Poets and Poetry," in *The Cambridge History of Literary Criticism*, vol. I: *Classical Criticism*, ed. George A. Kennedy (Cambridge University Press, 1989), pp. 1–77, at pp. 8–18; for the Renaissance, O. B. Hardison, *The Enduring Monument: A Study of the Idea of Praise in Renaissance Literary Theory and Practice* (Chapel Hill: University of North Carolina Press, 1962), pp. 40–48; Brian Vickers, "Epideictic and Epic in the Renaissance," *New Literary History* 14 (1983), 497–537; and Craig Kallendorf, *In Praise of Aeneas: Virgil and Epideictic Rhetoric in the Early Italian Renaissance* (Hanover: University Press of New England, 1989).

between author and patron?[44] Specifically, what should a poet do when the patron is not praiseworthy? In theory, the poet was supposed to offer praise anyway: not as propaganda, to deceive the outside world, but to force the patron's hand, thanking him in advance for favors which, in fact, he had not yet decided to grant, or for virtues which, outside of fiction, he did not already possess.

In the *Eclogues*, Virgil praises Augustus retrospectively, for favors already granted, and prospectively, for favors he hopes to obtain. Retrospective praise is the occasion of Eclogue 1, in which Virgil is said to praise Augustus for restoring his lands.[45] In Eclogue 9, however, the petition has to be renewed, either because Virgil is under threat from the veteran who would otherwise stand to gain his property (Servius and Badius) or because Virgil, having already obtained his own lands, wants now to save those of his fellow townsfolk (Mancinelli and Badius).[46] Either way, his strategy is to praise Augustus. First, he describes the comet which attended Julius Caesar's funeral and was received as a sign of his apotheosis (vv. 46–49); Badius, in his summary of the poem, calls this "a respectful reference" to the emperor's adoptive father.[47] Then in vv. 51–52, Virgil mentions the "long suns" of summer; according to Servius, Mancinelli, and Badius, this alludes to the months of July and August, which were named in honor of Julius Caesar and Augustus. Together, these compliments reveal Virgil's intention: according to Badius, "all things aim (*tendunt*) here: for Maro to redeem back the fields that have been seized and to obtain entry to the favor of Augustus."[48] To this end, the eclogue concludes with a promise for more praise: "we shall sing better songs" (v. 67), either when the lands are returned (Mancinelli, Badius) or when the battle of Actium is concluded (Servius), at which point, presumably, Virgil will have another occasion to praise Augustus.

---

[44] The scholarship on authors and patrons is a dense forest, in which the following are trustworthy guides: for Virgil's period, Peter White, *Promised Verse: Poets in the Society of Augustan Rome* (Cambridge, MA: Harvard University Press, 1993); Phebe Lowell Bowditch, *Horace and the Gift Economy of Patronage* (Berkeley and Los Angeles: University of California Press, 2001); and for our period, *Patronage in the Renaissance*, ed. Guy Fitch Lytle and Stephen Orgel (Princeton: Princeton University Press, 1981); Graham Parry, "Literary Patronage," in *The Cambridge History of Early Modern English Literature*, ed. David Loewenstein and Janel Mueller (Cambridge University Press, 2002), pp. 117–40; and Julio Vélez-Sainz, *El parnaso español: Canon, mecenazgo y propaganda en la poesía del siglo de oro* (Madrid: Visor, 2006).

[45] Badius, summary of Eclogue 1 (Giunta 1544, sig. *x^v).

[46] Another possibility, raised by Servius in his introduction (Giunta 1544, fol. 1^r), is that Eclogue 9 was written before Eclogue 1.

[47] Badius, summary of Eclogue 9 (Giunta 1544, fol. 45^r).   [48] Badius on *Ecl.* 1.1 (fol. 46^r).

WAS VIRGIL A FLATTERER?

The question comes up more in discussions of Virgil's epic than of his *Eclogues*, but we will deal with it here, as an aspect of patronage. As Tasso explains in *Discourses on the Epic Poem* (1594), it is the duty of an epic poet to give praise, and for this Virgil is the great model. Thus Tasso: in choosing a subject for his epic, a poet "should consider the glory of his country, the origins of cities and famous families, and the foundations of kingdoms and empires, as did beyond all others Virgil."[49] But the bid for patronage must not be too obvious; the key terms, therefore, are origins (*origine*) and foundations (*principi*). Like Ariosto, Tasso was patronized by the ducal family of Ferrara; unlike Ariosto, who applauded his benefactors by name, Tasso worked indirectly, and praised them *a parentibus*, by means of their *famiglie*. His model in this was Virgil, as expounded by Servius. In both poems, a mythical ancestor functions as a surrogate for the living patron. Thus, in Virgil's epic, Augustus is usually glorified obliquely, in the person of Aeneas;[50] direct references to Augustus, when they appear in the text at all, are always in the form of prophecy.[51] Tasso's method is more severe: apart from the dedication to Alfonso d'Este, there are no direct references to living patrons in the text of Tasso's epic. Instead, Tasso traces the history of the family and celebrates its founder, a fictional warrior named Rinaldo.[52]

That was in 1581. Five years later, Tasso entered the service of a rival prince and, when he revised the poem for a new edition (1593), he deleted all references to Alfonso, including the oblique ones. The story is complicated: Tasso was irritable and took offense easily; Alfonso put up with him for a long time. Still, he was no Rinaldo.

But who is? According to Badius, Virgil did not portray Aeneas "as he always was, but as he ought to have been." His model in this was Xenophon's portrait of Cyrus. Aeneas was chosen, not because he *is* Augustus, but because he is Augustus' ancestor (by way of Julius Caesar), and therefore Augustus would naturally want to imitate him; or, failing that, would at least be ashamed to be *worse* than Aeneas.[53] Sidney has a similar theory. If you want, he says, to know what someone looked like, then it is

---

[49] Torquato Tasso, *Discorsi del poema eroico* (1594), Bk. 2, in *Prose*, ed. Ettore Mazzali (Milan: Ricciardi, 1959), p. 554.
[50] For examples from Servius, see Michael O'Connell, *Mirror and Veil: The Historical Dimension of Spenser's* Faerie Queene (Chapel Hill: University of North Carolina Press, 1977), pp. 3–15.
[51] *Aen.* 1.293–96; 6.791–805; 8.675–722.
[52] The most important passage is *GL* 17.64–81, in which Rinaldo beholds the founders of the Este dynasty depicted on a metal shield. Cf. *Aen.* 6.756–886 and esp. 8.608–731.
[53] Badius, preface to *Aeneid* (Giunta 1544, fol. 147ʳ).

best to have the painter give a faithful rendering. "But if the question be for your owne vse and learning, whether it be better to haue it set downe as it should be, or as it was, then certainly is more doctrinable the fained *Cirus* in *Xenophon* then the true *Cyrus* in *Iustine*, and the fayned *Aeneas* in *Virgil* then the right *Aeneas* in *Dares Phrigius*."[54]

Sidney was satisfied, but not Ariosto. In his reading, Virgil's Aeneas is a portrait of Augustus, and the portrait is a lie. "Augustus was neither so saintly, nor so kindly, as the trumpet of Virgil proclaimed" (*OF* 35.26). In particular, Ariosto is troubled by the proscriptions that accompanied Octavian's rise to power. In 43 BC, Octavian and Mark Antony made a list of citizens who were unfavorable to their cause, declaring them outlaws and seizing their property. This was unjust, continues Ariosto, but Augustus had good taste in poetry and that pardons his crime – at which point, Ariosto begins a long tribute to the House of Este, modeled on Virgil's praise of Augustus. The sequence (and the implication) are crass: Virgil was a flatterer – and so am I, when I sing of you.[55] Now, can I have my pension?

MAECENAS AS THE MODEL PATRON

The charge of flattery never went away. We hear it from France in the twelfth century: "Virgil's muse gave color to many lies / And wove false mantles over the face of truth."[56] From Italy in the fourteenth century: "But to flatter (*ut ... adularetur*) the emperor, [Virgil] mixed many lies with the truth."[57] And from England in the seventeenth: "I cannot flatter with smooth *Virgils* pen / Or giue *Augustus* more then he should haue."[58]

But this, as we have said, was more a problem for epic poets than for pastoral. In pastoral, the problem for Virgilian poets is not whether to flatter, but where to find, a patron. The key figure here was Virgil's other "friend," Maecenas. For poets after Virgil, Maecenas was the image of a model sponsor to the extent that, even today, his name is used as a synonym for *patron* in dozens of languages, including not only the Romance languages but also Finnish (*mesenaatti*) and Russian (меценат). This usage was already established in the Renaissance: for example, in Thomas Cooper's

---

[54] *An Apologie for Poetrie* (c. 1583), in *ECE*, vol. 1, p. 168. Tasso makes the same argument and uses the same pair of examples in *Apologia in defesa della* Gerusalemme liberata (1585), in *Prose*, pp. 434–36.
[55] See David Quint, "Astolfo's Voyage to the Moon," *Yale Italian Studies* 1 (1977), 398–408.
[56] Alain de Lille, *Anticlaudianus* 1.142–43 (qtd. *VT*, p. 309).
[57] Domenico di Bandino, *Vita Virgili* (*VT*, p. 309).
[58] Thomas Heywood, *Troia Britanica*, 12.2, in *Troia Britanica: or, Great Britaines Troy* (STC 13366; London: W. Jaggard, 1609), p. 304.

Latin-English dictionary (1565), Maecenas is identified as "A gentleman of Rome[,] minion to Augustus the Emperour: and bycause hee was the supporter of great learned men, all fauourers and succourers of learned men be so called."[59]

When the name is used this way, generically, it is normally tied to a complaint: if only we had a Maecenas, our poetry would blossom just as Horace's and Virgil's did. The *locus classicus* is Martial, writing in AD 86, a century after Virgil died:

> Often you say to me, dearest Lucius Julius,
>   "Write something important, you lazy creature."
> But give us leisure (*otia*), such as once
>   Maecenas did for Horace and his Virgil:
> I'd apply myself to such exertions as would outlive the ages
>   And rescue my name out of the flames.[60]

Eight years later, Martial is still making the same excuse (and the same promise) to another patron:

> You're shocked: "Talent like His Holiness, Virgil's, has disappeared
>   And no one can trumpet out wars in the same style."
> Flaccus, where there are Maecenases, Virgils won't be lacking:
>   A country estate will get you one for sure.[61]

Through these two poems, Maecenas would be remembered in aftertimes as the rich man who buys into existence a golden age of poetry. Thus in 1549, Joachim Du Bellay prophesies that modern poetry will flourish in France when it begins to receive adequate patronage: "Surely if we had Maecenases and Augustuses, Heaven and Nature are not so hostile to our century, that we should not also have our Virgils."[62] In 1589, Thomas Nashe (1567–1601?) makes the same pitch for English literature and uses the same examples: if English poetry "wanders abroade vnrewarded in the mouthes of vngratefull monsters," it is because "those of higher place" have neglected "the remembrance of *Mæcenas* liberalitie extended to *Maro*, and men of like qualitie."[63]

Such a one, he goes on to say, is the "diuine Master *Spencer*," and in the next century Spenser would indeed be remembered as the Elizabethan poet

---

[59] Thomas Cooper, *Thesaurus Linguæ Romanæ & Britannicæ* (STC 5688; London: [Henry Denham], 1578), sig. Llllll.vi[v].
[60] Martial, *Epigrams* 1.107. In [*Epigrammata cum commentariis Domitii Calderini*] (Venice: Baptista de Tortis, 1485), sig. c v[r].
[61] *Epigrams* 8.55.3–8 (1485 edn., sig. m viii[r]).
[62] *La deffence et illustration de la langue francoyse* 2.5, ed. Henri Chamard, 3rd edn. (Paris: Didier, 1966), pp. 132–33.
[63] Thomas Nashe, "To the Gentlemen Students of Both Vniuersities" (1589), in *ECE*, vol. 1, p. 318.

who, like Virgil, flowered in the shade of royal patronage; but this was in reference to Spenser's epic.[64] In his pastoral, Spenser grumbles about the decay of patronage:

> Indeede the Romish *Tityrus*, I heare,
> Through his *Mecœnas* left his Oaten reede,
> Whereon he earst had taught his flocks to feede,
> And laboured lands to yield the timely eare,
> And eft did sing of warres and deadly drede,
> So as the Heauens did quake his verse to here.
>
> But ah *Mecœnas* is yclad in claye,
> And great *Augustus* long ygoe is dead.   ("October," 55–63)

Complaints about the decay of patronage were common in the last decades of Elizabeth's reign, but the problem was not peculiar to England or even to the 1500s. Spenser was not the first poet to compose an eclogue on this theme, nor would he be the last. Mantuan had written one in the 1470s (from which Spenser borrows here), and Thomas Lodge would publish another one in 1596 (modeled on Spenser).[65] Each of the three follows the same pattern and uses the same examples.

Tityrus, in the verses quoted here, is of course the prosperous shepherd in Virgil's first eclogue, the one who finds favor with a young god and is allowed by him to keep his lands. As recognized by Virgil's contemporaries and (beginning with Donatus) recorded by almost every commentator, Tityrus stands for the poet and the young god represents Octavian, who gave Virgil back his farm and became his patron.[66] According to E. K., Spenser's official commentator, the next verses refer to "the three seuerall

---

[64] See George Wither, "Another to His Majestie," 21–34, in *Iuvenilia* (STC 25912; London: Robert Allott, 1633), pp. 264–65; and John Eliot, "To the Lord Chamberlain," 55–68, in *Poems consisting of Epistles and Epigrams, Satyrs, Epitaphs and Elogies, Songs and Sonnets* (Wing E524A; London: Henry Brome, 1658), p. 110.

[65] Mantuan, *Adulescentia* 5 (pub. 1498); Lodge, "To Rowland. Eclogue. 3"; lines 65–80 of Lodge's poem are modeled directly on Spenser.

[66] For the ancient reception, see Antonino Romano, "L'allegoria della prima ecloga di Vergilio secondo gli antichi commentatori," in *Miscellanea di archeologia, storia e filologia dedicata al Prof. Antonino Salinas nel LX anniversario del suo insegnamento accademico* (Palermo: Virzi, 1907), pp. 118–25; Raymond J. Starr, "Vergil's Seventh *Eclogue* and Its Readers: Biographical Allegory as an Interpretive Strategy in Antiquity and Late Antiquity," *Classical Philology* 90 (1995), 129–38, at 131–32; and Marianne Wifstrand Schiebe, *Vergil og Tityrus: En studie i selvbiografisk læsning af Bucolica* (Copenhagen: Museum Tusculanums, 1998). Renaissance commentaries made this identification in the first line of the first poem, citing Probus and Servius as their authority (Mancinelli and Badius, fol. 1ᵛ). Even Peter Ramus, who usually rejected allegory, endorsed this one; see Peter Mack, "Ramus Reading: The Commentaries on Cicero's *Consular Orations* and Vergil's *Eclogues* and *Georgics*," *Journal of the Warburg and Courtald Institutes* 61 (1998), 111–41, at 124–41.

workes of Virgile ... For in teaching his flocks to feede, is meant his Æglogues. In labouring of lands, is hys Georgiques. In singing of wars and deadly dreade, is his diuine Æneis figured." We shall say more on this in Chapter 3; as we shall see there, he is talking about style as much as genre. But he is also making a point about patronage: were it not for Maecenas, Virgil might never have written anything more than eclogues. This too comes from Martial. When Maecenas made a gift to Virgil of a handsome slaveboy (on whom more in Chapter 4), Virgil was said to switch immediately into high gear:

> Thunderstruck, the poet forgot all about ripe Galatea
>   And the harvester Thestylis, with her sun-tanned cheeks.
> On the spot he came up with *Italy* and *Arma virumque* –
>   The same one who, lately, was making clumsy moans over a gnat![67]

Galatea and Thestylis are characters from the *Eclogues*. *Italy* refers to the famous *laus Italiae* in *Georgics* 2.136–76 and *Arma virumque* is of course the opening phrase of the *Aeneid*. The gnat is Virgil's *Culex*, an allegory about an ungrateful patron; today scholars no longer attribute the *Culex* to Virgil, but in the Renaissance it was assumed to be his (partly on the strength of this epigram) and assigned to his juvenilia.[68] Spenser published a translation of *Culex* in 1591, prefaced with a complaint about the late Robert Dudley, one of his earliest would-be patrons.

In *The Shepheardes Calender* (1579), Spenser was angling for the patronage of Dudley's nephew, Sir Philip Sidney. Sidney died in 1586, so for his epic, *The Faerie Queene* (1590), Spenser went to (among others) Sidney's father-in-law, Sir Francis Walsingham, and reminded him of Virgil and Maecenas. His appeal was modeled on Martial:

> That Mantuane Poetes incompared spirit
> Whose girland now is set in highest place,
> Had not *Mecænas* for his worthy merit,
> It first aduaunst to great *Augustus* grace,
> Might long perhaps haue lien in silence bace,
> Ne bene so much admir'd of later age.

Spenser goes on to hail Walsingham as "the great *Mecenas* of this age" and hints that patronage would be requited with "bigger tunes," just as Martial

---

[67] Martial, *Epigrams* 8.55.17–20 (1485 edn., sig. m viii').
[68] The term *Appendix virgiliana*, as a collective title for Virgil's shorter, probably spurious works, was introduced by Joseph Scaliger, who investigated their authenticity. Prior to 1573, when Scaliger published his inquiries, poems such as *Culex* and *Catalepta* were known as Virgil's *opuscula*, his "minor works." The most popular commentaries, by Badius Ascensius (1501) and Domitius Calderinus (c. 1480), were reprinted upwards of thirty and even forty times, respectively.

had promised to write "something important" (*aliquid magnum*) for Lucius Julius. But Walsingham was no Maecenas; for one thing, he had no money (he was buried at night to save funeral expenses) and, so far as we know, he never gave Spenser anything.

Why did poets need patrons? The classical explanation came from one of Martial's contemporaries, Juvenal. "Who will be your Maecenas?" he asks in Satire 7. Poetry needs patrons because it comes from "a care-free mind" (*Anxietate carens animus*).[69] Spenser echoes this in the eclogue we quoted earlier: "The vaunted verse a vacant head demaundes, / Ne wont with crabbed care the Muses dwell" ("October," 100–1). To illustrate, Juvenal gives the example of Virgil: "Had Virgil lacked a slave, or a decent room, / All of the snakes would have fallen from the Fury's hair; / The trumpet been mute, no grave note sounded."[70] Ironically, Juvenal never names any of his own patrons, possibly because he was too rich to require one. But for poets who did, Virgil and Maecenas were the great pattern.

DARKNESS INVISIBLE

The extent to which patronage defined and even distorted Renaissance interpretations of Virgil's pastoral can be tested by studying the reception of Eclogues 1 and 9. Today, these poems are regarded as some of Virgil's darkest and most complex. In Eclogue 1, the happiness of Tityrus (rejoicing in his new patron, the young god Octavian) is balanced by the unmerited wretchedness of the shepherd Meliboeus, and the last image of the poem is one of lengthening shadows. In Eclogue 9, Mantuans are still having their lands seized and poetry seems powerless to change anything: "Our songs," says the old shepherd Moeris, "Avail only as much among the spears of Mars / As the proverbial Chaonian doves, when an eagle comes" (11–13).

The materials for such a reading – cautious about empire, critical of Augustus – are there in the text. What varies from age to age is how much weight they receive from critics and commentators. In the Renaissance, some weight was given, but less than we might expect. Sidney, when he defends the low-style genre of pastoral, sounds like one of us:

Is the poore pype disdained, which sometime out of *Melibeus* mouth can shewe the miserie of people vnder hard Lords or rauening Souldiours? and again, by *Titirus*,

---

[69] Juvenal, *Satires* 7.93, 57 in *Juvenalis [opera] cum tribus commentariis* (Venice: Simone Bevilaqua, 1497), sig. nn iiii[r–v].
[70] *Satires* 7.69–71 (1497 edn., sig. nn iiii[r–v]).

what blessednes is deriued to them that lye lowest from the goodnesse of them that sit highest?[71]

But this oft-quoted passage is not representative; it is an example, rather, of Sidney's originality. Badius, whose commentary is a better guide to what most Europeans would have learned about the *Eclogues*, describes Meliboeus, not as a victim of "hard Lords," whose suffering offsets or even nullifies the prosperity of Tityrus, but as a literary foil. His plight (says Badius), which Virgil dramatizes in detail, makes the benefit conferred by Augustus more weighty and more splendid, by showing the effect of its absence – just as in Homer the departure of Achilles illustrates his value to the Greeks.[72]

The ancient commentators were more open to the idea of criticism. According to Probus, Eclogue 9 "condemns" Augustus, but was written early; after Virgil received his lands back, he praised Augustus in Eclogue 1, and to avoid offending him, buried Eclogue 9 in a less conspicuous place: not at the beginning of the book, and not at the end. Servius goes farther, and finds elements of dispraise in both eclogues. In Eclogue 1, he says that verses 12 and 27 criticize Augustus "privily" (*latenter*); and in Eclogue 9, that verse 5 does so "almost openly" (*pæne aperte*).[73]

These were seeds, though, not full-blown readings. For Servius, the overall aim (*intentio*) of the *Eclogues* was still "to imitate Theocritus and to praise Caesar." The question that we have to ask, then, is what became of the seeds? Did they germinate and grow up into a tradition? Or did they lie dead in the ground, for lack of tending? The answer, to some, will be disappointing: the seeds died with Servius. The most important modern commentators, Mancinelli and Badius, do not refute, but they do not elaborate, amplify, or even transmit the suggestion that, in some verses of the *Eclogues*, Virgil criticized his patron.[74] The reason has less to do with social piety and more with readerly inertia. Unless they have great willpower, most readers and scholars find only what they are looking for. In this case, modern commentators already had a strong hint from classical commentators that the *Eclogues* were about Virgil getting his lands back, and that he used the poems to praise Augustus, even to flatter him into granting further benefits (such as giving back all of Mantua's lands, not just Virgil's). One scholar, Vives, thought this approach too limited and looked for new

---

[71] *Apologie* (*ECE*, vol. 1, p. 175).   [72] Badius on *Ecl.* 1.1 (Giunta 1544, fol. 2ʳ).
[73] Giunta 1544, fols. 2ᵛ, 4ᵛ, 45ᵛ; see also *Ecl.* 2.73 (fol. 15ᵛ), where Servius makes a cross-reference.
[74] I have also checked the *Eclogues* commentaries of Landino (1488), Paulo Manuzio (1558), and Jacobus Pontanus (1599).

levels of allegory that were unrelated to patronage.[75] Most, though, were content to provide fresh examples of an already-established theory: to show how Virgil fulfilled his intention of praising the emperor in more poems and more verses than just the ones Servius had noticed. What did not conform (in this case, the verses where Servius found criticism) was either ignored or reexplained. Servius, like many learned teachers, turned out to have broader interests than most of his disciples. He worried about Virgil's grammar,[76] but not his orthodoxy, as Badius did.[77] On the other hand, Badius also wrote commentaries on Terence, Cicero, and Horace; translated Thucydides; and ran one of Europe's greatest printing presses.

Today's reading of the *Eclogues*, in which there is just as much darkness as light, was not automatic in the Renaissance, but it was not "unthinkable" either; Sidney seems to have thought it, and structured his own eclogues accordingly.[78] The hints for this duality were there in Servius, and poets were free to develop them. But what, for us, is almost a reflex would have been for Sidney an act of independence, even willfulness. And here is another use of old commentaries: to show what was normal, yes, but also what was novel, brave, or just odd.[79]

IMITATING THEOCRITUS: THE BOOKISHNESS OF VIRGILIAN PASTORAL

Patronage was the main, but not the only, motif in Renaissance commentary on the *Eclogues*. It was used to explain Eclogues 1, 2, 4, 5, 8, and 9 but not all ten. What else was there? What patronage did not explain can be summarized under five or six headings: bookishness, love, Epicureanism, Christian prophecy, variety, and style. These gave clues for the remaining Eclogues, 3, 6, 7, and 10.

The most important of these submotives was bookishness. In Umberto Eco's novel *The Name of the Rose* (1980), there is a sex scene – the only one in

---

[75] See Claudie Balavoine, "Vie et mort de l'allégorie dans les commentaires des *Bucoliques* virgiliennes à la Renaissance," in *Hommages à Henry Bardon*, ed. Marcel Renard and Pierre Laurens (Brussels: Latomus, 1985), pp. 10–40; and Annabel Patterson, *Pastoral and Ideology: Virgil to Valéry* (Berkeley and Los Angeles: University of California Press, 1987), pp. 85–92.
[76] Robert A. Kaster, "The Grammarian's Authority," *Classical Philology* 75 (1980), 216–41.
[77] See Mark L. Crane, "A Conservative Voice in the French Renaissance: Josse Bade (1462–1535)," unpublished dissertation (University of Toronto, 2005).
[78] Robert E. Stillman, *Sidney's Poetic Justice*: The Old Arcadia, *Its Eclogues, and Renaissance Pastoral Traditions* (Lewisburg, PA: Bucknell University Press, 1986).
[79] Sidney's famous summation of Eclogue 1 is followed immediately by a less-famous summation of Eclogue 7, which he quotes to illustrate the vanity of all human striving (*ECE*, vol. 1, pp. 175–76). Cf. Mancinelli's approach, summarized below (pp. 68–69).

the whole book – which consists entirely of quotations from the Song of Songs. It dramatizes what C. S. Lewis called the "overwhelmingly bookish or clerkly character of medieval culture."[80] The Renaissance was, if possible, even more book-reliant (or, as Lewis charged elsewhere, text-credulous);[81] and this affected, not just the approach to Virgil's *Eclogues*, but Virgil's status in the curriculum. As we shall see in Chapter 4, Virgil was the paradigm of an imitative poet: the kind who lives, moves, and has his being in books – his own and other poets'. This accounts, perhaps, for why there is so little actual shepherding in Virgil's pastoral.

According to both ancient and modern commentators, the first aim (*intentio*) of the *Eclogues* was "to imitate Theocritus," perhaps the most bookish goal that has ever been proposed. Servius pointed out some of Virgil's borrowings, but in the centuries after Servius, knowledge of Greek fell into decay; and with Greek, knowledge of Theocritus. In the fifteenth century, when Greek got on its feet again, scholars began to compare the two authors in detail. Theocritus was usually allowed to have written the better pastorals,[82] but Virgil offered something that, for students, was ultimately more important. Insofar as its goal (and not just its method) was "to imitate Theocritus," the *Eclogues* was, as we might say, poetry about poetry. Specifically, it was a model of how to imitate another author. This (and probably their brevity) was what made Virgil's eclogues attractive to educators. For learning morality, Mantuan's pastorals were more useful – and they sometimes preceded Virgil's in the curriculum. But for learning composition, Virgil's poems were superior: by comparing Virgil with his Greek source, students could study at first-hand how a great writer operates, digesting his materials and reusing them for his own purposes.

Badius, who would later translate Theocritus into Latin, notes some of Virgil's borrowings; and Mancinelli, for each eclogue of Virgil, specifies which idyll of Theocritus he seems to be imitating. But the best commentator for this kind of study was Eoban Koch (1488–1540), better known to

---

[80] C. S. Lewis, *The Discarded Image* (Cambridge University Press, 1964), p. 5.
[81] Lewis, *English Literature in the Sixteenth Century Excluding Drama* (Oxford: Oxford University Press, 1954), ch. 1. See now Anthony Grafton, *Defenders of the Text: The Traditions of Scholarship in an Age of Science, 1450–1800* (Cambridge, MA: Harvard University Press, 1991); and Grafton, *New Worlds, Ancient Texts: The Power of Tradition and the Shock of Discovery* (Cambridge, MA: Harvard University Press, 1992).
[82] In his introduction to the *Georgics*, Servius writes that Virgil surpassed Hesiod, was far from equalling Homer, and was close to equalling Theocritus (fol. 53ʳ). This judgment was echoed by various Renaissance critics, including Vives (1782 *Opera* vol. 11, pp. 76–77), Du Bellay (*Deffence* 1.7; ed. Chamard, pp. 43–44), Thomas Nashe (*ECE*, vol. 1, p. 316), and William Webbe (*ECE*, vol. 1, p. 262). A notable exception was Julius Caesar Scaliger, who weighed the two poets passage by passage and found the Greek author wanting; see his *Poetices libri septem* 5.4 (Lyon: Antonius Vincentius, 1561).

his Latin readers as Helius Eobanus Hessus. Hailed as the "King of the Humanists," Hessus was a hard drinker and a prolific writer.[83] He translated the Psalms of David, then the *Idylls* of Theocritus, then the whole of Homer's *Iliad* (Poliziano had stopped after four books). His Latin verse, which he revised and reissued over several decades, was read all over Europe and included epic poems on the Harrowing of Hell and the history of Nuremberg, a satire on love-madness, a didactic poem on diet and medicine, elegiac couplets on how not to get drunk, topical eclogues modeled on Theocritus, and a series of fictional letters from Christian heroines modeled on Ovid's *Heroides*. Mutianus Rufus praised Hessus as "a modern Pindar"; Erasmus called him "the Christian Ovid." But what endeared Hessus to students and teachers was his commentary on Virgil. For the *Eclogues*, he indicated the passages that were borrowed from Theocritus and provided a Latin translation of Theocritus' Greek. For the *Georgics*, Hessus pointed out Virgil's debts to Hesiod and translated the relevant passages, again into Latin. By our standards, Hessus is strong on documentation, weak on interpretation. But Hessus gave students what they needed and, in consequence, his notes stayed in print. After their initial publication in Hagenau in 1529, they were bundled with the Latin text of Virgil's works and reprinted in that form first in Cologne (1535, 1537, 1540, 1542, 1545, 1556, 1568, 1577?), then Venice (1539), Strasbourg (1540, 1555, 1556), Antwerp (1542, 1543), Basel (1544), and Lyon (1545?). Forty years after the first edition, they were still being mentioned by the tutor of Queen Elizabeth, as an aid to students who are learning the art of imitation.[84] What seems to have replaced them was a new commentary by Peter Ramus (1515–72), which collected Virgil's borrowings and showed the structure of each eclogue. This commentary, which first appeared in 1555, was reprinted every decade for the rest of the century and seems, judging from surviving book inventories, to have been popular at Cambridge.[85]

What did all of these collations produce? Better writers, presumably. But what about literary criticism? In Eclogue 7, Mancinelli points out that Virgil's singing contest has a winner, but in Theocritus the contest is a draw.[86] Today, this would lead to some general remarks, if not a reading of

---

[83] For an overview of Hessus's life and works, see Harry Vredeveld, "Eobanus Hessus," *Dictionary of Literary Biography* (Detroit: Bruccoli Clark-Gale Research, 1978–), vol. CLXXIX, pp. 97–110.
[84] Roger Ascham, *The Scholemaster* (1570), in *ECE*, vol. I, p. 8.
[85] E. S. Leedham-Green, *Books in Cambridge Inventories: Book-Lists from Vice-Chancellor's Court Probate Inventories in the Tudor and Stuart Periods*, 2 vols. (Cambridge University Press, 1986), vol. II, pp. 777–80.
[86] Mancinelli on *Ecl.* 7.1 (Giunta 1544, fol. 38ʳ).

the whole poem, but for Mancinelli the *aperçu* is enough, and the point goes no further. This is disappointing, but Hessus and Ramus are no different, only more detailed.

The one generalization that does get repeated goes back to Aelius Donatus, who says in his *Life of Virgil* that, whereas Theocritus was *simplex*, "one-layered," Virgil is allegorical: "not never and not everywhere" (*neque nusquam neque ubique*), but only where it pertains to praise of Caesar and his lost lands.[87] This distinction between the two authors (and the limit of its application in Virgil) was adopted by Servius and, in the Renaissance, by most of the major commentators.[88] Over the long term, it had two effects. First, it established a basic chronology for literary history. Before Virgil, pastoral was a genre about shepherds. After Virgil, shepherds were allegorical: in Virgil, of poets; after Virgil, of poets, priests, and princes. The second consequence was to shift the subject of pastoral, from the lives of shepherds to the life of the author. This might seem to go without saying, except that it did not happen with Virgilian epic. Until Wordsworth, nobody wrote epics about the growth of a poet's mind, but they did write eclogues. With Virgil, pastoral joined lyric as a genre of allegorical autobiography. It might have happened otherwise and, in the Middle Ages, other topics entered the mix. But in the classical tradition, as exemplified by Virgil and defined by his commentators, the author's life became the primary, though never the exclusive, subject of pastoral as a genre.

LOVE AMONG THE SHEPHERDS

The other major subject was love: in Eclogue 2, the hopeless love of a field hand for a house slave; in Eclogue 3, the bitterness of unrequited love; in Eclogue 8, love magic; and in Eclogue 10, the folly of love. Actually, if you believe Badius, *all* of these poems illustrate the folly of love. But he was writing for adolescents; also, he had four children. What he really thought about love is hard to guess.

Why are there so many love songs in the *Eclogues*? In the Renaissance, the most (indeed, the only) comprehensive theory of pastoral as a genre was that of Julius Caesar Scaliger (1484–1558). Scaliger argued that pastoral was the oldest form of poetry, older than drama, and that the first pastorals were love songs (*amatoriae*). He gives several reasons. First, nature has endowed

---

[87] Donatus 66 (Giunta 1544, sig. *ii^v, printer's error for *iii^v).
[88] See Romano, "L'allegoria"; Starr, "Biographical Allegory"; Schiebe, *Vergil og Tityrus*; Balavoine, "Vie et mort de l'allégorie."

all living things with the desire to perpetuate their species. Second, shepherds would have observed their animals copulating and the example would, he says, have "inflamed" them. Third, shepherds are young, feed on rich foods, live in solitude free from care, and wear almost no clothes; this disposes them to think of love. Fourth (and Scaliger dwells on this reason more than any other), the female companions of shepherds wear revealing attire; you can see this, says Scaliger, when you look at paintings of nymphs, with their shoulders bare and their thighs exposed. With these provocations, it was inevitable that shepherds would be the first poets, and that their first songs would be of love.[89]

CHRISTIAN PROPHECY AND EPICUREANISM

There were other subjects, of course, but not always the ones that we think of as pastoral. There are women in the *Eclogues*, but none with a speaking part; the *pastourelle* does not exist as a character in Virgil, or even as a word in classical Latin. There is nothing in Virgil about the care of sheep, except occasional reminders that they need feeding, and no description of the shepherd's raiment or gear.[90] Finally, Virgil seems uninterested in the contrast between urban and rural, court and country. In the Renaissance, all three of these subjects were established elements of pastoral, and today the last one seems indispensable. But each of them, as Helen Cooper has shown, originated in French-language pastoral during the Middle Ages, among poets who seem not to have studied Virgil at all.[91] Renaissance commentators did sometimes recognize ingredients of this later tradition in Virgil, but they didn't – probably couldn't – elaborate; in Virgil's first

---

[89] Julius Caesar Scaliger, *Poetices libri septem* 1.4 (Lyon: Antonius Vincentius, 1561), pp. 6–7.
[90] "Someone who reads pastoral will not learn a method (*rationem*) for feeding the herd ... nor will he want to become a shepherd." Gulielmus Modicius, *Virgilius a calumniis vindicatus* (1575), qtd. in Alice Hulubei, *L'églogue en France au XVIe siècle: époque des Valois (1515–1589)* (Paris: Droz, 1938), p. 6 n. 1.
[91] Helen Cooper, *Pastoral: Mediaeval into Renaissance* (Totowa, NJ: Rowman & Littlefield, 1977), ch. 2. For the periods it covers, Cooper's survey is still the best in English; see also Hulubei, *L'églogue en France*; W. Leonard Grant, *Neo-Latin Literature and the Pastoral* (Chapel Hill: University of North Carolina Press, 1965); and Sukanta Chaudhuri, *Renaissance Pastoral and Its English Developments* (Oxford: Clarendon Press, 1989), which also covers pastoral on the Continent. William Empson, *Some Versions of Pastoral: A Study of the Pastoral Form in Literature* (London, 1935) has been criticized for defining pastoral too broadly. Paul Alpers, *What Is Pastoral?* (Chicago: University of Chicago Press, 1996) dismisses Renaissance theories of pastoral as lacking "critical power or coherence" (p. 9); his own theory has both, but uses concepts and categories which the pastoralists themselves might not have recognized. For Renaissance categories, see Hulubei, *L'églogue en France*, pp. 1–25; J. E. Congleton, *Theories of Pastoral Poetry in England, 1684–1798* (Gainesville: University of Florida Press, 1952), chs. 1 and 2; and Fred J. Nichols, "The Development of Neo-Latin Theory of the Pastoral in the Sixteenth Century," *Humanistica lovaniensia* 18 (1969), 95–114.

eclogue, there was enough town and country to make a snack, but not a whole meal.[92]

Other than love and patronage, the two subjects that commentators did develop were Epicureanism and Christian prophecy. Again, both traditions are ancient if not classical.

Beginning in the third century, Virgil was enrolled as a Christian prophet, largely on the basis of his fourth eclogue, "Pollio."[93] The poem is a birthday ode (*genethliacon*), occasioned by the arrival of an unnamed child who will usher in a Golden Age of righteousness and prosperity, and whose identity is still unsettled even today. The consulship of Virgil's patron Pollio is mentioned at the beginning of the poem and, according to Servius, it is possible that some of the prophecies allude to Pollio's son Saloninus; but most of them Servius explains as referring to Augustus, the boy-god of Eclogue 1.[94] Servius was not the first critic to notice a gap between putative subject (a consul's infant) and Golden Age prophecy. In the third century Lactantius ("the Christian Cicero," as he was known in the Renaissance) proposed that Virgil was an unwitting prophet, almost four decades before the event, of the true Messiah, Jesus. For Lactantius, Virgil was the hierophant of an *unapprehended* inspiration; whatever Virgil might have intended, the true meaning of the prophecy could only be understood retrospectively, after its fulfillment. This would be Dante's view as well, when he described Virgil as "one who goes by night, / Who carries the light behind, and does not profit himself, / But teaches those who follow after" (*Purgatorio* 22.67–69). Others made Virgil more active. In the fourth century Constantine, the first Christian emperor, was credited with saying that Virgil prophesied knowingly about the Messiah, but disguised his true meaning behind a veil of allegory, lest he be accused of impiety by the pagan authorities.[95] In the Middle Ages,

---

[92] Conrad of Hirsau (*c.* 1070–1150) claimed that Virgil "aimed in these works to describe the ways (*mores*) of shepherd life, its character, its serious business and its games; to exhibit the difference between country retirement and the city; and to show his gratitude to Caesar for protecting him" (*VT* 740). Conrad, though, was writing an introduction and did not have to give specifics. Badius, in his opening remarks on the *Eclogues*, says that Virgil aimed "to imitate Theocritus and to disclose the ways of shepherds (*pastorum mores explicare*)" (sig. *x^v). In the body of his commentary, he substantiates the first claim at length, but not the second.

[93] For the Christian reception, see Pierre Courcelle, "Les exégèses chrétiennes de la quatrième Églogue," *Revue des études anciennes* 59 (1957), 294–319; and Sabine MacCormack, *The Shadows of Poetry: Vergil in the Mind of Augustine* (Berkeley and Los Angeles: University of California Press, 1998), pp. 21–31.

[94] Servius on *Ecl.* 4.6, 7, 10, 12, 13, 15, 17 (Giunta 1544, fols. 24^r–25^v).

[95] But see Mario Geymonat, "Un falso cristiano della seconda metà del IV secolo (sui tempi e le motivazioni della 'Oratio Constantini ad sanctorum coetum')," *Aevum antiquum* n.s. 1 (2001), 349–66.

stories circulated that Virgil corresponded with St. Paul, or even was converted by Paul after his death.[96]

The moderns were more cautious. According to Mancinelli, Virgil borrowed an authentic prophecy about Christ (uttered by the pagan oracle at Cumae), but grafted or replanted it (*inseruit*), in order to praise Pollio and Augustus. That is to say, Virgil was using prophecy the same way he used Theocritus, as grist for his own mill. But, says the commentator, Virgil did not believe that the prophecies would actually come to pass.[97] I.e., so far as he knew, Virgil was not foretelling the Messiah, but flattering his mortal patrons. Badius holds a similar position. "There is great controversy," he begins, "among learned and saintly men" about whether the poem refers to Christ's nativity. Badius thinks it does, but that Virgil was not aware of this; when he wrote the poem, Virgil probably was thinking of Pollio; Pollio's son; Augustus; or Augustus' heir Marcellus, whose death Virgil memorializes in *Aen.* 6.860–86.[98]

Why were modern critics so cautious? As we shall see in the next chapter, Virgil was not tied firmly to any one school of philosophy. The *Eclogues*, however, were associated with Epicureanism, perhaps the least Christian of all pagan sects. Virgil was believed (correctly it now seems) to have been a student of Siro, sometimes spelled Silo, around whom gathered a circle of thinkers known as the Garden of Epicurus. Virgil mentions Siro by name in two epigrams, *Catalepton* 5 and 8. Today, these little poems – the title suggests trifles – are no longer attributed to Virgil, but Donatus mentions them, and in the Renaissance they were accepted as Virgil's. Together with the *Eclogues*, they form a portrait of the artist as a young Epicurean.

Servius finds examples of Epicurean doctrine in three of Virgil's ten eclogues: 2, 6, and 8. Modern commentators ignored two of these and focused on Eclogue 6. In this poem, known as "Silenus," the old wino is captured, sleeping off a hangover, by two young men (Servius says by two satyrs). A moment later they are all joined by a naiad, and Silenus sings a series of stories, beginning with creation. As Servius explains it, Silenus is really the teacher Siro and his song is Epicurean doctrine. The two satyrs are Virgil and his classmate Varus; and the girl represents pleasure (*voluptas*), which Epicureans think must be present for anything to be complete (*perfectum*).[99] This explains why the two students are pictured as satyrs (a species that lives for bodily pleasure) and why Silenus, of all creatures, is

---

[96] Spargo, *Virgil the Necromancer*, pp. 20–21, 100–16.   [97] Mancinelli on *Ecl.* 4.4 (Giunta 1544, fol. 24ᵛ).
[98] Badius, summary of Eclogue 4 (Giunta 1544, fol. 23ᵛ).
[99] Servius on *Ecl.* 6.13 (Giunta 1544, fol. 33ʳ). The Varus who studied under Silo has been identified elsewhere as P. Quinctilius Varus. The dedicatee of the poem, named in line 7, is probably Alfenus Varus, but Servius does not distinguish.

supposed to represent Virgil's teacher. It is a daring leap that Servius makes here, not only for what it says about Virgil's career as an intellectual, but also for what it suggests about Virgil's character: that he was capable, among other things, of self-mockery.

Badius is slightly wary: the foregoing is true "if Servius is to be believed."[100] What makes him reluctant is not sex or liquor but cosmology. Servius says that the creation story which Silenus sings is Epicurean, because it derives everything in the universe from two elements, *corpus* (which consists of atoms) and *inane* (void).[101] Mancinelli notes this as well, and cites Lucretius as Virgil's probable source.[102] Badius agrees – Virgil sounds like Lucretius here – but worries that students will imbibe a heresy. He emphasizes, therefore, that the true account is found in Genesis, where God created the world *ex nihilo*, not (as here) from nothing and atoms.[103] Virgil may have been an unwitting prophet in Eclogue 4, but he was not (as Justin Martyr called Plato) a Christian before Christ.

VARIETY AND THE LOW STYLE

The other thing that commentators noticed about the fourth and sixth eclogues was their style, which is elevated above the rest. According to a popular etymology, the word *eclogue* was thought to mean "goat-speech," from Greek *aix* "goat" and *logos* "word." The etymology was mistaken, but survived anyway for two reasons: because most scholars had only fuzzy knowledge of Greek; and because it confirmed something that critics already knew, that the language of pastoral is supposed to be uncombed, coarse, and homely.[104] Servius, in writing about the *Eclogues*, calls this the groundling (*humilis*) style, Donatus the eked-out (*tenuis*) style. The latter is a term that implies poverty but also thrift: as if words were in short supply, like butter in war-time, and have to be rationed out. According to the commentators, Virgil announces that he is going to use this style in the first sentence of the *Eclogues*, when he describes Tityrus, his *alter ego*, as plying his music on a slender (*Tenui*) oaten reed. "By saying this," Servius explains, "Virgil indicates in a hidden way the kind of groundling style (*stili genus*

---

[100] Badius on *Ecl.* 6.16 (Giunta 1544, fol. 33ʳ). [101] Servius on *Ecl.* 6.31 (Giunta 1544, fol. 33ʳ).
[102] Mancinelli on *Ecl.* 6.31 (Giunta 1544, fol. 34ᵛ).
[103] Badius on *Ecl.* 6.31 (fol. 35ʳ). To make Virgil more Christian, Valens Guellius (1575) argued that the end of Silenus' song, an "empty fable" about Phoebus, was chosen by Virgil to expose the *vanitas* of Epicurean philosophy. This suggestion was quoted by Pontanus (1599), col. 144, but does not seem to have been widely adopted.
[104] The correct derivation, *choice* or *select* (from Greek *eklegein* "to choose out"), was given by Scaliger, *Poetice* 1.4 (1561 edn., p. 7). Cf. the popular etymology of *satire* from *satyr*.

humilis) which, as we said before, is usual for bucolics."[105] This interpretation was repeated by the modern commentators Mancinelli and Badius, except that Mancinelli calls it the skinny (*gracilis*) style and Badius the *tenuis* style, a term which he explains (citing Landino's commentary) as "thinned out" rather than "precise" (*subtilis*).[106]

In the ancient world after Virgil, *sermo humilis* became associated with Christianity – a slave-religion for many decades – and with the topsy-turvy, first-shall-be-last message of Jesus and the Epistles.[107] But that was not how critics, classical or Christian, explained low style in the *Eclogues*. Among Elizabethan critics, the low style is sometimes described as a "vaile" or "cloake of simplicitie," which the author dons in order to comment on current affairs.[108] This comes, as we have seen, from the tradition of reading Virgil's *Eclogues* allegorically. For Servius, though, the style of the *Eclogues* is dictated by the need, not for disguise, but for decorum. "The characters (*personæ*) are country people (*rusticae*), and there is nothing citified (*urbanum*) in them, or oratorical (*declamatorium*)." That is to say, there are no references to the urban culture of Rome, with its busy markets, noisy law courts, senate debates, lavish dinners, gladiators, or chariot races. Second, there is an absence of certain rhetorical figures, such as epic simile, apostrophe, and personification, which were considered marks of the high style.

In place of these, the low style is marked by metaphors from country life – Servius gives the example of "after many ears of grain" (*Ecl.* 1.69) for "after many years" – and archaisms (such as adjectival *cuium* in *Ecl.* 3.1). In the Renaissance, archaisms were controversial. In Castiglione, it is assumed that peasant speech preserves certain archaic forms, but whether these forms should be restored is never decided.[109] Sidney objected to archaisms, even in pastoral, as being unclassical – a mistake, as we can see from Virgil.[110] Ben Jonson observed (more correctly) that Virgil uses archaism sparingly.[111] But he also criticized Sidney for making all of his characters, including shepherds, "speak as well as himself," i.e., like courtiers.[112] The principle that

---

[105] Servius on *Ecl.* 1.2 (Giunta 1544, fol. 1ʳ).
[106] Mancinelli and Badius on *Ecl.* 1.2 (Giunta 1544, fols. 1ᵛ, 2ʳ).
[107] Erich Auerbach, "Sermo humilis," in his *Literary Language and Its Public in Late Antiquity and the Middle Ages*, trans. Ralph Mannheim (Princeton: Princeton University Press, 1965), pp. 27–66.
[108] Puttenham, *Arte of English Poesie* 1.18 (ed. Willcock and Walker, p. 38); William Webbe (*ECE*, vol. I, p. 262).
[109] Castiglione, *Il cortegiano* 1.31 and 35, ed. Giulio Preti (Turin: Einaudi, 1965).
[110] Sidney, *Apologie* (*ECE*, vol. I, p. 196).
[111] Jonson, *Timber* 1931–48, in *Ben Jonson*, ed. C. H. Herford, Percy Simpson, and Evelyn Simpson, 11 vols. (Oxford: Clarendon Press, 1925–52), vol. VIII, p. 622.
[112] Jonson, *Conversations with Drummond* 3 (in *Ben Jonson*, ed. Herford and Simpson, vol. I, p. 132).

theorists agreed on everywhere – in Europe as well as England – was that shepherds ought to speak like members of their own class; and for eclogues modeled on Virgil, that meant using the low style.[113]

There were three exceptions, which Donatus mentions in his *Life of Virgil* and Servius in his preface to the *Eclogues*: "Gallus" (Eclogue 10), for reasons which are never spelled out; "Silenus" (Eclogue 6), which merits a higher style because its subject is cosmology; and "Pollio" (Eclogue 4). This was the poem that, for Servius, heralded the Golden Age of Augustus and, for Christian authors, predicted the Advent of Christ. Beginning with Donatus, commentators explained its opening verse, "Muses of Sicily, let us sing of slightly greater matters," as Virgil's acknowledgement that this particular eclogue was going to stretch – "slightly" – the traditional subject matter of Sicilian (i.e., Theocritean) pastoral to include, not just shepherds, but world events and universal peace.[114] For Renaissance critics, this meant that Virgil also had to adopt "a somewhat swelling stile," on the principle that "stile ought to conforme with the nature of the subject."[115] Again, though, Eclogue 4 was an exception; the normal style for Virgilian pastoral was low, threadbare, and thrifty.

Why did Virgil depart from this norm in three of his poems? In one sense, the answer has already been given: to accommodate abnormal subject matter. What compelled him, though, to admit this subject matter in the first place? The classical answer was that pastoral needs variety. According to Servius, "whoever writes bucolics must be careful, above all things, that his eclogues should not be like each other. This is why the first eclogue has one character who is content and another who is complaining, because he has been driven away from his own land; the second eclogue portrays a boorish lover; and the third eclogue has quarreling and back-and-forth (*altercationem*)." This is also, Servius continues, why Virgil sometimes speaks in his own voice (e.g., Eclogue 4), sometimes in the voice of his characters (e.g., Eclogue 1), and sometimes in a mixture of both (e.g., Eclogue 10).[116] Variety is essential, but pastoral only allows so many permutations. According to Donatus, this is why Virgil only wrote ten eclogues (and of these, only seven are really about shepherds).[117] The other three, explains Servius, were grafted on (*insertis*) either because it was pleasing to have loftier subject matter or because,

---

[113] For examples, see Cooper, *Pastoral*, ch. 4.
[114] Donatus 65–66 (Giunta 1544, sig. *ii^v, for *iii^v); Servius and Badius on *Ecl.* 4.1 (fols. 24$^{r, v}$).
[115] Puttenham, *Arte of English Poesie* 3.5 (ed. Willcock and Walker, pp. 150, 151). See also Badius on *Ecl.* 4.2–3 (fol. 24^v).
[116] Servius on *Ecl.* 3.1 (Giunta 1544, fol. 18^v). [117] Donatus 65, 68 (sig. *ii^v, printer's error for *iii^v).

without these three, "it was impossible to supply enough variations."[118] Non-pastoral eclogues, such as "Silenus" and "Pollio," increased the range of subject matter, but also the range of styles. As we shall see in the next chapter, both types of variety were key to Virgil's reputation in the Renaissance.

---

[118] Servius, preface to *Eclogues* (Giunta 1544, fol. 1ʳ).

CHAPTER 3

Variety and the Georgics

> We do not display greatness by going to one extreme, but in touching both at once, and filling all the intervening space.
> Pascal, *Pensées* §353 (trans. W. F. Trotter)

Virgil's *Georgics* was sometimes assigned in schools, but it was never as widely studied as his *Eclogues* – almost no poem was – or his *Aeneid*. The *Georgics* was imitated, but not to the extent of defining a genre, as the *Eclogues* defined pastoral and the *Aeneid* defined epic (especially for readers who did not know Greek). One reason was terminology. In the sixteenth century there were, as we shall see, many poems modeled on the *Georgics*, but "georgic" was not established yet as a separate genre; it was the name of a book (as in the phrase "Virgil's third georgic") but not of a mode or kind. In the Renaissance there were commentaries on the *Georgics*, but no theories of georgic poetry.

The theme was different as well. In scholarship today, the phrase *labor omnia vincit* (*Geo.* 1.145, "labor conquers everything") is routinely cited as "[t]he central principle of the *Georgics*."[1] The orthodoxy on this point is so secure that it seems self-evident, but it was not so in the Renaissance. In the fifteenth and sixteenth centuries, the most popular commentators on the *Georgics* were the same ones who were popular on the *Eclogues*: the ancients Servius and Probus, and the moderns Mancinelli and Badius Ascensius.[2] Naturally, when Virgil does write about labor, the commentators do so as well; but they do not make it the theme of the whole poem. Servius, for example, when he explains *labor omnia vincit*, says only that no one loves labor; Mancinelli, that Virgil's phrase has an echo in the newly discovered

---

[1] Annabel Patterson, "Pastoral versus Georgic: The Politics of Virgilian Quotation," in *Renaissance Genres: Essays on Theory, History, and Interpretation*, ed. Barbara Kiefer Lewalski (Cambridge, MA: Harvard University Press, 1986), pp. 241–67, at p. 244.
[2] See Appendix B.

text of Manilius on astronomy; Badius, that necessity is the mother of invention; and Probus says nothing at all.³

Instead of labor, what defined the *Georgics* was variety. Servius, for example, in his preface to the *Georgics* says that it was planned in four books "because the whole earth ... is divided into four parts. For either there is plowed land, for sowing; or planted land, fit for trees; or pasture land, which is empty but for grass and beasts; or flowering land, in which there are gardens agreeable for bees and flowers."⁴ Badius, in his preface, says the same.⁵ Variety was a central concept in Renaissance architecture, music, and literary criticism; and its history has been studied thoroughly.⁶ It resembles, in a way, our own ideal of diversity, but differs in its goal. Whereas, for us, diversity is an end in itself, variety was, for the Renaissance, a means to an end. Today an artist or critic is usually content just to multiply alternatives; variety, though, was exhaustive. It was not satisfied until it had filled every niche, catalogued every variation, anatomized every combination. This project was conceivable because, while vast, the variety of the created world was not considered to be infinite. For most of the sixteenth century, it still seemed possible to know everything.⁷ This confidence did not last, but while it did, the poet who seemed to justify it was Virgil.

THE ANCIENT TRADITION OF VIRGIL'S ERUDITION

Variety, as applied to Virgil, usually refers either to his erudition or his versatility. The *Georgics* was special in this regard though not unique. As we saw in the previous chapter, Virgil's *Eclogues* was also noted for its philosophical learning; as we shall see in this chapter, so was Virgil's *Aeneid*. What made the *Georgics* different was its method of presentation.

---

³ Giunta 1544, fols. 62ᵛ, 63ʳ.   ⁴ Giunta 1544, fol. 53ʳ.   ⁵ Giunta 1544, fol. 53ᵛ.
⁶ See Bernard Weinberg, *A History of Literary Criticism in the Italian Renaissance*, 2 vols. (Chicago: University of Chicago Press, 1961), chs. 19–20 and index, s.v. *Variety*; Terence Cave, *The Cornucopian Text: Problems of Writing in the French Renaissance* (Oxford: Clarendon Press, 1979); Dominique de Courcelles, ed., *La varietas à la renaissance* (Paris: Champion, 2001); Perrine Galand-Hallyn and Luc Deitz, "Le style au quattrocento et au xvɪᵉ siècle," in *Poétiques de la renaissance*, ed. Perrine Galand-Hallyn and Fernand Hallyn (Geneva: Droz, 2001), pp. 532–65. Homer and Ovid were also praised for their variety. See, respectively, Hermogenes, *Images of Style* 2.10, in *Hermogenis opera*, ed. Hugo Rabe (Leipzig: Teubner, 1913), pp. 389–95; and Raphael Regius, "Enarrationem in Ouidii Metamorphosin præfatio," in *P. Ovidii Nasonis metamorphosis cum integris ac emendatissimis Raphaelis Regii enarrationibus* (Venice: Simon Bevilaqua, 1497), sigs. Aiiʳ⁻ᵛ.
⁷ Jean Lecointe, *L'idéal et la différence: la perception de la personnalité littéraire à la Renaissance* (Geneva: Droz, 1993).

As with patronage, the image of Virgil as a learned poet dates back to the classical world. Before Virgil was born, there was a tradition of interpreting Homer allegorically, as a repository of scientific knowledge.[8] Virgil was aware of this tradition and, in imitating Homer, made scientific allegory part of his epic.[9] This was noticed by the early commentators. According to Servius, "Virgil is everywhere full of knowledge (*scientia plenus*),"[10] which he documents in various disciplines: philosophy, what we would now call history of religion, and most of the natural sciences.[11] Macrobius, whose dates overlap with Servius, claims that Virgil was never trammeled by error in any discipline, and there was no branch of learning in which he was not a master.[12] To demonstrate this, he devotes long and detailed chapters of the *Saturnalia* to subjects such as Virgil's knowledge of astronomy and philosophy, Virgil's knowledge of pontifical law, Virgil's knowledge of rhetoric, and (in the last surviving chapter) Virgil's knowledge of human physiology, household remedies, and personal hygiene. This was in the fourth century, but the tradition was already established in the second: according to Aulus Gellius, Virgil was "a man well versed in antiquarian lore, though he did not make himself tedious by showing it off."[13] Elsewhere, Gellius praises Virgil for knowing that a child gets its character from breast milk.[14]

The tradition of the learned poet was disseminated through biography as well as commentary. Aelius Donatus records that Virgil gave himself three years to revise the *Aeneid*, after which he intended to devote his remaining life to philosophy.[15] In the humanistic version, this theme becomes more elaborate. When Donatus tells us that Virgil left Cremona in his youth to go

---

[8] See Don Cameron Allen, *Mysteriously Meant: The Rediscovery of Pagan Symbolism and Allegorical Interpretation in the Renaissance* (Baltimore: Johns Hopkins University Press, 1970), ch. 4; Howard Clarke, *Homer's Readers: A Historical Introduction to the* Iliad *and the* Odyssey (Newark: University of Delaware Press, 1981), ch. 2; Robert Lamberton, *Homer the Theologian: Neoplatonist Allegorical Reading and the Growth of the Epic Tradition* (Berkeley and Los Angeles: University of California Press, 1986); and Fernand Hallyn, "Poésie et savoir au quattrocento et au xvie siècle," in *Poétiques de la renaissance*, ed. Galand-Hallyn and Hallyn, pp. 167–209, at pp. 167–80.

[9] See Robin R. Schlunk, *The Homeric Scholia and the* Aeneid: *A Study of the Influence of Ancient Homeric Literary Criticism on Vergil* (Ann Arbor: University of Michigan Press, 1974); Michael Murrin, *The Allegorical Epic: Essays in Its Rise and Decline* (Chicago: University of Chicago Press, 1980), ch. 1; Philip R. Hardie, *Virgil's Aeneid: Cosmos and Imperium* (Oxford: Clarendon Press, 1986); and David O. Ross, *Virgil's Elements: Physics and Poetry in the Georgics* (Princeton: Princeton University Press, 1987).

[10] Servius, on *Aen.* 6.1 (Giunta 1544, fol. 322ᵛ).

[11] See J. W. Jones, Jr., "Allegorical Interpretation in Servius," *Classical Journal* 56 (1961), 217–26.

[12] Macrobius Ambrosius Theodosius, *Commentarii in Somnium Scipionis* 2.8.1, in *Opera* (Venice: s.n., 1492), fol. xxiᵛ; *Saturnalia* 1.16.12 (fol. viiiʳ) and 1.24.10–20 (fols. xiiiᵛ–[xiiiiʳ]).

[13] Aulus Gellius, *Noctes atticae* 5.12.13, in *Auli Gellii noctes atticae* (Paris: Joannes Tornaesius, 1592), p. 190.

[14] Gellius, *Noctes atticae* 12.1.20 (1592 edn., pp. 370–71). [15] Donatus 51 (Giunta 1544, sig. *iiᵛ).

to Milan, the fifteenth-century *vita* adds, "There, although he labored earnestly at literature, Greek as well as Latin, he also gave himself to medicine and mathematics, with all zeal and diligence."[16] A humorous anecdote follows to illustrate Virgil's wit and his knowledge of zoology. Later, we are informed that "Virgil learned the teachings of Epicurus from Silo ... And although he seems to have inserted the opinions of opposing philosophers in his books (especially regarding the soul), he himself was of the Academy. For he preferred the opinions of Plato to all others."[17]

Like most of the humanistic interpolations, this statement is a derivative mixture of scholarship and intuition. "Silo" is a misspelling of "Siro" and is probably taken from Servius, who says that Virgil was an Epicurean "for the most part";[18] this is in contrast with the humanistic life, which makes Virgil a Platonist. The difference is important, but so is the caveat: Virgil is a Platonist, or an Epicurean, "for the most part" (*ex maiore parte*).[19] Servius explains: "We know that the opinions of the various schools are contrary to one another. That is why we find some contradictions in the work even of a single poet: not because of a defect in him, but the diversity of the schools." For example, in Book 4 of the *Aeneid*, Virgil claims that Dido died before her time, *ante diem* (697); this, says Servius, is the opinion of the Epicureans, who attribute everything to chance. In Book 10, however, Jupiter says that a day is fixed for everyone, *Stat sua cuique dies* (467); this, says Servius, is the opinion of the Stoics, who teach that what the fates have set down is inviolable. Servius makes no attempt to reconcile the two views; what matters, rather, is that in each passage, the opinion fits the speaker. When he speaks in his own voice, as the narrator, Virgil gives the Epicurean view which, being fluid and unsettled (*fluxam et vagam*), is appropriate for a human being. But when a god speaks, his opinion should

---

[16] Donatus auctus 7 (Giunta 1544, sig. *ii^r).
[17] Donatus auctus 79 (Giunta 1544, sig. *ii^r, printer's error for *iii^r). Cf. Landino, *Disputationes camaldulenses*, ed. Peter Lohe (Florence: Sansoni, 1980), pp. 257–58. It would take a long time, says Landino, to summarize the opinions of all the ancient philosophers about the immortal gods, because the schools are various and contradict one another. In one passage, Virgil follows the doctrine of the Stoics, because he did not wish to contradict his fellow poets: Orpheus, Musaeus, Hesiod, and Homer. "But everywhere else, he never parts company with his Plato."
[18] Servius on *Aen.* 6.264 (Giunta 1544, fol. 333^v). The name *Siro* also appears in the *Appendix virgiliana*; see *Catalepton* 8.1. Once studied as Virgil's apprentice-work, the *Appendix* poems are now dismissed as spurious; this one, however, may be genuine (Nicholas Horsfall, *A Companion to the Study of Virgil* [Leiden: Brill, 1995], pp. 9–11). In the Renaissance this was reversed: most of the *Appendix* was regarded as genuine, except the *Catalepton* poems: these were grouped with the *Priapeia* and shared their fate; see pp. 108–9, below.
[19] Cf. Petrarch on *Aen.* 6.713–15: "Virgilium *in multis* esse Platonicum certum est" (emph. mine). Qtd. in Mary Louise Lord, "The Use of Macrobius and Boethius in Some Fourteenth-Century Commentaries on Virgil," *International Journal of the Classical Tradition* 3.1 (1996), 3–22, at 5.

be robust (*validus*), and this is why, when Jupiter talks, Virgil makes him sound like a Stoic. "For the Stoics are cherishers, both of an excessive manliness (*nimiæ virtutis*) and of the gods."[20]

SCIENCE OR POETRY?

The idea that Virgil was a philosopher, as well as a poet, continues to animate criticism and commentary well into the seventeenth century.[21] "Philosophy," though, does not just include ethics, metaphysics, and epistemology, but also "natural philosophy," which we would call science. Already by the fourth century AD, there was a school of allegorists known as *physici* (because they studied *physis*, "nature") who specialized in scientific interpretation (*ratio physica*). Servius invokes them throughout his commentary, especially when a passage's literal meaning makes no sense.[22] For example, when Virgil says that the moon over Troy was *tacita*, "silent," Servius explains this as poetic license; either that, or Virgil means something scientific. "For there are seven circles: Saturn, Jupiter, Mars, the Sun, Venus, Mercury, and the Moon. The first of these, Saturn, sounds loudly; the rest sound less loudly, according to their order ... Therefore, the moon is 'silent' compared with the other planets, because its circle is nearest to the earth, which does not move."[23]

This approach to Virgil persisted for more than a thousand years after Servius. In the Renaissance, translators took it for granted that Virgil's text was a repository for scientific information. Richard Stanyhurst (1547–1618), who Englished four books of the *Aeneid*, praises its author for "ferreting out the secretes of Nature."[24] The physician Thomas Phaer (1510?–1560), who

---

[20] Servius on *Aen.* 10.467 (Giunta 1544, fol. 461ᵛ). See also *Aen.* 1.227, on Stoic and Epicurean views of whether gods take notice of human affairs (Giunta 1544, fol. 168ᵛ). For syncretism in Virgil, see R. G. M. Nisbet, "Virgil's Fourth *Eclogue*: Easterners and Westerners," *Bulletin of the Institute of Classical Studies* 25 (1978), 59–78; for eclecticism, Susanna Morton Braund, "Virgil and the Cosmos: Religious and Philosophical Ideas," in *The Cambridge Companion to Virgil*, ed. Charles Martindale (Cambridge University Press, 1997), pp. 204–21. As a rule, Servius favors eclecticism; see Philip North Lockhart, "The Literary Criticism of Servius," diss., Yale University (1959), pp. 142–45.
[21] Allen, *Mysteriously Meant*, ch. 5.
[22] See J. F. Mountford and J. T. Schultz, *Index rerum et nominum in scholiis Servii et Aelii Donati tractatorum* (Ithaca, NY: Cornell University Press, 1930), s.vv. *physici (et res physica)*. For absurdity as a trigger for allegory, see Michael Murrin, *The Veil of Allegory* (Chicago: University of Chicago Press, 1969), pp. 146–47, 142–43.
[23] Servius on *Aen.* 2.225 (fol. 212ʳ).
[24] *ECE*, vol. 1, p. 137. For Stanyhurst's translation and its critical reception (which was caustic), see O. B. Hardison, *Prosody and Purpose in the English Renaissance* (Baltimore: Johns Hopkins University Press, 1989), pp. 203–6.

translated nine books, also mentions "misticall secretes" – but, he adds, not all of these can be rendered in English![25]

The *Georgics* was read in a similar way, especially Book 1. What we think of as a poem about agriculture was, for the Renaissance, also a poem about cosmography (mapping the universe) and weather prediction.[26] Unlike the *Aeneid*, however, the *Georgics* conveyed its lore directly. In his epic, Virgil was believed to have disguised his learning, so that it remained secret or at least unobtrusive. For example, at the end of Book 5, Virgil says that dewy night is more than halfway over (738–39); according to Aulus Gellius, Virgil was alluding to the Roman concept of a "civil" day, which was calculated from midnight rather than dawn. Yet Virgil displayed his learning "not openly and in plain sight, but, as became a man dealing with things poetical, with a buried and, as it were, veiled indication of the ancient rite."[27] In the Renaissance, this notion of "things poetical" was nearly fatal to the *Georgics*, because in most of the poem Virgil gives information openly, without a veil. For some critics, this disqualified the *Georgics* as poetry.[28] Poetry, as defined by Aristotle, was imitation; and for these critics that meant fiction. Except for the last book, the *Georgics* did not seem to be fiction and was dismissed, therefore, as versified science; it might have meter, but it was not poetry. Lucan and Lucretius were waved off in the same way: Lucan for being too historical, Lucretius for not telling a story. None of this, however, stopped poets from reading the *Georgics* or writing imitations.

LABOR AND THE PLOW

Today most of these imitations are not well known, because they were not written in English. The result has been a cascade of misunderstanding. Until 1599, there is nothing in English that resembles the *Georgics* closely. Noticing this, scholars should have looked for equivalents in other languages; instead, what most have done is to write about georgic values, especially labor, and georgic images, especially the plow. On this basis, *The Shepheardes Calender* and *The Faerie Queene* have both been classified as "georgic" poems, even though one is pastoral and the other is epic.[29]

---

[25] "Maister Phaers Conclusion to His Interpretation of the Æneidos of Virgill," in *The .xiii. Bookes of Æneidos* (STC 24802; London: William How, for Abraham Veale, 1584), sig. Vi^v.
[26] Margaret Tudeau-Clayton, *Jonson, Shakespeare and Early Modern Virgil* (Cambridge University Press, 1998), ch. 3; see also Andrew Wallace, "Virgil and Bacon in the Schoolroom," *ELH* 73 (2006), 161–85.
[27] Gellius, *Noctes atticae* 3.2.14 (1592 edn., p. 113).
[28] Hallyn, "Poésie et savoir," pp. 180–96, 202–9.
[29] Alastair Fowler, "The Beginnings of English Georgic," in *Renaissance Genres*, ed. Lewalski, pp. 105–25. See also Fowler, *Kinds of Literature: An Introduction to the Theory of Genres and Modes* (Cambridge,

As a definition of georgic, "labor and the plow" is at once too vague and too narrow. Too vague, because labor and the dignity of labor are also major themes in the *Aeneid*,[30] not to mention the Reformation. Labor, as a theme, is characteristic of georgic poetry, but not distinctive; nor (as we have said) did commentators in the Renaissance give it the same prominence that we do. As for plowing, it only occurs in Book 1 of the *Georgics* (on grain crops) and in Book 2 (on vines and trees). After Book 2, we move on to animal husbandry (in Book 3) and bees (in Book 4). Indeed, most of the famous set-pieces, even in the books on agriculture, have nothing to do with raising crops: these set-pieces include, in Book 1, the description of winter (287–310) and the portents of civil war (463–97); in Book 2, the praise of Italy (136–76) and the blessings of country life (459–74, 495–540); in Book 3, the effects of lust (209–83) and the description of a plague (470–532); in Book 4, the politics of a bee hive (67–115) and the story of Orpheus (453–527). According to L. P. Wilkinson, these are the passages that were remembered and imitated by poets, not the parts of the plow (1.160–75).[31]

LOOKING FOR THE *GEORGICS* IN RENAISSANCE POETRY

What, then, if not a plowman's tale, is georgic poetry? In the Renaissance, poems were classified in two ways: by content and by form. Let us begin with content. Printed editions of the *Georgics* were sometimes bound up with other classical treatises on farming, in volumes labeled *De re rustica*.[32] If we are looking for Renaissance equivalents, we shall find them in poems about farming. In English, there was *The Boke of Husbandrye* (1533?) by John

---

MA: Harvard University Press, 1982), pp. 108, 202–6; William A. Sessions, "Spenser's *Georgics*," *English Literary Renaissance* 10 (1980), 202–38; Andrew V. Ettin, "The *Georgics* in *The Faerie Queene*," *Spenser Studies* 3 (1982), 57–71; Anthony Low, *The Georgic Revolution* (Princeton: Princeton University Press, 1985), ch. 2; Jane Tylus, "Spenser, Virgil, and the Politics of Poetic Labor," *ELH* 55 (1988), 53–77; John N. King, *Spenser's Poetry and the Reformation Tradition* (Princeton: Princeton University Press, 1990), pp. 216–20; Bruce Thornton, "Rural Dialectic: Pastoral, Georgic, and *The Shepheardes Calender*," *Spenser Studies* 9 (1991), 1–20; Maurice Hunt, "Hellish Work in *The Faerie Queene*," *Studies in English Literature* 41 (2001), 91–108; and Joshua Scodel, *Excess and the Mean in Early Modern Literature* (Princeton: Princeton University Press, 2002), pp. 79–89.

[30] Variations on the word *labor* appear three times in the *Eclogues*, thirty-five times in the *Georgics*, and seventy-eight times in the *Aeneid*. Examples from this last group include such famous lines as "Quæ regio in terris nostri non plena laboris?" (*Aen.* 1.460), "Hoc opus, hic labor est" (*Aen.* 6.129), "Vitam oro, patiar quemuis durare laborem" (*Aen.* 8.577), and "Disce puer virtutem ex me, verumque laborem" (*Aen.* 12.435).

[31] L. P. Wilkinson, *The Georgics of Virgil: A Critical Survey* (Cambridge University Press, 1969), pp. 293–95.

[32] See Rosalie Colie, *The Resources of Kind: Genre-Theory in the Renaissance*, ed. Barbara K. Lewalski (Berkeley and Los Angeles: University of California Press, 1973), p. 16.

Fitzherbert and *A Hundreth Good Points of Husbandrie* (1556) by Thomas Tusser. This was eventually expanded to *Fiue Hundreth Points of Good Husbandry, Vnited to as Many of Good Huswiferie* (1573), in which form it was reprinted at least eighteen times, and did not go out of print until the 1670s.[33]

But most of the poems on this subject – and all of the poems that seem to have imitated Virgil directly – were written in languages other than English. This was noticed in 1591 by the Elizabethan critic William Webbe, who tried to think of English equivalents for the *Georgics* and could name only two: Tusser's *Hundreth Points* and a Latin poem by Conradus Heresbachius, *Res rusticae* (1570), which Barnabe Googe translated as *Foure Bookes of Husbandrie* (1577). According to Webbe, the reason that English authors have not done more in this vein is "there haue beene always plenty of other wryters that haue handled the same argument very largely."[34]

By "other wryters," Webbe means foreign authors.[35] In Latin, there was *Rusticus* (1483) by Angelo Poliziano and *De hortis Hesperidum* (1501) by Giovanni Pontano; the first of these is an oration on country life, organized by season; the second is a poem in two books on the care of orange trees. Another tree poem, *De arboribus* (c. 1494–97) by Bartolomeo della Scala, describes the effect of a recent plague.[36] In Italian, there was *Il podere* (composed 1560; published 1769) by Luigi Tansillo and *La coltivazione* (1546), a blank-verse poem in six books by Luigi Alamanni; both of these poems were still being reprinted in the latter part of the eighteenth century, Alamanni's with a commentary. In addition, there was at least one instance of what we might call "dirty" or "blue" georgic. This was Tansillo's *Il vendemmiatore* (1532), a chronicle in three books of debauchery at the local grape harvest. In 1559, the poem was placed on the Index of Prohibited Books, for obscenity. Publishers, though, were not deterred: between 1537 and 1849, the poem was reprinted seventeen times. In 1792, it was translated into French; a second translation, also in French, was published six years later.[37]

And those are just the poems on agriculture. The *Georgics* also inspired (or at least gave license to) a long series of poems on hunting and

---

[33] See Andrew McRae, *God Speed the Plough: The Representation of Agrarian England, 1500–1600* (Cambridge University Press, 1996), p. 207.
[34] *ECE*, vol. 1, p. 265.
[35] The best guide to these, and the only one in English, is still Marie Loretto Lilly, *The Georgic: A Contribution to the Study of the Vergilian Type of Didactic Poetry* (Baltimore: Johns Hopkins Press, 1919).
[36] *Bartolomeo Scala: Humanistic and Political Writings*, ed. Alison Brown (Tempe, AZ: Medieval & Renaissance Texts & Studies, 1997), pp. 426–45.
[37] Gino Raya, introduction, *Il vendemmiatore: poemetto* (Catania: Tirelli-Guaitolini, 1928), pp. xiv–xxii.

gardening: themes that Virgil alluded to in the *Georgics*, but did not develop.[38] But the most popular spin-offs were poems on the care of insects. In 1524, Giovanni Rucellai published a beekeeping poem, *Le api*, which was directly modeled on Virgil's fourth georgic. A great success, *Le api* was still being reprinted – with a commentary – in the second half of the eighteenth century. Also inspired by Virgil's beekeeping discourse was a string of poems on silkworms: the most famous of these was Marco Girolamo Vida's *De bombycum cura et usu* (1527), but there was also *Il bombyx* (1493) by Lodovico Lazzarelli, *De sere* (1510) by Pierfrancesco Giustulo da Spoleto, *La sereide* (1585) by Alessandro Tesauro, and in English *The Silkewormes* (1599) by Thomas Moffet.

"ILLE EGO QUI QUONDAM"

Moffet was a physician as well as a farmer. In English, his is the first poem that actually sounds like the *Georgics*. But its direct source was Vida, not Virgil,[39] and it was not published until 1599. The Renaissance in England was notoriously belated, compared with the rest of Europe, but that does not explain everything: by this date English writers were already producing Virgilian eclogues and Maronian epics. What was it, then, about Virgil's middle poem, the *Georgics*, that seemed skippable?

If anyone should have written an English version of the *Georgics*, it was Edmund Spenser (who died the same year that Moffet published his *Silkewormes*). Spenser's first original poem, *The Shepheardes Calender* (1579), was partly modeled on Virgil's *Bucolics*; and his epic, *The Faerie Queene* (1590), began with an imitation of Virgil's *Aeneid*:

> Lo I the man, whose Muse whylome did maske,
> As time her taught, in lowly Shephards weeds,
> Am now enforst a farre vnfitter taske,
> For trumpets sterne to chaunge mine Oaten reeds:
> And sing of Knights and Ladies gentle deeds.   (*FQ* I.proem.1)

As has been said many times, this is a close paraphrase of Virgil's opening verses: not *Arma virumque cano*, but the first lines of the *Aeneid* as printed both in Renaissance editions of the Latin text and in translations:

---

[38] See Lilly, *The Georgic*, pp. 101–23 and 75–79, respectively.
[39] Victor Houliston, ed., *The Silkewormes and their Flies* (Binghamton, NY: Medieval & Renaissance Texts & Studies, 1989), pp. xi–xiii.

86 *Variety and the* Georgics

> Ille ego qui quondam gracili modulatus auena
> Carmen, & egressus syluis, vicina coegi,
> Vt quamuis auido parerent arua colono:
> Gratum opus agricolis. At nunc horrentia Martis
> Arma virumque cano.[40]

> I that my slender Oten Pipe in verse was wont to sounde
> Of woods, and next to that I taught for husbandmen the ground,
> How fruite vnto their greedy lust they might constraine to bring,
> A worke of thanks: Lo now of Mars, and dreadfull warres I singe,
> Of armes, and of the man.[41]

The verses are doubtful and do not appear in any of the oldest manuscripts, except as insertions.[42] Aelius Donatus,[43] however, says that the verses are authentic, as does Servius,[44] and on this basis they were accepted as genuine in the Renaissance. Pierio Valeriano, whose textual criticism we discussed earlier, testifies that "insofar as the ancient manuscripts are concerned, I have discovered none so far in which the *Aeneid* begins with these verses – though in some codices they have been added separately by a later hand (*postscripti*)." Also troubling for Valeriano is the fact that Persius and Martial both refer to the poem as *Arma virumque*, as if that were the poem's opening phrase. Nevertheless, Valeriano thinks that the contested verses are useful: like the colophon at the end of *Georgics* Book 4, they identify the author and connect the new poem with its predecessors, the *Eclogues* and *Georgics*, "binding it to the earlier pair in order to form, as it were, one body (*vnum quasi corpus*), knit together by an indissoluble bond." Ergo the "Ille ego" verses are in.[45]

---

[40] Giunta 1544, fol. 149ʳ. Typographically, the verses beginning "Ille ego" are indistinguishable from the ones beginning "Arma virumque." This differs from medieval practice, in which the "Ille ego" verses were usually set off from the rest of the text; see Christopher Baswell, *Virgil in Medieval England: Figuring the* Aeneid *from the Twelfth Century to Chaucer* (Cambridge University Press, 1995), pp. 42–43.

[41] Trans. Thomas Phaer and Thomas Twyne (1584 edn.), sig. B1ʳ. The lines are also printed in Richard Stanyhurst, *Thee First Foure Bookes of Virgil His Aeneis Translated intoo English Heroical Verse* (STC 24806; Leiden: John Pates, 1582), sig. B3ʳ. Again, the interpolated verses are not distinguished typographically from the rest of the text.

[42] See Mario Geymonat, ed., *P. Vergili Maronis opera*, rev. edn. (Rome: Edizioni di Storia e letteratura, 2008), pp. 173–74. My own theory is that the verses are not authentic, but correct and elaborate Ovid, *Tristia* 4.10.1, "Ille ego qui fueram, tenerorum lusor amorum," in *Publii Ovidii Nasonis sulmonensis poetae clarissimi opera* (Venice: Lazarus Soardus de Saviliano, 1492), (4.10.1; 1497 edn., sig. &iiiᵛ).

[43] Donatus 42 (Giunta 1544, sig. *iiᵛ).

[44] Servius, preface to *Aeneid* (Giunta 1544, fol. 146ʳ).

[45] Giunta 1544, fol. 151ʳ⁻ᵛ. The other main textual critic of Virgil in the Renaissance was Georg Goldschmidt, who declares that the verses are "undoubtedly Virgilian"; see *Opera P. Virgilii Maronis* (STC 24789; London: Henry Middleton, 1580), p. 581.

Valeriano's explanation is an example of how a Renaissance critic thinks, and is our best guide to what was in Spenser's mind when he imitated Virgil's opening. By beginning his epic, "Lo I the man, whose Muse whylome did maske, / As time her taught, in lowly Shephards weeds," Spenser is linking his new poem with *The Shepheardes Calender* and establishing a corpus, a coherent body of work. Prior to this, Spenser did literally "maske" his meaning, behind a veil of allegory, and his authorship of *The Shepheardes Calender*, behind the pseudonym "Immerito." In *The Faerie Queene*, he abandons the mask, and also writes in a new style: "trumpets sterne" in place of "Oaten reeds." The importance of this last change will become clear later.

GENERIC SUBSTITUTION

The sequence of Virgil's career – *Eclogues, Georgics, Aeneid* – was spelled out in three main places. One was the "Ille ego" verses that Spenser imitated at the beginning of *The Faerie Queene*. Another was Virgil's epitaph, which the poet composed for his own tombstone. The monument is gone, but the text is quoted in Donatus:

Mantua gave birth to me; the Calabrians snatched me away; now it holds me fast, The city where Parthenope is buried. I sang of pastures, fields, and princes.[46]

In the Renaissance there were more than a dozen variations on this distich, nearly all of which describe (always in two verses) the subject matter of Virgil's three poems: woods, fields, and arms; sheep, corn, and Mars; pastures, husbandry, and wars; sheep, fields, and battles; shepherds, country, and combats; pasturage, tillage, and armies; Pan, Ceres, and Bellona; goats, grounds, and enemies.[47] Spenser, however, composed no poem on the care of "grounds."

Not everything in Spenser's career can or should be explained with reference to Virgil. Ovid is a major influence as well, and to a lesser extent Cicero.[48] Spenser actually began his career by writing sonnets – and to

---

[46] Donatus 36, in Giunta 1544, sig. *i^v.
[47] "Epitaphs vpon Virgil, by diuers illustrious persons," in John Penkethman, *The Epigrams of P. Virgilius Maro, and Others. With the Praises of Him and His Workes* (STC 24825; London: George Purslowe, 1624), sigs. D2^v–D3^r.
[48] See Raphael Lyne, *Ovid's Changing Worlds: English Metamorphoses 1567–1632* (Oxford: Oxford University Press, 2001), ch. 3; Rebeca Helfer, "The Death of the 'New Poete': Virgilian Ruin and Ciceronian Recollection in Spenser's *The Shepheardes Calender*," *Renaissance Quarterly* 56 (2003), 723–56; and Syrithe Pugh, *Spenser and Ovid* (Aldershot: Ashgate, 2005).

sonnets he returned, in the middle of his epic, with no regret, and with no precedent in Virgil.⁴⁹ One critic suggests that, for Spenser, the middle term between private pastoral and public epic was actually epithalamion, the social genre.⁵⁰ The principle is one of substitution, one genre for another.⁵¹ Another critic extends this idea, but defines the middle term more broadly: after *pastoral* comes *love lyric*, Petrarchan or Ovidian; followed by *epic*; which is then followed in Spenser's case by a fourth term, the Christian *hymn*.⁵²

The only fixture, it would seem, is where one begins. But even this, if we look outside of England, was negotiable. In Lope de Vega's epic, *Jerusalén conquistada* (1609), one of the first stanzas reads,

> Yo que canté para la tierna vuestra
> los amores de Angélica y Medoro
> en otra edad, con otra voz màs diestra;
> de vuestro sol el vivo rayo adoro;
> en tanto, pues, que a la marcial palestra
> la fama os llama en al metal sonoro,
> oíd, Felipe, las heroicas sumas
> de España triunfos, de la fama plumas.

[I who in other times sang for you in your tender years with a more skilled voice the loves of Angelica and Medoro, I adore the bright rays of your sun. While now fame with resounding trumpet calls you to the lists of war, listen, Philip, to the supreme heroic achievements: the triumphs of Spain, the pens of fame.]⁵³

Like Spenser's "Lo I the man," this is an adaptation of the *Ille ego* verses that were prefixed to Virgil's *Aeneid*. But instead of pastoral, Vega begins with a continuation of Ariosto: *los amores de Angélica y Medoro*. What is the rule here, if there is one?

---

⁴⁹ Joseph Loewenstein, "Spenser's Retrography: Two Episodes in Post-Petrarchan Bibliography," in *Spenser's Life and the Subject of Biography*, ed. Judith H. Anderson, Donald Cheney, and David A. Richardson (Amherst: University of Massachusetts Press, 1996), pp. 99–130, at pp. 115–19.
⁵⁰ Richard T. Neuse, "Milton and Spenser: The Virgilian Triad Revisited," *ELH* 45 (1978), 606–39.
⁵¹ See Anne Lake Prescott, "The Laurel and the Myrtle: Spenser and Ronsard," in *Worldmaking Spenser: Explorations in the Early Modern Age*, ed. Patrick Cheney and Lauren Silberman (Lexington: University Press of Kentucky, 2000), pp. 63–78.
⁵² Patrick Cheney, *Spenser's Famous Flight: A Renaissance Idea of a Literary Career* (Toronto: University of Toronto Press, 1993), p. 23.
⁵³ Qtd. and trans. C. P. Brand, "The Grand Style: Italy, France, and Spain," in *The Old World: Discovery and Rebirth*, ed. David Daiches and Anthony Thorlby (London: Aldus, 1974), pp. 201–37, at p. 233.

The problem is obvious in Elizabethan poetry, where the *Georgics* have almost no equivalent until Moffet. But even Moffet's source, Vida, did not think of the *Georgics* as a natural sequel for someone who has just written a pastoral. In his *Art of Poetry* (1527), Vida says that Parnassus is steep and should be scaled in stages; a youngster unskilled in poetry

> ought not to venture to compose long *Iliads*, but should gain experience little by little, making his debut by playing on the shepherd's slender pipes. Soon he will be able to tell in verse of the fearsome fates of a gnat, or of how in boundless battle the thundering mouse dealt death to the croaking troops of marsh-loving frogs, or weave a tale of stratagems and webs of the subtle spider.[54]

For Vida, what comes after pastoral is not georgic but mock-epic: either a battle of mice and frogs such as Homer's *Batrachomyomachia*; a spider ambush such as Homer's *Arachnomachia*; or an insect epyllion such as the *Culex*, which Spenser translated as *Virgils Gnat* (1591).

A SPECTRUM OF STYLES

The third *locus classicus* for the sequence of Virgil's poems was a passage in Aelius Donatus. According to the ancient *vita*, Virgil wanted to describe the simplicity of the world's first occupation, which is shepherding, "before moving on to other kinds of poetry."

> For afterwards he took up the cultivation of fields, and last of all, in place of lands well-tilled and fertile, war. What Virgil meant to teach when he sang first of herdsmen, then of farmers, and finally of warriors is evident, therefore, in the very order of his works. We still need to consider what cause prompted the poet's desire to write a bucolic poem first. For either he was enticed by admiration for Theocritus and the sweetness of his song, or he followed the order of the ages with regard to human existence (as we said above). Or he followed the three styles of speech (what the Greeks call *charaktērai*): *ischnos*, which is understood to mean "meager" (*tenuis*), *hadros*, "powerful" (*validus*) and *mesos*, "temperate" (*moderatus*). One might think that Virgil desired to devote his *Bucolics* to the first mode, his *Georgics* to the second, and the *Aeneid* to the third, in order to distinguish himself in every kind of poetry. Or rather, did he write the *Bucolics* first because a poem of that kind is somewhat freer and sturdier than the rest, thinking thereby to gain an opportunity to capture the Emperor's favor and regain his lost land?[55]

---

[54] *De arte poetica* 1.459–65, translation adapted from *The* De arte poetica *of Marco Girolamo Vida* (1527), ed. and trans. Ralph G. Williams (New York: Columbia University Press, 1976), pp. 32–33.

[55] Donatus 58–60/auctus 91–94 (Giunta 1544, sig. *ii*ʳ, printer's error for *iii*ʳ). The humanistic text, translated here, has several errors; e.g., according to the oldest manuscripts, Virgil's *Eclogues* is *magis varium quam cetera* (more varied than the other poems), not *magis validum* (sturdier).

Donatus begins with a sociological explanation: Virgil's career recapitulates the progress of civilization. After that, he gives a biographical explanation: Virgil began with pastoral because he was enamored of Theocritus. Then he offers a literary explanation: Virgil wanted "to distinguish himself in every kind of poetry": i.e., in each of the three styles. Then he offers another biographical explanation.

This is typical. Like Servius, Donatus was trained as a *grammaticus*: strict about usage, but a pluralist about interpretation. Where there is more than one explanation, he transmits it to the next generation, sometimes indicating his own preferences, sometimes not. A thousand years later, Badius Ascensius is still explaining Virgil's career in the same four ways.[56] What Donatus does not say, and what Badius does not repeat, is that Virgil instituted a sequence of genres.

Instead what Donatus describes is a range of styles: meager, temperate, and powerful; or, as the styles were also called, low, middle, and high. The boast here is completeness. Virgil did not write in all of the available genres – and georgic, we have said, was not considered a genre – but he did exhaust all of the available styles.

THE MYTH OF VIRGIL'S WHEEL

Another, medieval source for this idea was the Wheel of Virgil (*rota Virgilii*).[57] Today, the Wheel is probably more familiar than any of the classical sources, but its importance has been overstated and its meaning misconstrued. The term originates with John of Garland in the early thirteenth century; and (to my knowledge) it also dies there. Today, one meets with the phrase "Wheel of Virgil" in scholarship *about* the Renaissance, but never (that I have seen) in texts *from* the Renaissance. The real problem, however, is not anachronism so much as inaccuracy. Too many scholars (especially ones writing in English) write about the Wheel as if it were a progression of genres, beginning with pastoral and culminating with epic. This makes as much sense as saying that a color wheel begins with red and ends with violet; by definition, circles do not have end-points. What is more, the actual *rota* never says anything about genres. Table 2 shows the original contents, arranged vertically.

---

[56] Badius Ascensius, praeambula (Giunta 1544, sig. *ix^v–x^r).
[57] Edmond Faral, *Les arts poétiques du xiie et du xiiie siècle: Recherches et documents sur la technique littéraire du moyen age* (Paris: Champion, 1924), pp. 86–89; *VT*, pp. 744–50.

Table 2 *The spokes of Virgil's Wheel*

Lowly (*humilis*) style	Middle (*mediocris*) style	Weighty (*grauis*) style
shepherd at ease	farmer	soldier, ruler
Tityrus, Meliboeus	Triptolemus, Coelius	Hector, Ajax
sheep	cow	horse
crook	plow	sword
pasture	field	city, camp
beech	apple, pear	laurel, cedar

The columns of the Wheel, as John himself calls them, are organized (*ordinantur*) according to styles – lowly, middle, and weighty – not according to genres. The purpose of the Wheel, as explained in the text, is not to dictate which genre should be attempted first, but to teach decorum: for example, poems in the middle style should not feature swords or shepherds, because the former belong to the high style and the latter to the low. Again, there is no mention of genres, much less of progressions.

STYLE AND GENRE

As I have said, the Wheel of Virgil was not a phrase that authors used in the Renaissance. But the conception of Virgil's career, as extending to every level of style, was (as we have seen) classical and was also echoed in Renaissance commentaries. One of these that has not been mentioned so far is Agostino Dati's commentary on the opening verses of the *Aeneid*. Dati died in 1478, but his commentary was popular and remained in print until 1555. Like many commentaries, it was based on a public lecture. But this was a special event: Dati was a public intellectual and did not want, it would seem, to spend his sweetness on rudimentary items like grammar, vocabulary, and syntax. That task was assigned to Dati's nephew, whose job it was to warm up the audience and explain the grammar. He began with the apocryphal "Ille ego" lines that we quoted earlier. In these verses,

> the poet describes for us his three principal works in a three-fold style (*triplici stylo*). For the *Bucolics*, which describes things in a slender style (*gracili stylo*), he has memorialized with slender words (*gracilibus verbis*); the *Georgics*, which describes things in a middle (*mediocri*) style, he has remembered in middling (*mediocris*) words; and the *Aeneid*, which describes things in a lofty (*sublimi*) style, he has honored with lofty (*sublimis*) words.

The first verse, continues the nephew, is slender (or should we say fragile?) because all of the words are open (*aperta*) and welcoming (*propitia*); this verse describes the *Eclogues* and is an example of the low style. The next three verses are about the *Georgics*, a poem that uses middle-style figures of speech and that farmers welcome because it uses "familiar language" (*translatitijs locutionibus*).[58] The description of Virgil's *Aeneid*, in verses four and five, is constructed on the same principle: in lofty language, as befits an epic. Indeed, so closely has Virgil adhered to the style of each work, that all of the lines were deleted by mistake: because the first line is in the "slender" style, and is too lowly (*humilius*) for an epic, which should commence in majesty! Noticing the discrepancy, Virgil's editors decided to eliminate the first four lines, so that the poem begins on a loftier note, with "Arma virumque cano."[59]

Again, this was just the warm-up act. The main event was the lecture by Dati. A student of Filelfo, Dati knew Greek and some Hebrew. He was well read in scholastic philosophy, gave public orations on every conceivable occasion, and left behind a popular handbook on letter-writing and speech-making.[60] Dati was a celebrity: today there is even a street named after him in Rome. Yet his approach to Virgil's text was substantially the same as his nephew's. According to Dati, the "Ille ego" verses are a catalogue of the poet's major works, and each poem is characterized by a style: humble and delicate for the *Eclogues*; well tempered (*moderatus*) and pleasant (*amœnus*) for the *Georgics*; grave and dignified for the *Aeneid*. Dati is more erudite than his nephew and can explain the science (*physica*) behind a phrase like "the shuddering arms of Mars." Mars is the third planet, which is hot and dry: when combined in succession, heat and aridity inflame men's minds to violence, and the result is *arma*, or war.[61] But that is a grace note. For both men, the senior lecturer no less than the graduate assistant, what defines Virgil's career is mastery of the three styles.

The same principle was used to analyze the career of Ariosto. In 1560, a Venetian cartographer named Girolamo Ruscelli (*c.* 1504–*c.* 1569) assembled a new edition of Ariosto, complete with illustrations, a biography of the poet, and allegorical commentary. Like his predecessors, Ruscelli compiled a list of parallels between Ariosto and Virgil, including parallels in their careers:

---

[58] Middle-style figures of speech are the Gorgian figures of parallelism, isocolon, antithesis, and homoeoteleuton. *Translatitiae locutiones* are words and phrases sanctioned by custom.
[59] Petrus Fundius, preface to *Explanatio primæ Virgilii Aeneidos* by Agostino Dati, in Giunta 1544, fols. 147^v–148^r.
[60] James Hankins, *Plato in the Italian Renaissance*, 2 vols. (Leiden: Brill, 1990), vol. II, p. 408.
[61] Agostino Dati, *Explanatio primæ Virgilii Aeneidos*, in Giunta 1544, fol. 148^r.

What is said about the three styles of Virgil [that he mastered all of them] might also be said of Ariosto, since his comedies are in the humble style (*l'humiltà*), his satires in the middle style (*la mediocrità*), and his *Furioso* in the high style (*l'altezza*), no less than the *Eclogues*, the *Georgics*, and the *Aeneid* of Virgil.[62]

This confirms something that scholars today have long suspected, that genres in the Renaissance could be exchanged. A comedy could be substituted for *Eclogues*, a satire for *Georgics*. Again, what defines Virgil's achievement is not a sequence of genres but a spectrum of styles; and it is the spectrum, not the sequence, that the modern poet must imitate. In Ariosto's case, the spectrum was probably imposed on him retrospectively, by his biographer. In Spenser's case, it was probably deliberate. As we have seen, the "Ille ego" verses that Spenser imitated at the beginning of *The Faerie Queene* were thought to be a catalogue of the poet's writing in each of the three styles. In *The Shepheardes Calender*, Spenser had already written a poem in the low style; in *The Faerie Queene* he intended to write a poem in the high style. This is what the transition from "Oaten reeds" to "trumpets sterne" signifies. But what about the middle style? That would be Spenser's *Georgics*: we should probably look for it in Spenser's *Complaints* (the equivalent of Ariosto's satires) or possibly in *The Faerie Queene* itself – much of which is actually written in the middle style, not the high style. I shall say more about this in my next book.

STYLE AND VARIETY

Our conclusion is surprising, but the tradition was well established. Macrobius, in Book 5 of the *Saturnalia*, compares the achievement of Virgil with that of Cicero and says that Cicero was master of only one style, the "copious." Virgil, however, was master of four styles: the copious (*copiosum*), the curt (*breue*), the dry (*siccum*), and the "fat and florid" style (*pingue & floridum*). "Vergil's eloquence comprises many elements, takes many forms, and embraces every kind of style; in your fellow countryman, Cicero, you will observe that the tenor of his language is uniform, although his words flow forth like a copious torrent." He continues, "There are all these widely differing styles, and in Vergil alone do you find all of them united ... Vergil is the one writer in whom you will find all of these four kinds represented."[63]

---

[62] "La Vita dell'autore," in *Orlando Furioso*, ed. Girolamo Ruscelli (Venice: Vincenzo Valgrisi, 1560); the Italian is qtd. in Daniel Javitch, *Proclaiming a Classic: The Canonization of* Orlando furioso (Princeton: Princeton University Press, 1991), p. 174 n. 25.
[63] Macrobius, *Saturnalia* 5.1.1, 4–7 (Venice 1492, fol. lvi^r), trans. Percival Vaughan Davies, *The Saturnalia* (New York: Columbia University Press, 1969), pp. 282–83.

The number of styles and their names was a matter of debate, even in antiquity.[64] In the Renaissance, most critics sided with Donatus, and settled on three styles, with Virgil the master of all. Examples can be cited from both volumes of Bernard Weinberg's *History of Literary Criticism in the Italian Renaissance*.[65] Aulo Giano Parrasio, in his commentary on Horace's *Ars poetica* (1531), "recommend[s] Vergil as the model to be followed unfailingly for all three styles." Niccolo Liburnio, in his treatise on *The Three Fountains* (1526), cites Virgil as the "consummate master" of the three styles. Francesco Filippi Pedemonte, again in a commentary on Horace (1546), makes the same observation, as does Antonio Minturno in *De poeta* (1559), and Landino, both in a commentary on the *Ars poetica* (1482) and at greater length in the third book of his *Camaldulensian Dialogues* (c. 1473):

> No one can have been so indifferently instructed that he never doubted that this man, in the power and plenitude of his speech, surpassed, so to speak, eloquence itself. For there are three general styles and if anybody excels in any one of them, whether it be in figures of speech or other stylistic devices, he has achieved very great glory. Anyone can see that to have fulfilled all of them in each of one's books, and often indeed in a few verses to have so blended and mixed them all with that marvelous proportion such as different voices make in perfect harmony is to have prepared an unbelievable delight for the ears. Moreover, he so constructed his work with the four kinds of speaking that leisure matters did not lack their plenitude, nor more business-like matters their brevity. You will see that certain things please by their severity and plainness; others are pleasing inasmuch as they are set forth and adorned with the flowers of rhetoric; finally, all have been constructed with such art that you will find no other writing so full of all the examples of rhetorical grace. Add to that the knowledge of history. Add also that he [Vergil] stood out as the most diligent possible investigator of antiquity, and not only our antiquity, but that of the Greeks and of all nations. He was extremely careful of the old words, and yet how elegantly he formed new ones for himself. It was characteristic of him to master the power of all things. I say nothing of civil law; I omit the law of the high priests; I say nothing of the law of the Augurs – all of which he so mastered that he seems not to have received them from others but to have established them himself.[66]

At the end here, praise of style shades into praise of erudition (which we have seen already). What links the two is variety.

---

[64] See Tasso, *Discorsi del poema eroico* (1594), Bk. 4 (*Prose*, pp. 648–50).
[65] Weinberg, *Criticism*, vol. I, pp. 100 (Parrasio), 95 (Liburnio), and 117 (Pedemonte); vol. II, p. 742 (Minturno); and vol. I, p. 80 (Landino).
[66] Trans. Thomas H. Stahel, S. J., "Cristoforo Landino's Allegorization of the *Aeneid*: Books III and IV of the *Camaldolese Disputations*," diss., Johns Hopkins University (1968), pp. 49–50 (= Lohe, ed., p. 117). See also Arthur Field, "An Inaugural Oration by Cristoforo Landino in Praise of Virgil (from Codex «2», Casa Cavalli, Ravenna)," *Rinascimento* 2nd ser. 21 (1981), 235–45.

LISTING VARIETY

Ben Jonson, writing in 1601, called the poetry of Virgil "a direct and *analyticke* summe / Of all the worth and first effects of artes."[67] Sicco Polenton, in his biography of the poet (1426), wrote that a lamb could step in Virgil and a camel could swim – a claim usually reserved for Scripture.[68] But the Elizabethans said the same thing: "children do wade in *Virgill*, and yet strong men do swim."[69]

The usual way of proving this was a list. One of the shortest, from Sir Thomas Elyot, spills over onto four pages.[70] J. C. Scaliger (1561) has a similar list, but twice as long, which he offers under the heading of *Varietas*; for example, he claims that no two people in Virgil ever die the same way, but the *modus* is always varied.[71] Elsewhere, under the heading "Gradations of Style," Scaliger says that Virgil moved from style to style in order to produce *varietatem*. In proof of this he quotes descriptions from the *Aeneid* of five different thunderstorms, each one different; then he does the same thing for two funerals, two burial mounds, four eulogies, and three tempests.[72]

An even longer demonstration is given by the neo-Latin poet Giovanni Pontano in the dialogue known as *Actius* (c. 1599). According to Pontano, Virgil's poetry is chiefly notable for its variety, and especially the variety of his metrical effects, which he enumerates for the space of forty-two pages. "But the first praise of Virgil is that he achieves *varietas*." When Virgil breaks up the rhythm of a dactylic line with a slow pair of spondees, the result is not only "graceful," but also "desirable on account of *varietas*." And again, "The *varietas* of his rhythm is artful."[73] Minturno, in a treatise titled *On the Poet* (1559), praises Virgil for the same quality:

Indeed, by the immortal gods, what style (*dicendi genus*), what trope, what choiceness of words (*verborum delectus*), what arrangement, what ornament of speech, what splendors do not appear in him with the greatest of all possible brilliance? And what is more, is there ever something that seems to stick out in a picture, whether it be times, places, events, passions of the soul, that he has not placed before the eyes far better, and far more clearly? Moreover, is there any aspect of virtue, any

---

[67] Jonson, *Poetaster* (1601) 5.1.134–35, in *Ben Jonson*, ed. C. H. Herford, Percy Simpson, and Evelyn Simpson, 11 vols. (Oxford: Clarendon Press, 1925–52), vol. IV, p. 293.
[68] *VT*, p. 328/340.
[69] Sir John Harington, preface to Ariosto (1591), in *ECE*, vol. II, p. 212.
[70] Thomas Elyot, *The Boke Named the Gouernour* 1.10 (STC 7635; London: Thomas Berthelet, 1531), fols. 32^v–34^r.
[71] J. C. Scaliger, *Poetices libri septem* 3.28 (Lyon: Antonius Vincentius, 1561), pp. 119–20, at p. 119.
[72] Scaliger, *Poetice* 4.23 (p. 194).
[73] Giovanni Pontano, *I dialoghi*, ed. Carmelo Previtera (Florence: Sansoni, 1943), pp. 146, 178, 188.

consideration of conduct, that he has not depicted distinctly (*planissimè*)? Which branch of knowledge (no matter how complicated and obscure the inquiry), which pursuits of learning (no matter how strange and recondite), – of which of these did he not give an account and scatter their essential principles (*principia seminaque*) in his poems?[74]

Again, as in Landino, praise of style shades into praise of erudition. Again, what links the two is *varietas* (or as we might say, comprehensiveness). As in Pontano and Macrobius, the demonstration takes the form of a list. The same point is made, and in the same way, a few years later, by Bartolomeo Maranta, in his *Lucullianae quaestiones* (1564), five dialogues on the virtues of the poet Virgil:

[H]ow variedly – and always wherever he wishes – he draws away the souls of men, inflames, calms, teaches, impels, excites, diverts, discourages them; and how distinctly and clearly and abundantly and luminously he writes, with respect both to content and to expression; and how also, without ever neglecting brevity, to both matter and form he so adapts all things that if you were to add, or change, or remove anything it would be wholly faulty and less perfect.[75]

Virgil's brevity was another cliché of Renaissance literary criticism, and will be discussed in the next chapter. Notice, though, what the critic says about Virgil's versatility: not only does Virgil produce a variety of effects (*distrahat, incendat, leniat, doceat, impellat*, etc.), but he does so in various ways (*varie*). Tributes to Virgil's *varietas* are also found in the works of Juan Luis Vives (1492–1540)[76] and Fabius Paulinus (d. 1605);[77] in both, the demonstration takes the form of a list.

VIRGIL AS SECOND NATURE

The other way of showing Virgil's versatility was comparison. Sometimes, as in Macrobius, the comparandum is another author: Cicero, or Homer. Thus Angelo Decembrio (*c.* 1415–*c.* 1466), in a dialogue on *Literary Refinements* (1462):

The gods lavished such abundance and such grace of eloquence (*tanta dicendi copia gratiaque*) on this poet, so much elegance, that the more he is read, the more one is moved to read him. I know for a fact that some of the most distinguished speakers,

---

[74] Minturno, *De poeta*, Bk. 1; as qtd. in Jacobus Pontanus, *Symbolarum libri XVIJ Virgilij* (Augsburg: J. Prætorius, 1599), facsimile repr., 3 vols. (New York: Garland, 1976), vol. 1, p. 24.
[75] Trans. Weinberg, *Criticism*, vol. 1, p. 172.
[76] *Joannis Ludovici Vivis Valentini opera omnia* (1782), facsimile repr., 8 vols. (London: Gress, 1964), vol. 11, p. 76.
[77] *Hebdomades* (1589), Bk. 1 (qtd. in Pontanus, *Symbolae*, vol. 1, p. 24).

no matter what the type of speech they are working on, can find it, most appropriately, quite as easily in Vergil's works as in those of Cicero or of Homer; nor is it surprising that whatever is flowery, fruitful, and most pleasant in the Greek poet, can be found equally in the Latin poet, even though Homer wrote forty-eight books – Greek authors are always long-winded – while Vergil wrote barely half that total.[78]

We shall see both of these – the comparison with Homer and praise of Virgil's brevity – again in the next chapter. Also popular was the comparison with Nature. On November 9, 1482, Poliziano delivered a public lecture in the form of a poem. The subject was Virgil, and the poem concluded with a peroration on the varied contents of Virgil's poetry:

And now, young people of Florence, as you behold the miracles of such eloquence, who would not think that he was looking out over a measureless stretch of land and sea? Here the fields abound with rich plenty; here the cattle are grazing on the tender grains; here is the elm beloved of the supple vine; on one side, the oak trees rise up with mossy trunk; over there, the seas are stretched out in their spaciousness; the shore is rough with thirsty sand; from the mountains there are cold streams running down; to one side, there are bare cliffs, leaning down; on the other, there are bays, opening up onto rocky caves; over there, sheltered valleys nestle. And so the glory of the world is moderated by an appearance of disharmony. Thus, in various faces, does the wealth of his eloquence clothe itself. And now it tumbles down like a river, with savage attack; now it trickles in a dry stream; now it opens itself up; and when it has wandered, it confines itself again; now it glories in its rawness; now it glitters once more, in a profusion of polished ornaments; and all the while it mixes everything beautifully.[79]

The phrasing of this passage is largely Virgil's own, or from other classical authors.[80] The content, however, is almost entirely from Macrobius, and so is most of the imagery:

You see – do you not? – that the use of all these varied styles is a distinctive characteristic of Vergil's language. Indeed, I think that it was not without a kind of foreknowledge that he was preparing himself to serve as a model for all, that he intentionally blended his styles, acting with a prescience born of a disposition divine rather than mortal. And thus it was that with the universal mother, Nature, for his only guide he wove the pattern of his work – just as in music different sounds are combined to form a single harmony. For in fact, if you look closely into the

---

[78] Trans. Mario di Cesare, *Vida's Christiad and Vergilian Epic* (New York: Columbia University Press, 1964), pp. 52–53.
[79] *Manto* 351–67, in *Silvae*, ed. Francesco Bausi (Florence: Olschki, 1996), pp. 42–43.
[80] Bausi's edition traces the sources. On Poliziano's method, see Thomas M. Greene, *The Light in Troy: Imitation and Discovery in Renaissance Poetry* (New Haven: Yale University Press, 1982), ch. 8; and McLaughlin, *Literary Imitation*, ch. 10.

nature of the universe, you will find a striking resemblance between the handicraft of the divine craftsman and that of our poet. Thus, just as Vergil's language is perfectly adapted to every kind of character, being now concise, now copious, now dry, now ornate, and now a combination of all these qualities, sometimes flowing smoothly or at other times raging like a torrent; so it is with the earth itself, for here it is rich with crops and meadows, there rough with forests and crags, here you have dry sand, here, again, flowing streams, and parts lie open to the boundless sea. I beg you to pardon me and not charge me with exaggeration in thus comparing Vergil with nature, for I think that I might fairly say that he has combined in his single self the diverse styles of the ten Attic orators, and yet not say enough.[81]

Six years later, Landino (Poliziano's former teacher) would quote the same passage in the preface of his 1488 commentary.[82]

In 1483, the year after his public lecture on Virgil, Poliziano composed a long poem on farming, closely modeled on Hesiod and Virgil's *Georgics*. Why the *Georgics* instead of the *Aeneid*? Because, for Poliziano, the *Georgics* was the poem that best exemplified the protean resourcefulness of its author: an inventiveness, not just of theme and subject matter, but also of style and tone.[83] Virgil's resourcefulness would also be linked with the *Georgics* in Vida's *Art of Poetry* (1527). "The power of speech," Vida advises the poet-in-training,

is variable and assumes numberless shapes and aspects involving a thousand shades of utterance and varying significance ... Again, since a thousand modes and figures of speech are at your disposal, if you are not hard-pressed by narrow limitations, introduce those thousand modes and figures, each in its turn; remember to practice variety (*mutare memento*) by diligently adopting first one set of expressions and then another. For thus a boundless pleasure holds our ears in your power and pervades our breast with an impulse of delight. Poets therefore bend every effort to ensure that, as among the examples which nature supplies, one may never find [in their works] two forms quite alike, since all things which breathe the living winds beneath the stars – every species of beasts and men, the gorgeously plumed birds and the silent swimmers of the sea – all are of varying appearance.[84]

---

[81] *Saturnalia* 5.1.18–20 (Venice 1492, fol. lvi^{r–v}), trans. Davies, p. 285. For the image of the river, see also *Sat.* 5.1.10: "Quis fons: quis torrens: quod mare tot fluctibus: quot hic uerbis inundauit" (Venice 1492, fol. lvi^r). "What spring, what torrent, what sea in flood can match with waves the number of his words?" This line is quoted, silently, by Erasmus in *De copia* 1.3; see *Collected Works of Erasmus*, gen. eds. R. J. Schoeck and B. M. Corrigan, 84 vols. (Toronto: University of Toronto Press, 1974–), vol. XXIV, p. 298. On the river as a metaphor for literary influence, see David Quint, *Origin and Originality in Renaissance Literature: Versions of the Source* (New Haven: Yale University Press, 1983).
[82] Giunta 1544, sig. *viii^v.
[83] Perrine Galand-Hallyn, *Le reflet des fleurs: Description et métalangage poétique d'Homère à la renaissance* (Geneva: Droz, 1994), ch. 7; see also McLaughlin, *Literary Imitation*, ch. 10.
[84] Marco Girolamo Vida, *De arte poetica* (1527), 3.23–25, 3.32–43, ed. and trans. Williams, pp. 86–87.

Vida was devoted to Virgil: earlier in the same work, he urged the reader, "Revere Maro in your mind before all others ... follow him only, and as far as you are able, keep to his steps" (1.208–9). In the longer passage, the injunction is more subtle, but the reference is unmistakable. Imitate, says Vida, the variety of nature, which never repeats itself: all are of varying appearance, "genus omne ferarum, / Atque hominum, pictæ volucres, mutæque natantes." This last phrase is almost a direct quotation from Virgil's third georgic, where he describes the dominion of Eros over all creatures:

> Omne adeo genus in terris hominumque, ferarumque,
> Et genus æquorum, pecudes, pictæque volucres
> Infurias, ignemque ruunt. amor omnibus idem.[85]

[And so every species in the world – men and beasts, every kind of fish, the cattle and the painted birds – all run into the madness, into the fire. Love is the same in all of them.]

For ancient critics, Virgil was the universal poet: everywhere full of knowledge, versatile and various, the one who does all things well. His poetry described the whole scope of human society, in all of its classes and stages, and in their diversity his works suggest and imitate the fecundity and profusion of Nature itself. Vida was heir to this long tradition, but he also added something to it. It is not just that the poet is supposed to imitate Nature; rather, the modern poet is supposed to imitate Virgil imitating Nature. Once the imitator, now the imitated, Virgil is the new and improved Nature. Or, as Julius Caesar Scaliger would put it, the poetry of Virgil is a kind of second Nature (*altera natura*), in which the beauties of Nature have been gathered into one place, and the defects purged. Thus Scaliger:

Up until this point we have used examples from Virgil to show how the forms of things are to be drawn from nature itself. For I believe that it has come about in poetry, just as in paintings ... In each of many things, whatever the painters discover of excellence, they transfer it to one of their own works; and so it seems that they have not learned from nature, but that they have been able to give laws to nature. For who would think that there was ever such beauty in any given woman, that a discriminating judge would not find something lacking? For although there is in nature's pattern and scope a general completeness (*vniversa perfectio*), there are also many shortcomings (*impedimenta*), brought about by the mixing of either parent, the season, the weather, or the place. And so we could not take from any

---

[85] *Geo.* 3.242–44 (Giunta 1544, fol. 112ᵛ).

single product of nature the examples that we have borrowed from the one archetype (*idea*) of Virgil.[86]

Scaliger uses the term *idea* in its Platonic sense, to indicate one of the Forms. Sidney uses the same term in his *Defence of Poesie* (*c.* 1583), to describe the golden world of poetry. According to Sidney, the poet describes Nature, not as she is, but as she ought to be (what the French call *la belle nature*). This, explains Sidney, is the "idea" or "fore-conceit" of a poem. Again, the problem with Nature is that she never gathers her beauties into one place; in consequence, she has never produced "so excellent a man euery way as *Virgils Aeneas*."[87] The important phrase is "euery way." For indeed Nature has made many good men, but she has never made a perfect man, one who is good in each way. This was left to poets, and to Virgil in particular; we shall say more about this in Chapter 6.

---

[86] Scaliger, *Poetice* 3.25 (1561 edn., p. 113). Cf. Cinzio: "Virgil gathered up ... all of the good that can be found in each of the Greek and Roman writers, and collected it in one place ... And in this ... [he] imitated the great painters, who ... looked at all of the beautiful women they could and took the best parts from each one." *Discorso dei romanzi* (1554), in *Scritti critici*, ed. Camillo Guerrieri Crocetti (Milan: Marzorati, 1973), pp. 62–63.

[87] *ECE*, vol. 1, pp. 156–57; for Sidney's debt to Scaliger, see pp. 182, 191, 193, and 206. Oscar Wilde's dialogue "The Decay of Lying" (1891) is a variation on the same theme: "Nature is so uncomfortable."

CHAPTER 4

Morals and minimalism

Leibniz has a parable about two libraries: one of a hundred different books of different worth, the other of a hundred books that are all equally perfect. It is significant that the latter consists of a hundred Aeneids.

Jorge Luis Borges (trans. Eliot Weinberger)

VIRGIL THE REVISER

The richest and perhaps most interesting of the clichés about Virgil was his refinement. As we have seen, Virgil's poetry was revered almost universally for its scope and versatility; its variety resembled Nature in seeming to be endless. But Nature is careless, undependable; it requires supervision, guidance, and cultivation. What it wants is refinement, and refinement was supposed to be Virgil's specialty.

Again, the tradition begins in antiquity. In Horace, Virgil's song is described as "smooth and polished" (*molle atque facetum*).[1] Varius Rufus, who was assigned to edit and publish the *Aeneid* after Virgil's death, records that the poet composed slowly, only a few lines a day.[2] According to Aulus Gellius, Virgil boasted of making verses

after the manner and fashion of a bear. For as that beast, he said, brought forth her young formless and misshapen (*ineffigiatum informemque*), and afterwards by licking the young cub gave it form and shape (*conformaret & fingeret*), just so the fresh products of his mind were rude in form and imperfect, but afterwards by working them over and polishing them (*tractando colendoque*) he gave them a definite form and expression.

---

[1] Horace, *Satires* 1.10.44, in *Horatius cum quattuor commentariis* (Venice: J. Alvisius, 1498), fol. ccv^r.
[2] Recorded by Quintilian, *Institutio oratoria* 10.3.8, in *M. Fabii Quintiliani oratorium institutionum [libri duodecim]. Vna cum annotationibus Raphaelis Regii in depra[u]ationes eiusdem* (Venice: Georgius de Rusconibus, 1572), fol. clxviii^v.

This is why, continues Gellius, Virgil in his will directed his executors to burn the unfinished *Aeneid*:

For the parts that he left complete and polished (*perfecta expolitáque*), to which his judgment and approval had applied the final hand, enjoy the highest praise for poetical beauty; but those parts which he postponed, with the intention of revising them later ... are in no way worthy of the fame and taste (*iudicio*) of the most elegant of poets.[3]

The reference to "those parts which he postponed (*procrastinata*)" is explained by Aelius Donatus, who says that Virgil "would let certain things pass unfinished, lest anything should impede his momentum; others he propped up, as it were, with lightweight (*levissimis*) verses, joking that they were placed there as little struts or props (*tigillis vel tibicinibus*), to support the structure until the solid columns arrived";[4] these struts or props are the famous half-lines, of which there are about fifty. Donatus also knows about the bear-licking anecdote, and makes it the climax of a story about Virgil's writing habits. According to Donatus, the poet usually began the morning by dictating a great many verses, which he had devised beforehand; he would then spend the rest of the day revising, until he had reduced them to a very small number (*retractando ad paucissimos redigere*). As in Gellius, Virgil is reported to have said that he fashioned a poem "like a she-bear, by licking it for a long time."[5] The important phrase here is "for a long time": according to Donatus, Virgil labored at the *Aeneid* for eleven years; he was fifty-two when he died, and had hoped to spend the next three years on revision.

This gave rise, in the Renaissance, to the image of Virgil as a perfectionist. Giraldi Cinzio (1504–73) calculated his rate of production at two lines per day and quoted the anecdote about the she-bear.[6] This was perhaps the most famous of Virgil's *bons mots*, and was repeated endlessly.[7] Ben Jonson, when he censures Shakespeare for not revising, gives the example of Virgil,

---

[3] Aulus Gellius, *Noctes atticae* 17.10.2–6 (Loeb translation); the Renaissance text is printed in *Auli Gellii noctes atticae* (Paris: Joannes Tornaesius, 1592), p. 556.
[4] Donatus 35 (Giunta 1544, sig. *ii^(r–v)).
[5] Donatus 33 (Giunta 1544, sig. *ii^r). On the dangers of writing too much and too quickly, see Horace, *Satires* 1.4.9–13 (1498 edn., fol. clxi^v); 1.9.23–24 (fol. ccii^r); and 1.10.56–61 (fols. ccv^(r–v)).
[6] Cinzio, *Scritti critici*, ed. Camillo Guerrieri Crocetti (Milan: Marzorati, 1973), p. 134.
[7] E.g., Thomas Freeman, *Rubbe, and A Great Cast* 2.74, 75 (STC 11370; London: Nicholas Okes, 1614), sig. J4^v–K^r; Samuel Wesley, *Maggots* (Wing W1375; London: John Dunton, 1685), p. 3.

who "brought forth his verses like a Beare, and after form'd them with licking."[8]

Jonson was a disciple of Horace. "[T]hings wrote with labour," he goes on to say, "deserve to be so read, and will last their Age."[9] Or as Horace wrote in his *Satires*: "To write things that are worthy of a second reading, you must erase often."[10] In his *Ars poetica*, Horace urged would-be poets to delay the publication of a new work for nine years, during which time the poet is "free / To erase."[11] Horace does not mention Virgil by name here, but Virgil's example was thought to lie behind the precepts: according to Antonio Minturno (1500–74) and Lorenzo Gambara (1496–1586), Horace's *Ars poetica* was based on Virgil, in the same way that Aristotle's *Poetics* was based on Homer.[12]

STYLE AND CHARACTER

Why did it matter? In the Renaissance, Virgil was used as a standard textbook, not just for poetry but also for morality; in classrooms the world over, he was offered to students as a formal model (*norma loquendi*) and as a moral guide (*norma vivendi*).[13] In part, this was a function of how humanism began, as an attempt to write a purer Latin style, first in verse and afterwards in prose.[14] Purity is a word with moral as well as linguistic connotations, and there is always a temptation, especially among literary types, to set up style as an index to morality; it helps that, in Greek, the word for style is *charactēr*. Experience contradicts this equation at every turn, and

---

[8] Jonson, *Timber* 650, 2440–65, in *Ben Jonson*, ed. C. H. Herford, Percy Simpson, and Evelyn Simpson, 11 vols. (Oxford: Clarendon Press, 1925–52), vol. VIII, pp. 583, 637–38.
[9] Jonson, *Timber* 2465 (vol. VIII, p. 638). Cf. Cinzio, *Scritti critici*, p. 133 and Samuel Johnson: "What is written without effort is in general read without pleasure."
[10] Horace, *Satires* 1.10.72–73 (1498 edn., fol. ccv^v).
[11] Horace, *Ars poetica* 386–90 (1498 edn., fol. clxxvii^r).
[12] Bernard Weinberg, *A History of Literary Criticism in the Italian Renaissance*, 2 vols. (Chicago: University of Chicago Press, 1961), vol. II, p. 973 and vol. I, p. 306, respectively.
[13] Margaret Tudeau-Clayton, *Jonson, Shakespeare and Early Modern Virgil* (Cambridge University Press, 1998), ch. 2. See also Craig Kallendorf, *Virgil and the Myth of Venice: Books and Readers in the Italian Renaissance* (Oxford: Clarendon Press, 1999), ch. 2 and, for conditions in the classroom, Anthony Grafton and Lisa Jardine, *From Humanism to the Humanities: Education and the Liberal Arts in Fifteenth- and Sixteenth-Century Europe* (London: Duckworth, 1986); Paul F. Grendler, *Schooling in Renaissance Italy: Literacy and Learning, 1300–1600* (Baltimore: Johns Hopkins University Press, 1989), ch. 9 (on Virgil in particular); and Gerald Snare, "The Practice of Glossing in Late Antiquity and the Renaissance," *Studies in Philology* 92 (1995), 439–59.
[14] Ronald G. Witt, *In the Footsteps of the Ancients: The Origins of Humanism from Lovato to Bruni* (Leiden: Brill, 2000).

so do some of the poets. Thus Martial: "My page is wanton, but my life is sound"; Catullus says the same thing, and so does Ovid.[15] Yeats seems to argue, in "The Choice," that the split is inevitable: one can have perfection of the work or perfection of the life, but not both. Apparently one may sing and paint – and be a villain. On the other side, we have Milton: "he who would not be frustrate of his hope to write well hereafter in laudable things, ought him selfe to bee a true Poem, that is, a composition of the best and honourablest things; not presuming to sing high praises of heroick men, or famous Cities, unlesse he have in himselfe the experience and the practice of all that which is praise-worthy."[16] In the words of Quintilian, "Speech (*oratio*) often reveals character (*mores*); wherefore the Greeks say, and not without reason, 'As a man lives, so also does he speak.'"[17] Or, as Oscar Wilde would say, "It is only shallow people who do not judge by appearances." Beauty is truth, truth beauty – there is more ye need to know, but in the Renaissance, style is character.[18] Thus Jonson: "Language most shewes a man: speake that I may see thee. It springs out of the most retired, and inmost parts of us, and is the Image of the Parent of it, the mind. No glasse renders a mans forme, or likenesse, so true as his speech."[19]

It was important, therefore, that Virgil's verse be pure. In his play *Poetaster* (1601), Jonson praised Virgil as

> a rectified spirit,
> By many reuolutions of discourse
> (In his bright reasons influence) refin'd
> From all the tartarous moodes of common men;
> Bearing the nature, and similitude
> Of a right heauenly bodie: most seuere
> In fashion, and collection of himselfe,
> And then as cleare, and confident, as IOVE.

In the play, the speech is assigned to Horace; but the phrasing of the compliment derives from *Aeneid* 6.724–47, which tells how souls are

---

[15] Martial 1.4.8, in [*Epigrammata cum commentariis Domitii Calderini*] (Venice: Baptista de Tortis, 1485), sig. bi[r]. Cf. Catullus 16.4–5, in *Catullus, Tibullus, Propertius: His accesserunt Cornelii Galli fragmenta* (Lyon: Sebastianus Gryphius, 1537), p. 17, and Ovid, *Tristia* 2.354, in *Publii Ovidii Nasonis sulmonensis poetae clarissimi opera* (Venice: Lazarus Soardus de Saviliano, 1492), sig. viii[v].
[16] *The Complete Prose Works of John Milton*, ed. Douglas Bush *et al.*, 8 vols. (New Haven: Yale University Press, 1953–82), vol. I, p. 890.
[17] Quintilian, *Institutio oratoria* 11.1.30; cf. Seneca, *Epistulæ* 114.1: "talis ... oratio qualis vita."
[18] Exceptions, who defended style for the sake of style, were Étienne Dolet (1509–46) and Pietro Bembo (1470–1547); see respectively Marc Fumaroli, *L'âge de l'éloquence* (1980; repr. Paris: Michel, 1994), pp. 111–15; and Martin L. McLaughlin, *Literary Imitation in the Italian Renaissance* (Oxford: Clarendon Press, 1995), pp. 262–64.
[19] Jonson, *Timber* 2031–35 (vol. VIII, p. 625).

purified in the underworld. Ordinarily, this process begins after death; Jonson, however, states that Virgil "refin'd" himself in this life, "By many reuolutions of discourse." What are these? The context suggests planetary orbits. Elsewhere, though, when writing about Virgil and the she-bear, Jonson uses turning (either on a lathe or an anvil) as a metaphor for revision: "beate not the poore Deske; but bring all to the forge, and file, againe; tourne it a newe."[20]

The next speech, which is given to Gallus (Virgil's friend from the *Eclogues*), draws on the ancient story about Virgil's will, that he gave orders to burn the unfinished *Aeneid*. Gallus explains this command as an effect of Virgil's refined sensibility:

> so chaste, and tender is his eare,
> In suffering any syllable to passe,
> That, he thinkes, may become the honour'd name
> Of issue to his so examin'd selfe;
> That all the lasting fruits of his full merit
> In his owne *poemes*, he doth still distaste:
> As if his mindes peece, which he stroue to paint,
> Could not with fleshly pencils haue her right.

Self is to syllable, as parent to child, and mind to flesh; syllable-examination is but the outward growth and flourish of self-examination. Unfortunately, the flesh is weak, and the child, when it grows up, is always a disappointment. Perfection of the life is achieved, but perfection of the work falls behind.

Or so the poet feared when he died. But Jonson rejects Virgil's assessment of his own work and concludes,

> That, which he hath writ,
> Is with such iudgement, labour'd, and distill'd
> Through all the needfull vses of our liues,
> That could a man remember but his lines,
> He should not touch at any serious point,
> But he might breathe his spirit out of him.

The style is the man after all. And yet there seems, at first, to be a contradiction. On the one hand, Virgil's poetry serves in all the needful uses of our lives; this is his versatility. On the other hand, the poetry is described as the product of distillation: a rarefied essence, single and pure; this is his refinement. In fact, Jonson goes on to suggest, it is the process of distillation that

---

[20] Jonson, *Timber* 2441–43 (vol. VIII, pp. 637–38).

makes Virgil's poetry so versatile: it gathers experience, extracts what is essential, and leaves the reader with "a direct and *analyticke* summe / Of all the worth and first effects." The result, says Jonson in a memorable phrase, is poetry that is "ramm'd with life."[21]

VIRGIL'S CHASTITY

Distillation is a process that usually takes place in a kitchen or laboratory; again, though, the implications are moral, as well as culinary and chemical. What presides over it all, the poet's super-ego, is his ear, which Jonson describes as "chaste, and tender." The image is strange, but the concept is old. In our first chapter, we reviewed the textual criticism of Pierio Valeriano, the scholar who drowned Poliziano in a sea of ink and helped ensure that Virgil's admiring readers will probably misspell his name until the end of time. Valeriano, we recall, titled his great and terrible book *Chastenings and Variants*. Neither term was unusual. In editing parlance, the corruption of a text was termed a "violation" and restoring it was called "chastening" or even "castration" (a usage that was still current even in the 1940s).[22] In Virgil's text, if nowhere else, the metaphor did not seem strained. At Naples, his adopted home, Virgil was known as *Parthenias*, "the virgin," because of his sexual purity,[23] and this was believed by most critics to carry over into his poetry. The same two examples were recycled endlessly. The first was Virgil's description of Dido and Aeneas having sex in a cave (*Aen.* 4.160–72). Ben Jonson, in *Poetaster*, translated the scene as an example of what is distinctive about Virgil's poetry.[24] The choice seems odd, but Jonson was drawing on a well-established tradition. Vida mentions the cave scene as an example of how to handle delicate subject matter:

Finally, if you find yourself faced with an episode whose telling would bring even a faint blush to the [cheeks of] the virgin chorus of the Muses, conceal it, and either glide by it with a light touch only, or turn your narrative elsewhere and put fictitious material in its place. If the omnipotent father is to shake all heaven with this thunder, let Dido and the prince of Troy take shelter in the same cave; but modesty (*pudor*) must take care to add nothing further. For it will suffice if

---

[21] Jonson, *Poetaster* 5.1.100–7, 108–15, 118–23, 134–36 (vol. IV, pp. 292–93).
[22] See Stephanie H. Jed, *Chaste Thinking: The Rape of Lucretia and the Birth of Humanism* (Bloomington: Indiana University Press, 1989), ch. 1; and Debora Shuger, "Castigating Livy: The Rape of Lucretia and *The Old Arcadia*," *Renaissance Quarterly* 51 (1998), 526–48, at 528–30.
[23] Donatus 11/auctus 22 (Giunta 1544, sig. *ii^r).
[24] Jonson, *Poetaster*, 5.2.56–73 (ed. Herford and Simpson, vol. IV, p. 296).

primal Earth and the witnessing Air give the signal of the marriage, and the Nymphs keen on the peaks of the hills.²⁵

Tasso says much the same thing: Virgil, he writes, was *modestissimo* because he passed over the details of the event with a brief word, *con brevi parole*; later in the same treatise, he contrasts this with the practice of modern poets, who say too much.²⁶ Of course, some readers will want more than this: Cinzio, for instance, thought Virgil's poetry was too chaste, and recommended a good dose of *lascivia*.²⁷

The other scene that critics mentioned in this connection was the lovemaking of Venus and Vulcan (*Aen.* 8.387–406). The first critic to comment on this passage was apparently the Stoic philosopher Annaeus Cornutus (1st century AD), who says that, for the most part, Virgil deals with sex at a distance, using figurative language, except for Vulcan's *membra*, which Virgil was "a little careless" to have mentioned directly. The treatise is lost now, but the anecdote is preserved in Aulus Gellius, who compares Virgil with Homer. Whereas Homer is timid in such matters and merely hints at them, Virgil observes propriety, but does not take refuge in euphemisms. "He alone has revealed the sacred mysteries of the bedchamber in words of such number and plainness: open words, yet pure and dignified (*puris honestisque*)."²⁸ Ausonius (c. 310–c. 394) praises the scene as well, for recounting in a seemly way (*decenter*) what would be obscene otherwise.²⁹

In the Renaissance, Virgil's description of the lovemaking was widely discussed and was closely associated with a famous piece of classical sculpture, the *Bed of Polyclitus*.³⁰ Taking their cues from Gellius, literary critics routinely cited the episode as an example of Virgil's refinement in sexual matters. Ronsard, for instance, mentions the passage in the third preface to his *Franciade* (1587), as a species of diction that is "distanced from trivial and vulgar prose."³¹ Sir John Harington, in his preface to Ariosto, quotes the same verses (albeit without an English translation) to prove that sex scenes

---

²⁵ Vida, *De arte poetica* (1527), 2.526–34, ed. and trans. Ralph G. Williams (New York: Columbia University Press, 1976), pp. 78–79.
²⁶ Tasso, *Discorsi del poema eroico* (1594), Bk. 2, in *Prose*, ed. Ettore Mazzali (Milan: Ricciardi, 1959), pp. 501, 545–52.
²⁷ Cinzio, *Scritti critici*, p. 61.
²⁸ Gellius, *Noctes atticae* 9.10 (1592 edn., pp. 287–88); see also Servius on *Ecl.* 8.406 and the ancient writers anthologized in *VT*, pp. 811–15.
²⁹ *VT*, p. 474.
³⁰ Leonard Barkan, *Unearthing the Past: Archaeology and Aesthetics in the Making of Renaissance Culture* (New Haven: Yale University Press, 1999), pp. 247–69.
³¹ *Les œuvres de Pierre de Ronsard*, ed. Isidore Silver, 6 vols. (Chicago: University of Chicago Press, 1966–68), vol. IV, p. 12.

should not be off-limits for an epic poem: "I hope they that vnderstand Latin will confesse this is plaine enough, & yet with modest words & no obscenous phrase." Harington also mentions the lovemaking of Dido and Aeneas, and says that Virgil describes it "mannerly and couertly."[32] A decade later, Harington would acquire an edition of Virgil by the Jesuit commentator Jacobus Pontanus, who said all of the same things: "Virgil speaks in a way that is moral and reserved (*honestè ac tectè loquitur*) . . . There is nothing in Virgil that is not chaste and modest (*castum ac pudicum*), not a single word that is obscene."[33] For examples, Pontanus cites the cave scene in Book 2 and the lovemaking of Venus and Vulcan in Book 8. Perhaps the most famous, and certainly the longest commentary on the Venus and Vulcan episode was Montaigne's essay "Sur des vers de Virgile" (*Essais* 3.5). Montaigne praises the description highly: "Venus is nowhere else so fair, all naked and quick and panting (*toute nue, et vive et haletante*), as she is here in Virgil." If he objects to anything, it is only that Virgil makes married love seem more passionate than is either usual or prudent. Like Gellius and Harington, Montaigne admires Virgil's plainness and contrasts it with the petty conceits, the *menues pointes*, of contemporary love poetry. The eloquence of Virgil, he says, is not "a soft eloquence that is merely inoffensive: it is sinewy and solid, an eloquence that does not please so much as cram and carry away (*remplit et ravit*) . . . When I consider these bold forms of self-expression, so lively, so deep, I say not that it is well-spoken (*bien dire*): I say it is well-thought (*bien penser*)."[34] Again, style is a revelation of character.

RUMORS ABOUT VIRGIL'S SEX LIFE

There was only one problem with this picture: according to Donatus, Virgil had a special fondness for adolescent boys. He was also the author (it was believed) of certain pornographic epigrams, the so-called *Priapea*, or *Songs of Priapus*. For the younger Pliny (AD *c.* 61–*c.* 112), the existence of these obscene little poems was a license to write more of them.[35] But Renaissance critics were uncomfortable. William Webbe, in *A Discourse of English Poetrie* (1586), gives the commonplace view that Virgil improved on his models by rendering them more grave and decorous. "But, notwithstanding hys sage grauity and wonderfull wisedome, dyd he not altogether

---

[32] Harington, "In Praise of Ariosto" (1591), in *ECE*, vol. II, pp. 215, 214.
[33] Pontanus, *Symbolarum libri XVIJ Virgilij* (Augsburg: J. Prætorius, 1599), facsimile repr., 3 vols. (New York: Garland, 1976), vol. I, p. 15.
[34] Montaigne, *Essais*, ed. Albert Thibaudet (Paris: Gallimard, 1950), pp. 949, 976, 977.
[35] Pliny, *Epistles* 5.3.6 (*VT*, p. 62).

restrayne his vayne, but that he would haue a cast at some wanton and skant comely an Argument, if indeede such trifles as be fathered vppon him were his owne."[36] The metaphor "have a cast" is from bowling, and implies that the "trifles" were meant as recreation; even so, it would be preferable if they could be "fathered" on someone else – as, in fact, they were.[37] Poliziano, for instance, argued that the epigrams were by Ovid; Virgil, he reasoned, could not have written them, "for he was called *Parthenias*, on account of his virginal modesty (*uirginea . . . uerecundia*)."[38] In the event, Poliziano was wrong about Ovid, but right about Virgil: most of the poems are now attributed to an anonymous poet writing in the first, golden century of the Roman Empire.

Another small triumph for textual scholarship. But philology could not solve everything. For one thing, Virgil seems to have led a rather complicated sex life. It was rumored, for instance, that he cohabited (*consuesse*) with a woman named Plotia Hieria; it was also said that she started the rumors herself, and that when her husband, the playwright Varius, offered to share her with Virgil, the poet refused. But Plotia was a sideshow: according to Donatus, Virgil's *libido* was "more inclined to boys (*pronioris ad pueros*). Best of all, he loved Cebes and Alexander. Alexander was a gift to him from Asinius Pollio; the second poem of his *Bucolics* refers to him as 'Alexis.' Nor was the other one unlearned; in fact, Cebes was also a poet."[39] This last piece of information was meant, presumably, to reassure. But it did not forestall the obvious question: was Virgil homosexual?[40]

NISUS AND EURYALUS

Scholars who would prefer to sidestep this question will point out that Donatus is not unfailingly reliable, or they will insist on the distinction

---

[36] *ECE*, vol. 1, p. 238.
[37] See Kallendorf, *Virgil and the Myth of Venice*, pp. 81–90.
[38] Poliziano, *Miscellanea* 1.71, in *Omnia opera* (Venice: Aldo Manuzio, 1498), sig. Gii[v]. Badius Ascensius endorsed Poliziano's attribution and wrote commentaries on all of Virgil's poems except the obscene ones: because they were by Ovid and because they contain things that would be painful to Christian ears (Giunta 1544, sigs. *ix[v] and *x[r]).
[39] Donatus 9–10/ auctus 20–21 (Giunta 1544, sig. *ii[r]). See also Servius on *Ecl.* 3.20; Martial, *Epigrams* 8.55 (qtd. above, p. 63), 5.16.12; Juvenal 7.69–70 (qtd. above, p. 64); and, on Plotia, Jean Hubaux, "La 'maîtresse' de Virgile," *Revue des études latines* 12 (1934), 343–59.
[40] There was, it used to be said, no such thing as a homosexual identity before the late nineteenth century, but the consensus on this has broken down; see Claude J. Summers, "Homosexuality and Renaissance Literature, or the Anxieties of Anachronism," *South Central Review* 9 (1992), 2–23. With Leonard Barkan, "I use the word 'homosexuality' as generically as possible to refer to erotic relations of any kind between those of the same gender, whatever mentality concerning psyche, society, or identity may accompany them." Barkan, *Transuming Passion: Ganymede and the Erotics of Humanism* (Stanford: Stanford University Press, 1991), p. 24.

between life and art. But for Renaissance critics, the art raised questions of its own.

In *Aeneid* 9, Virgil tells the story of a night raid carried out by two Trojans: an older man, Nisus, and a younger man, Euryalus. In the course of their foray, Euryalus is captured and killed:

> Purpureus veluti cum flos succisus aratro
> Languescit moriens.[41]
>
> [Like a dark-red flower when cut down by the plow,
> he droops over in death.]

Virgil is echoing Homer, as usual, but also Catullus:

> Nec meum spectet, uelut antè, amorem,
> Qui illius culpa cecidit, uelut prati
> Vltimus flos, prætereunte postquàm
> Tactus aratro est.[42]

[Let her not look for my love just as it was before: it is fallen on account of her failing, just like the last flower in a meadow, after it has been touched by the plow passing by.]

The "failing" Catullus refers to is Lesbia's sluttish infidelity: a few lines earlier, he claims that she has "embraced" 300 lovers (*mœchis*), but truly loves none of them. Elsewhere in Latin poetry, the man is the plow and the woman is the flower. Catullus inverts this, and imagines himself as "the last flower in a meadow." His friends must have had a good laugh over that one. There is a hint here, in "the plow passing by," of Lesbia's coldness, her casual disregard. The cut worm, as Blake says, may forgive the plow, but Catullus does not. The Latin becomes precise all of a sudden, even fussy: the flower falls, not "when touched" by the plow, but "after it has been touched." For a poem that was talking, just a moment earlier, about a woman who "breaks her lovers in the groin" (*ilia rumpens*), it is a delicate way to end.

Virgil is more concentrated, less fussy. Death is real here, and what in Catullus was hyperbole ("I am just like the last flower in a meadow") has become understatement. A dying boy is rather more pitiful than a wounded flower, but Virgil is restrained; there is no mention of blood, only a color, dark-red. The bitterness and the self-pity are all gone. Also gone is the woman.

To say that the simile retains its erotic charge, when so many other things have slipped away and been replaced, would be arbitrary. More importantly, Virgil's echo of Catullus was not noticed by any of the major

---

[41] *Aen.* 9.435–36 (Giunta 1544, fol. 434ᵛ).   [42] Catullus 11.21–24 (1537 edn., p. 14).

commentators.[43] And yet readers today (including this one) assume that the two men, Nisus and Euryalus, were lovers. In the Renaissance, commentators dismissed this idea, because Virgil describes their affection elsewhere as *amore pio* (*Aen.* 5.296). But what does *pius* mean? According to Tiberius Claudius Donatus, Nisus loves Euryalus with *amore pio*, because otherwise it might seem that Nisus loves Euryalus with a shameful love (*amore turpe*). Badius Ascensius puts the matter even more bluntly: in this passage, *pius* means *castus*, "chaste."[44] The one critic who comments on the episode at any length is Julius Caesar Scaliger, who goes into ecstasies of appreciation. What he loves, though, is not the two young men, but the mother's speech that comes afterward, when she finds out that Euryalus is dead.[45] For Sidney, Nisus and Euryalus are a "shyning" example of "friendship."[46] The pair is also so categorized in a Jacobean Virgil, where they are listed in the index under "friendship, model of" (*amicitiæ typus*).[47]

At one level, the poets went along with this. As Colin Burrow has shown, Ariosto and Spenser both include versions of the Nisus and Euryalus story, but they quickly separate the pair, and assign the younger man to a more suitable (i.e., female) partner. In *Orlando furioso* 18.165–19.42, two Moors, Cloridano and Medoro, go out on a raid by moonlight. The younger man, Medoro, is wounded. But instead of dying, like Euryalus, he meets Angelica, who heals him, takes him into her bed, and eventually marries him. Spenser's version does not end in marriage, but is still heterosexual.[48]

Tasso's response is complicated in a different way. The night raid of Argante and Clorinda, described in *Gerusalemme liberata* twelve, is clearly modeled on that of Nisus and Euryalus. The difference is that Argante is a

---

[43] I have checked the major commentators who were available in the sixteenth century: Servius, Tiberius Claudius Donatus, Landino, Badius Ascensius, and Valeriano.
[44] For T. C. Donatus and Badius Ascensius, see Giunta 1544, fols. 302^v and 303^r, respectively. *Pius* is also glossed as *castus* in the ancient commentary known as "Servius auctus" or "Servius Danielis"; however, this version of Servius was not published until 1600; see above, p. 22 n. 23.
[45] Scaliger, *Poetices libri septem* (Lyon: Antonius Vincentius, 1561) 5.3 (p. 233).
[46] Sidney, *Apologie for Poetrie* (c. 1583), in *ECE*, vol. 1, p. 165.
[47] *Pub. Vergilii Maronis opera, scholiis doctissimis marginalibus illustrata, cum verborum & rerum indice* (STC 24792; London: Richard Field, 1616), sig. Ii5^v. The scholia in this edition are unattributed, but the epistle "Ad lectorem" (also unattributed) is by Melanchthon.
[48] Colin Burrow, *Epic Romance: Homer to Milton* (Oxford: Clarendon Press, 1993), pp. 110–20. See also Barbara Pavlock, *Eros, Imitation, and the Epic Tradition* (Ithaca, NY: Cornell University Press, 1990), pp. 13–17, 87–112, 170–83; and Wiley Feinstein, "Ariosto's Parodic Rewriting of Virgil in the Episode of Cloridano and Medoro," *South Atlantic Review* 55 (1990), 17–34. In the same way that Spenser's imitation of Virgil is mediated through Ariosto, Ariosto's imitation is mediated through Statius, *Thebaid* 10.347–448; see Eduardo Saccone, "Cloridano e Medoro, con alcuni argomenti per una lettura del primo *Furioso*," *Modern Language Notes* 83 (1968), 67–99; and Daniel Javitch, "The Imitation of Imitations in *Orlando Furioso*," *Renaissance Quarterly* 38 (1985), 215–39, at 219–22.

man and Clorinda is a woman; therefore when they fall in love, there is no impropriety. This is the most obvious allusion to the story of Nisus and Euryalus. But in Canto 9, there is another allusion and this time it concerns a pair of men. Solimano, the commander of Jerusalem's defenses, has a young page named Lesbino. Lesbino is a combination of two characters from Virgil, the young Euryalus and the virgin warrior Camilla. Both characters die in battle under the eyes of a friend, who then takes vengeance. True to type, Lesbino dies and Solimano sees him: "il suo Lesbin quasi bel fior succiso" (*GL* 9.85). It is an echo, clearly, of Virgil's *flos succisus*. What does it mean, though, and how much weight should we place on the *il suo* part of *il suo Lesbin*?

There is a similar question in Ariosto. For, as in Tasso, there are two versions of the story. The longer version, which we have already mentioned, describes how Medoro discovered his true vocation, as a heterosexual. But there is another version, three cantos earlier, in which the outcome is closer to Virgil. Again there is a *giovinetto*, Olimpio, and an older man, Ferraù, who "holds him in great esteem" (*OF* 16.71–73). During the battle of Paris, Olimpio's skull is cracked in two. Ferraù sees it happen and slices the killer into neat, symmetrical halves. If he were Nisus, he would die at this point. But Ferraù has more adventures ahead of him and, besides, he is in love with Angelica. The story moves on and we are left to reflect: what manner of love is this? The name *Olimpio*, like the name *Lesbino*, suggests Greece and perhaps "Greek" love.[49] But the main clue is religion: Olimpio and Ferraù are both Moors from Spain.

The Koran forbids sodomy, but Islamic and pre-Islamic literature is full of poems and stories about men who are in love (or just having sex) with other men; the most famous example ought to be *The Arabian Nights*, but most of us have read that only in expurgated versions. Tolerance in the Islamic world was limited,[50] but what came through to Western eyes was a distorted image of pederasty and freestyle incest.[51] It is no coincidence, then, that Olimpio and Ferraù are both Muslim. So are Cloridano and Medoro, as are Solimano and Lesbino. It was a way of holding the issue at arm's length. Boys will be boys, until they meet Angelica. If not, they were heathens anyway. To be sure, in all of these stories, the poetry is tender.

---

[49] The term *lesbian*, as applied to homosexual women, seems not to have been used before the nineteenth century; in the Renaissance, the usual terms were *tribade* (French) or *fricatrix* (Latin).
[50] Khaled El-Rouayheb, *Before Homosexuality in the Arab-Islamic World, 1500–1800* (Chicago: University of Chicago Press, 2005).
[51] Adrienne L. Martín, "Images of Deviance in Cervantes's Algiers," *Cervantes* 15.2 (1995), 5–15.

Always, though, the tenderness happens to someone else, to someone far away and of a different faith or race.

Characters like Lesbino and Olimpio show what a poet could do. They do not show what he was expected to do. As we have seen, readers in the Renaissance were curious about Virgil's *amor pius*. But curiosity did not break out into open controversy. At the level of commentary, there was no debate, only denial. At the level of poetry, the response was more complex. There was the main response, safe and heterosexual, and there was the marginal response, homosexual and also safe.

VIRGIL'S GAY ECLOGUE

So far we have been speaking about epics. In shorter poems, such as Virgil's *Eclogues*, it was harder to hide things, or to hide from them. As we have seen, the *Eclogues* was a standard text in Renaissance grammar schools.[52] The challenge came in teaching the second eclogue, known as "Alexis," which begins,

> Formosum pastor Corydon ardebat Alexim,
> Delicias domini: nec quid speraret, habebat.[53]

Roughly translated, this says that the shepherd Corydon "was hot for" the shapely Alexis, but Alexis was already the master's boy-toy, and Corydon didn't stand a chance. The rest of the poem is a dramatic monologue in which Corydon woos his fellow manservant with gifts from the field: a pair of chamois rescued from a deep ravine, quinces, plums, and chestnuts. Alexis spurns the gifts and, in the final lines of the poem, Corydon is encouraged to find someone else. This poem spawned numerous imitations,[54] the most famous of which in English are Richard Barnfield's *Affectionate Shepherd* and Christopher Marlowe's "Passionate Shepherd." Spenser also knew the "Alexis" well, and alludes to it at least twice, once at the beginning of his career, and once at the end.[55]

According to Aelius Donatus, the character of Alexis was based on a historical figure, Alexander. Servius adds that Alexander was a slave and that Virgil met him in the house of his first patron, Asinius Pollio; Virgil asked for his help at dinner and received him from Pollio as a gift. In the poem,

---

[52] See also T. W. Baldwin, *William Shakspere's Small Latin & Lesse Greeke*, 2 vols. (Urbana: University of Illinois Press, 1944), index, s.vv. "Virgil, *Eclogues*."
[53] *Ecl.* 2.1–2 (Giunta 1544, fol. 10ʳ).
[54] See Stephen Guy-Bray, *Homoerotic Space: The Poetics of Loss in Renaissance Literature* (Toronto: University of Toronto Press, 2002), ch. 4.
[55] Spenser, "Januarie," 57–58; *FQ* 6.9.40.

says Servius, Corydon represents Virgil, who was said to have a "rustic look," and whose love for the beautiful boy was initially frustrated.[56] Now all of this a teacher might omit in the classroom. But even a student of very modest abilities was bound to notice that the main subject of the poem is one male's burning passion for another male: *Corydon ardebat Alexim*.

There were three or four solutions. According to Servius, Alexis might be a real-life slaveboy, or he might be a pseudonym for Caesar, or for Caesar's boy (*puerum*), "whom if anyone had praised, it would have been welcome to Caesar."[57] In which case, the poet's real "burning" would be for patronage. At the end of the poem Servius rejects this theory, because there is nothing in the text to connect it with Augustus.[58] The theory was endorsed, however, by Paolo Manuzio, whose commentary on Virgil (1558) was, as we saw in Chapter 1, exceedingly popular. "For Corydon, understand Virgil; for Alexis, Augustus." Early in his career, Augustus rewarded his armies with lands confiscated from Virgil and his neighbors. Thus, when Corydon says to Alexis, "You care nothing for us," this means "You have not restored to me the lands that were taken away."[59] What looks on the surface, then, like a homosexual lovesong is really a petition for return of lost property.

Another solution for the awkwardness of Eclogue 2 was suggested by Erasmus, who gives detailed instructions for teaching the poem in his *De ratione studii* (1512). He suggests using the eclogue as an example of friendship (*amicitia*). Friendship depends on equality, but Corydon is from the country and Alexis from the city: ergo their friendship is doomed. A good teacher will be able to supply parallels from classical mythology, and can even quote Plato on the difference between sacred and profane love. This, he says, will distract the students and "nothing shameful (*turpe*) will come into the mind of those who listen, unless he is already corrupt when he arrives."[60] One wonders whether this method actually worked.

A variant of this was proposed by Juan Luis Vives, who corresponded with Erasmus and in 1537 published an allegorical commentary on all of Virgil's *Eclogues*. According to Vives, Corydon is Virgil and Alexis is the

---

[56] Servius on *Ecl.* 2.1 (Giunta 1544, fol. 10ʳ). For withholding the principals' real names, see Apuleius, *Pro se de magia apologia* 10 (*VT*, p. 65). For Virgil's *facies rusticana*, see Donatus 8/auctus 19 (Giunta 1544, sig. *iiʳ).

[57] Servius on *Ecl.* 2.1 (Giunta 1544, fol. 10ʳ).   [58] Servius on *Ecl.* 2.73 (Giunta 1544, fol. 15ᵛ).

[59] Paolo Manuzio on *Ecl.* 2.1 and 2.7, in *Opera P. Virgilii Maronis. Pauli Manutii annotationes brevissimae in margine adscriptae* (STC 24789; London: Henry Middleton, 1580), p. 40. Cf. Servius on the same verses and Aelius Donatus, *Vita Virgilii* 61–63 (Giunta 1544, sig. *iiᵛ, for *iiiᵛ).

[60] Erasmus, *Opera omnia* (Amsterdam: North-Holland, 1969–), ord. I, vol. II, p. 142; see Anthony Grafton, "Renaissance Readers and Ancient Texts: Comments on Some Commentaries," *Renaissance Quarterly* 38 (1985), 615–49, at 637–39.

poet Cornelius Gallus, whom Virgil writes about more directly in Eclogue 10. The situation, as Vives describes it, is briefly this. Once the two poets were friends, but Gallus works for Augustus now and has no time for his old friend. The issue of sexual love is never raised. When, in the first line, Virgil describes Gallus as *Formosum*, "shapely," Vives answers the obvious question with another question: "What is more shapely than the features of the mind (*animi lineamenta*), as the Stoics say? And to the friend (*amico*) what is more shapely than his friend, to the learned (*docto*) than one who is learned, and especially to the pure (*candido*)?" Friendship, which for Erasmus was a screen for something else, is for Vives the real meaning of the poem. As in Erasmus, friendship requires equality, and when the friendship began the two poets were equals. When, though, Gallus joined Augustus as part of his administration and moved to the city, he began to look down on Virgil because of his rustic upbringing and his humble station. At the end of the poem, Virgil's only recourse is to publish more poetry.[61]

A fourth method of dealing with the poem (and the biography) was to neutralize all the words for love. The Romans never were as casual about same-sex love as the Greeks, and by the time Servius was writing, at the turn of the fifth century AD, attitudes had hardened to the point where Eclogue 2 was a potential embarrassment. An explanation was necessary and Servius provided one in his introduction: "Virgil is said to have had a love for boys (*in pueros . . . amorem*), but surely he would not have enjoyed that love in a shameful way (*turpiter*)."[62]

DEFENSE BY FORGERY

That was in the *Eclogues*. At the beginning of his *Aeneid* commentary, Servius gave a brief account of the poet's life and character, saying that he "was so intensely shy (*verecundissimus*) that his habits earned him a nickname; for he was called *Parthenias* [in Greek, 'the Virgin'], because he was found to be upright (*probatus*) in every area of life." He adds that Virgil suffered "from only one vice (*morbo*), for he could not control his lust (*libidinis*)."[63] Servius does not explain how someone with this particular failing could get the nickname of "virgin." But in the Middle Ages, Servius was almost the only source for Virgil's life and, in consequence, most of the biographies that were produced between the fifth and fifteenth centuries

---

[61] Vives, *Joannis Ludovici Vivis Valentini opera omnia* (1782), facsimile repr., 8 vols. (London: Gress, 1964), vol. II, pp. 14–19.
[62] Servius on *Ecl.* 2.1 (Giunta 1544, fol. 10ʳ).
[63] Servius, preface to *Aen.* (Giunta 1544, fol. 146ʳ); in *VT*, pp. 203/204.

include some mention of Virgil's "only vice"; sometimes, though not always, they specify boys.[64] One of the few biographies that are silent on this point, the tenth-century *Periochae vaticanae* says that Virgil's life should not be spoken of in detail, because it was not one to be imitated![65] There was also, in the same period, a series of vernacular stories that featured Virgil as a would-be womanizer.[66] These tales continued to circulate in the sixteenth century, but seem not to have been connected with Virgil's poetry: the commentaries never refer to them, and Virgil is described in them as casting spells, not composing verses.

In the Renaissance, all of this changes. As we have seen, Virgil in the fifteenth and sixteenth centuries was famous for his personal chastity and for his modesty in writing about sexual intercourse. What caused the change?

The differences between medieval and Renaissance culture have been overstated so many times and for so long that critics today are wary of both terms. But in classical scholarship, some of the differences were real, and this is one of them. What happened in the fifteenth century was that someone, probably in northern Italy, discovered a manuscript of Aelius Donatus, whose *vita* of Virgil had stopped circulating after the age of Charlemagne.[67] When the *vita* was rediscovered, the results were mixed. On the one hand, Donatus provided scholars with new information from an ancient source; some of it was even true. On the other hand, he confronted them with the problem of Virgil's sex life. The response was disarmingly direct: forgery. Whoever discovered the old text did not pass it on without first making some strategic alterations; the result was a new and longer document, which we described earlier as the interpolated vita or *Donatus auctus*. It was in this interpolated form that Donatus reentered the mainstream of European scholarship, and he stayed in this form until the end of the eighteenth century. Where the old text had, "Virgil's appetite was more inclined to boys," the new version read, "It was rumored (*Fama fuit*) that Virgil's appetite was more inclined to boys."[68] After this, it also inserted an *apologia*:

---

[64] *VT*, pp. 213/216 (Philargyrius I), 231/234 (Expositio monacensis II), 253/254 (Vita gudiana I), 307/315 (Domenico di Bandino), 332/345 and 382/395 (Sicco Polenton), 399/403 (Vita laurentiana).
[65] *VT*, p. 247.
[66] See John Webster Spargo, *Virgil the Necromancer: Studies in Virgilian Legends* (Cambridge, MA: Harvard University Press, 1934), ch. 5.
[67] On the fortunes of Donatus, see Fabio Stok, "Virgil between the Middle Ages and the Renaissance," *International Journal of the Classical Tradition* 1.2 (1994), 15–22.
[68] Donatus auctus 20 (cf. Giunta 1544, sig. *ii^r, which reads "Fama est"). For variants, see Giorgio Brugnoli and Fabio Stok, eds., *Vitae vergilianae antiquae* (Rome: Istituto Polygraphico, 1997), pp. 21 and 85. In one MS, Virgil's appetite for boys (*libidinis in pueros*) is said to be excessive (*nimie*); in another MS, the words *in pueros* have been partially erased.

"But good men have thought that he loved (*amare*) the boys as Socrates loved Alcibiades, and Plato *ta paidika*."[69] In most printed editions, the Greek was left out and in its place there was a Latin translation: *suos pueros*, "his boys." Or should that be "his sweethearts"? Badius Ascensius (who, as we saw in previous chapters, wrote one of the standard modern commentaries on Virgil) tried to clarify:

> Socrates often spent the night (*pernoctasse*) with Alcibiades not otherwise than with a son (*non aliter quam cum filio*). As for the rest, everyone agrees that Virgil was a man of integrity (*probum*), both in word and thought, and for that he was known in Naples as "the Virgin." I am getting most of this from Donatus. Surely "the mouth speaketh out of the abundance of the heart" [Mt. 12:34] (though Catullus might think otherwise, for he says "The poet should be chaste / Himself, not his verses necessarily"). But if the former is correct, and Virgil is found to be entirely chaste (*castissimus*) in all of his poetry, then we ought to go along with those who say that he pursued the boys with a chaste love (*casto amore*). Of course, when I say *all* of his poetry, some have a different view, e.g., of his second eclogue. I shall get to that, and when I do I shall say that no one will ever be able to prove (*conuicerit*) that Virgil was talking about a shameful kind of love (*impudico amore*).[70]

The official commentator on Spenser's *Shepheardes Calender* (known only by his initials, E. K.) makes the same point when Spenser imitates some lines from Virgil's second eclogue. "[S]uch loue," says E. K., as Spenser describes in his January eclogue "is muche to be alowed of and liked of ... as Socrates vsed it: who sayth, that in deede he loued Alcybiades extremely, yet not Alcybiades person, but hys soule, which is Alcybiades owne selfe."[71]

The tone here is defensive, as it was in Badius ("no one will ever be able to prove"). According to the Greek satirist Lucian, who is mentioned by E. K. in connection with "execrable and horrible sinnes of forbidden and vnlawful fleshliness," "Socrates was as given over to love (*Amori*) as anyone else, and when he lay down under the same blanket with Alcibiades, the latter did not get up again untouched (*intactus*)."[72] This comes from the end of a dialogue called *Erotes*; the dialogue begins with a description of that still-celebrated sculpture, the Cnidian Venus of Praxiteles. Upon inspection, the statue is found to have been "assaulted," not in the vagina but in the anus, and a discussion ensues,

---

[69] Donatus auctus 20 (Giunta 1544, sig. *ii^r).
[70] Badius Ascensius, "Praeambula" (Giunta 1544, sig. *ix^v). Cf. Plato, *Symposium* 216b–19d, in [*Opera Platonis*], trans. Marsilio Ficino (Venice: Bernardinus de Choris and Simon de Luero, 1491), fol. 157^v.
[71] Gloss on "January," 59, in Spenser's *Shorter Poems*, ed. Richard A. McCabe (London: Penguin, 1999), pp. 38–39. See also William Webbe (1586) on Spenser's "June" (*ECE*, vol. 1, pp. 264–65). I will say more about these poems and the scholarship on them in a separate article.
[72] Ps.-Lucian, *Erotes* 54, in *Luciani samosatensis opera ... a graeco sermone in latinum conuersa* (Paris: Michaël Vascosanus and Johannes Roigny, 1546), fol. 197^r.

whether it is better to have sex with women or young men. The winning argument is almost Kantian: sex with young men is more civilized than sex with women, because it serves no useful purpose beyond itself; also, women are ugly when they wake up next to you. Modern authors were sometimes less crude, but no less skeptical. In Castiglione's *Courtier* (1528), Cesare Gonzaga says that the story of Socrates and Alcibiades is unlikely for two reasons: because bed and night are strange circumstances for the contemplation of ideal beauty, and because beauty of the mind is more likely to be found in an old man than a young boy (3.45). Yet he affirms the possibility of chaste love between a man and a woman (3.43), and the dialogue as a whole ends with Pietro Bembo's famous meditation on platonic love (4.50–73).

This was how it stood with Virgil, too. Thanks to Servius, the poet was reputed to be incontinent, sometimes (in the medieval biographies) with young males. Then in the Renaissance, when the text of Donatus was rediscovered, Virgil's boyward libido was converted by forgery into platonic love. The defense was not fireproof, but it was adequate to the extent that even the hard-headed Sir Francis Bacon (1561–1626), writing at the end of our period, called Virgil "The chastest poet and royalest ... that to the memory of man is known."[73] Ben Jonson, Bacon's contemporary, begins one of his elegies,

> Let me be what I am, as *Virgil* cold;
>   As *Horace* fat; or as *Anacreon* old;
> No Poets verses yet did ever move,
>   Whose Readers did not thinke he was in love.[74]

For the poem to work, readers have to know that Horace was chubby and Virgil chaste. And as late as 1640, when Jonson's poem was published, they still did – in spite of gay shepherds, pornographic epigrams, and persistent rumors about Virgil's *paidika*. To my knowledge, the only modern critic who acknowledged even the possibility that Virgil committed homosexual acts was Coluccio Salutati (1331–1406), who conceded that Virgil, being a man of his times, might have been led astray by them. "However," the analysis continues, "Virgil was known to the writers of the past as 'Parthenias' ('chaste'). From this reputation, Salutati concludes that his sexual conduct was above reproach, so that one can simply reject the charges against him."[75] As we have seen, most readers did the same thing.

---

[73] Qtd. Elizabeth Nitchie, *Master Vergil: An Anthology in English on Vergil and Vergilian Themes* (Boston, MA: Heath, 1930), p. 1.
[74] Jonson, *The Under-wood* (1640) 42.1–4 (ed. Herford and Simpson, vol. VIII, p. 199).
[75] Craig Kallendorf, *In Praise of Aeneas: Virgil and Epideictic Rhetoric in the Early Italian Renaissance* (Hanover, NH: University Press of New England, 1989), p. 90.

PERFECT POETRY

Like Horace, Virgil grew up in the provinces. Mantua, where he was born, is 240 miles from the capital and did not receive Roman citizenship until 49 BC, when Virgil was already twenty. According to Castiglione, Virgil did not speak or sound like a Roman (*parlava romano*);[76] Castiglione adds, however, that the Romans did not hold this against him and, in the Renaissance, Virgil was known as the poet who refined and perfected the Latin language.

In his commentary on Dante (1481), Cristoforo Landino says that Virgil was the origin of *la uera, & perfetta poesia latina*. Not that Virgil was the first Latin poet. "But," he continues, "before Virgil, speakers of Latin did not have *la perfetta poesia*."[77] The key word in both sentences is obviously *perfetta*. Vasari (1511–74) is also fond of the term, and uses it in a similar way. The first phase of Renaissance art, says Vasari, was marked by increasing naturalism in the depiction of faces and draperies. The second phase was characterized by new discoveries in mathematical perspective, and a renewed interest in classical archaeology. The only thing lacking, says Vasari, was *la finezza et una certa grazia*. By definition, *la finezza* is something that is achieved only at the end (*la fine*) of a process, which Vasari believed himself to be witnessing and even contributing to. This is the third stage of art's rebirth, which is distinguished from the second stage by more delicacy, more refinement, and more confidence. The outcome, says Vasari, is *la perfezzione*: not the absence of flaws, but maturity, the results of a process or progression – as when Vasari speaks, in the preface to part one, of "the progress of art's rebirth (*rinascita*) and of that perfection (*perfezzione*) to which it has risen again in our own times."[78] The ripeness is all.

The same principle, of growth and maturation, was applied to language and literature. According to Peter Ramus, "Every language has a childhood (*infantia*), a youth (*iuventus*), a maturity (*perfectio*), and an old age (*senectus*). Nor does anything become great all at once."[79] Latin poetry obeys the same rule. First, says Landino, there was Livius Andronicus, then Ennius and Plautus, and Terence and Lucretius; finally there was Virgil,

---

[76] Castiglione, *Il cortegiano* 1.35. Tasso comments on this as well; see his *Apologia della Gerusalemme liberata* (1585), in *Prose*, p. 474.
[77] Landino on *Inf.* 1.79, in *Dante con l'espositioni di Christoforo Landino, et d'Alessandro Vellutello* (Venice: Giovambatista Marchio Sessa & Fratelli, 1578), fol. 6ᵛ.
[78] Vasari, *Le vite de' più eccellenti pittori scultori e architettori, nella redazioni del 1550 e 1568*, ed. Rosanna Bettarini and Paolo Barocchi, 6 vols. (Florence: Sansoni, 1966–87), vol. III, p. 16 (preface to part 2) and vol. II, p. 31 (preface to part 1).
[79] Ramus, *Ciceronianus* (1557), qtd. in Kees Meerhoff, *Rhétorique et poétique au XVIᵉ siècle en France: Du Bellay, Ramus et les autres* (Leiden: Brill, 1986), p. 38.

the source of *la perfetta poesia*. This is the mature poetry that can only come about after decades and even centuries of experimentation and refinement.

VIRGIL AND ENNIUS

The details of this history would change over time, but the outlines, and especially the outcome, were consistent. According to Vida, Ennius was the first Latin poet, "rude of speech"; then there was Lucretius; and

> at last crude verses began little by little to assume excellence of form. The Latin poets freed themselves of their rustic manner until, like purest-shining day after clouds and squalls of rain have left the heavens, that most certain of Phoebus' sons, Vergil, godlike in voice and spirit, raised up his sacred voice, cleansed the filth and neglect left by the ancients, and set forth everything anew, made more excellent by his miraculous art ... Of no other time can Latium so boast herself, for then the Ausonian tongue achieved its highest excellence, and the mighty fame of Italy was borne to the sky. It would be blasphemous for poets to hope for anything excelling this.[80]

This little history of Latin literature was published in 1527; it was not new then, and it would not grow old for many years to come. In 1549, Du Bellay names Virgil on three occasions as one who labored to refine, not merely his own verse, but also his native language. When Virgil and Horace began writing, Roman "eloquence and poetry were still in their infancy"; by imitating the Greeks, however, they equaled Homer and Demosthenes. Modern France, says Du Bellay, is no different from ancient Rome: what Virgil and Horace did for Latin, our poets can do for French. In the meantime, he himself will do what he can for *la perfection* of his native tongue.[81] In 1570, Roger Ascham (1515–68) urged English poets to do the same. As in Du Bellay, the model is to be Virgil and Horace, who forsook the "faultes" of their fathers and "by right *Imitation* of the perfit Grecians ... brought Poetrie to perfitnesse also in the Latin tongue." A few pages later, he names the fathers, and contrasts the "perfitnes" of Virgil and Horace with the "vnperfitnes" of that faulty pair, Plautus and Ennius.[82]

As in Landino, the key word is *perfit*; again, it describes a stage of maturity in Roman literature, which is illustrated by a brief roll-call of the

---

[80] Vida, *De arte poetica* 1.155, 161–68 (trans. Williams, pp. 13, 15).
[81] Du Bellay, *Deffence et illustration* 1.3, 1.7, 2.12, and 2.1, ed. Henri Chamard, 3rd edn. (Paris: Didier, 1966), pp. 23–24, 44–45, 188–89, 89.
[82] Roger Ascham, *The Scholemaster* (1570), in *ECE*, vol. 1, pp. 29, 33, and 35. See also Webbe (1586), in *ECE*, vol. 1, pp. 278–79, 301; and on efforts to perfect English in the sixteenth century, Richard Foster Jones, *The Triumph of the English Language* (Stanford: Stanford University Press, 1953), chs. 1, 3–5.

important authors. Naevius (*c.* 270–*c.* 199 BC), it will be noticed, is not mentioned in either of these little histories. Livius Andronicus (*c.* 284–204 BC) makes a token appearance in Landino's sketch, but no more: as far as the Renaissance was concerned, the real history of Roman literature began with Quintus Ennius (239–169 BC). There were two reasons for this. First, none of these authors survives in any great quantity, but the fragments of Ennius outnumber the other two by a wide margin. Second, Renaissance critics had it on Cicero's authority that "there were none wrytt woorth the reading twyce in the Romaine tongue, before the Poet *Ennius*."[83]

A playwright as well as a poet, Ennius is still known as the father of Latin poetry; he was the first Roman poet to employ dactylic hexameter; and his *Annals*, a long poem on the history of Rome, was a major source for the *Aeneid*. Today scholarship remembers Ennius as "the most notable of the archaic poets, the most quoted, admired, criticized, and revived."[84] Cicero quotes him frequently and refers to him as *noster Ennius*. Under Nero, Ennius' reputation declined; by the end of the fourth century, it was hard to find even one copy, and by the end of the fifth century, it was impossible – the work was lost, apparently for ever, except in scattered fragments. Some of these were preserved in Cicero and Servius, and in that form they reached a sizable audience, including Petrarch. But for the most part, Renaissance scholars had to be content with second- and third-hand knowledge, much of it framed in hostile terms.[85] Quintilian, who was merely condescending, suggests that we ought to worship Ennius "as we do places that antiquity has made sacred, in which the oak trees, grand and ancient, are reverend, rather than beautiful."[86] Aulus Gellius defends Ennius against some of his detractors, but he also passes on their criticisms: according to Seneca the Younger (*c.* 4 BC–AD 65), Ennius came from "goatish" people (*hircosos*), and his verses are "ridiculous." (Virgil, he admits, also made some bad verses, which are "harsh and unmetrical." But these verses, Seneca insists, were made in imitation of Ennius!) Apparently, the old man wasn't funny, either: in a ranking of comic playwrights compiled by Vulcacius Sedigitus (fl. 100 BC), Ennius comes last, and even this, apparently, was an honorable mention:

---

[83] Webbe (*ECE*, vol. 1, p. 235). Cf. Cicero, *Brutus* 71–76, an important text for the early history of Latin literature that was only rediscovered in 1421.
[84] Gian Biagio Conte, *Latin Literature: A History*, rev. Don Fowler and Glenn W. Most, trans. Joseph B. Solodow (Baltimore: Johns Hopkins University Press, 1994), p. 77.
[85] What follows is only a sketch; for a more detailed treatment of the early reception, see Otto Skutsch, ed., *The Annals of Q. Ennius* (Oxford: Clarendon Press, 1985), pp. 8–46.
[86] Quintilian, *Institutio oratoria* 10.1.88 (1572 edn., fol. clxiiii^v). For places (*locos*), today's editions read groves (*lucos*).

I add him, says the ancient critic, on account of his age (*causa antiquitatis*).⁸⁷

The problem, by most accounts, was Ennius' style, which seemed, in retrospect, rough and slapdash. According to Propertius, "Ennius girds his words with a shaggy crown (*hirsuta ... corona*)."⁸⁸ Ovid opines, in the *Amores*, that Ennius "lacks art," and in the *Tristia* that "nothing is shaggier (*hirsutius*) than the *Annals*"; later in the same poem, Ovid writes that Ennius was unsurpassed with respect to invention (*ingenio*), but crude in craftsmanship (*arte*).⁸⁹ Horace is kinder, and praises Ennius for enriching the language with new words; at one point, he even calls him a second Homer (*alter homerus*). But his dramatic verse, says Horace, was written carelessly and in haste. Horace also claims that "Father Ennius" never sang of war except when drunk (*nisi potus*).⁹⁰ This was trivia, but schoolboys remember that kind of thing, and one finds echoes of it in unexpected places. The following verses are taken from a Latin poem entitled *The Overthrow of the Gout*, as Englished by Barnabe Googe:

> Of Martiall acts in stately stile,
>   did *Ennius* alwaies write:
> And in his cups did blase the deeds,
>   of many a worthy knight.
> Yet of the Gout at last he dyed,
>   nor could his verses saue:
> (With all the sweetnes that they had)
>   their maister from the graue.⁹¹

Gout and drink were bad, but this was not the worst of it. Far more damaging was the verdict attributed to Virgil, who, "when asked why he was reading Ennius, was said to reply, 'I am combing dung (*stercore*) in search of gold,' for that poet possessed extraordinary thoughts, but did not furnish them well with words." This is catty; it is reassuring, therefore, to

---

⁸⁷ Gellius, *Noctes atticae* 12.2, 15.24 (1592 edn., pp. 373–74, 499).
⁸⁸ Propertius, *Carmina* 4.1.61, in *Catullus, Tibullus, Propertius: his accesserunt Cornelii Galli fragmenta* (Lyon: Sebastianus Gryphius, 1537), p. 284.
⁸⁹ Ovid, *Amores* 1.15.19 (1492 edn., sig. giiiiʳ); *Tristia* 2.259 (sig. v iiᵛ), 424 (sig. v iiiiʳ). The latter passage was quoted by Coluccio Salutati, *De laboribus Herculis* 1.3.2, ed. B. L. Ullman, 2 vols. (Zurich: Thesaurus Mundi, 1951), vol. I, p. 17: "Of the poet who everyone agreed was the best before Virgil, and by many was even preferred to Virgil, Ovid said in *De tristibus*, 'Ennius ingenio maximus, arte rudis.'"
⁹⁰ Horace, *Ars poetica* 56–57 (1498 edn., fol. clxviiʳ); *Epistles* 2.1.50 (fol. ccxlixᵛ); *Ars poetica* 259–61 (fol. clxxiiiiʳ); *Epistles* 1.19.7–8 (fol. ccxliiᵛ).
⁹¹ Christophe Arbaleste, *The Ouerthrow of the Gout* (1525 or 1528), trans. Barnabe Googe (STC 1312.7; London: [J. Allde for] Abraham Veale, 1577), sig. B2ᵛ. The tradition that Ennius suffered from gout begins with Ennius himself, and was transmitted by the grammar textbook of Priscian; see Edward Courtney, ed., *The Fragmentary Latin Poets* (Oxford: Clarendon Press, 1993), pp. 17–18.

know that this anecdote is not recorded before AD 562, in Cassiodorus (*c.* 490–*c.* 585).⁹² From there, it made its way into the humanistic version of the ancient *Life of Virgil*, where it remained ensconced as biographical fact until the early nineteenth century.⁹³

Deprived of a text and dependent on hearsay, Renaissance critics made do with what they had. The results, for Ennius, were almost uniformly bad. Again, most of the comments focus on style. Petrarch, for instance, had access to only four of the six fragments that are still preserved. Nevertheless, he knew from Valerius Maximus that Ennius composed his epic "in a crude and unpolished style" (*rudi et impolito . . . stilo*).⁹⁴ Elsewhere, Petrarch said that Ennius was coarse (*ruvido*), in spite of his high subject matter. Richard Stanyhurst, in his preface to the *Aeneid* (1582), wrote that the "ragged verses [of Ennius] are nothing current, but sauoure soomwhat nappy of thee spigget, as one that was neauer accustomed too strike vp thee drum, and to cry, in blazing martiall exploytes, 'alarme,' but when hee were haulfe tipsye, as *Horace* recordeth."⁹⁵ The sentiment was, as we have seen, not original. But originality was not to be looked for. Lacking a proper text, Renaissance critics deferred to classical critics, not out of reverence only, but from necessity. Of the fragments that did survive, perhaps the most famous was *O Tite, tute, Tati, tibi tanta, tyranne, tulisti*. "Tyrant, thou has taken upon thyself these terrible troubles, Titus Tatius!" The line was notorious in the Renaissance as an example of too much alliteration ("hunting the letter").⁹⁶

Ennius was reduced, in consequence, to being Virgil's foil. Virgil was patient, virginal, abstemious, a perfectionist. His verse, wrote Webbe, runs "smoothely."⁹⁷ His narrative, said Stanyhurst, is "smooth" and every sentence "smoothlye slyckte."⁹⁸ Ennius was none of these things: his verses ragged and nothing current, his lips stained with wine, his speech a mingled skein of gold and dung. This is the version of literary history that was in place at the end of Elizabeth's reign; and it persisted well into the next century. Thus, in Jonson's *Poetaster* (1601), we are told to "Shun PLAUTVS, and old ENNIVS," as being "meates / Too harsh for a weake stomacke."⁹⁹

---

⁹² Cassiodorus, *De institutione divinarum scripturarum* 1.1.8, in *Variarum libri* XII. *De Anima liber I. De Institutione divinarum scripturarum libri* II . . . (Paris: Sebastianus Nivellius, 1589), p. 312.
⁹³ Donatus auctus 71 (Giunta 1544, sig. *iiʳ, printer's error for *iiiʳ).
⁹⁴ Francesco Petrarca, *Le familiari* 10.4.34, ed. Vittorio Rossi, 3 vols. (Florence: Sansoni, 1933–37), vol. II, p. 309; cf. Valerius Maximus 8.14.1.
⁹⁵ *ECE*, vol. I, pp. 136–37.
⁹⁶ Skutsch, *Annals* §104, qtd. in *ECE*, vol. II, p. 276 and 439–40 n. Another famous line was "At tuba terribili sonitu taratantara dixit" (*Annals* §451), which is preserved in Servius on *Aen.* 9.501.
⁹⁷ *ECE*, vol. I, p. 256.   ⁹⁸ *ECE*, vol. I, pp. 136, 137.
⁹⁹ Jonson, *Poetaster* 5.3.542–43 (ed. Herford and Simpson, vol. IV, p. 314).

The speaker, fittingly, is Virgil, for it was Virgil who refined and tamed Latin's asperity. Some years later, Jonson returned to this idea, when he passed sentence on the archaisms in *The Faerie Queene*: "*Spencer*, in affecting the Ancients, writ no Language: Yet I would have him read for his matter; but as *Virgil* read *Ennius*."[100] The meaning of this last phrase has, to my knowledge, never been properly explained, but the allusion is unmistakable: for Jonson, reading Spenser was like sifting dung.

This illustrates why, for reception history, it is necessary to read even classical texts in Renaissance editions. In the texts of Donatus that scholars produce today, the anecdote about Virgil reading Ennius is consigned (as it should be) to the apparatus criticus. For our purposes, the OCT and Teubner editions are too scrupulous and, in a sense, too classical. But only in a sense: so far as Jonson knew, the judgment he rendered of Ennius was the classical one framed by Virgil himself: that he besmeared great deeds with awkward style.[101] Whether Jonson was being fair, in likening Spenser to Ennius, is a separate question. At the end of the seventeenth century, critics were still making the comparison, but the terms were reversed now, and favored *The Faerie Queene*. For Samuel Cobb (1675–1713), it was Chaucer who made the dung and Spenser who sifted it, Virgil-like, for gold and diamonds.[102]

VIRGIL AS IMITATOR OF HOMER

Virgil, as we have seen, was famous for his perfectionism; this was established by the anecdote of the she-bear and it was matched, in the personal sphere, by his reputation for chastity, as the "Virgin." Virgil was remembered, both as a reviser of his own poetry and as one who, in Eliot's phrase, purified the dialect of his tribe. According to the critics, Virgil did so not by force of will but by imitating the Greeks: Theocritus, Hesiod, and especially Homer. But even these he improved on, by refining them. In the *Georgics*, Virgil was said to have imitated Hesiod "more grauely, and in a more decent

---

[100] Jonson, *Timber* 1806–8 (ed. Herford and Simpson, vol. VIII, p. 618).
[101] Cf. Thomas Cooper, *Thesaurus Linguæ Romanæ & Britannicæ* (STC 5688; London: [Henry Denham], 1578), sig. Iiiiiij.iij': Ennius "made manye bookes in sundrie kinds of verses, but the stile that he vsed was very auncient and homely, but they contained graue and substanciall sentences of great wisedom."
[102] Qtd. in R. M. Cummings, ed., *Spenser: The Critical Heritage* (New York: Barnes & Noble, 1971), pp. 231–32. For Chaucer as Ennius see also, in the same volume, Charles Fitzgeoffrey (p. 109), Sir Aston Cockayne (p. 194), and Dryden (p. 205).

style."¹⁰³ Similar claims were made, though not as frequently, for Virgil and Theocritus.¹⁰⁴ But most of the attention was on Virgil and Homer.

The nature of Virgil's borrowings, and therefore of Virgil's originality, was already a subject of debate in antiquity. Macrobius, for example, provides an extensive list of parallels, which he divides into three sections: passages in which Virgil improves on Homer, passages in which Virgil equals his model, and passages in which Virgil falls short.¹⁰⁵ According to Aelius Donatus, there was also an eight-volume list of "correspondences," compiled by Quintus Octavius Avitus, and a list of "thefts," compiled by Perellius Faustus. The charge of theft was already current in Virgil's lifetime, and Virgil is said to have answered his detractors with a stinging rebuke: "Why is it that they, too, do not attempt the same 'thefts'? Indeed, they will perceive that it is easier to steal the club from Hercules than a line from Homer."¹⁰⁶

This did not silence Virgil's detractors, nor did it settle the question of who was better, Virgil or Homer. Long before it was finished, Propertius proclaimed the *Aeneid* "a greater work than the *Iliad*," and Augustus was said to have begged Virgil, even for a rough draft or a few verses.¹⁰⁷ Virgil was an instant classic, a standard text, not only in Roman grammar schools, but also in Roman washrooms.¹⁰⁸ After the initial enthusiasm, though, Virgil was still in second place, after Homer. Quintilian recalls that when he asked his teacher, Domitius Afer (d. AD 59), who was next to Homer in the ranks of epic poetry, Domitius replied, "Virgil is second, but closer to first than to third." Virgil, Quintilian goes on to say, was more refined than Homer: for

although we must yield to Homer's heavenly and immortal nature, yet there is, if you will, more care and discrimination (*curæ et diligentiæ*) in Virgil, albeit he had

---

¹⁰³ Webbe (*ECE*, vol. I, p. 238). See also Marcantonio Maioragio (d. 1555), qtd. in Weinberg, *Criticism*, vol. I, p. 269. According to Scaliger, "Hesiod's whole book cannot compare with even a single verse of the *Georgics*" (qtd. in Pontanus, *Symbolae*, vol. I, p. 23).

¹⁰⁴ For examples, see Pontanus, *Symbolae*, vol. I, pp. 26–28; Cinzio, who refers in passing to *la semplicità di Teocrito* and *la maturità di Virgilio* (*Scritti critici*, p. 128); and Servius, commentary on *Ecl.* 2.51: whereas Theocritus recorded a dirty word openly (*aperte*), Virgil suppressed it modestly (*verecunde*).

¹⁰⁵ Macrobius, *Saturnalia* 5.2–13 (1492 edn., fols. lviᵛ–lxviᵛ). See also the blue-stocking in Juvenal 6.434–37 who, "as soon as she sits down, praises Virgil, excuses doomed Dido, sends the poets into combat, and compares them, with Virgil dragging down one end of the scale, and Homer in the other." *Juvenalis cum tribus commentariis* (Venice: Symon Papiens, 1497), sig. ll vᵛ.

¹⁰⁶ Donatus 44–46/auctus 62–64 (Giunta 1544, sig *iiᵛ). On borrowings from Homer, see also Gellius, *Noctes atticae* 9.9, 12.1.20, 13.25 (= 13.27 in modern edns.), 17.10 (in 1592 edn., pp. 283–87, 370–71, 440, 556–59), and J. F. Mountford and J. T. Schultz, *Index rerum et nominum in scholiis Servii et Aelii Donati tractatorum* (Ithaca, NY: Cornell University Press, 1930), s.vv. *Homerus (et Vergilius)*.

¹⁰⁷ Propertius, *Carmina* 2.34.66; qtd. with Augustus in Donatus 30–31/auctus 45–46 (Giunta 1544, sig *iiᵛ).

¹⁰⁸ For Virgil in grammar schools, see Horsfall, *Companion*, pp. 250–52; for washrooms, Salvatore Ferraro, *La presenza di Virgilio nei graffiti pompeiani* (Naples: Loffredo, 1982).

to work more. We are won by [Homer's] loftier peaks (*eminentioribus*), but we might give an even finish (*æqualitate*) just as much weight. All the rest follow from a distance.[109]

This established the terms of subsequent discussion for roughly the next 2,000 years. Homer is the poet of nature, Virgil the poet of art. Homer towers over us and conquers, like an army; his charms are obvious. Virgil, by contrast, is smooth, persuasive; he does not overpower, but appeals to our judgment.[110]

In the Renaissance, Homer's reception was shaped, for the most part, by three big events. All of them have to do with the recovery of something that was lost and all of them give weight to the old but not quite discredited notion that the Renaissance really was a time of rebirth and rejuvenation.[111] The first of these was the rediscovery of this passage from Quintilian. For most of the Middle Ages, the text of Quintilian was available only in mutilated form; the famous survey of Greek and Latin literature (10.1.46–131), from which this passage is excerpted, was one of the more unfortunate lacunae. In the twelfth century, this section began to circulate – on an occasional basis – as a fragment.[112] Then, in 1416, Poggio Bracciolini discovered a copy of the complete text, "begrimed with mold and dust," in the basement of the St. Gall monastery. The survey of classical literature was restored, and the contrast between Homer – nature's child – and Virgil – study's step-son – was introduced once again into the mainstream of European literary criticism.

That was one event. The second was the reappearance, in the late thirteenth century, of pseudo-Plutarch's *Life of Homer*. Among other things, it argued that Homer's poetry contains the seeds (*spermata*) of all subsequent discoveries in science and philosophy.[113] It did not, however, mention Virgil.

---

[109] Quintilian, *Institutio oratoria* 10.1.86 (1572 edn., fol. clxiiii^v).
[110] Cf. Ovid, *Amores* 1.15.14 on Callimachus, son of Battus: "Battiades toto semper cantabitur orbe. / Quanuis ingenio non ualet, arte ualet" (1492 edn., sig. giiii^r). A. D. Melville translates, "Callimachus throughout the world will shine, / In art supreme, in genius less fine." *The Love Poems* (Oxford: Oxford University Press, 1990), p. 27.
[111] Fumaroli, commenting on the discovery of new Cicero manuscripts in 1421, argues that "The chief difference between 'gothic' man and the man of the Renaissance is that the latter has at his disposal an incomparably richer and more complete knowledge of the Ancients' *ars rhetorica*" (*L'âge de l'éloquence*, p. 47). But there were losses as well as gains; see Lewis on "New Learning and New Ignorance," in his *English Literature in the Sixteenth Century, Excluding Drama* (Oxford: Oxford University Press, 1954), pp. 1–65.
[112] See Michael Winterbottom, "The Textual Tradition of Quintilian 10.1.46 f.," *Classical Quarterly* n.s. 12 (1962), 169–75; and Winterbottom, *Problems in Quintilian* (London: University of London Institute of Classical Studies, 1970), pp. 22–31.
[113] Pseudo-Plutarch, *Essay on the Life and Poetry of Homer* §91, ed. and trans. J. J. Kennedy and Robert Lamberton (Atlanta: Scholars, 1996), p. 157. The *Life* was often printed with Homer's text and was available, from 1537 onward, in a Latin translation.

The third big event was the direct experience of Homer's poetry. In the Middle Ages, access to Homer had been almost entirely limited to the *Homerulus*, or *Ilias latina*: this was a short summary of the *Iliad* in Latin hexameters. Then, in 1360, Boccaccio commissioned a Byzantine refugee, Leonzio Pilato (d. 1365), to translate the *Iliad* and the *Odyssey* into Latin prose.[114] The rendering was crude, but for the first time in almost a thousand years, Western scholars could examine Homer, for themselves and in large numbers. They were also learning Greek.

The results, for Homer, were not entirely favorable: in gaining readers, he also gained critics. Prior to this, Homer and Virgil could only be compared on the basis of their reputations. Dante, for example, was innocent of Greek; yet he knew, on good authority, that Homer was the greatest poet of all time, "the lord of high song, who flies above the rest like an eagle."[115] Beginning with Boccaccio, readers could compare Homer and Virgil on the basis of their merits. Few of them could read Homer's Greek with the same fluency that they brought to Virgil's Latin; nevertheless, it was now possible – even respectable – to express a preference for Virgil.[116]

Not that Homer lacked advocates: he was, after all, the great original, *fons et origo* of European literature. If water tastes best at the source then Homer, almost by definition, is the greatest poet of all time.[117] But if progress is possible – if poetry, like painting, is susceptible of refinement – then Homer is just a prototype or first draft: more accomplished than Ennius, but a founder, not a finisher.

---

[114] See Agostino Pertusi, *Leonzio Pilato fra Petrarca e Boccaccio: Le sue versioni omeriche negli autografi di Venezia e la cultura greca del primo umanesimo* (Venice: Istituto per la collaborazione culturale, 1964).

[115] Dante, *Inferno* 4.95–96 (1578 edn., fol. 27ʳ).

[116] For the reception of Homer on the Continent, see Noémi Hepp, "Homère en France au xvɪe siècle," *Atti dell'Accademia delle scienze di Torino* 96, pt. ɪɪ (1961–62), 389–508; Hepp, *Homère en France au xvɪɪe siècle* (Paris: Klincksieck, 1968); Pertusi, *Leonzio Pilato*; Don Cameron Allen, *Mysteriously Meant: The Rediscovery of Pagan Symbolism and Allegorical Interpretation in the Renaissance* (Baltimore: Johns Hopkins University Press, 1970), ch. 4; Howard Clarke, *Homer's Readers: A Historical Introduction to the* Iliad *and the* Odyssey (Newark: University of Delaware Press, 1981), ch. 3; Christiane Deloince-Louette, *Sponde: Commentateur d'Homère* (Paris: Champion, 2001), pt. I, ch. 2; Philip Ford, "Homer in the French Renaissance," *Renaissance Quarterly* 59 (2006), 1–38; and, for the history of Latin translations in the Renaissance, Alice Levine Rubinstein, "Imitation and Style in Angelo Poliziano's *Iliad* Translation," *Renaissance Quarterly* 36 (1983), 48–70. For England, see George de Forest Lord, *Homeric Renaissance: The* Odyssey *of George Chapman* (London: Chatto & Windus, 1956) and David G. Hale, "Virgil and Homer in the Early Tudor Period," in *The Early Renaissance: Virgil and the Classical Tradition*, ed. Anthony L. Pellegrini (Binghamton, NY: Center for Medieval and Early Renaissance Studies, 1985), pp. 121–29.

[117] This was assuming Homer had no predecessors, a premise that at least one critic, Jacques Pelletier, rejected. See his *Art poétique* (1555), 1.5, in *Traités de poétique et de rhétorique de la Renaissance*, ed. Francis Goyet (Paris: Librairie générale française, 1990), p. 257.

Youth is ripe for exploits and mighty enterprises, but perfection is the child of time. This was the modernist argument, as set forth by Cinzio in his *Discourse on Romances* (1554). Cinzio is defending Ariosto, but unlike most of his fellow advocates,[118] Cinzio makes no attempt to show that his client conforms to the example of Virgil, much less the canons of Aristotle. Instead, Cinzio borrows a page from Erasmus, in his famous attack on the Ciceronians, and insists that modern authors, living in the Christian dispensation, should not be constrained by the classical forms of pagan antiquity. New ideas demand new words, new rules, and new genres. Virgil, however, is special: not, as Dante and others have alleged, because he was a proto-Christian, but because Virgil teaches poets how to be modern. Although he imitated Homer, he did not imitate the barbarous customs and ethics of Homer's age, but those of his own, more enlightened epoch.[119] In doing so, he not only surpassed his predecessor, but also supplanted him. For Cinzio, the purpose of imitation is not to resemble the original, but to make something that is itself worthy of being imitated; not to reproduce the model, but replace it *qua* model. Thus, when Virgil was writing, the object of imitation was Homer; now, for us moderns, the object of imitation is Virgil himself.[120]

REFINING HOMER

Homer was vulnerable mainly on two fronts, the first of which was decorum. In Book 2 of the *Iliad*, Homer compares the attacking Greeks with swarming flies (469–73). In Book 11, he likens Ajax in retreat to

> a donkey, stubborn and hard to move, [when he] goes into a cornfield
> in despite of boys, and many sticks have been broken upon him,
> but he gets in and goes on eating the deep grain, and the children
> beat him with sticks, but their strength is infantile; yet at last
> by hard work they drive him out when he is glutted with eating.[121]

If description is the only goal of poetry, then this one is hard to improve on: "Everything fits," says Vida, "and the image, I confess, is exactly like the event. But the animal is disgusting (*turpis*)." Vida continues: if you are

---

[118] Weinberg, *Criticism*, vol. II, ch. 19; Daniel Javitch, *Proclaiming a Classic: The Canonization of Orlando furioso* (Princeton: Princeton University Press, 1991), ch. 2.
[119] Cinzio defended his own stage plays with the same argument; see Weinberg, *Criticism*, vol. II, pp. 914–15.
[120] Cinzio, *Scritti critici*, p. 62 *et passim*; see also Castiglione, *Cortegiano* 1.30.
[121] Homer, *Iliad* 11.558–62, trans. Richmond Lattimore (Chicago: University of Chicago Press, 1951), p. 249.

going to describe a warrior on the run, it is far better to compare him with a lion, as Virgil does. As for the flies in the other simile, they are filthy (*fœdissima*) and indecorous.[122] Several years later, Vives would echo Vida's complaint, noting that Homer's similes are "humble and sometimes mean ... as when he compares the soldiers to flies in a meal-sack, or Ajax to an ass, which will not leave its pasture although beaten with sticks. Virgil speaks more fittingly, for he compares the armies to ants and bees, which are more noble insects than flies."[123]

Decorum, then, was one problem. As the poet of nature, Homer was, almost by definition, unsophisticated and unrefined. The way Quintilian describes it, there seems to be a trade-off: one can have a vigorous imagination, or one can have critical judgment, but not both in combination. Homer, in this scheme, was fancy's child, and favored imagination at the expense of judgment. Thus J. C. Scaliger, in the fifth book of a seven-book treatise on the subject of *Poetics* (1561): "Homer's inventiveness (*ingenium*) was unsurpassed, but his craftsmanship (*ars*) was such that he seemed rather to have stumbled upon it, than to have cultivated it."[124] Homer did not revise, and in consequence, his writing was often "cold, or childish, or poorly suited (*inepta*) to the situation."[125] Elsewhere Homer is said to be no better than a mob spectator: "his descriptions have no craftsmanship (*arte*) and no purpose, no shaping tendency (*affectu*)."[126] Admittedly, Virgil borrowed much from Homer, but what he found there was little more than a heap of broken images, "a mass of crude and undigested material." This last phrase, *rudis indigestaque molis*, comes from Ovid, who uses it to describe the chaos of the elements, before the creation of the world. What resolved their quarrel? "A god," says Ovid, "and better nature." According to Scaliger, this god, this *melior natura*, was Virgil;[127] for "he did not so much imitate Homer, as teach us how Homer ought to have spoken."[128]

BREVITY AS CHASTITY

There is a second problem: according to Scaliger, Homer is repetitive and uses too many words. "Homer poured (*fudit*), and Virgil gathered; that one

---

[122] Vida, *De arte poetica* 2.286–303.
[123] Vives, *De tradendis disciplinis* 3.7, trans. Foster Watson, *Vives on Education* (Cambridge University Press, 1913), p. 146.
[124] Scaliger, *Poetice* 5.2 (1561 edn., p. 214). [125] Scaliger, *Poetice* 5.3 (p. 216).
[126] Scaliger, *Poetice* 5.3 (p. 228).
[127] Scaliger, *Poetice* 5.3 (p. 223); cf. Ovid, *Metamorphoses* 1.7 and 21 (1492 edn., sig. B^r).
[128] Scaliger, *Poetice*, 5.3 (p. 219).

scattered and this one arranged (*composuit*)." To be sure, Homer scatters his words with great fluency and power. "Yet greatness," says Scaliger, "does not consist in mass (*mole*) or frequency of speech, but in chastity and frugality."[129] These are Virgil's virtues, and they are matched, on the other side, by a series of Homeric vices: *licentia, luxuria, prolixitas*.[130] Looseness, lechery, and long-windedness: in Latin, these are cognates, each of which describes a form or permutation of "letting go" (cf. *liceo*). Not that Scaliger was opposed to any of these things in private. Later in life, the critic used poetry the way old men use worry beads, as a way to relax. To his son Joseph he would dictate, in Latin, between eighty and a hundred verses *per diem*: an impressive rate, but not Virgilian. The public face was rather different: not a word of "letting go" or "spontaneous overflow," except in disapproval: "But Homer flows (*fluit*), without any forethought (*sine vllo apparatu*), just as it takes his fancy (*more suo*)."[131] What he needs, in a word, is to be chastened (*castigandus*);[132] naturally, the man to do it is Virgil, the Virginal One.[133]

Virgil, says Scaliger, imitates Homer *castigatissime*, and is "almost everywhere *castigatior* than Homer."[134] As we have seen, the chastity that Scaliger refers to is both moral and stylistic. In Jacques Pelletier's *Art poétique* (1555), Virgil is said to have "imitated what seemed admirable to him in Homer. But he chastened (*châtié*) Homer in several places." The main complaint is that Homer is repetitious and wordy: what Virgil can do in only twelve books, Homer does in forty-eight. In particular, he fastens on the epithets. In Homer, the sea is always "the black sea," the ships are always "the hollow ships," the Greeks are always "the long-haired Greeks," Menelaus is always "the blond Menelaus," and so on.[135]

The criticism goes back to Macrobius.[136] Today, we recognize this as a feature of Homer's oral formulaic style. But Pelletier has never heard of oral formulaic style and asks the poet's question instead: is this a good style? Pelletier thinks not. Scaliger agrees: the epithets in Homer are repetitive,

---

[129] Scaliger, *Poetice* 5.2 (pp. 214, 215); the first quotation also appears in Pontanus, *Symbolae*, vol. 1, p. 24.
[130] For *licentia, luxuria*, and *prolixitas*, see Scaliger, *Poetice* 5.3 (pp. 245, 242, and 233, respectively).
[131] Scaliger, *Poetice* 5.3 (p. 230). A few pages later, Homer's voice is described as "superflua atque otiosa" (5.3/p. 235).
[132] Scaliger, *Poetice* 5.3 (p. 229).
[133] For refinement as a characteristic of modern poetry, cf. Horace, *Satires* 1.4.6–18 (1498 edn., fols. clxi^v–clxii^r) and 1.10.67–71 (fol. ccv^v).
[134] Scaliger, *Poetice* 5.3 (pp. 222, 243); for Virgil's "virginal modesty" and Homer's "satyr-like wantonness," see also pp. 227 and 241 in the same chapter.
[135] Pelletier, *Art poétique*, 1.5 (ed. Goyet, p. 257).
[136] Macrobius, *Saturnalia* 5.15.7 and 14 (1492 edn., fol. lxvii^r).

redundant, and – what is worse – ill-suited to their context. For it makes no sense to describe Achilles as "swift" when he is sitting in his tent. Also clumsy is the repetition of speeches. In contrast, Virgil has a "settled hatred of loquacity" and chooses every word with care.[137] For Scaliger, this is what makes him a better stylist than Homer: "The divine Maro chastened (*castigauit*) the free and loose way of speaking from Homer,"[138] and he refused the blandishments of Homeric *prolixitas*.[139]

Again, Scaliger is drawing on an ancient biographical tradition, in which Virgil achieved refinement by paring down in the afternoon what he had poured forth in the morning. He is also drawing on an ancient critical tradition, in which Virgilian poetry was distinguished by "aptness (*decoris*) and a kind of polished elegance (*excultæ . . . elegantiæ*)." Thus Quintilian.[140] Decorum and polish have already been mentioned, but what is *elegantia*? According to Aulus Gellius, Virgil was *elegantissimus poëta*, the most elegant of poets.[141] Elsewhere he says that Virgil was *poeta verborum diligentissimus*, very discriminating in his choice of words.[142] The root word in both phrases, *elegantissimus* and *diligentissimus*, is *legere*, to gather or choose. To be *elegant*, in this sense, is to be choosy, selective.[143] The Latin word for choosing is *electio*, which (according to Scaliger) is the chief virtue in a poet; that, and self-criticism (*sui fastidium*), which Homer did not have. "As soon as he thinks of something, he thinks it good" and writes it down; as a result, his verses are *longa & laxa*, long and loose. This is why Virgil, in chastening Homer, "frequently changed things, and left many things out."[144]

Scaliger did nothing by halves. Virgil, he argues, is nothing less than the alpha and omega of classical poetry. At the end of Book 6, there is even an "altar," erected in the text, where author and reader can pause to venerate the Virgilian *diuinitas*.[145] As for Homer, Scaliger has an eye for the weak points in his narrative, and pounces on them greedily, with the eagerness of a graduate student. Why, for instance, does Homer say, in the fourth book of the *Iliad*, that Contention strikes the heavens with her head? Critics of Virgil allege this as the source for Virgil's Rumor, "the goddess [who] strides the earth and buries her head among the clouds" (*Aen.* 4.177). But they are mistaken – at which point, Scaliger switches to the first person, and gives the response from

---

[137] Scaliger, *Poetice* 5.3 (p. 242).   [138] Scaliger, *Poetice* 5.10 (p. 263).   [139] Scaliger, *Poetice* 5.3 (p. 242).
[140] Quintilian, *Institutio oratoria* 6.3.20 (1572 edn., fol. c^r).
[141] Gellius, *Noctes atticae* 20.1.54 (1592 edn., p. 643).
[142] Gellius, *Noctes atticae* 2.26.11 (1592 edn., p. 99).
[143] Cf. Gellius, *Noctes atticae* 10.11.6–7, where Virgil is said to distinguish apparent synonyms *elegantissime* (1592 edn., p. 314).
[144] Scaliger, *Poetice* 5.3 (pp. 245, 242).   [145] Scaliger, *Poetice* 6.conclusion (p. 345).

Virgil's point of view: "I did not imitate this passage. I did not want to imitate this passage. The description is not pleasing. It is not true that Contention puts her head in the sky. It is ridiculous. It is fatuous. It is Homeric. It is Greekling (*Græculum*). It is not Virgilian. It is not Roman."[146]

This sounds like a string of tautologies. It draws, however, on widely accepted stereotypes, each with a classical pedigree. Greek was now being taught in some of the better grammar schools, but the road to Athens still had to pass through Rome. That is, the Latin authors came first on the syllabus. As a result, one tended to read the Greek authors (if one read them at all) through Latin-tinted spectacles. For example, when at the age of fifteen Poliziano began to translate Homer's *Iliad*, he did so in the style of Virgil's *Aeneid*, so that (for example) the heroes in the poem are no longer "horse-driving" but *magnus* and even *magnanimus*.[147] By the time a boy got to Homer (even a prodigy like Poliziano, who started Greek at age ten), he had already imbibed a certain idea – a Roman idea – of what poetry sounds like and what it means (for example) to be a hero.[148] He would also have imbibed certain Roman prejudices: for instance, that Greeks are "licentious, luxurious, frivolous, bibulous, venereal, insinuating, perfidious, and unscrupulous."[149]

DEFENDERS OF HOMER AGAINST VIRGIL

Scaliger was a critic in the grand style: irascible, intemperate, what Dr. Johnson calls "a very good hater." Yet despite the vehemence of his rhetoric, the substance of his views was never far from the mainstream of informed opinion. Virgil is concise, Greek authors talk too much, and Homer, in particular, is a chatterbox – one finds the same ideas, phrased with more politeness, in the critical writings of Decembrio, Vida, Vives, Maranta, Cinzio, Torquato Tasso, and (as we have seen already) Jacques Pelletier.[150]

---

[146] Scaliger, *Poetice* 5.3 (p. 227). For more examples of the same, see Lewis, *Sixteenth Century*, p. 25 and Hepp, "Homère en France au XVIe siècle," 496–500.

[147] Rubinstein, "Imitation and Style," pp. 50–55. Cf. Hepp, "Homère en France au XVIe siècle," 501: "The name of Homer, at the end of the sixteenth century, remained for many poets the symbol of an admirable perfection, but when they sought to define perfection, it was the Virgilian canons, not the Homeric ones, that they tended to make use of."

[148] Robin Sowerby, "Early Humanist Failure with Homer," *International Journal of the Classical Tradition* 4.1 (1997), 37–63, 4.2 (1997), 169–94.

[149] T. J. B. Spencer, "'Greeks' and 'Merrygreeks': A Background to *Timon of Athens* and *Troilus and Cressida*," in *Essays on Shakespeare and Elizabethan Drama in Honor of Hardin Craig*, ed. Richard Hosley (Columbia: University of Missouri Press, 1962), pp. 223–33, at p. 231.

[150] Maranta and Decembrio are quoted above. Examples from Cinzio and Tasso are given below. For Vida and Vives, see *De arte poetica* 2.190 (trans. Williams, p. 55) and *De tradendis disciplinis* 3.7 (trans. Watson, pp. 146–47), respectively.

Scaliger was demonstrative, even to the point of idolatry; like his namesake, Julius Caesar, he was also dictatorial. But he was not eccentric.[151]

Prior to 1600, the only major critics who reject this view are Lodovico Castelvetro (1505–71) and Sperone Speroni (1500–88). Both critics prefer Homer, and for similar reasons. The first reason will be familiar to anyone who has ever taught both authors in the same class: Virgil is derivative. The second reason is more subtle, and returns to the question of style. Like most of their contemporaries, Castelvetro and Speroni observed that Homer sows from the bag, Virgil from the hand. Castelvetro argues that this is a defect in Virgil, because brevity is inimical to wonder. In order to experience wonder, the reader of a poem must be able to visualize what is being described. Detailed descriptions – of thoughts, actions, costumes, scenery, and emotions – are therefore necessary.[152] Homer provides these things in abundance, and in doing so shows himself a true poet; Virgil, however, mars all with his perverse addiction to minimalism.[153]

Speroni agrees, but for slightly different reasons. According to Speroni, the essence of poetry is ornament. "This leads him," as Bernard Weinberg says,

> to place a premium on two qualities, "ornateness" and "floridity," both of which he finds in Homer, both of which are lacking in Vergil. Vergil's error lies in the fact that he "was concerned with brevity, in which the poet should take no delight if he wishes to delight the reader; for brevity cannot be ornate, and consequently is not pleasurable." The comparison between the two poets is concluded thus: "I return to speak again of the brevity of Vergil and the floridity of Homer. The latter delights properly, pleasantly ornamenting and amplifying his subjects, whence he always abounds in epithets; but Vergil delights through the marvelous, speaking as he does with so much brevity and precision and without affectation. But from the delightfulness of Homer is born joyfulness and gaiety, from that of Vergil is born astonishment (*stupore*) and melancholy, which is not proper to the poet but rather to the historian."[154]

Speroni, it would seem, does not just want to deprive Virgil of his throne, but even of the title of poet. Elsewhere, Speroni recalls the well-known anecdote about Virgil's last will and argues that, instead of publishing the

---

[151] "Outlandish though it may seem to us, this conception of Homer merits our attention, because it would reign in France for nearly two decades." Hepp, "Homère en France au XVIe siècle," p. 499.
[152] See Baxter Hathaway, *Marvels and Commonplaces: Renaissance Literary Criticism* (New York: Random House, 1968), pp. 62, 82.
[153] Lodovico Castelvetro, *Poetica d'Aristotele vulgarizzata e sposta*, ed. Werther Romani (Rome: Laterza, 1978–79), vol. II, pp. 161–74.
[154] Weinberg, *Criticism*, vol. I, p. 170; see also vol. II, p. 689.

Aeneid, Augustus ought to have burned it.[155] Speroni's conclusions are eccentric, but their premises are orthodox: Virgil is brief and Homer is flowery. Everyone knows that, even a rebel like Speroni. For Speroni, ornament is the very essence of poetry; therefore flowery is good and brevity is bad. I shall return to this idea in my next book.

WHY BREVITY IS BETTER

Speroni and Castelvetro were outlaws and outriders; they are important, however, for three reasons: because a fair account must acknowledge what does not conform; because Speroni was Tasso's teacher; and because Tasso rejected both of them. I will summarize his reasons for doing so, and conclude with some remarks about style.

The biographical tradition, preserved by Aulus Gellius and Aelius Donatus, described Virgil as a kind of minimalist. In the morning he would weave and in the afternoon he would unweave, until the loom was almost empty again. "Admittedly," said one commentator, "Virgil's field is smaller than Homer's. But it is well tilled (*bene cultus*)."[156] To be sure, Virgil could expand, at need and if the situation called for it; hence his reputation for versatility. "One moment, he is marvelously copious; the next moment, he is marvelously brief." So Vives.[157] Brevity, though, was Virgil's specialty.

But is brevity appropriate for an epic? According to Aristotle, epic poetry describes high personages in a grand style. From a literary standpoint, Virgil's choice of subject was unassailable: the first half of the *Aeneid* describes the journey of a hero (as in the *Odyssey*) and the second half describes a war (as in the *Iliad*). By combining the two subjects in a single poem, Virgil had actually proposed for himself a "somewhat larger" subject. "All the same," says Tasso,

> Virgil is sometimes so restrained and so sparing of ornament in the way he proceeds that, although that purity (*purità*) and that brevity (*brevità*) of his are marvelous and inimitable, there may be more of the poetical in the florid and fertile plenty (*la fiorita e faconda copia*) of Homer.

Again, brevity goes with purity. Also typical is the contrast between Virgil's *brevità* and Homer's flowery *copia*. But which is better? "Flowery," as we

---

[155] See Jean-Louis Fournel, "Le travail de la critique dans les écrits sur Virgile de Sperone Speroni," in *Les commentaires et la naissance de la critique littéraire: France/Italie (XIVe–XVIe siècles)*, ed. Gisèle Mathieu-Castellani and Michel Plaisance (Paris: Aux Amateurs des Livres, 1990), pp. 235–43.
[156] Raphael Regius, marginal commentary on Quintilian, *Institutio oratoria* 10.1.85–86 (1572 edn., fol. clxiiii^v).
[157] Vives, *De tradendis disciplinis* 3.7 (trans. Watson, pp. 146–47).

recall, was Speroni's word and, sure enough, in the next sentence, Tasso recalls something that the master said to him, when he used to attend the old man in his private chamber. Virgil, said Speroni, sounds like a speech-maker, rather than a poet. For instead of writing like Homer, he writes like Demosthenes. Cicero, says Speroni, makes the opposite error: instead of writing like Demosthenes, he writes like Homer. "And in truth," comments Tasso,

> whoever wishes to examine in detail the manner of each of them will see that the copious eloquence of Cicero is very similar to the generous fertility (*larga facondia*) of Homer; likewise Virgil and Demosthenes resemble one another closely in the sharpness and fullness and sinew of a glorious brevity.[158]

Tasso endorses Speroni's parallel: Virgil, indeed, is like the orator. But the phrasing of his endorsement hints that pupil and master are beginning to disagree. Though spare, the style of the *Aeneid* is not ineffectual: it is pointed, muscular, and it has its own kind of fullness (*pienezza*).

What kind of fullness is suggested by Macrobius, who says that Virgil's brevity was such that Brevity itself could not be more compact. The example he gives is a phrase:

> Et campos ubi troia fuit.
> [And the fields where Troy was.] (*Aen.* 3.11)

"Notice," says Macrobius: "with a few words, [Virgil] has consumed and swallowed up a great city; not even a ruin is left behind."[159] The same passage is quoted by Erasmus in the opening chapters of *De copia* (1512), as an example of "compressing the subject to such an extent that you can subtract nothing."[160] Brevity, then, is more than leaving things out; it is also a matter of putting things in.

Hence Tasso's reference to "fullness," in the *Discourses on the Art of Poetry* (1587). This was Tasso's first attempt to formulate a general theory of poetry and it was composed in a period when Speroni's influence was especially strong: Tasso studied with Speroni from 1560 to 1562, and he worked on the *Discourses* c. 1562–65. After that, the relationship frayed, badly – at one

---

[158] Tasso, *Discorsi dell'arte poetica* (c. 1562–65; pub. 1587), discourse 1 (*Prose*, pp. 364–65). The contrast between Demosthenean pointedness and Ciceronian fullness comes from Quintilian; see Ezio Raimondi, "Poesia della retorica," in *Retorica e critica litteraria*, ed. Lea Ritter Santini and Ezio Raimondi (Bologna: Mulino, 1978), pp. 123–50, at p. 137.
[159] Macrobius, *Saturnalia* 5.1.8 (1492 edn., fol. lvi^r).
[160] Erasmus, *Collected Works of Erasmus*, gen. eds. R. J. Schoeck and B. M. Corrigan, 84 vols. (Toronto: University of Toronto Press, 1974–), vol. XXIV, p. 298 (trans. Betty I. Knott). Erasmus also gives several examples of Virgilian *copia*; see pp. 297–98, 577, 580–82, and 586–87. Most of these are clustered in Bk. 2, on methods for achieving variety (*variandi rationes*).

point, Speroni even accused his former student of plagiarism.[161] In 1594, Tasso expanded the earlier treatise, from three books to six, and published it under the title of *Discourses on the Art of Poetry and, in Particular, the Poem Heroical*. It might have been spite, or it might have been reluctance to rebuke a former teacher. For once, though, Tasso did what was dignified: he passed over their quarrel in silence and directed his arguments instead to Castelvetro. Again the question is framed in terms of a comparison between Virgil and Homer. This time, however, Tasso approaches the question obliquely, with an observation about Dante. According to Tasso, the author of the *Divine Comedy*

is more like Homer than Virgil, in his boldness, in his freedom, and in his mixture of words archaic and barbaric. There is also a further similarity in what the Latins call *evidentia* ["vividness"]. Yet Dante calls himself an imitator and a disciple of Virgil – and perhaps there is a similarity, in brevity (*brevità*). But comparing the virtues of the two masters together, one hesitates to say which is greater. For one sets things before the eyes and particularizes them (*le particolareggia*), to use Castelvetro's phrase. The other (that is, Virgil) dwells more on the universal – not, as Castelvetro would have it, because he lacks art, but, as I think, in order to say things with more magnificence and more gravity. For to describe them in the minutest detail (*minutissimamente*) does not convey either of these virtues. Yet the virtue of Homer is the virtue that is proper to a poet, indeed, to every poet; Virgil's is the virtue that is proper to an epic poet, whose chief duty, above all else, is to preserve decorum and maintain magnificence (*grandezza*).[162]

Dante wanted to be like Virgil, but in practice (and apparently by accident), he was more like Homer.[163] He specialized in making strange things vivid, and to do that he was willing to use barbarisms and even obscenities such as would never occur to a chaste mind like that of Virgil or Petrarch.[164] This made trouble with Dante's critics in the same way and for the same reasons that the flies and donkey made trouble for Homer.[165] Flies are dirty, and donkeys are undignified. Nevertheless, when Homer says that the Argives were swarming like flies, we get the picture. And this is Tasso's point, precisely: what Homer says, the reader sees, vividly. That is the essence of poetry.

---

[161] See Lawrence F. Rhu, *The Genesis of Tasso's Narrative Theory: English Translations of the Early Poetics and a Comparative Study of Their Significance* (Detroit: Wayne State University Press, 1993), pp. 18–20.
[162] Tasso, *Discorsi del poema eroico*, Bk. 6 (*Prose*, p. 715). Cf. *Inf.* 10.20–21 (1578 edn., fol. 60ᵛ), where Virgil is said to have encouraged Dante – more than once – "to speak briefly" (*dicer poco*).
[163] The source for this comparison is Piero Vettori's commentary on *De elocutione* (1562); see Raimondi, "Poesia della retorica," pp. 135–36.
[164] For example, see Cinzio on Dante's use of *forba* (*Scritti critici*, p. 145).
[165] Weinberg, *Criticism*, vol. II, chs. 16 and 17.

But, Tasso continues, it is not enough to accumulate details: rather, the details must convey magnificence and gravity. This is where Virgil excels and Homer stumbles. Homer talks too much. What is more, he talks about things that do not matter. A famous example is the description of Hera's chariot in *Iliad* 5.720–32. "What is the use," asks Vida, "of depicting chariots encrusted with jewels, and pausing lovingly over their wheels and lengthily over their axles, at a time when the wars demand close combat and Mars is brandishing his weapons?"[166] Another example is the description of Thersites in *Iliad* 2.216–19. It is only four lines, but in Vida's opinion this is far too long: "If while you are recounting tales of outstanding heroes in arms you should tell of a camp follower who is shamefully lacking in courage and has a thorough distaste for battles, your eager readers will not be anxious to hear of the expression on his face, or whether he has lost an eye, his left foot is lame, or he has a pointed head atop an elongated neck."[167] Virgil, on the other hand, dwells more on the universal. "He does not number the streaks of the tulip, or describe the different shades in the verdure of the forest." Whatever is not conducive to grandeur and magnificence, he banishes with rigor pitiless. This perhaps is why Spenser's friend Gabriel Harvey says that Virgil achieves majesty, not only in his versification (which everyone admired), but also in his choice of words (*vocabulorum*).[168] It also explains why everyone in this period comments on Virgil's brevity: more than a trick of style, omitting what is trivial and mean is a key to Virgil's power and *gravità* – that high seriousness in which, says Tasso elsewhere, "Virgil surpassed all of the poets heroical."[169]

Brevity also creates mystery. According to Tasso, that is why we never tire of reading him: always in Virgil there is something left over, because in Virgil there is always something left out, "like sand without lime."[170] That

---

[166] Vida, *De arte poetica* 2.176–78 (trans. Williams, p. 55). Tasso says that if someone is going to paint a cavalry engagement, he will need to focus on the horses and their riders, for it would be a big mistake to fritter away his skill on microscopic details, like flowers and little birds (*Discorsi del poema eroico*, Bk. 4, in *Prose*, p. 652); the example comes from ps.-Demetrius Phalereus, *De elocutione* 2.76.
[167] Vida, *De arte poetica* 2.179–85 (trans. Williams, p. 55).
[168] *Gabriel Harvey's Ciceronianus*, ed. Harold S. Wilson and trans. Clarence A. Forbes (Lincoln: University of Nebraska Press, 1945), p. 70.
[169] Tasso, *Discorsi del poema eroico*, Bk. 5 (*Prose*, p. 687). For Virgil's gravity, see also Benedetto Varchi's *Lezzion della poetica*, delivered in Florence 1553–54, which attributes Virgil's greatness to "his erudition, his eloquence, [and] his gravity" (Weinberg, *Criticism*, vol. 1, p. 431). Webbe uses the same term in *A Discourse of English Poetrie* (1586), where Virgil is said to have imitated Hesiod in the *Georgics*, "yet more grauely, and in a more decent style" (*ECE*, vol. 1, p. 238). Virgil's mastery of the "serious" style is also noted by Vives (*De tradendis disciplinis* 3.7) and by Cinzio, who says that Virgil is "the rule by which things serious and grand (*gravi e magnifiche*) are judged" (*Scritti critici*, 62).
[170] Tasso, letter to Scipione Gonzaga (Oct. 1, 1575), in *Lettere poetiche*, ed. Carla Molinari (Parma: Guanda, for Fondazione Pietro Bembo, 1995), p. 225.

phrase is how Caligula described the loose, concatenated prose style of Seneca. Tasso remembers it, though, as a description of what happens to verse when you remove all of the conjunctions. What remains is concentrated and powerful, but also ambiguous. When he first noticed it, Tasso viewed this as a defect. But ten years later, Tasso would defend ambiguity, because an epic poem must be weighty.[171] Ambiguity contributes to the sense of weight, because it creates mystery. When mystery is dispelled, gravity goes away. As in the temple, so in the forest: reverence and fear, *l'onore con l'orrore*, grow side by side and always in shadow.[172]

The opposite of this shadowy mystique is *claritas*. This was (and still is) considered to be Homer's specialty: not the half-lights of the forest crepuscular, but "externalized, uniformly illuminated phenomena, at a definite time and in a definite place, connected together without lacunae in a perpetual foreground."[173] The virtues of this poetry are precision and fidelity. For these, Homer will sacrifice everything: decorum, gravity, everything. But the price, says Tasso, is too high. Homer, he suggests, was probably the greatest poet – the greatest imitator – of all time. But he did not write the greatest poem.[174] He purchased a crown at the price of his kingdom, and another man – more cautious, less chatty – ruled in his place.

STYLE: VIRGIL'S LAST STAND

That man, the prince of poets if not their rightful king, was Virgil. But Virgil does not emerge from this history unscathed. His reign was long and glorious, but it was not perpetual. And at the end of the eighteenth century, the race was given to the swift man after all. The story of how Homer recovered his kingdom has been told elsewhere: it is wrapped up with Romantic primitivism and the cult of *Volkspoesie*, and most of it falls outside our period.[175] But there are hints already of what will come.

---

[171] See Raimondi, "Poesia della retorica," pp. 139, 142, 148–50.
[172] Tasso, *Apologia della* Gerusalemme liberata (1585), in *Prose*, pp. 464–5.
[173] Erich Auerbach, *Mimesis: The Representation of Reality in Western Literature* (1946), trans. Willard Trask (1953; repr. Princeton: Princeton University Press, 1968), p. 11.
[174] This would be Samuel Johnson's judgment, as well: "We must consider (said he,) whether Homer was not the greatest poet, though Virgil may have produced the finest poem." James Boswell, *Life of Johnson*, ed. R. W. Chapman (Oxford: Oxford University Press, 1980), p. 870 (Sept. 22, 1777).
[175] See Donald M. Foerster, *Homer in English Criticism: The Historical Approach in the Eighteenth Century* (New Haven: Yale University Press, 1947); H. L. Lorimer, "Homer and the Art of Writing: A Sketch of Opinion between 1713 and 1939," *American Journal of Archaeology* 52 (1948), 11–23; Kirsti Simonsuuri, *Homer's Original Genius: Eighteenth-Century Notions of the Early Greek Epic (1688–1798)* (Cambridge University Press, 1979), pt. 11; and Tanya M. Caldwell, *Virgil Made English: The Decline of Classical Authority* (New York: Palgrave, 2008).

Virgil's greatness was rhetorical, in the sense that it was greatness for a particular purpose, a given audience, a special situation. Homer, on the other hand, was simply great: his virtues, said Tasso, were the virtues of poetry as such. Virgil's virtues – seriousness, grandeur, magnificence – were the virtues of a great epic poem. Tasso adds, however, that every virtue is closely allied to a corresponding vice: courage is neighbor to rashness, frugality to avarice, and so on. It is the same with style: there is a fine line between magnificence (*il magnifico*) and coldness (*il freddo*).[176] Homer's defenders put the point more strongly: correct imitation is no substitute for a vigorous original. According to George Chapman (1559?–1634),

Homers Poems were writ from a free furie, an absolute & full soule, *Virgils* out of a courtly, laborious, and altogether imitatorie spirit: not a *Simile* hee hath but is *Homers*: not an inuention, person, or disposition, but is wholly or originally built vpon *Homericall* foundations, and in many places hath the verie wordes *Homer* vseth.[177]

This was published in 1598. As we have seen, the complaint is traditional: the stigma of imitation varies in strength, but it never disappears. In Chapman's case, it coincides with a preference for the "strong lines" of what would later be called metaphysical poetry, and with a general distaste for the elaborate style of Chapman's immediate predecessors: Spenser, Sidney, the early Shakespeare.

There were other ways of digging at Virgil, most of them (like this) variations on Quintilian. For instance, Quintilian said that there was "more care and discrimination (*curæ et diligentiæ*) in Virgil, because he had to work more (*ei fuit magis laborandum*)." Chapman shifts the emphasis – not by much – and says that Virgil was "laborious," a plodder whose vaunted refinement was simply a function of time, and had nothing to do with inborn ability, which expresses itself in the free fury of an "absolute" (in the sense of "unrestrained") inspiration, the spontaneous overflow of powerful feelings. One finds the same idea ten years earlier in Thomas Nashe (1567–1601?):

Let other men praise the mountaine that in seauen yeares brings foorth a mouse, or the Italianate pen that of a packet of pilfries affordeth the presse a pamphlet or two in an age, and then in disguised arraie vaunts *Ouids* and *Plutarchs* plumes as their owne; but giue me the man whose extemporall vaine in anie humor will excell our greatest Art-masters deliberate thoughts, whose inuention, quicker than his eye, will challenge the proudest Rhetoritian to the contention of like perfection with like expedition. What is he amongst Students so simple that he cannot bring forth

---

[176] Tasso, *Discorsi del poema eroico*, Bk. 6 (*Prose*, p. 715).
[177] Chapman, Preface to *Achilles Shield* (1598), in *ECE*, vol. II, pp. 298–99.

(*tandem aliquando*) some or other thing singular, sleeping betwixt euerie sentence? Was it not *Maros* xij. years toyle that so famed his xij. *Æneidos*? Or *Peter Ramus* xvj. yeares paines that so praised his pettie Logique? Howe is it, then, our drowping wits should so wonder at an exquisite line that was his masters day labour?[178]

This is from the preface to Robert Greene's *Menaphon: Camillas alarum to slumbering Euphues in his melancholie Cell at Silexedra* (1589). As the title suggests, the targets of his attack are the ornamental curlicues of John Lyly's *Euphues* (1580). Prior to his "conversion," Greene had been a disciple of that style. But refinement can only be carried so far, or praised so long, before a reaction sets in. The eye tires of smoothness and the ear strains after uncouth melodies. Farewell, therefore, to trailing arabesques and branching symmetries! Farewell to pomps and vanities! Farewell, laborious refinement! Hello spontaneity, bed tricks, incest, and criminal slang!

In 1572, Ronsard published the first installment of his *Franciade*, boasting that he had patterned his epic "more on the untutored genius (*la naïve facilité*) of Homer than the minute industry (*la curieuse diligence*) of Virgil."[179] The contrast goes back to Quintilian and anticipates the distinction Schiller would later draw between naïve and sentimental poetry. In this version of literary history, Homer is the Shakespeare of the ancient world, warbling his woodnotes wild, and Virgil is its Ben Jonson. Ronsard evolves, though, and in the final edition of the *Franciade* (1587) he cites Virgil's example at every turn: with approval, and with fond recollections of reading and memorizing Virgil in his schooldays, "always carrying his book in my hand."[180] How to account for the change?

As a young man, Ronsard was in love with Greek and Greek poetry. As an adult, he did not outgrow Homer, but he himself grew into a different kind of poet. The Pléiade admired Homer's freshness, his "naïve félicité."[181] As a

---

[178] "To the Gentlemen Students of both Universities" (1589), in *ECE*, vol. 1, pp. 308–9. *Laborious* is also a critical term in Du Bellay, who says that some enterprising poet should turn the old stories about King Arthur into a long poem that will be, for the French people, "une admirable *Iliade* & laborieuse *Eneide*" (Du Bellay, *Deffence* 2.5; ed. Chamard, p. 129). But Du Bellay is older than Nashe by a generation and a half; *laborieuse* is a compliment, and a poet who wants to be remembered should expect to sweat, shiver, starve, thirst, and spend his nights in wakefulnesss (*Deffence* 2.3; pp. 105–6).

[179] Ronsard, *Œuvres complètes*, ed. Gustave Cohen, 2 vols. (Paris: Union, 1938), vol. II, p. 1013. The keyword is *curieuse*, from Latin *curiosus* "careful, painstaking, scrupulous." Cf. Tailboys Dymoke, *Caltha Poetarum: or The Bumble Bee* (STC 6151; London: Thomas Creede, 1599), sig. A5^r, where Virgil is described as "the curious Ape of *Homer*."

[180] Ronsard, *Les œuvres de Pierre de Ronsard*, ed. Isidore Silver, 6 vols. (Chicago: University of Chicago Press, 1966–68), vol. IV, p. 418. See Walter Henry Storer, *Virgil and Ronsard* (Paris: Champion, 1923); and François Rigolot, "Homer's Virgilian Authority: Ronsard's Counterfeit Epic Theory," in *Discourses of Authority in Medieval and Renaissance Literature*, ed. Kevin Brownlee and Walter Stephens (Hanover, NH: University Press of New England, 1989), pp. 63–75.

[181] Hepp, "Homère en France au XVIe siècle," 435, 477–94.

group, though, they were moving away from primitivism; by 1587, they had abandoned the native (we would say, medieval) tradition in French poetry without so much as an *au revoir*. For the poet that Ronsard was becoming, Homer was too spontaneous and too unrefined. He was also too long: Ronsard never finished the epic *Franciade* and preferred the shorter genres (of sonnet, ode, and hymn) at which he excelled. His gifts ran to sweetness and satire. A big book, for Ronsard, was not so much a bad book, as a book that would never get written. His domain was eloquence in a brief compass, and for that, Virgil was an obvious model.

Virgil's eloquence was one of the great, undeniable facts of literary criticism in the Renaissance. Speroni liked to say (with some exaggeration) that Virgil had invented nothing, but borrowed both his plot and its treatment (*dispositio*) from Homer. He allowed, though, that the Roman's style, his *elocutio*, is excellent – although it is deformed somewhat by Virgil's stubborn, manneristic brevity.[182] It was a grudging admission, and evasive. But apparently it was necessary: Virgil's eloquence, his skill with words and figures, was an axiom of Renaissance criticism.[183] When all else failed, it was always safe to praise his eloquence.[184] In particular, Virgil would continue to be singled out for verbal sound effects in which the movement of the verse seems to imitate the thing that it describes.[185] But the value of Virgil's eloquence was dependent on the value of rhetoric in general, and when that began to decline, Virgil's reputation was bound to suffer.

---

[182] See Weinberg, *Criticism*, vol. I, pp. 169–71.
[183] Examples have been given; to these might be added two more. According to Giovanni Pietro Capriano, Virgil was superior to Homer, because more learned and because his diction was better (*ibid.*, vol. II, p. 736). According to Antonio Maria de' Conti, Virgil was better than Hesiod for the same reason, by virtue of his "elegance" and the clarity of his diction (*ibid.*, vol. I, p. 269).
[184] For examples, see Kallendorf, *Myth of Venice*, pp. 126–27 (on Ermolao Barbaro); and Di Cesare, *Vida's* Christiad, p. 45 (on Coluccio Salutati).
[185] For examples, see Vida, *De arte poetica*, 3.373–435; Giovanni Pontano, *I dialoghi*, ed. Carmelo Previtera (Florence: Sansoni, 1943), pp. 150–51, 185–88; Tasso, *Discorsi del poema eroico*, Bk. 6 (*Prose*, 713–14); Webbe, *Discourse* (in *ECE*, vol. I, pp. 256–57, 260); and Omer Talon (Meerhoff, *Rhétorique et poétique*, p. 231). For *la doctrina de la sonoridad expresiva o adecuada* which Virgil's sound effects were taken to exemplify, see María José Vega Ramos, *El secreto artificio*: Qualitas sonorum, *maronolatría y tradición pontaniana en la poética del Renacimiento* (Madrid: Consejo superior de investigaciones científicas, Universidad de Extremadura, 1992) and Jean-Charles Monferran, "*Declique un li clictics*: La poésie sonore de Jacques Peletier du Mans," in *À haute voix: Diction et pronociation au XVIe et XVIIe siècles*, ed. Olivia Rosenthal (Paris: Klincksieck, 1998), pp. 35–54. Virgil's reputation for verbal sound effects persisted well into the seventeenth century. In England, see Abraham Cowley's note on the first book of his *Davideis*, in *Poems* (Wing C6683; London: Humphrey Moseley, 1656), sigs. Dddd5ᵛ–Eeeeiʳ. In France, see Pierre Nicole, "Dissertatio de vera pulchritudine & adumbrata" (1659), trans. J. V. Cunningham, in *The Problem of Style*, ed. J. V. Cunningham (Greenwich, CT: Fawcett, 1966), p. 174.

The process began, in England at least, with Bacon's attack on Ciceronian humanism: "for words are but the images of matter; and except they have life of reason and invention, to fall in love with them is all one as to fall in love with a picture."[186] It did not happen all at once, but the taste for rhetoric, the undisguised appetite for eloquence as such, was a casualty, first of the scientific revolution in the late 1600s,[187] and once again, of the Romantic revolution in the late eighteenth century. The result is what C. S. Lewis called an "invisible wall" between us and our ancestors. "Nearly all our older poetry was written and read by men to whom the distinction between poetry and rhetoric, in its modern form, would have been meaningless."[188] The point is not that good writing has joined Astraea and disappeared from the face of the earth. Rather, what has disappeared is the climate of taste in which a poet could prosper solely on the basis of style. Coleridge, at supper, was heard to say that Virgil's "metre and composition" make "*sobs* of harmony"; but "what one deep feeling that goes to the human heart? I see not one."[189] Of course, Coleridge himself was obsessed with prosody, claiming to have spent weeks perfecting the meter of *Christabel*.

In retrospect, it seems that Virgil was cursed with eloquence, as some women are cursed with beauty. It dazzles the eye and makes the mind suspicious. It also excites envy. Today there is a renewed interest in Virgil's style and especially its sources: the linguistic background, the literary context. But Tasso's interest was different, discipleship more than scholarship. He wanted to imitate what he studied, become what he understood. Today there are still those who want to share Virgil's vision, but the ambition to speak with Virgil's voice, to master what Dante called *lo bello stilo*, seems alien now through long disuse.

---

[186] Bacon, *The Advancement of Learning* 1.4.3, in *Francis Bacon*, ed. Brian Vickers (Oxford: Oxford University Press, 1996), p. 139. Cf. *Aen.* 1.464: "animum pictura pascit inani."
[187] See Richard Foster Jones, "Science and English Prose Style, 1650–75," *PMLA* 45 (1930), 977–1009.
[188] Lewis, *Sixteenth Century*, p. 61; see also and more recently Fumaroli, *L'âge de l'éloquence*, pp. 17–28 et passim.
[189] Samuel Taylor Coleridge, *Table Talk*, ed. Carl Woodring, 2 vols. (Princeton: Princeton University Press, 1990), vol. 1, p. 58 n. Cf. Mark Van Doren: "Homer is a world; Virgil, a style." Qtd. in Allen Mandelbaum, trans., *The Aeneid of Virgil* (New York: Bantam, 1971), p. v.

PART III
Interpretation

CHAPTER 5

Virgil's Odyssey

Indeed, the safest road to Hell is the gradual one – the gentle slope, soft underfoot, without sudden turnings, without milestones, without signposts.

Screwtape

PRIORITIZING EPISODES

The previous chapters were about reputation as much as interpretation: what did the *Eclogues* and *Georgics* mean, but also who was their author? What were his virtues? his vices? his methods of working? their results, compared with those of other writers? This chapter and its sequel are, if possible, even more ambitious. The goal of them is to give a survey of the whole *Aeneid*, as it was understood by European readers from about 1300 to 1600.

To accomplish this goal many even of the poem's most luminous episodes will have to be passed over in silence. For these sins of omission no contrition is forthcoming. Mapping every crest and crevice of interpretation would not only be impossible, it would defeat the purpose of a survey, which is to sketch the big picture; to limn large-scale features of the interpretive landscape; to draw connections between seemingly discrete authors; and to locate specialized research in its historical, pan-European context. Whereas an inventory should be exhaustive, a survey must needs be selective. Our task here is not to catalogue details, but to place them in perspective.

A few episodes, such as the night raid of Nisus and Euryalus, are discussed elsewhere in this book. But most episodes – even some controversial ones, such as the transformation of ships into sea nymphs (in Book 9) – will not be discussed at all. For such as these, the place to begin is with the commentaries listed in Appendix B, especially the ones singled out in Chapter 1, on account of their wide distribution. Some things will be missed this way: for example, one will not learn from a commentary that Castelvetro found the whole notion of ships turning into sea nymphs ridiculous, absurd, and implausible.¹ Still, for studying individual episodes, the commentaries are the easiest places to start.

The hard task, the real labor, is to comprehend the tradition about Virgil's *Aeneid* as a whole: not to claim omniscience, but to see continuities, indicate structure. Without this skeleton, the significance of individual episodes will be weakened where it is not distorted. One can work up to this structure through case studies of individual scholars. Thanks to Kallendorf, for example, we know what Landino thought about the *Aeneid* as a whole.² But what did Europe think?

At the highest level of generality, the answer can be summarized in a few words. From ancient times to the present, readers of Virgil have always divided the *Aeneid* into units of six books. The first six, modeled on Homer's *Odyssey*, are about wandering. The last six, based on Homer's *Iliad*, are about war.³ This will be our starting point.

TROY IN THE ODYSSEY

What happens in Virgil's Odyssey? To construct a survey that is really an overview and not just a collage, we must first decide which items should receive the most weight and which should be omitted altogether. Montaigne's favorite was Book 5, the funeral games of Anchises.⁴ But Montaigne was more independent than most readers, then or since. Better indications of popular taste are the episodes that poets and scholars liked to translate. In France, there were three: the fall of Troy (Book 2), the affair with Dido (Book 4), and the descent to the underworld (Book 6).⁵ These, it seems, were Shakespeare's favorites as well: according to T. W. Baldwin, "Only three episodes of the *Aeneid* seem to have made a deep

---

¹ Lodovico Castelvetro, *Poetica d'Aristotele vulgarizzata e sposta*, ed. Werther Romani (Rome: Laterza, 1978–79), vol. I, pp. 245, 274–79; vol. II, pp. 189, 191, 207, 217, 235, 251, 267. See also Servius on *Aen.* 3.46 (Giunta 1544, fol. 237ᵛ).
² Craig Kallendorf, *In Praise of Aeneas: Virgil and Epideictic Rhetoric in the Early Italian Renaissance* (Hanover, NH: University Press of New England, 1989), ch. 6.
³ Servius on *Aen.* 7.1 (Giunta 1544, fol. 362ᵛ); see also Badius, preface to *Aen.* (Giunta 1544, fol. 147ʳ).
⁴ Montaigne, *Essais* 2.10 ("Des livres"), ed. Albert Thibaudet (Paris: Gallimard, 1950), p. 451.
⁵ See Alice Hulubei, "Virgile en France au XVIᵉ siècle: Éditions, traductions, imitations," *Revue du seizième siècle* 18 (1931–32), 1–77, at 53.

impression on Shakspere – the account of the fall of Troy ..., the grief of the forsaken Dido, and the infernal machinery of Vergil's Hades."[6]

Dido is going to be dealt with in the next chapter, in contrast with Lavinia. About Troy I have my own theory, that its fall in Book 2 is an allegory of the Roman Republic; but of this I can find no trace in the old commentaries. Instead, for them, Troy signifies sensuality.

Why? According to Landino, because Troy is where Aeneas' father, Anchises, compounded for two weeks with the goddess Venus. Also, because Troy is associated with Paris, who chose harlotry (Venus again) instead of wealth (Juno) or wisdom (Minerva).[7] This is confusing, slightly, because Venus is also the goddess who rescues Aeneas and takes him to Italy. Ah, says Landino, that was a different Venus. The Venus who coupled with Anchises and who bribed Paris with carnal pleasure was the earthly Venus, *Venus vulgaris*. The one who rescued Aeneas was *Venus caelestis* (what Spenser calls in his fourth hymn "Heavenly Beautie"). By removing her son from the burning city, she directs his soul away from appetite and fastens it on goods of intellect (symbolized for Landino, a Florentine, by Italy).[8]

The notion that Troy equals dominion of the senses was also held by Petrarch, Coluccio Salutati, and Natale Conti.[9] It seems plausible, until we go back and actually read Book 2. There is nothing here about making love, it is all about making war: the wooden horse and the fog of war. We associate this, naturally, with the *Iliad*. But here is an example of where the division between Odyssean and Iliadic halves becomes important. Even though the subject is war, Book 2 of the *Aeneid* is technically part of Virgil's Odyssey, a homecoming narrative rather than a war narrative. In consequence, the episode gets interpreted according to a different set of expectations, which were already well established. From ancient times onward, Homer's *Odyssey* was interpreted allegorically as the soul's journey from flesh to spirit, from the body which imprisons the soul to the stars which are its spiritual home.[10] Thus Plotinus, writing in the third century AD:

---

[6] T. W. Baldwin, *William Shakspere's Small Latine & Lesse Greeke*, 2 vols. (Urbana: University of Illinois Press, 1944), vol. II, p. 420. But see Patricia Parker, "Romance and Empire: Anachronistic Cymbeline," in *Unfolded Tales: Essays on Renaissance Romance*, ed. George M. Logan and Gordon Teskey (Ithaca, NY: Cornell University Press, 1989), pp. 189–207.

[7] Natale Conti, *Mythologia siue explicatio fabularum* (Padua: P. P. Tozzi, 1616), 6.23 (p. 353).

[8] Kallendorf, *Praise of Aeneas*, pp. 139–40.

[9] Kallendorf, *Praise of Aeneas*, pp. 28–29 (Petrarch) and p. 95 (Salutati); for Conti, see n. 7 above.

[10] See Howard Clarke, *Homer's Readers: A Historical Introduction to the* Iliad *and the* Odyssey (Newark: University of Delaware Press, 1981), ch. 2; Robert Lamberton, *Homer the Theologian: Neoplatonist Allegorical Reading and the Growth of the Epic Tradition* (Berkeley and Los Angeles: University of California Press, 1986); Judith Yarnall, *Transformations of Circe: The History of an Enchantress*

Let him who can arise, withdraw unto himself, forego all that is known by the eyes, turn aside forever from the bodily beauty that was once his joy ... "Let us flee then to the beloved Fatherland" [*Iliad* 2.140]. Here is sound counsel. But what is this flight? How are we to "gain the open sea"? For surely Odysseus is a parable for us here when he commends flight from the sorceries of a Circe or a Calypso, being unwilling to linger on for all the pleasure offered to his eyes and all the delight of sense that filled his days. The Fatherland for us is there whence we have come. There is the Father. What is our course? What is to be the manner of flight? Here is no journeying for the feet; feet bring us only from land to land. Nor is it for coach or ship to bear us off. We must close our eyes and invoke a new manner of seeing, a wakefulness that is the birthright of us all, though few put it to use.[11]

Ithaca, the "beloved Fatherland," is man's spiritual nature, which he fulfills and realizes through contemplation.

There is something here which is perverse. But for a long time, the perversion outlived the poem, like a parasite that survives its host. After the estrangement of Rome from Constantinople – the one that resulted in the Great Schism – scholars in the West did not actually read Homer until the tail-end of the Middle Ages. The story of Odysseus was still well known, but Homer's winged words, the hard, vertical light of his objective style – those were lost. What remained were certain images: the giant with one eye, the temptress, the journey home.

The allegorical tradition about Homer is older even than Socrates; and Virgil, in the first century BC, was demonstrably well versed in it,[12] as were his early commentators Servius and Macrobius.[13] Such was their authority and the momentum of tradition that scholars in the Middle Ages and Renaissance continued to apply the old patterns of Homeric allegory, even when the text of Homer was not being studied. Like the voyage of

---

(Urbana: University of Illinois Press, 1994), chs. 3–6; and Andrew Ford, "Performing Interpretation: Early Allegorical Exegesis of Homer," in *Epic Traditions in the Contemporary World: The Poetics of Community*, ed. Margaret H. Beissinger *et al.* (Berkeley and Los Angeles: University of California Press, 1999), pp. 33–53. For the afterlife of this interpretation in the Renaissance, see George de Forest Lord, *Homeric Renaissance: The* Odyssey *of George Chapman* (London: Chatto & Windus, 1956) and Don Cameron Allen, *Mysteriously Meant: The Rediscovery of Pagan Symbolism and Allegorical Interpretation in the Renaissance* (Baltimore: Johns Hopkins University Press, 1970), ch. 4. The tradition gives most of its energy to the first half of the *Odyssey*, especially the temptations. After the hero makes landfall back in Ithaca (Book 13), the allegorists find less to talk about.

[11] Plotinus, *Enneads* 1.6.8, trans. Elmer O'Brien, S. J., *The Essential Plotinus*, 2nd edn. (Indianapolis: Hackett, 1964), pp. 41–42.

[12] Robin R. Schlunk, *The Homeric Scholia and the* Aeneid: *A Study of the Influence of Ancient Homeric Literary Criticism on Vergil* (Ann Arbor: University of Michigan Press, 1974); Michael Murrin, *The Allegorical Epic: Essays in Its Rise and Decline* (Chicago: University of Chicago Press, 1980), ch. 1; Philip R. Hardie, *Virgil's* Aeneid: Cosmos *and* Imperium (Oxford: Clarendon Press, 1986).

[13] Julian Ward Jones, Jr., "Allegorical Interpretation in Servius," *Classical Journal* 56 (1961), 217–26; and Murrin, *Allegorical Epic*, p. 32.

Odysseus from Troy to Ithaca, Aeneas' journey from Troy to Italy was understood as a spiritual pilgrimage, by means of contemplation.

This did not change, even in the late fourteenth century, when it became possible again to read Homer's text. Again, Landino is an example. Like many of the early humanists, Landino had only a rudimentary knowledge of Greek. He knew, though, that Virgil was an imitator of Homer, and that Dante was an imitator of Virgil. Combining, then, what he knew of Dante and Virgil, Landino inferred what Homer's allegory "must" have been: the liberation of soul from body by way of philosophy.[14] He was not *very* far from being right, either: the allegory of the spiritual voyage did originate in commentaries on Homer (if not in Homer himself) and from there it was transmitted to Virgil and his commentators. Dante, in turn, did know Virgil, did interpret him allegorically,[15] and did know Virgil's allegorizing commentators.[16] For Landino, this last link in the chain was the most important: reading backwards through Dante, Landino made Homer and Virgil seem almost Christian.[17] Landino was a syncretist, and syncretism tends to homogenize. But for someone whose direct knowledge of Homer was limited, Landino arrived at a reading of him that was similar to the one an Athenian schoolboy would have received, living in the fifth or sixth century BC. It was not Homer, to be sure, but it was the ancient idea of Homer.

THE WEIGHT OF THE UNDERWORLD

Between Homer's *Odyssey* and Virgil's there was at least one major difference. When ancient scholars allegorized the *Odyssey*, they focused on the obstacles and temptations that impede the soul on its return journey: Circe, Calypso, the sirens. These signify the appetites: not only the desire for sex, but the instinct for generation. Dido, too, can be allegorized as appetite, but refusing her is not the point of Aeneas' journey. In her life, he is the climax, but in his life, she is an episode. His climax, or at least the climax of his

---

[14] Kallendorf, *Praise of Aeneas*, ch. 6.
[15] Dante, *Convivio* 4.26, in *Opere minori*, ed. Domenico De Robertis *et al.*, 2 vols. in 3 pts. (Milan: Ricciardi, 1979).
[16] See Edward Kennard Rand, "Dante and Servius," *Dante Studies* 33 (1916), 1–11; Erich von Richthofen, "Traces of Servius in Dante," *Dante Studies* 92 (1974), 117–28; and Georg Rabuse, "Macrobio," in *Enciclopedia dantesca*, ed. Umberto Bosco, 6 vols. (Rome: Istituto della enciclopedia italiana, 1970–78), vol. III, pp. 757–59. In addition to the ancient commentators, Dante was probably aware of the twelfth-century commentary associated with Bernardus Silvestris; see David Thompson, *Dante's Epic Journeys* (Baltimore: Johns Hopkins University Press, 1974), chs. 2 and 9.
[17] See Kallendorf, "Philology, the Reader, and the *Nachleben* of Classical Texts," *Modern Philology* 92 (1994), 137–56.

Odyssey, is the *katabasis* in Book 6, the *descensus ad inferos*. This is where the commentators would spend all their ingenuity, lavish all their learning.

Homer invents the *katabasis* and locates it at the approximate midpoint of his poem (Book 11 in the division established by Aristarchus). But he does not make it the climax – that will come later, when Odysseus has actually arrived in Ithaca and takes up the bow to exact his revenge. Virgil, in contrast, has arranged matters such that the hero's arrival – the conclusion of his Odyssey – will coincide with his *katabasis*. When Aeneas makes his final landfall, it is at Cumae, where he seeks passage underground.

This arrangement gives the underworld more weight and, for interpreters, imposes a new challenge. Servius, at the beginning of his commentary on Book 6, claims that "Virgil is everywhere full of knowledge (*scientia*), especially in this book."[18] Medieval commentators accepted this as a premise: the bulk of what they wrote was either borrowed or paraphrased from Servius, but when they did say something original, most of it was about the underworld.[19] Landino, writing in the second half of the fifteenth century, is the direct heir of this tradition. When, in his *Camaldulensian Dialogues* (c. 1473), he unfolds the allegory of the *Aeneid*, fully half of his explanation is devoted to the underworld.

There was a price for this: as a rule, commentaries that focused on Book 6 stopped after Book 6; or if they did go on, they stopped being interesting. After Landino, commentators became more evenhanded. So did poets, who began to imitate with more frequency episodes from Virgil's *Iliad*; I shall say more about this in the next chapter. Even so, the underworld was still primary. Spenser refers, in his collected writings, several times to the death of Turnus. But these are allusions. Longer and more numerous in *The Faerie Queene* are the many episodes which have been constructed as underworld journeys: in Book 1, the Forest of Error (Canto i), Archimago's errand to Morpheus (i), the House of Pride (v), Duessa's errand to Night (v), Orgoglio's dungeon (viii) and the Cave of Despair (ix); in Book 2, Mammon's Cave (vii) and the Bower of Bliss (xii); in Book 3, Merlin's Cave (iii), the Garden of Adonis (vi), and perhaps Busirane's mansion (xi, xii); in Book 4, the Delve of Ate (i) and perhaps Florimell's dungeon (4); in Book 5, Malengin's Cave (ix); and in Book 6, the pirate den from which Calidore rescues

---

[18] Servius on *Aen.* 6.1 (Giunta 1544, fol. 322ᵛ).
[19] See my "Lavinia and Beatrice: The Second Half of the *Aeneid* in the Middle Ages," *Dante Studies* 119 (2001), 103–24, at 106–9.

Pastorella (xi).[20] The underworld is so pervasive in *The Faerie Queene*, appears in so many guises and so many cantos that, according to one school of thought, Fairyland *is* the underworld, an Elysium of sorts in which British heroes, dead and unborn, relive or rehearse their deeds in life.[21]

Spenser, as we shall see, was not unique. Quantitatively, his epic has more underworld episodes than other poets', which makes him useful as a fund of examples. But what these episodes illustrate is a tradition of interpretation that was both ancient (everything in it comes from or through Servius) and international (readers in England said the same things as readers in France or Italy).

Why is the underworld so ubiquitous, not just in *The Faerie Queene*, but in epic as a genre? We sometimes hear that Aeneas is changed by the journey: becoming, for example, more resolved. But to me, when he comes out, he seems just as dogged, dutiful, and grim as when he went in. Is *katabasis*, the journey down, compelling to readers because it combines something universal (death) with something unusual (resurrection)? Does the hero, going down, acknowledge his own mortality? Or, coming back up, assert the immortality of the soul? Do the laws of life and narrative require, before going up, a going down? As Eliot says, "the way forward is the way back." Or Conrad: "The way is to the destructive element submit yourself." But there is no reason to choose only one reason. By 1600, when our coverage ends, commentary on Homer, Virgil, and (surprisingly) Lucan had made the underworld one of the richest, most pregnant symbols that poets and their critics have ever devised between them.

To illustrate, let us consider briefly Coluccio Salutati's unfinished masterpiece, *De laboribus Herculis* (1406). For Salutati, the most interesting labor is the last one, stealing Cerberus from Hades. Salutati devotes a whole book to this subject, taking up such topics as whether hell exists, where it is located, and why various epic heroes go there. Yes, hell exists, although most of the pagan philosophers did not believe in it. Why then did the pagan poets write about hell? Salutati suggests they were inspired by God to anticipate certain

---

[20] See Bernard Francis Beranek, "Forgotten Excellence: The Sins of the Flesh and the *Sententiae* of the Bower of Bliss," diss., Duquesne University (1979), ch. 3; Thomas E. Maresca, *Three English Epics: Studies in Chaucer, Spenser, and Milton* (Lincoln: University of Nebraska Press, 1980), ch. 1; and Matthew Fike, *Spenser's Underworld in the 1590 Faerie Queene* (Lewiston, NY: Mellen, 2003).

[21] Isabel E. Rathborne, *The Meaning of Spenser's Fairyland* (New York: Columbia University Press, 1937), ch. 2, esp. pp. 149–54. Angus Fletcher and Wayne Erickson give this hypothesis qualified endorsement in, respectively, *The Prophetic Moment: An Essay on Spenser* (Chicago: University of Chicago Press, 1971), pp. 86–88, 196 and *Mapping* The Faerie Queene: *Quest Structures and the World of the Poem* (New York: Garland, 1996), pp. 60–61, 72–74, 93–95.

elements of Christian dogma. Whether hell is really like the poets' description of it, with nine rivers and a three-headed dog, he does not know. Salutati's task is to relate what these things signify, "or, to speak more properly, what they might signify."[22] Where is hell? "According to the ancients, hell is the human body; or, as some Platonists believed, the sphere of the four elements; or the all-encompassing sphere of three elements, arranged in three bodies (or seven spheres plus the region of corruptible things where nature reigns over the four elements); or the region under the sea, as Theodontius believed; or the West, as Lactantius thought; or the hollows of the earth; or, as Gregory defined hell, the gloomy air and the depths of the earth."[23] Why do heroes go there? In the case of Hercules, it is fitting that the end of his labors should correspond with the end of human life. But it really depends on the hero: Orpheus, when he goes to the underworld, represents the Epicurean view that pleasure is the goal of life; Theseus and Perithous, the mob's view that we ought to seek what is useful and lucrative; Aeneas and Hercules, the Stoic view that we ought to seek virtue.[24] But even in Virgil, the descent can mean more than one thing. "For that is the way of poets, when they create some fiction, to find pleasure in more than one meaning (*pluralitate sensuum delectari*)."[25]

Salutati's treatise on the labors of Hercules, which he died before finishing, is one of the great monuments of Renaissance mythography. Its influence was limited, though, because it remained in manuscript until 1951; it is doubtful whether most poets, even in Italy, knew of its existence. But Salutati was not unique. We think of him as a humanist, but much of his learning was in fact derived from medieval sources. His Latin was new and as one of Florence's leading citizens – he was chancellor from 1375 until his death – he enjoyed access to some of the city's best libraries. But his curiosity about the underworld, and his pluralistic approach to interpreting it, were typical of a long tradition, which he did not invent, exhaust, or even perpetuate. His book is a sounding, his learning a sample.

For the rest of this chapter, we are going to follow Salutati's example and examine the various meanings that were assigned to the underworld. To someone who was ignorant of the sources, such minute scrutiny might seem disproportionate, especially in a survey. But we are following the grain of our materials. As was said already, the most popular episodes – for imitators

---

[22] Coluccio Salutati, *De laboribus Herculis*, ed. B. L. Ullman, 2 vols. (Zurich: Thesaurus Mundi, 1951), vol. II, pp. 457–62.
[23] Salutati, *De laboribus Herculis*, vol. II, p. 470.   [24] Salutati, *De laboribus Herculis*, vol. II, pp. 487–89.
[25] Salutati, *De laboribus Herculis*, vol. II, p. 485.

and translators – were the fall of Troy, the encounter with Dido, and the underworld. Troy, in Book 2, has been dealt with already; and Dido, in Book 4, will receive her due in the next chapter. As an influence on later poetry, Dido did not inspire more episodes than the underworld; and, as a symbol, she suggested fewer shades of meaning. With the possible exception of *Arma virumque cano*, there was nothing else in the whole *Aeneid* that generated more commentary than *katabasis*. What dreams are to the unconscious, the underworld is to Virgil's Odyssey: a royal road, a heart of darkness, where meanings converge and problems ramify. At least, that is how it was treated by scholars and commentators in the Renaissance. For them, the underworld was the climax of the first six books, but it was also an epitome of their meaning: the way down was also the way inside. When we are done mapping its pathways, we shall look back and see that the circle we have traveled is very wide indeed. We shall also be in a position to ask a general question about how epics were written: specifically, what did a classically trained poet think he was imitating? Was it an author? a text? or an idea?

THE GATES OF SLEEP

There were many views of the underworld. Many of them were not exclusive and could be held simultaneously (as they were, in fact, held by Servius and Salutati). What most of them had in common was skepticism. Consider, for example, a list of defects in the *Divine Comedy*, which was compiled in 1572 by someone named Ridolfo or Anselmo Castravilla. The first item is lack of plausibility: "Nobody will believe that a living man, in the flesh, could make a voyage through the three regions of the other world. The verisimilitude of our times cannot admit such an action."[26] Apparently Castravilla has never heard of "that willing suspension of disbelief for the moment, which constitutes poetic faith." This is from someone who probably believes in witchcraft, demons, and miracles. But that is not *poetic* faith. Also, Dante is cheating. Nowhere does he even hint that maybe the voyage did not really take place. "The fiction of the *Divine Comedy* is that it is not fiction."[27] But in the classical tradition that Dante invokes – by making Virgil his guide – the voyage is always a fiction and the poet always gives hints.

---

[26] Bernard Weinberg, *A History of Literary Criticism in the Italian Renaissance*, 2 vols. (Chicago: University of Chicago Press, 1961), vol. II, p. 833.
[27] C. S. Singleton, *Dante's* Commedia: *Elements of Structure* (Cambridge, MA: Harvard University Press, 1954), p. 62.

The reason, as Castravilla suggests, is that no one believes in a literal *katabasis*. And this not only in "our times," as he says, but in ancient times. Cicero, for example, says that the torments which Homer describes in the *Odyssey* for mythical sinners like Tantalus have no objective reality and are merely a bedtime story, the "hobgoblins (*portenta*) of poets and painters."[28]

The response to Virgil's underworld was more serious, but still skeptical, and it always came up in the same place: in commentaries on the Gates of Sleep. According to Virgil,

> Sunt geminæ somni portæ, quarum altera fertur
> Cornea: qua veris facilis datur exitus vmbris:
> Altera candenti perfecta nitens elephanto:
> Sed falsa ad cœlum mittunt insomnia manes.
> His vbi tum natum Anchises unaque Sibyllam
> Prosequitur dictis, portaque emittit eburna.[29]

> [There are twin gates of Sleep, of which one is said
> to be of horn, through which an easy exit is given to true shades.
> The other, shining gate is finished with gleaming ivory:
> thus do the *manes* send false dreams up to the sky.
> There now with these words, Anchises, together with the Sibyl,
> escorts his son and sends him out through the ivory gate.]

In 1559, Marc-Antoine Muret (1526–85), the French humanist who was nicknamed "Orator of the Popes," published an essay on the gates, using Cicero as a gloss. Like Cicero, Muret is skeptical. Not of eternal punishment: "that wicked men are punished in hell after death there is hardly any doubt." What is doubtful, rather, is the form of punishment: boulders and sieves and three-headed dogs. These are things, says Muret, that "the more judicious sort (*cordatiores*) have always taken either for dreams or old wives' tales (*anilium fabularum*)." And that is the meaning of the gates of sleep: it is Virgil's way of confirming for wise readers (*sagacibus lectoribus*) that their doubts are justified.[30]

Why does Aeneas leave the underworld through the gate of false dreams, instead of true? Was it, as some critics argue today, Virgil's way of hinting that the Roman empire is really a bad idea, a misleading and destructive illusion? Servius, at first glance, seems to endorse this view. "For in painting," he observes,

---

[28] Cicero, *Tusculanæ disputationes* 1.6.11 (trans. Loeb); see also *De natura deorum* 2.2.5.
[29] *Aen.* 6.893–98 (Giunta 1544, fol. 361ʳ).
[30] Marcus Antonius Muretus, *Variæ lectiones* 2.7, cited by Pontanus for *Aen.* 6.893, in *Symbolarum libri XVIJ Virgilij* (Augsburg: J. Prætorius, 1599), col. 1547.

we recognize sleep by its horn. And those who have written about dreams say that those dreams come true which are possible, given our fortunes and character. These dreams are associated with the horn [of sleep], and therefore the truthful gate is described as "horn." But those dreams which are beyond our fortunes, which have too much art (*ornatum*) and empty boasting, those dreams they say are false: wherefore the ivory gate, because it seems too artful (*ornatior*), is described as "false."[31]

This sounds like it is getting ready to say something negative about the imperial mission. But that something never comes. Servius holds the door open for criticism, but doesn't actually walk through. Nor was the hint amplified, or even taken up, by any of the major commentators after Servius. The same thing, as we saw in Chapter 2, happened in the *Eclogues*. Instead, what interested commentators after Servius was a question about common sense. Did Virgil really believe that a living man could go to Hades and come back?

Of course not. According to Servius, that is the primary reason why Aeneas goes out of hell through the gate of false dreams:

Poetically, the meaning is wide open (*aperta*): now Virgil wants it to be understood that everything he wrote is fictional (*falsa*). For in scientific terms, the horn gate means the eyes, which are colored like horn and hardy (hardier than the rest of the body in that they do not feel cold). So also says Cicero in his book *On the Origin of the Gods*. But the ivory gate means the teeth. And therefore this is how we interpret it: what we say can be made up (*falsa*), but what we see is true without a doubt. That is why Aeneas is sent out through the ivory gate.[32]

It is the same logic that we saw in Cicero and Muret: everyone knows that Cerberus and the rest are an old wives' tale, which intellectuals (like Virgil) do not actually believe in. Therefore, when Anchises sends Aeneas through the ivory gate, it is Virgil's way of winking at the reader: "This did not really happen. I know, you know, and I want you to know that I know." As for *falsa insomnia*, these are not misleading ideas, but fictions. Thus, for Landino, going out through the gate of false dreams "shows what [Virgil] wrote to have been all feigned (*omnia ficta*)."[33] According to Badius Ascensius, it "shows that all these things were dreams: not actual events, something that happened (*rem ... gestam*), but a poetical invention."[34]

What, exactly, is "a poetical invention" (*rem ... poetice excogitatam*)? Paulo Manuzio, one of the most popular Renaissance commentators and

---

[31] Servius on *Aen.* 6.893 (Giunta 1544, fol. 361ʳ).   [32] Servius on *Aen.* 6.893 (Giunta 1544, fol. 361ʳ).
[33] Landino on *Aen.* 6.898, in *Publii Virgilii Maronis ... opera cum commentariis* (Venice: Philippus Pincius Mantuanus, 1499), fol. ccxliiiiʳ.
[34] Badius on *Aen.* 6.893 (Giunta 1544, fol. 361ʳ).

almost the only one who was actually published in England, suggests that we ought to compare the gate of false dreams with the tree of empty dreams (*somnia ... Vana*) which stands at the entrance to hell.[35] The dreams that depend from the branches of that tree are all freaks (*monstra*): hybrid creatures like the centaur and scylla, a giant with a hundred hands, a hydra, a chimera, gorgons, and harpies. None of these exists, except in poetry. By implication, then, the things that Virgil describes within Hades do not exist either: the punishments, the people – all are fiction. Thus reasons Servius: "If the entrance and the exit are both feigned (*simulata*) and fictional (*falsa*), it shows all things to have been feigned (*simulata*)."[36]

If there is no such thing as a chimera, what does Aeneas see? The easiest, most popular, and probably correct interpretation is that the whole underworld experience takes place in a dream.[37] The authority for this was Macrobius, who explains that in dreams there are various degrees of lucidity. The ivory gate, through which Aeneas goes, indicates a dream in which the truth is veiled: "for whereas horn is translucent, ivory is dense and opaque."[38] This was a standard reading in the Middle Ages,[39] and it continued to hold sway in the Renaissance. Rabelais gives a close paraphrase of it in the *Tiers livre* (1546),[40] and Landino cites it with approval: "Servius is satisfying, but what Macrobius thinks is even better (*excellentissima*)."[41] There is no contradiction: for Servius, the main point is that the episode is fiction; for Macrobius, that it happens in a dream. The dream, while unreliable, is not deceitful either; rather, like one of Plato's myths, it is a

---

[35] Paulo Manuzio on *Aen*. 6.282, in *Opera P. Virgilii Maronis. Pauli Manutii annotationes brevissimae in margine adscriptae* (STC 24789; London: Henry Middleton, 1580), p. 265. Manuzio, as usual, is excerpting Servius.

[36] Servius on *Aen*. 6.282 (Giunta 1544, fol. 334ʳ).

[37] Cf. Latinus' dream at the beginning of *Aen*. 7. The king, we are told, goes to sleep in order to take counsel with gods "and to address Acheron in deep Avernus" (90–91). Avernus is the cave where Aeneas finds hell and Acheron is one of its rivers, so Latinus is now "in" hell, but this time we are told how he got there: in a dream. Both times, the dream trance is probably induced by hallucinogenic fumes: the forest where Latinus goes to sleep "breathes in the darkness a dire and pestilential vapor" (7.84) and the cave where Aeneas begins his journey reeks with vapors so foul that even birds avoid the surrounding airspace (6.239–42).

[38] Macrobius, *In somnium Scipionis* 1.3.17–20, in [*Opera*] (Venice: s.n., 1492), sig. aiiiⁱⁱⁱᵛ–ivʳ. See also Vives, preface to Cicero's *Somnium Scipionis*, in *Somnium et vigilia in Somnium Scipionis* (*Commentary on the Dream of Scipio*), ed. and trans. Edward V. George (Greenwood, SC: Attic, 1989), pp. 32–35.

[39] See John of Salisbury, *Policraticus* 2.14.428d, in *Ioannis Saresberiensis episcopi Carnothensis policratici sive De nugis curialium et vestigiis philosophorum libri VIII*, ed. Clemens C. I. Webb, 2 vols. (Oxford: Clarendon Press, 1909).

[40] Rabelais, *Gargantua* 3.13, in *Œuvres complètes*, ed. Jacques Boulenger, rev. Lucien Scheler (Paris: Gallimard, 1955), pp. 375–76.

[41] Landino on *Aen*. 6.898 (1499 edn., fol. ccxliiiiʳ).

story "not unlike the truth," a verity conveyed through fiction. As John Skelton says at the end of his dream vision *The Bowge of Court* (c. 1498),

> I wolde therwith no man were myscontente,
> Besechynge you that shall it see or rede,
> In every poynte to be indyfferente,
> Syth all in substaunce of slumbrynge doth procede.
> I wyll not saye it is mater in dede,
> But yet oftyme such dremes be founde trewe;
> Now constrewe ye what is the resydewe.

Skelton emphasizes the truthfulness of dreams, but of course dreams can deceive as well. In Spenser's epic, the Bower of Bliss has a gate made of ivory (*FQ* 2.12.44). Spenser's Bower is a sex park: does this mean that lechery is like death (or leads to hell)? Probably.[42] Also that sex is a kind of reverie: "Before, a joy proposed; behind, a dream."

DESCENT BY MURDER

By now we can see that, when Castravilla complains about Dante's ridiculous journey into the afterlife, he is not just being a spoil-sport. The standard method for going to hell was in a dream, but to this urbane and reasonable convention Dante makes no concessions. Within the *Divine Comedy*, there are faintings and dreams, but the *Comedy* itself is not a dream.

And yet such was the force of skepticism and of the epic tradition that even Dante's own children knew that a physical journey was impossible. Dante had one daughter and three sons. The daughter entered a convent and took the name of Beatrice. The sons, two of them, wrote commentaries on their father's masterpiece. Iacopo (d. 1348) was a wastrel and his commentary is worthless. But Pietro's (d. 1364) commentary, which he revised twice, is learned and intelligent. It knows what Dad was really like, that in the year 1300 he did not go to hell during Holy Week, but was still in Florence studying Virgil. Like his father, Pietro has also studied the commentaries on Virgil. The strangest and most original of these commentaries was attributed to the Spanish cosmographer Bernardus Silvestris (fl. 1136).[43] Like every other commentary, it assumes that a literal *descensus ad inferos* is

---

[42] See Beranek, "Forgotten Excellence"; Fike, *Spenser's Underworld*, ch. 4.
[43] The commentary's authorship is disputed; I retain the name "Silvestris," because that is how it was known. See Julian Ward Jones, Jr., "The So-Called Silvestris Commentary on the *Aeneid* and Two Other Interpretations," *Speculum* 64 (1989), 835–48.

impossible for someone still alive. Ergo, descent must mean something else. There are four possibilities:

1. *Descensus naturae*: the confinement or entombment of the soul in a material body.
2. *Descensus virtutis*: the wise man's contemplation of matter's frailty.
3. *Descensus vitii*: the enslavement of the mind to temporal and sensual things.
4. *Descensus artificii*: necromancy, pursued "by means of a certain abominable sacrifice."[44]

Pietro, in his preface to the *Commedia*, posits the same four types, and in the same order.[45] Dante, he claims, descended into hell by means of the "virtuous descent," through philosophy. But the hero of the *Aeneid* was not so scrupulous: according to Pietro (who is repeating what he finds in Silvestris), Aeneas descended "artificially," conversing with his father's ghost by means of necromancy.

The particulars of this ritual are hinted at in Servius. Before Aeneas goes into the cave, the Sibyl tells him to bury Misenus, his trumpeter (*Aen.* 6.149–235). Aeneas complies and, in the process, finds the golden bough which will be his passport into the underworld. The sequence sounds innocent, but Servius thinks the Sibyl was being coy. When she mentions the corpse, she does so casually. "And so she ought," writes Servius. But the burial of Misenus

> is also an advantage (*opportunitas*) for going down to the underworld, i.e., for performing the rites of Proserpina. Now of these rites there are said to have been two kinds: the one, of necromancy, which Lucan describes, and the other of sciomancy, which one reads about in Homer (whom Virgil imitated). According to Lucan, blood is necessary in necromancy to raise the corpse, because [the witch] *begins by filling its breast with hot blood* [*Pharsalia* 6.667]. But in sciomancy, because it is only the summoning of a shade, only a burial is necessary – which is why Misenus washes up dead on the tide.[46]

Already this is bizarre. What was lurid in Servius, though, becomes positively sinister in later tradition.

The key, which Servius mentions, was Lucan's *Pharsalia*. From his epic, Lucan banishes all of Virgil's gods, but he cannot dispense quite with

---

[44] Preface to *Aen.* 6, in *Commentum quod dicitur Bernardi Silvestris super sex libros Eneidos Virgilii*, ed. Julian Ward Jones and Elizabeth Frances Jones (Lincoln: University of Nebraska Press, 1977), p. 30. See also Jane Chance Nitzsche, *The Genius Figure in Antiquity and the Middle Ages* (New York: Columbia University Press, 1975), pp. 42–64.

[45] Pietro Alighieri, *Il Commentarium di Pietro Alighieri*, ed. Roberto della Vedova and Maria Teresa Silvotti (Florence: Olschki, 1978), pp. 11–17.

[46] Servius on *Aen.* 6.149 (Giunta 1544, fol. 328ᵛ).

Virgil's underworld. The difference is that, in Lucan's version, no one actually goes to the underworld. Instead, the underworld comes to us, by means of a witch and a talking corpse. As in Virgil, there is still an element of the supernatural, but subdued now and subject to human agency. Servius approves, though perhaps Lucan goes rather too far with all of the blood and guts. Fortunately, there is sciomancy, which does not require an actual corpse. Like necromancy, it is more believable than actually going to Hades. But it is less messy than necromancy, and also more Homeric. Therefore Aeneas must have performed sciomancy.

For Servius, Lucan is a foil: more sensational, less civilized than Virgil. But he is also more truthful. Indeed, from classical times onward, the standard complaint about Lucan was that he is no poet, because he writes history instead of fiction.[47] A possible corollary is that Lucan and Virgil are describing the same kinds of events, except that Lucan does so without the veil of fiction. Servius does not explore this, but in Renaissance scholarship the corollary is explicit. Thus, in Landino's commentary, the "artificial descent" means "calling out spirits with certain rites and with necromancy, as appears more openly (*latius patet*) in Lucan."[48] There is no mention here of Homer. Landino cites Lucan instead, because he has actually read Lucan and because Lucan, as a historian rather than a poet, tells the unvarnished truth, openly. Salutati says the same thing and gives the same example: "Properly speaking, it seems to me, [the descent by magic] is not a descent but a wicked calling up from the underworld. But because wizards 'pierce hell with speech' (as Lucan said) and are taken to hell in the mind, not unfittingly did the poet assert that the wizard 'descended.' For wizards descend into hell, not with speech only, but mental perception."[49]

In the idiom of epic tradition, *descensus* does not mean "going down," but "dreaming" or even "demon-mongering." Dreaming is the preferred explanation, but if Aeneas did summon demons, how did he perform the ritual? Badius Ascensius records but does not necessarily endorse the view of some scholars, that necromancy "required a fresh corpse, and that is why the death of Misenus follows."[50] What is he referring to? In the text of Virgil, Aeneas buries the remains of his shipmate, who has died at sea and washed up on shore. But in medieval tradition, Aeneas murders Misenus in order to use his corpse for necromancy. This tradition begins, apparently, with Bernardus Silvestris, who says that whatever *descensus* means allegorically,

---

[47] E.g., Servius on *Aen.* 1.382 (Giunta 1544, fol. 179ʳ).
[48] Landino on *Aen.* 6.126 (1499 edn., fol. ccxxᵛ).   [49] Salutati, *De laboribus Herculis*, vol. II, p. 485.
[50] Badius on *Aen.* 6.126 (Giunta 1544, fol. 329ʳ).

the literal meaning is magic. Not that Aeneas actually goes to the underworld, or even converses with dead people. Rather, he consults with demons and the demons require a human sacrifice. So he kills Misenus.⁵¹

As interpretation, this was outrageous. But as gossip, it was too juicy not to repeat. Thus, in a late medieval commentary edited by Julian Ward Jones, we are told that, when the Sibyl orders Aeneas to bury Misenus, what she really means for him to undertake is the "descent by necromancy," and this "cannot be accomplished except by sacrificing human blood – and blood of the better sort, at that. But in reality, Aeneas slew Misenus in order to converse with demons. Virgil, however, did not dare to say it as plainly as this, on account of Augustus." On account of Augustus! Necromancy also explains the golden bough. Allegorically, it signifies "true wisdom." But in order to obtain the bough, Aeneas must first "bury" Misenus. Ergo, the golden bough is how Aeneas proves to the queen of hell that he has performed a human sacrifice. Likewise, when the Sibyl tells Aeneas to hurry up, it is because of human sacrifice: apparently, the demons have established a fee schedule in which one human sacrifice purchases one day of conversation. "If you wish to have more, you will need to renew the sacrifice."⁵²

How widely held was this interpretation? This last commentary is only preserved in two manuscripts. The Silvestris commentary circulated more broadly, and was still being copied out by hand *c.* 1480. It was late, though, in making the jump to print: the first extracts were not published until 1836 and there was no edition of the complete text until 1924.⁵³ It had some influence in the fifteenth century, but after that its influence was almost entirely indirect. Landino, we know, studied Silvestris intensively and reproduced his discussion of the various *descensus* types in two different languages and three separate publications: his *Camaldulensian Dialogues* (*c.* 1473), his Dante commentary (1481), and his Virgil commentary (1487).⁵⁴

---

⁵¹ Preface to *Aen.* 6, in *Commentum quod dicitur Bernardi Silvestris*, p. 30.
⁵² *An* Aeneid *Commentary of Mixed Type: The Glosses in MSS Harley 4946 and Ambrosius GIII inf., a Critical Edition*, ed. Julian Ward Jones (Toronto: Pontifical Institute of Mediæval Studies, 1996), pp. 129, 126, and 171.
⁵³ For the text's history, see Giorgio Padoan, "Tradizione e fortuna del commento all'"Eneide" di Bernardo Silvestre," in Padoan, *Il pio Enea, l'empio Ulisse: Tradizione classica e intendimento medievale in Dante* (Ravenna: Longo, 1977), pp. 207–22; and the Jones edition, pp. xiv–xx.
⁵⁴ Landino, *Disputationes Camaldulenses*, Bk. 4, ed. Peter Lohe (Florence: Sansoni, 1980), pp. 212–18; Landino's preface to *Inf.* 3 in *Dante con l'espositioni di Christoforo Landino, et d'Alessandro Vellutello* (Venice: Giovambatista Marchio Sessa & Fratelli, 1578), fol. 18ʳ; Landino's commentary on *Aen.* 6.126 (1499 edn., fol. ccxxᵛ). On Landino's knowledge of Silvestris, see Lohe's edition of the *Disputationes*, index, s.n. "Bernardus Silvestris" and Thomas H. Stahel, "Cristoforo Landino's Allegorization of the *Aeneid*: Books III and IV of the *Camaldolese Disputations*," diss., Johns Hopkins University (1968), pp. 9–12. Another Florentine, Coluccio Salutati, also used Silvestris; see Ullman's edn. of *De laboribus*

Unlike Silvestris, Landino does not actually affirm that Aeneas made use of necromancy; he prefers, rather, to think that Aeneas was like Dante and descended via contemplation. Nor does Landino mention human sacrifice. Still one does find the occasional mention. When Aeneas says "Learn virtue from me" (*Aen.* 12.435), Petrarch sneers back: What virtue is that, pray tell? The virtue of betraying your fatherland, which Virgil with his eloquence glosses over? Or the virtue of sacrificing to demons, slaughtering your friends and using their blood?[55] This is Petrarch in his quasi-monastic phase. Melanchthon, though, was also familiar with this tradition and records in his commentary that "some people (*nonnulli*) think Misenus was slain by Aeneas, because necromancy cannot be performed without a corpse."[56]

There were other, more benign readings of Misenus' burial in circulation. For example, Nascimbaenus Nascimbaenius of Ferrara (fl. 1570) praises Aeneas for having compassion on Misenus by giving him sepulture.[57] Salutati knows about the different kinds of *descensus*, and believes that Aeneas made the "moral and virtuous" (*honestus et virtuosus*) kind, through contemplation. But this does not rule out a descent by necromancy! For that, fresh blood *would* be necessary, and the death of Misenus *would* be convenient. But Salutati prefers to dwell on the allegorical meaning of Misenus. We know he was a companion of Hector (a fighter) and that he died in competition. Therefore he signifies irascibility. Why does he die? Literally, because he is competing with a god. Allegorically, because Aeneas is leaving behind the irascible appetite that Misenus represents. "In preparation for contemplation . . . there is the death of what can die (*mors est ipsa mortalium*)."[58] Landino also interprets Misenus allegorically, but as the desire for praise (because Misenus was a trumpeter); ergo the death of Misenus means the death of worldly ambition.[59]

What the commentators agreed on is that no one goes to the underworld alive: either the journey is a euphemism for necromancy, or it occurs in a dream. Both explanations were current through the end of our period. In Jacobean England, the same Sir John Harington (1539/40–1613) who,

---

Herculis, index auctorum, s.n. "Bernardus Silvestris." Salutati never refers to Silvestris by name, calling him "Maro's allegorizer," and when he lists the four kinds of *descensus* he attributes them to someone else (vol. II, pp. 483–86). This suggests that he used excerpts of Silvestris, not the text itself.

[55] See Kallendorf, "Historicizing the 'Harvard School': Pessimistic Readings of the *Aeneid* in Italian Renaissance Scholarship," *Harvard Studies in Classical Philology* 99 (1999), 391–403, at 394–95.

[56] Melanchthon on *Aen.* 6.149, in *P. Vergilii Maronis poemata quae extant omnia* (Zurich: Christoph Froschauer, 1561).

[57] Cited in Pontanus's commentary on *Aen.* 6.149.

[58] Salutati, *De laboribus Herculis*, vol. II, pp. 484–85, 577–81.

[59] Landino, *Disputationes Camaldulenses*, Bk. 4 (ed. Lohe, pp. 226–29).

during Elizabeth's reign, translated *Orlando furioso* and invented a flush toilet, also composed in Gatehouse prison a commentary on *Aeneid* 6, which he dedicated to King James for the use of his nine-year-old heir. Like every other commentator I have read, Harington is skeptical about a literal descent: the journey is either a dream (induced by gluttony) or a "trawnce" into which the Sibyl falls when she is visited by a "speryt or dyvell."[60] This is what Servius would call sciomancy, and Harington writes about it at some length. Partly this is because his would-be patron, King James, has written a treatise on demonology, from which Harington is eager to quote.[61] But he is also concerned about the little prince, "least the example of Eneas vsing the helpe of Sibilla to see his fathers ghost, though yt seem to proceed of pyety should make any excuse for such negromancy or witchcraft."[62]

Harington's understanding of what happens in sciomancy is based on 1 Samuel 28:6–25, in which King Saul commands a witch in the town of Endor to summon the ghost of Samuel and make him prophesy. Samuel predicts that Saul and his sons will all die in battle the next day, and so it comes to pass. But was it Samuel's ghost who spake or, as Harington speculates, "some speryt in his lykeness"? According to the orthodox view, witches do exist and they do converse with spirits, but the spirits who come are demons in disguise.[63] This is to make witchcraft enticing; otherwise, Harington says, no one would bother.[64]

Spenser, who was younger than Harington by about ten or fifteen years, is familiar with this tradition and incorporates it in *The Faerie Queene*. When, in Book 3, the ancestor of Queen Elizabeth goes down to Merlin's cave, she sees a pantomime of her descendants, acted out by demons. The model for this, ultimately, is the parade of Roman worthies that is staged for Aeneas in the underworld. The difference is that magic, which was latent in Virgil and had to be pried up by commentary, is on the surface of Spenser's text, in plain view as the literal meaning. Merlin, says Spenser, takes "counsel" with demons (*FQ* 3.3.7), commands them to build his palace

---

[60] Harington on *Aen.* 6.46, in *The Sixth Book of Virgil's* Aeneid, *Translated and Commented on by Sir John Harington*, ed. Simon Cauchi (Oxford: Clarendon Press, 1991), p. 9. For dreaming brought on by "excesse of meats & drinks," see p. 61 (on *Aen.* 6.893).
[61] See Cauchi's edn., index, s.v. "James VI and I, King ... *Dæmonologie*."
[62] Harington, "The Comment," ch. 1 (ed. Cauchi, p. 65).
[63] Pietro Martire Vermigli (1499–1562) gives an authoritative summary of the various opinions in his *Common Places* 1.10.3–7, trans. Anthonie Marten (STC 24669; London: Henry Denham and Henry Middleton, 1583), pt. 1, pp. 73–77.
[64] Harington, "The Comment," ch. 1 (ed. Cauchi, p. 65); see also *Mixed Type* (ed. Jones, p. 124) on *Aen.* 6.126.

(3.3.10–11), and prophesies when he is in "the spirites powre" (3.3.50). Spenser is getting this from Ariosto. In the third canto of *Orlando furioso*, the ancestor of Ariosto's patron, the Duke of Ferrara, stumbles into the cave of Merlin and sees the history of her race acted out by demons (st. 21). This seems like a distortion of Virgil, who of course says nothing about fallen angels. But according to Virgil's commentators, this is what a real *descensus* would look like: magic would be involved and if any spirits appeared, they would be demons. The material comes from Virgil, the treatment of it from Lucan.

CHARACTER BY EXAMPLE

So far we have been talking about the literal meaning of *descensus ad inferos*. Can a person physically journey down to the underworld? And if not, what is the poet describing? The other meanings of *descensus* were classified as allegorical: the descent of embodiment, the descent of vice, and the descent of virtue.

As a rule, heroes in epic avoid the vicious descent. Sometimes a character will die and go to hell – Rodomonte in *Orlando furioso* (46.140), Cymochles in *The Faerie Queene* (2.8.45) – but these are always villains. The honorable descent is that of virtue; this occurs, says Landino, when we devote ourselves to "examining the nature of evil and of all the vices."[65] This is not to satisfy an idle, much less a salacious curiosity. Instead, we study the vices "in order that we might abstain from them, by understanding their harmfulness."[66]

In particular, we should study the punishments of the damned. Donatus puts it bluntly: "Virgil did not even pretend to be concerned about what happens in the underworld; his concern, rather, was through the fear of suffering to steer (*conuerteret*) individuals to good character (*bonos mores*) ... For the more he made them to fear, the less they would sin."[67] Badius concurs: "Maro describes all of these crimes for the sake of the living, to lead them back to good character through the fear of punishment."[68] This aspect of the underworld was emphasized by the humanist educator Sir Thomas Elyot (*c.* 1490–1546), who advocates the reading of Virgil "before any other autor latine" and who praises the usefulness of Book 6 in particular, because it teaches a boy to be good:

---

[65] Landino, *Disputationes camaldulenses*, Bk. 4 (ed. Lohe, p. 218).
[66] Landino on *Aen.* 6.126 (1499 edn., fol. ccxx^v).
[67] Tiberius Claudius Donatus on *Aen.* 6.625 (Giunta 1544, fol. 348^v).
[68] Badius on *Aen.* 6.622 (Giunta 1544, fol. 348^v).

howe shall he abhorre tyranny / fraude / & auarice / whan he doth se the paynes of duke Theseus / Prometheus / Sisiphus / and suche other / tourmented for their dissolute and vicious lyuing: Howe glad soone after shall he be / whan he shall beholde in the pleasant feldes of Elisius / the soules of noble princes & capitaines / which for their vertue and labours / in aduauncing the publike weales of their countrayes / do lyue eternally in pleasure inexplicable.[69]

Elyot was a promoter of the New Learning, but his method of teaching the underworld (as examples to imitate and shun) was hundreds of years old.[70] It was also international. Tasso, in the prose allegory of his *Gerusalemme liberata* (1581), says that when Aeneas undertakes his journey to the underworld, "it signifies his contemplation of punishments and rewards, which in the age to come are reserved for good and guilty souls."[71] Likewise in 1603, when Harington writes his commentary for the royal heir, he dwells at length on Virgil's description of "præmium et pœna," reward and punishment: for "hope of reward & fear of punishment" are "the band of all good goverment publique and pryvat."[72]

This sounds crude. Let us pause, though, and remind ourselves of how poetry was supposed to work. According to Sir Philip Sidney, poetry is more effectual than philosophy, because it teaches by example rather than by precept.[73] There were two kinds of example, *de bono* and *de malo*, and both were used in preaching as well as poetry: the one to inspire, the other to deter.[74]

Morals would change, but the underworld always remained a place of admonishment. William Baldwin's *A Myrroure for Magistrates* (1559) is a collection of stories that was enlarged and reprinted several times; Shakespeare used it for *The Rape of Lucrece* and probably for his history plays. The frame of the *Myrroure*, composed by Sir Thomas Sackville, is a *descensus ad inferos*, complete with sibyl. Her name is Sorrow and she leads the narrator into an underworld modeled on *Aeneid* 6. Here she will tell of peers and princes, how they perished in their pride (which is a vice for Christians, though not for pagans). In each case, the purpose of the story (as

---

[69] Elyot, *The Boke Named the Gouernour* 1.10 (STC 7635; London: Thomas Berthelet, 1531), fol. 33ᵛ.
[70] See Christopher Baswell, *Virgil in Medieval England: Figuring the* Aeneid *from the Twelfth Century to Chaucer* (Cambridge University Press, 1995), ch. 4.
[71] Tasso, *Le prose diverse di Torquato Tasso*, ed. Cesare Guasti, 2 vols. (Florence: Le Monnier, 1875), vol. 1, p. 302.
[72] Harington, "The Epistle" (ed. Cauchi, p. 2).
[73] Sidney, *An Apologie for Poetrie* (c. 1583), in *ECE*, vol. 1, pp. 160–74.
[74] See Carol V. Kaske, *Spenser and Biblical Poetics* (Ithaca, NY: Cornell University Press, 1999), ch. 2. Although Spenser used example, he seems also to have questioned its effectiveness; see Jeff Dolven, *Scenes of Instruction in Renaissance Romance* (Chicago: University of Chicago Press, 2007), chs. 4 and 6.

explained in Baldwin's preface) is "to shewe the slyppery deceytes [of Fortune], and the due rewarde of all kinde of vices."[75]

There is something that mislikes us here: the emphasis on fear. The Milanese mythographer Natale Conti (1520–82) explains why it is necessary, in the preface to his section on the underworld. According to Conti, the majority of men are pretty raw (*rudiores*) and can be persuaded to abstain from crime only by the rather crude method (*crassiore modo*) of punishments and rewards. Virgil's descriptions of these are vivid and effective.[76]

What is the less crude method? In the epic tradition, it is to persuade readers that wickedness is painful: not just in the sequel, but *in delicto*. The poet who does this most successfully is Dante. Anyone who has studied the *Inferno* even casually will have noticed that Dante matches crime and punishment with exquisite care. But the punishment is never just payback; it is also a diagnosis. For example, when Dante describes gluttons who wade through mud, sleet, and stinking rain, he is not predicting what will happen in the next life so much as picturing what happens in this one, when a spirit is weighed down by something more crudely material than itself.

Many of the punishments in hell Dante invented. But the idea of his hell – punishment as diagnosis – was neither new nor Christian. He probably found it in Servius, which is ironic, since Servius seems not to have believed in a literal afterlife. This comes out in several places, including his discussion of Tityos, the sinner who is stretched out on a rock for vultures to gnaw at his liver. For Servius, the author who "deals with all of these things in a healthy way (*sane*)" is Lucretius, the philosopher who

affirms that everything described in the underworld takes place in this life (*nostra vita*). For Tityos, he says, is *amor*, meaning *libido* [*De rerum natura* 3.978]. According to those who study nature and medicine, desire is in the liver, just as laughter is in the spleen and angriness in the gall-bladder. And this explains why the liver grows back when the vulture consumes it: for *libido*, once it has been acted on, is never satisfied but always comes back fresh.[77]

Servius goes on to explain the punishments of Sisyphus, Tantalus, and Ixion in the same way, as the unhappy state of all who give themselves up to ambition, avarice, or usury.[78] Quoting Horace, he urges readers to apply

---

[75] William Baldwin, *The Mirror for Magistrates*, ed. Lily B. Campbell (Cambridge University Press, 1938), p. 68. Sackville's "Induction" (1563) is on pp. 297–317 of this edition.
[76] Conti, *Mythologia* 3 (p. 96).
[77] Servius on *Aen.* 6.597 (Giunta 1544, fol. 347^r); see also his remarks on the gates of sleep (discussed above, pp. 155–56) and *descensus naturae* (discussed below, p. 173).
[78] Servius on *Aen.* 6.596, 603, 616 and 602 (Giunta 1544, fols. 347^{r-v}). See also Macrobius, *In Somnium Scipionis* 1.10.12–16, qtd. by Badius Ascensius on *Aen.* 6.98 (Giunta 1544, fol. 326^v).

these examples personally: "Why are you laughing? Change but the name, and the story is about you."[79]

Dante believes all of this, but he also believes in hell. So do his commentators and – in the Renaissance – so do the commentators on Virgil. Thus, according to Badius Ascensius, it is true what Servius wrote about Tityos' liver, that it grows back because lust is never satisfied. "Therefore," he adds, "our people say that the damned are always dying and yet can never die."[80] Our people (*nostri*) means Christians. Badius wants to be generous: here and elsewhere in his commentary, he is eager to find parallels between Christian theology and pagan understanding (*Ethnicorum sententia*). Still he is aware of gaps. In his preface to Virgil, Badius quotes from Servius to show that "the Romans did not listen to any poetry except what promotes both good character and the community (*reipublicam*)." Badius wants to extend this: "Without a doubt, Virgil's poetry promotes these things as much as can be, for he teaches the noble rewards established for virtues and the weighty punishments for vices, both in this age (*in hoc sæculo*) and in the age to come (*& in futuro*)."[81] Servius, could he have read this, would have smirked.

PLUTO'S DAUGHTER: HELL AS RICHES

As Michael Murrin has shown, the instinct of the allegorical commentator is always to seek out what is most fanciful in a story and substitute something hard-headed, usually science or morality.[82] "For it is blameworthy," writes Servius, "when a poet feigns (*fingere*) something that is absolutely untrue." Servius gives three examples: the story of Polydorus in Book 3, the ships that become nymphs in Book 9, and the golden bough in Book 6.[83] Why is the bough made of gold? Servius knows of several interpretations, all of which are unromantic. First, gold is the fee (*reparationem*) for magic. Actually, the real fee is human blood, of which gold is a symbol! Also the branch stands for moral choice. Servius imagines a branch shaped like the letter *Y*, and this reminds him of Pythagoras, who likened *Y* to a fork in the road of life: those who choose the left fork (*partem sinistram*) are those who follow vice, whereas those who go right follow virtue.

---

[79] Servius on *Aen.* 6.603 (Giunta 1544, fol. 347^v), quoting *Satires* 1.1.68–69.
[80] Badius, on *Aen.* 6.580ff. (Giunta 1544, fols. 347^v–48^r).
[81] Badius, praeambula (Giunta 1544, sig. *10^r).
[82] Michael Murrin, *The Veil of Allegory* (Chicago: University of Chicago Press, 1969), pp. 146–47; *Allegorical Epic*, passim.
[83] Servius on *Aen.* 3.46 (Giunta 1544, fol. 237^v).

Therefore Virgil, in imitation of the letter *Y,* says by way of the branch to pursue the virtues. He says that the branch is "hidden in the forest" because – in reality – virtue and innocence are hidden, by the confusion of this life and especially by our vices. Others say that one seeks the underworld with a golden branch because mortals perish easily in pursuit of riches (*diuitijs*). Tiberianus, that gold is the payment (*pretio*) which unlocks Dis's threshold.[84]

As usual, Servius rejects none of these interpretations. As a result, each of them will have a life of its own in subsequent commentaries and in poems based on the *Aeneid*. Magic we have discussed already. It remains then to speak of riches and choosing. As we shall see, these are often connected.

According to Servius, the golden bough is shaped like *Y* and represents the choice between virtue and vice. This choice, he continues, occurs in youth; for our first age, *prima ætas*, is *incerta*, "unfixed." In the Renaissance, this interpretation gets repeated letter for letter. For Petrarch, the choice is between Tartarus and Elysium. So too for Landino, Salutati, and Badius, each of whom mentions *Y* and the teaching of Pythagoras.[85] It is doubtful whether any of them had actually read Pythagoras, but they knew about him, and about the parable of *Y*, from Servius. Or they could have learned about them from one of the Church Fathers, Jerome or Lactantius, or from one of the early Christian poets, Sedulius or Prudentius.[86] Failing that, they could also have read about the doctrine in a short poem "On the Letter *Y*," which (in the Renaissance) was assigned to Virgil's juvenilia and printed as one of his minor works.[87] Badius even wrote a commentary.

So far, so classical. The shift, if there is one, occurs in poetry. What, in Virgil, was a scene of choosing becomes, in Boiardo and Spenser, a scene of temptation. In both poets, the temptation is gold. Boiardo's tempter is female, the treasure fairy Morgana, who lives underground and entices the hero with a magical stag. The stag has golden antlers, which it can moult six times every day, but the hero refuses, because the pursuit of wealth is unchivalrous and the desire for it can never be

---

[84] Servius on *Aen.* 6.136 (Giunta 1544, fol. 328ᵛ).
[85] For Petrarch, see Kallendorf, *Praise of Aeneas*, pp. 32–35; for Landino, Murrin, *Allegorical Epic*, p. 46; for Salutati, *Praise of Aeneas*, p. 96; for Badius, Giunta 1544, fol. 346ʳ (on *Aen.* 6.548).
[86] See Pierre Courcelle, "Interprétations néo-platonisantes du livre vi de l'*Énéide*," in *Recherches sur la tradition platonicienne*, ed. W. K. C. Guthrie (Vandoeuvres: Hardt, 1955), pp. 93–136, at pp. 100–2.
[87] There is an English translation in John Penkethman, *The Epigrams of P. Virgilius Maro, and others. With The Praises of him and his Workes* (STC 24825; London: George Purslowe, 1624), sig. B5ᵛ. The first lines are also echoed in the ninth book of Palingenius's popular encyclopedia, *The Zodiake of Life*, trans. Barnabe Googe (STC 19151; London: Raufe Newberie, 1576), p. 176.

satisfied.⁸⁸ Spenser's tempter, Mammon, makes a similar offer and receives the same response.⁸⁹ Like Morgana, he lives underground, in what seems to be a gold mine.

This seems modern: according to one scholar, Mammon's gold mine is in the New World.⁹⁰ But the setting is classical – Mammon's den is decorated like Pluto's basement – and so is the moral. We have quoted Servius on this point already: "one seeks the underworld with a golden branch because mortals perish easily in pursuit of riches." But the interpretation is older than Servius. Pluto, as everyone knows, is married to Persephone, the most famous child of Demeter. But Demeter also has a son, Ploutos, who is the god of wealth. According to Plato, this is not a coincidence: the name *Plouton* actually derives from *Ploutos*, because all wealth comes from the ground,⁹¹ whether gold from a mine or wheat from a field (since Ploutos is the child of Demeter). This etymology was widely known, and was available even to scholars with no knowledge of Greek.⁹² There was also a parallel in Latin. The Roman name for Pluto is *Dis*, which is a contraction of *diues*, "wealthy"; as Cicero explains, "All the forces of the earth and everything that originates there belong to Father Dis. The Greeks call him Plouton, meaning wealthy *(diues)*, because everything both returns to the ground and rises up out of the ground."⁹³

In the Renaissance, this account was routine. When Virgil speaks of "mighty Dis" (*Aen.* 6.541), Badius explains that Dis is "Pluto, who has his riches *(diuitias)* underground *(apud inferos)*."⁹⁴ Boccaccio, in his *Genealogies of the Pagan Gods* (1350–74), says that Pluto means riches *(diuitias)* and he notes that, in Virgil, the pure man does not venture into Pluto's city (*Aen.* 6.563). "From this it is clear," reasons Boccaccio, "that one cannot seek or guard riches without injustice." He goes on to explain almost the whole underworld in terms of avarice, saying that what Dante describes as the

---

⁸⁸ Boiardo, *Orlando innamorato* 1.25.9–16. See Charles S. Ross, "Angelica and the Fata Morgana: Boiardo's Allegory of Love," *Modern Language Notes* 96 (1981), 12–22; and Michael Murrin, "Trade and Fortune: Morgana and Manodante," in *Fortune and Romance: Boiardo in America*, ed. Jo Ann Cavallo and Charles Ross (Tempe, AZ: Medieval & Renaissance Texts & Studies, 1998), pp. 77–95.
⁸⁹ *FQ* 2.7.8–12, 33. See David Quint, "The Anatomy of Epic in Book 2 of *The Faerie Queene*," *Spenser Review* 34.1 (winter 2003), 28–45, at 33–39.
⁹⁰ David Read, *Temperate Conquests: Spenser and the Spanish New World* (Detroit: Wayne State University Press, 2000), pp. 72–74.
⁹¹ Plato, *Cratylus* 403a, qtd. by Conti, *Mythologia* 2.9 (p. 91). Conti's work first appeared in 1568.
⁹² See Conti, *Mythologia* 2.9, Badius on *Aen.* 6.124ff (Giunta 1544, fol. 327ʳ), and Fulgentius, *Mitologiae* 1.5, qtd. by Boccaccio, *Genealogiae deorum gentilium* 8.6 (Vicenza: Simon Bevilaqua, 1487), fol. lxxviiiʳ.
⁹³ Cicero, *De natura deorum* 2.66; I am indebted for this reference to Leofranc Holford-Strevens.
⁹⁴ Badius on *Aen.* 6.541 (Giunta 1544, fol. 345ʳ).

punishments of hell are, in many cases, really the anxieties that rich people have. Cerberus is real, too, but he is a type of personality, the type who is always on guard. This, says Boccaccio, means avarice. Why does Cerberus have three mouths? Because there are three types of avarice: prodigal spending, miserly hoarding, and the lazy exploitation of other peoples' sweat (*sudoribus*). Why does he have snakes for a collar? Those are the cares of greed.[95]

Boccaccio, along with Conti, was Spenser's main reference work for classical mythology,[96] which is why Spenser's Mammon has a daughter, Philotime (*FQ* 2.7.49). Her name means "love of tribute," but what is her connection with Mammon? The name Mammon is biblical: Mammon is a demon and demons do not have daughters. Pluto, though, does have a daughter and her name is Veneratio, "reverence"; Boccaccio mentions her in the next chapter after Pluto. What kind of reverence is Veneratio? The key, says Boccaccio, is her father, whose name means wealth. Veneratio, therefore, is the awe reserved for money, by men who are too "stolid, brutish, ignorant, and twisted" to be impressed by anything else.[97]

As the climax of Virgil's Odyssey, the underworld was supposed to recapitulate and amplify themes that had already been announced. Greed was one of these. The first, most famous, and most widely imitated episode of *Aeneid* 3 was the story of Polydorus, a Trojan prince who sails to Thrace, is murdered there for his treasure, and becomes a myrtle tree with bleeding branches. Today this sounds like a parable about history and cultural transformation.[98] But for Servius, Donatus, Landino, and Badius, it was a story about greed: what Virgil himself calls the "cursed hunger for gold" (*Aen.* 3.57). As related in Book 1, Dido's brother was also murdered for gold and that is why (in Book 3) Aeneas tells the anecdote of Polydorus: to gain Dido's sympathy.[99] Also and in general, to show that "greed is the parent of all crimes."[100]

---

[95] Boccaccio, *Genealogiae deorum gentilium* 8.6 (1487 edn., fols. lxxviii^(r-v)). Cf. Conti, "On Cerberus Understood Scientifically": "Cerberus is avarice and desire for riches ... He has many heads because many are the crimes that spring from this one source, avarice" (*Mythologia* 10, p. 535).
[96] Henry Gibbons Lotspeich, *Classical Mythology in the Poetry of Edmund Spenser* (Princeton: Princeton University Press, 1932), pp. 14–22.
[97] Boccaccio, *Genealogiae deorum gentilium* 8.7 (1487 edn., fol. lxxix^r).
[98] Douglas Biow, *Mirabile Dictu: Representations of the Marvelous in Medieval and Renaissance Epic* (Ann Arbor: University of Michigan Press, 1996).
[99] Servius on *Aen.* 3.57, T. C. Donatus on 3.45, Badius on 3.56 (Giunta 1544, fols. 237^v–38^v).
[100] Landino on *Aen.* 3.54 (1499 edn., fol. clxvii^r). Cf. 1 Tim. 6:10, qtd. below.

MOURIR, C'EST FACILE: HELL AS HABIT

"A gold mine," wrote Petrarch, is "a road that slopes down to hell" (*Pronum iter ad inferos*).[101] Spenser makes the proverb literal, by telling us that the doorway to Mammon's lair is "adioyning" to "the gate of Hell" and between them is only "a litle stride" (*FQ* 2.7.24). The allegory here is transparent: "they that will be rich, fall into tentation and snares, and into many foolish and noysome lustes, which drowne men in perdition and destruction. For the desire of money is the roote of all euill" (1 Tim. 6:9–10). This is what the commentators on Virgil would call the descent of vice. Unlike the descent of magic, which is a performance, the descent of vice is something we become, a habit of the soul. As we shall see, the main symbol for this was the gates of Dis.

When Aeneas requests a tour of Hades, the Sibyl smiles back grimly:

> facilis descensus Auerni,
> Noctes atque dies patet atri ianua Ditis:
> Sed reuocare gradum, superasque euadere ad auras,
> Hoc opus, hic labor est: pauci, quos æquus amauit
> Iuppiter, aut ardens euexit ad æthera virtus:
> Diis geniti potuere.[102]
>
> [Easy is the descent of Avernus,
> night and day the gates of gloomy Dis lie open.
> But to call back one's step, and wade out to the air above –
> that is the task, the hardship. Few have been able:
> those whom Jupiter, in his justice, favored,
> or whom burning virtue raised up to the skies,
> children of the gods.]

This speech was recognized by Virgil's contemporaries as an instant classic of Roman literature.[103] It is a rare instance of Virgil's sarcasm. The normal descent is death: it is easy, because people die all the time, "night and day." The trick is to come back from death. This is possible, sometimes, for a demigod such as Theseus or Hercules. But do such beings really exist? Servius, as usual, is skeptical and scientific: "those whom Jupiter loves" and "children of the gods" are people conceived under propitious stars.[104]

---

[101] Petrarch, "De inuentione auri dialogus," in *De remediis utriusque fortunae* (Cremona, 1492), sig. g2ʳ. Qtd. in James Nohrnberg, "Orlando's Opportunity: Chance, Luck, Fortune, Occasion, Boats, and Blows in Boiardo's *Orlando Innamorato*," in *Fortune and Romance*, ed. Cavallo and Ross, pp. 31–75, at p. 68.
[102] *Aen.* 6.126–31; Giunta 1544, fol. 328ʳ.
[103] Ovid, whose dates overlap Virgil's by about twenty-five years, echoes the speech on several occasions: *Met.* 4.439–40, 12.43–46; *Ars* 1.453.
[104] Servius on *Aen.* 6.129 (Giunta 1544, fol. 328ᵛ).

Badius does not believe in demigods either, and thinks immediately of two verses from the Gospel: "Broad is the way, which leads to perdition" (Mt. 7:13) and "Many are called, but few are chosen" (Mt. 20:16).[105]

In Spenser this becomes the "broad high way" to the House of Pride, which road is traveled "Both day and night, of each degree and place," though "few returned," except "With balefull beggery, or foule disgrace" (1.4.2, 3). It is a picture of what happens to young men when they go to court for the first time: most are swallowed up by various bad habits (depicted in this episode by a parade of the seven deadly sins); and those who do manage to come home again are usually ruined by the expense of living at court.[106] The image recurs in *The Faerie Queene*, Book 2, when Belphoebe says, "easy is the way, and passage plaine / To pleasures pallace; it may soone be spide, / And day and night her dores to all stand open wide" (2.3.41). "Pleasures pallace" is Belphoebe's term for "Princes court" (2.3.42), which is imagined, again, as a kind of hell. The Bower of Bliss, at the end of Book 2, is also an image of court ("Pleasures pallace") and, again, the gate is always open (2.12.46).[107]

Why? The gate is open, the way down easy, because no one becomes greedy or prideful all at once. Rather, they *do* greedy or prideful things, and the deeds become habits.[108] The way back is laborious because habits are hard to undo. As Landino explains, "when appetite, through the habit of vices, is sunk down to the very bottom, it is difficult for it to return up again, i.e., to virtue."[109] This is why, in Spenser, no one ever returns from the Gulfe of Greedinesse, which he compares with hell and Tartarus:

> But noght that falles into this direfull deepe,
> Ne that approcheth nigh the wyde descent,
> May backe returne, but is condemned to be drent.[110]

The descent of vice – in epic language, the fall into gulf, delve, cave, or declivity – is the formation of a bad habit. It is "easy" in the sense of being gradual. Thus Landino: "it is easy for the mind to descend into the senses,

---

[105] Badius on *Aen.* 6.129 (Giunta 1544, fol. 329ʳ).
[106] The biggest expense seems to be clothing; cf. Spenser's *Colin Clouts Come Home Again* 711–30.
[107] For the Bower as court, see Louis Montrose, "The Elizabethan Subject and the Spenserian Text," in *Literary Theory/Renaissance Texts*, ed. Patricia Parker and David Quint (Baltimore: Johns Hopkins University Press, 1986), pp. 303–40, at pp. 329–30; and Patricia Parker, *Literary Fat Ladies: Rhetoric, Gender, Property* (London: Methuen, 1987), ch. 4.
[108] Aristotle, *Nicomachean Ethics* 2.1 (1103).
[109] Landino on *Aen.* 6.128 (1499 edn., sig. Ciiiiᵛ).
[110] *FQ* 2.12.6. Cf. the fraudulent schemes of Malengin's cave: "Ne none can backe returne, that once are gone amis" (*FQ* 5.9.6); also the quarrels of Ate's lair: "many waies to enter may be found, / But none to issue forth when one is in: / For discord harder is to end then to begin" (4.1.20).

but not easily is the mind called back from the senses, for that is to withdraw from hell (*ab inferis*)."[111]

LIFE IN HELL

He is referring specifically to the descent of nature,[112] which is the easiest descent of all and has happened to everyone who is reading this book. In the beginning, says Plato, we were all pure souls. Our domain was the sphere of fixed stars, where we lived in beatitude, with neither bodies nor longing "for what we on earth call 'life.'" The decision to quit this happy existence was not rational; yet somehow it happens that,

> looking out from on high, staring down from perpetual light, the soul will begin to meditate a lurking desire until, weighed down with its own earthly thoughts, little by little it slips down into the lower regions. Not immediately does the soul, from complete incorporeality, put on this vesture of clay. But almost imperceptibly (*sensim*), through silent erosions (*detrimenta*) and through moving farther away from oneness and unconditional purity, it begins to swell up. At every step there is a planet, for in each sphere that lies under the heavens, the soul is robed with a layer of aether. And through these layers the soul is gradually reconciled to being joined with this garment of earth. Each sphere that it passes through in this way is a death, until it arrives here, at what we on earth we call "life."[113]

This is Plato's version of the Fall. Our so-called life is really the death of the soul and the body (*soma*) is its tomb (*sema*). It is a literal fall, from heaven to earth, and it happens not once, to our primeval parents, but to each of us individually.

Plato's influence on Renaissance art has sometimes been exaggerated, but the account I have just been quoting was the opposite of esoteric. It is from Macrobius, in his commentary on Cicero's "Dream of Scipio," and there was never a time, in the Middle Ages or Renaissance, when that document was not available, widely. Badius, in his commentary on *Aeneid* 6, gives an excerpt from Macrobius that fills almost two folio pages and gives more details about the spheres and planets; my translation is from this excerpt.[114]

---

[111] Landino, *Disputationes Camaldulenses*, Bk. 4 (ed. Lohe, p. 220).
[112] For the history of this idea prior to the Renaissance, see Jane Chance Nitzsche, *The Genius Figure in Antiquity and the Middle Ages* (New York: Columbia University Press, 1975), pp. 42–50; and Marilynn Desmond, "Bernard Silvestris and the *Corpus* of the *Aeneid*," in *The Classics in the Middle Ages*, ed. Aldo S. Bernardo and Saul Levin (Binghamton, NY: Center for Medieval & Early Renaissance Studies, 1990), pp. 129–39.
[113] Macrobius, *In somnium Scipionis* 1.11.11–12, as qtd. by Badius Ascensius on *Aen.* 6.98 (Giunta 1544, fol. 327ᵛ).
[114] Salutati, *De laboribus Herculis*, vol. II, pp. 464–68, gives long excerpts from the same passage.

For Macrobius, the underworld is really a parable about human existence. The moral is simple: to have a body – to inhabit this sublunary world – is to be in hell. Servius agrees: the earth is solid, and therefore a literal underworld would be absurd. Ergo,

> the "underworld" is the world we live in, because it is "under" all of the circles, namely of the seven planets – Saturn, Jupiter, Mars, the sun, Venus, Mercury, the moon – and of the two great circles [beyond]. And this is why, philosophers believe, the underworld is encompassed by the river Styx with its nine folds: because the earth is girded round with nine circles. Therefore, everything that is feigned (*fingitur*) to be in the underworld, we should acknowledge is here instead.[115]

Again, this world is hell. The only escape is for the body to die and the soul to go back where it came from. For Servius, this is what it means "to call back one's step, and wade out to the air above" (*Aen.* 6.128).

> Virgil is speaking poetically and according to the profound understanding of philosophers, who would have it be understood that the souls of those who live well go back to the upper circles, i.e., to their origin. And this is why Pompey says (in Lucan), "Behold, how much of our day lies under night" [*Phars.* 9.13–14]. For the souls of those who live wickedly remain in these bodies for a longer duration, with various changes, and are always in the "underworld."[116]

Notice that the soul does not automatically return to its origin after death. As Plato explained in the *Timaeus* (for centuries the only one of his dialogues available in Latin), the soul that entombs itself in a body derives from that body certain passions, such as desire, fear, and anger. If a soul conquer its passions, it may return to its native star. But the soul which is conquered by its passions will be reborn in the body of a woman – and if that does not reform it, the soul will be reborn yet again, as a beast.[117] These are the "changes" that, according to Servius, the wicked must endure while they are in hell, i.e., for the duration of their bodily existence.

PURGATORY

Virgil alludes to this doctrine directly. In the underworld, Aeneas happens upon a group of souls who are waiting to be reclothed in human flesh. He is

---

[115] Servius on *Aen.* 6.124 (Giunta 1544, fols. 328^(r–v)). He gives the same explanation of Styx at *Aen.* 6.439 (fol. 340^v).
[116] Servius on *Aen.* 6.128 (Giunta 1544, fol. 328^v).
[117] *Timaeus* 42. I paraphrase the Latin translation by Chalcidius (fourth century AD), *Timaeus a Calcidio translatus commentarioque instructus*, ed. J. H. Waszink (London: Warburg, 1962), p. 37. This translation was widely known in the Middle Ages and was available in print from 1520 onward.

puzzled with a kind of Platonic puzzlement: why would someone who has escaped the body return? Anchises explains:

> At the source, the heavens and the earth and the watery fields,
> the glowing orb of the moon and Titan's stars [725]
> are nourished by a spirit within them. A mind infusing every member
> animates the whole mass and mingles with its great body:
> thence the race of men and beasts, the being in birds,
> and the wonders that the sea brings forth under its marble surface.
> Fiery is the life in these things, celestial the origin of these seeds –
> insomuch as they are not congested by noisome bodies,
> dulled by earthly limbs and mortal members.
> On account of these they fear and desire, grieve and rejoice;
> closed in by shadows, by a blind prison, they do not perceive the sky.
> But even when the life departs with the last light, [735]
> still not all of the evil, not all of the body's plagues
> are utterly departed from these wretched ones: it is inevitable,
> over a long time, that many things should congeal, ingrain themselves in strange ways.
> For this reason they are schooled with punishments, and for their former sins
> they pay the penalty. Some are stretched out,
> exposed to the empty winds; in others, the guilty stain
> is washed away under a corrosive tide, or consumed by fire –
> each of us suffers his own shade. And then a few of us
> are sent through broad Elysium, to live in these gladsome fields –
> until time's circle is complete and the duration of days [745]
> has purged the stubborn taint, leaving pure
> the consciousness of heaven and the fire of unadulterated spirit.
> But all these, when they have rolled the wheel through a thousand years,
> a god summons to Lethe's stream in a long column
> as you can see, so that, having forgotten, they might revisit the skies
> and begin once more to have the will to turn back into bodies.[118]

Here, finally, is the answer to Aeneas' question: only when they have forgotten what it was like the first time will free spirits resume their fleshly tabernacle, which is really a prison. There is something in the last verse, *Rursus & incipiant in corpora velle reuerti*, which I have tried not to disguise by translation, a quality of labor and redundancy – as if the mind, anticipating its future state, were beginning already to slow down and succumb to the body's sluggishness. In contrast, the opening of the speech is lordly, expansive: *Principio cœlum, ac terras, camposque liquenteis*. For Scaliger, this verse was an example of the epic style at full tide, the grandest of the grand.[119]

---

[118] *Aen.* 6.724–51 (Giunta 1544, fol. 353ᵛ).
[119] J. C. Scaliger, *Poetices libri septem* 4.23 (Lyon: Antonius Vincentius, 1561), p. 194.

But that was the style. The content of the speech was problematic for several reasons.[120] First, there is the suggestion in lines 724–27 of pantheism. Virgil's supposed adherence to this "weak" and "vngodly" doctrine was denounced by Calvin and censured by his followers.[121] Second, Anchises asserts that guilt is contracted by the soul from contact with the body (731–38). Third, between death and beatitude, the souls even of the righteous will undergo a period of purgation (739–43). Finally, there is the suggestion that most souls will be purged of the ills that beset them only to take on new bodies, and with them new corporeal stains (743–51).

In England, the doctrine of purgatory was abandoned after 1534, but it continued to serve as a reference point, both in popular culture and in commentary on the *Aeneid*. Why? Culturally, because the idea of a middle space between heaven and hell was too useful to give up all at once.[122] But there was a scholarly reason as well. Even if, as Jacques Le Goff argues, the details of purgatory did not get worked out until the eleventh and twelfth centuries, the idea of purgatory was almost coeval with Christianity itself.[123] Among other places, it can be traced in the mature writings of St. Augustine (AD 354–430).

For a non-biblical author, the bishop of Hippo enjoyed a unique and privileged status among Protestant theologians of the 1500s. Luther studied him intensely and quoted from him freely. So did Calvin. In consequence certain ideas that ought, by rights, to have been killed by the Reformation were preserved, with Augustine as a vector. As everyone knows, Augustine was a teacher of rhetoric before he was a theologian. Even when he disagreed with Virgil, Augustine framed much of his thinking in terms and images

---

[120] John Watkins, *The Specter of Dido: Spenser and Virgilian Epic* (New Haven: Yale University Press, 1995), pp. 105–6, is a useful starting point.

[121] Jon A. Quitslund, *Spenser's Supreme Fiction: Platonic Natural Philosophy and* The Faerie Queene (Toronto: University of Toronto Press, 2001), pp. 124–26. The patristic response was more complicated; see Pierre Courcelle, "Virgile et l'immanence divine chez Minucius Felix," *Jahrbuch für Antike und Christentum* 1 (1964), 34–42. Landino, in his commentary on *Aen*. 6.730, avoids pantheism by interpreting *spiritus* (726) as a viceroy of God, appointed by the divine mind but not identical with it (1499 edn., fol. ccviii^v).

[122] See Alan Kreider, *English Chantries: The Road to Dissolution* (Cambridge, MA: Harvard University Press, 1979); Eamon Duffy, *The Stripping of the Altars: Traditional Religion in England 1400–1500* (New Haven: Yale University Press, 1992), ch. 10; Elizabeth Mazzola, *The Pathology of the English Renaissance: Sacred Remains and Holy Ghosts* (Leiden: Brill, 1998), pp. 55–63; and Stephen Greenblatt, *Hamlet in Purgatory* (Princeton: Princeton University Press, 2001).

[123] See Jacques Le Goff, *La naissance du Purgatoire* (Paris: Gallimard, 1981). Responses to Le Goff are summarized in Takami Matsuda, *Death and Purgatory in Middle English Didactic Poetry* (Cambridge: Brewer, 1997), ch. 1.

that were borrowed from the *Aeneid*.[124] Purgatory is a case in point. In *The City of God*, Augustine poses several questions about pains in the afterlife: are they to purify or punish, and how long will they last? To illustrate the view that punishments in the afterlife are for purification, Augustine quotes Anchises: some are purified by wind, some by water, and some by fire (*Aen.* 6.733–40). The three pains, says Augustine, refer to three of the four primal elements; the fourth element, earth, is omitted because that is where the taint comes from. He goes on to explain that not all pains are like the ones Anchises describes: some will be permanent, and will be for punishment, not for reform; these are the eternal pains of hell. But other pains will be temporary – and these will be for reform.[125] Several chapters later, Augustine associates the temporary pains with an obscure verse in 1 Corinthians: "If anie mans worke burne, he shal lose, but he shalbe safe him self: neuertheles yet as it were by the fyre" (3:15). Augustine is cautious: he does not commit himself to the view that Paul is referring to purgatorial fire. But he is unwilling to rule out the possibility.[126] Others were less cautious and, over the centuries, this verse became the central proof text for the doctrine of purgatory. As a result, when Protestants decided to refute that doctrine, it became necessary to explain that Paul must have been speaking metaphorically.[127]

But until that happened, Christian readers were just as delighted as modern scholars to discover in Virgil's text a confirmation of their own cherished beliefs. In the 1380s, an anonymous commentator based at Norwich explained that when Aeneas finds his helmsman, Palinurus, among the unburied dead, the steersman is *in purgatorio*,[128] a Latin word that did not even exist in Virgil's day, but was now part of the general vocabulary. Gavin Douglas (*c.* 1474–1522), who translated the *Aeneid* into Middle Scots, mocked Virgil's doctrine of soul migration.[129] But the bishop of Dunkeld (to give him his proper title) praised Book 6 in particular, because of how Virgil described the afterlife:

---

[124] See Sabine MacCormack, *The Shadows of Poetry: Vergil in the Mind of Augustus* (Berkeley and Los Angeles: University of California Press, 1998). For Book 6 in particular, see Pierre Courcelle, "Les pères de l'église devant les enfers virgiliens," *Archives d'histoire doctrinale et littéraire du moyen âge* 30 (1955), 5–74.
[125] Augustine, *De civitate dei* 21.13, in *Aurelij augustini de ciuitate dei* (Venice: Nicholas Jenson, 1475), n.p.
[126] Augustine, *De civitate dei* 21.26 (1475 edn., n.p.).
[127] See, for example, Luther's *Table Talk* §3695, in *Luther's Works*, gen. eds. Jaroslav Pelikan and Helmut T. Lehmann, 55 vols. (St. Louis, MO: Concordia, and Philadelphia, PA: Fortress, 1958–86), vol. LIV, p. 259; and Vermigli, *Common Places* 3.9.26 (trans. Marten, pt. III, p. 239).
[128] Baswell, *Virgil in Medieval England*, p. 156.
[129] Watkins, *Specter of Dido*, p. 106.

> Twichand our faith mony clausis he fand,
> Quhilk bene conforme or than collaterall.
> Schawis he nocht heir the synnis capitall?
> Schawis he nocht wickit folk in endles pane?
> And purgatorie for synnis veniale,
> And virtuus peple into the plesand plane?[130]

Douglas, we know, relied heavily on the commentary by Badius Ascensius,[131] and Badius, among the most popular modern commentators, was the one most eager to point out even possible resemblances between Virgil and Christianity. On the subject of wind, water, and fire, he begins with a quotation from *The City of God*, about the two kinds of pain, punitive and purgatorial. Maybe, he speculates, Virgil's corrosive tide (*gurges vastus*) is the holy water (*aqua benedicta*) that purges venial sins. Or, he submits, it may correspond with the ice where souls in torment have been observed by the saints. Or perhaps it is purgatory, as many believe and as St. Paul's reference to fire in 1 Corinthians seems to indicate.[132]

When Badius wrote this, c. 1500, Martin Luther was sixteen years old and planning to enter law school. Fifty years later, the face of Christendom had changed dramatically. But it was not unrecognizable. Moreover, in most areas of life, classical scholarship included, the pace of change was uneven. The Reformation was one of those big ideas that ought to have changed everything, and didn't. (The printing press was another.) As we saw in Chapter 1, the Reformation did not change which commentaries got published in which countries. Nor did it alter in any significant way the interpretation of Virgil. Harington, for example, in his preface to *Aeneid* 6 laments the "affynity" between Virgil's description of expiation through fire and the "popysh" doctrine of purgatory.[133] But when he translates the description, Harington is faithful to record Augustine's use of it, as an illustration of temporary pains in the afterlife. What is more surprising, he also gives the traditional cross-reference to "safe as yt wear by fyre" (from

---

[130] *The Poetical Works of Gavin Douglas, Bishop of Dunkeld*, ed. John Small, 4 vols. (Edinburgh: Patterson, 1874), vol. III, p. 2.

[131] See Charles R. Blyth, "*The Knychtlyke Style*": *A Study of Gavin Douglas' Aeneid* (New York: Garland, 1987), pp. 26–41.

[132] Badius on *Aen.* 6.793 (Giunta 1544, fol. 354ᵛ). Landino held similar views; see Kallendorf, *Praise of Aeneas*, pp. 159–60.

[133] See also Harington's remarks on the limbo of the infants – "Heer virgills opinion is moch lyke the papists of *Limbus Infantum*" (on *Aen.* 6.426, ed. Cauchi, p. 31) – and on the funeral of Misenus: "thease ceremonyes wowld make one suspect virgill for halfe a papist, but that in his tyme the world had neyther pope nor byshop" (on *Aen.* 6.213, p. 21). But cf. "Of Paradise and the state of the godly," where Harington praises Virgil for placing married priests in Elysium (on *Aen.* 6.661, p. 79).

1 Corinthians).[134] Harington held Augustine in high regard (he read *The City of God* in debtor's prison),[135] and on his authority gave what was essentially a Catholic interpretation of Virgil's purgatory. Shakespeare, whether he was Catholic or not, was certainly familiar with the doctrine and (what is more interesting) conceived of it in Virgilian images. In Shakespeare's plays, there are at least two characters who make reference to purgatory: the ghost of Hamlet's father and Claudio in *Measure for Measure*, who shrinks from death because he could not bear

> To bathe in fiery floods, or to reside
> In thrilling region of thick-ribbed ice;
> To be imprison'd in the viewlesse winds
> And blown with restless violence about
> The pendant world. (3.1.121–25)

As others have noted, this is a description of purgatory, not damnation, and it is couched in terms that distinctly recall the triple purgations of wind, water, and fire in Virgil's underworld.[136] This is consistent, both with the play's Catholic setting (Claudio's sister, Isabella, is planning to enter a convent) and with Shakespeare's education (he would have studied Virgil in grammar school).

"SINFULL MIRE": THE MORAL STATUS OF MATTER

To Protestants, purgatory was repugnant because it had no warrant in Scripture;[137] tended to "obscure the benefits and grace of Christ" by extending penance into the next life;[138] and gave license to the wicked practice of buying and selling indulgences.[139] With reincarnation, Christians of all creeds could afford to be more indulgent, because nobody believed in it. Thus Arthur Golding (1535/6–1606), Ovid's Elizabethan translator:

---

[134] Harington on *Aen.* 6.739 (ed. Cauchi, p. 51).
[135] See Cauchi's edn., p. 1 and index, s.v. *Augustine*. See also Douglas, prologue to *Aen.* 6: "How oft rehersis Austyne, cheif of clerkis, / In his gret volume of the Cetie of God, / Hundreth of versis of Virgile ... / ... / And of this sax buik walis he mony a scoir: / Nocht but guid ressoun; for, thocht Christ ground our faith / Virgilis sawis ar worth to put in stoir" (*Poetical Works*, vol. III, p. 3).
[136] Baldwin, *Small Latine*, vol. II, pp. 491–93; John E. Hankins, "The Pains of the Afterworld: Fire, Wind, and Ice in Milton and Shakespeare," *PMLA* 71 (1956), 482–95, at 487–94.
[137] Luther, *Table Talk* §3695 (*Luther's Works*, vol. LIV, p. 259). See also Vermigli, *Common Places* 3.9.26 (trans. Marten, pt. III, p. 239).
[138] Luther, *Table Talk* §3695 (*Luther's Works*, vol. LIV, p. 259); Calvin, *Institutes* 3.5.6; Vermigli, *Common Places* 3.9.18 (trans. Marten, pt. III, pp. 236–37).
[139] Vermigli, *Common Places* 3.9.21 (trans. Marten, pt. III, p. 238); Harington, "Of hel and the state of the damned" (ed. Cauchi, pp. 76–77).

> Of this I am ryght well assurde there is no Christian Wyght
> That can by fondnesse be so farre seduced from the ryght.[140]

Ben Jonson could allude to soul migration wittily in turning a compliment,[141] and Donne could use it savagely for satire.[142] Shakespeare referred to it in three plays that I know of, but always in jest or mockery.[143] In particular, what seems to have interested him was the migration of souls across species boundaries, from human to animal and animal to human. The latter was for mockery, as when Shylock is said to have a wolf's soul in a man's body. But the former transformation was always explained allegorically, as an image of what happens to men when they yield to bestial appetites.[144] Servius, it is true, seems to have taken reincarnation seriously.[145] Plato, too, refers to reincarnation at least eight times in five different dialogues – apparently, it was part of his mental furniture, if not his creed.[146] But for Plato's disciples in the Renaissance, the references to reincarnation were a stumbling block: either they had to concede

---

[140] Arthur Golding, "The Epistle," in *The .xv. Bookes of P. Ouidius Naso, entytuled Metamorphosis, translated oute of Latine into English meeter* (STC 18956; London: Willyam Seres, 1567), sig. aii^v.

[141] Jonson, *Epigrams* 95.1–4.

[142] According to Jonson, the "conceit" of Donne's unfinished *Metempsycosis* (1601) "was, that he sought the soul of that apple which Eve pulled, and thereafter made it the soul of a bitch, then of a she wolf, and so of a woman. His general purpose was to have brought in all the bodies of the heretics from the soul of Cain, and at last left it in the body of Calvin" (ed. Herford and Simpson, vol. I, p. 136).

[143] For jest, see *As You Like It* 3.2.176–78 ("I was never so berhym'd since Pythagoras' time, that I was an Irish rat, which I can hardly remember") and *Twelfth Night* 4.2.50–60; for mockery, *Merchant of Venice* 4.1.130–38 ("Thou almost make'st me waver in my faith / To hold opinion with Pythagoras / … / … for thy desires / Are wolfish, bloody, starv'd, and ravenous"). On Shakespeare's use of the idea, see A. C. Bradley, *Shakespearean Tragedy* (1904; repr. London: Penguin, 1991), pp. 244–46.

[144] Thus Landino: "It is the thinking of many Platonists … that Plato did not understand our souls to migrate into the bodies of birds and animals, but into their habits (*mores*)" (1499 edn., fol. ccxlv^r, comm. on *Aen.* 7.20). Cf. Chalcidius, *Commentarius* CXCVIII (ed. Waszink, p. 219). See also Golding, "Epistle," in *Metamorphosis* (1567), sig. aii^v and "[Preface] too the Reader," sig Aii^r: "Not that they lost theyr manly shape as too the outward showe, / But for that in their brutish brestes most beastly lustes did growe." An early source for this interpretation is Boethius, *Consolatio* 4.pr.3.17–25, qtd. by Silvestris, *Commentum*, pp. 22–23 to explain *Aen.* 3.386. Cf. Macrobius, *In somnium Scipionis* 1.9.5, quoting a piece of Anchises' sermon: "After death, however, the soul does not let go of the body easily … But either it wanders around its own corpse, or seeks to house itself in a new body – not always a human one, either, but also one of a beast, selecting a species to suit the habits (*moribus*) that, as a man, it exercised by choice (*libenter*)." Petrarch copied out this passage in his manuscript of Virgil, adding, "It is the way of learned men (*doctorum*) to marvel at childish absurdities (*pueriles ineptias*)"; see Mary Louise Lord, "The Use of Macrobius and Boethius in Some Fourteenth-Century Commentaries on Virgil," *International Journal of the Classical Tradition* 3.1 (1996), 3–22, at 6.

[145] Anchises' teaching about the soul is one of the few aspects of the underworld which Servius does *not* allegorize. He also alludes to soul migration when the text does not seem to require it, e.g., in his remarks on *Geo.* 1.243 (Giunta 1544, fol. 69^r), *Aen.* 6.448 (fol. 341^v), and *Aen.* 6.532 (fol. 344^r).

[146] Plato, *Laws* 10.903d–05b; *Meno* 81b–d; *Phaedo* 70c–d, 81–84b, 112e–13a; *Republic* 10.617d–21b; *Timæus* 41d–42c, and 90e–91a.

that the master was mistaken, or (they argued) it was one of his Noble Lies.[147]

One of the few places in Renaissance literature where reincarnation is not a joke or embarrassment is Spenser's Garden of Adonis. This episode is notoriously confusing.[148] It is not my intention here either to resolve the old controversies or to add to them. Instead, I want to show how an old, discredited heresy became useful again and productive.

The Garden of Adonis, like Virgil's underworld, has "double gates … which opened wide." But these portals have a doorman, whose name is Genius:

> He letteth in, he letteth out to wend,
>   All that to come into the world desire;
>   A thousand thousand naked babes attend
>   About him day and night, which doe require,
>   That he with fleshly weedes would them attire:
>   Such as him list, such as eternall fate
>   Ordained hath, he clothes with sinfull mire,
>   And sendeth forth to liue in mortall state,
> Till they againe returne back by the hinder gate.
>
> After that they againe retourned beene,
>   They in that Gardin planted bee agayne;
>   And grow afresh, as they had neuer seene
>   Fleshly corruption, nor mortall payne.
>   Some thousand yeares so doen they there remayne,
>   And then of him are clad with other hew,
>   Or sent into the chaungefull world agayne,
>   Till thether they returne, where first they grew:
> So like a wheele arownd they ronne from old to new.   (*FQ* 3.6.32–33)

This certainly sounds like soul migration: the babes enter the material world "faire and fresh," and when they have grown "old and dride" (*FQ* 3.6.31) they leave the material world and return to the Garden for a thousand-year convalescence, at which point the process starts over again.[149] Most of this seems to come from Ovid or Virgil.[150] Between the various sources there is

---

[147] James Hankins, *Plato in the Italian Renaissance*, 2 vols. (Leiden: Brill, 1990), vol. 1, pp. 257–59.
[148] For a summary of the debate, see Quitslund, *Supreme Fiction*, ch. 6.
[149] See Josephine Waters Bennett, "Spenser's Garden of Adonis," *PMLA* 47 (1932), 46–80, at 57.
[150] For Ovid as intertext in the Garden, see Brents Stirling, "The Philosophy of Spenser's 'Garden of Adonis,'" *PMLA* 49 (1934), 501–38; Colin Burrow, *Epic Romance from Homer to Milton* (Oxford: Clarendon Press, 1993), pp. 116–20; and Raphael Lyne, *Ovid's Changing Worlds: English Metamorphoses 1567–1632* (Oxford: Oxford University Press, 2001), pp. 107–11. There may also be some Lucretius: see Edwin A. Greenlaw, "Spenser and Lucretius," *Studies in Philology* 17 (1920), 439–64, at 442–43.

considerable overlap, but three details are unique to Virgil. First is the role of "fate" in assigning new bodies (st. 32; cf. *Aen.* 6.713–14).[151] This point receives special emphasis in Servius and Badius, both of whom note that not all souls receive new bodies, but only those appointed by fate.[152] A second borrowing from Virgil is the image of time's wheel (st. 33; cf. *Aen.* 6.748);[153] according to Landino, this refers to the cycle of physical reproduction.[154] Finally, there is the odd fact that Spenser's babes "require" – solicit – Genius for their "fleshly weedes" (st. 32). Virgil says that when souls forget what the material world is really like, "they begin to wish (*incipiant . . . velle*) to turn back into bodies" (*Aen.* 6.751). According to Landino, this means that the souls who undergo reincarnation "are not compelled, but drawn at fixed times by a bent (*procliuitate*) of nature."[155]

Christians, though, do not believe in reincarnation. According to Hebrews 9:27, "it is appoynted vnto men that they shal once die, and after that commeth the iudgement." So what is Spenser referring to? Since 1960, the usual explanation has been that Spenser's "babes" are not rational souls but "the forms of bodies which souls later assume" – what the Stoics and St. Augustine called "seminal reasons."[156] But what if the "babes" really are "men," as Spenser calls them in stanza 31? And why is the "mire" in which Genius clothes them "sinfull" (st. 32)?

RESURRECTION

There are two problems here. At one level, there is heresy; or, at the very least, a discrepancy between poet's creed and poet's mythology. At another level, there is the moral status of matter. For Anchises, the body is a source of contagion. As in Plato, the "descent of nature" and the fall of man are really the same thing. This is in contrast with the teaching of St. Augustine, who quoted Virgil and then refuted him, arguing that "the corruptible flesh made not the soule to sinne; but the sinning soule made the flesh corruptible."[157]

---

[151] Noted by John Erskine Hankins, *Source and Meaning in Spenser's Allegory: A Study of* The Faerie Queene (Oxford: Clarendon Press, 1971), p. 271.
[152] Servius and Badius on *Aen.* 6.713 (Giunta 1544, fol. 353ʳ).
[153] Noted by Hankins, *Source and Meaning*, p. 274.   [154] Landino on *Aen.* 6.748 (1499 edn., fol. ccixʳ).
[155] Landino on *Aen.* 6.751 (1499 edn., fol. ccixʳ).
[156] Robert Ellrodt, *Neoplatonism in the Poetry of Spenser* (Darby, PA: Darby, 1960), pp. 77–86. See also Hankins, *Source and Meaning*, pp. 248–86; James Nohrnberg, *The Analogy of* The Faerie Queene (Princeton: Princeton University Press, 1976), pp. 533–62; and Quitslund, *Supreme Fiction*, pp. 105–7, 122–24, 201–2, 228, 246–49, 261–63.
[157] Augustine, *De dei civitate* 14.3, as paraphrased by George Sandys in *Ovid's* Metamorphosis *Englished, Mythologized, and Represented in Figures* (1626), ed. Karl K. Hulley and Stanley T. Vandersall (Lincoln: University of Nebraska Press, 1970), p. 695. See MacCormack, *Vergil in the Mind of Augustine*, ch. 3.

For Augustine, the flesh is "weake" (Mt. 26:41), but not inherently sinful. At some level, Spenser probably believed both: that flesh is weak, and spirit too. It is a question of emphasis, and the deciding factor is tone. In religions that take it seriously (I am not talking here about Hollywood fads), reincarnation is always a curse or punishment. But in the Garden of Adonis, there is only one "enimy" and that is "wicked *Tyme*" (*FQ* 3.6.39). Spenser's wish, apparently, is for the body to last indefinitely. Virgil is more like Hamlet: Oh, that this too, too solid flesh would melt, thaw, and resolve itself into adieu! When he finds out that we are all, most of us, going to want bodies a second time, Aeneas is disgusted: *quæ lucis miseris tam dira cupido?*[158] "What is this craving, so loathsome, that wretches have for light?" The key phrase, *dira cupido*, comes from Lucretius, who uses it to describe the greedy, unquenchable desire of romantic love (*De rerum natura* 4.1090). That kind of longing – which cannot be satisfied with mere copulation – is a burden; and it repels Lucretius with the same force, apparently, that having a body repels Aeneas. He is afraid, like Hamlet, of tainting his mind. Spenser, though, is not squeamish at all. Indeed, the Garden is almost the only place in his writing where there seems to be no moralizing of any kind. We call this pagan, but the tone is wrong for that. Precisely where the real pagans were dour, Spenser is famously cheerful, with frank courtship, "goodly meriment, and gay felicity" (*FQ* 3.6.41). Anchises would say that Spenser is missing the point. He has got the details of reincarnation right, because they all come from classical texts. But the spirit of those texts he has perversely ignored.

Yet Anchises would be mistaken (not for the first time). Spenser is reading the texts, but he is doing so through the filter of patristic response. This response is well documented.[159] The Fathers all knew their *Aeneid*, especially the sixth book, and they all rejected its doctrine of soul migration. Indeed, Lactantius and Augustine both quote the description of reincarnation to illustrate what (for the Christian) is so unsatisfying about Plato's idea of the afterlife: that it permits no rest to the soul after death, but thrusts it back repeatedly into the material world, where it suffers all the heartache and the thousand natural shocks that flesh is heir to.[160] "Yet," says

---

[158] *Aen.* 6.721 (Giunta 1544, fol. 353ʳ).
[159] See Courcelle, "Pères de l'église"; and Courcelle, *Lecteurs païens et lecteurs chrétiens de l'Énéide*, 2 vols. (Paris: Institut de France, 1984, 1989), vol. 1, pp. 483–93.
[160] Lactantius, *Divinae institutiones* 7.22; and Augustine, *De civitate dei* 10.30 (citing *Aen.* 6.719–21 and 750–52, respectively). In the same chapter, Lactantius cites Virgil's reference to the thousand-year interval between death and reincarnation (*Aen.* 7.748–51) in order to correct it: according to Lactantius, there *will* be a millennial period, but it will follow the resurrection, not precede it.

Lactantius, "I cannot blame those who hold this opinion, because they perceived this truth," namely, that the soul survives the death of the body.[161] Jerome makes the same argument.[162] Augustine goes even further, saying that if only one combined the insight of Plato (who understood that the soul must return to the body after death) with that of Porphyry (who perceived that the beatified soul does not return to misery) and Varro (who correctly observed that the reincarnate soul would seek out its own body, not a new one), the result was Christian resurrection. So Plato and Virgil were on the right track after all.[163]

Lactantius and Augustine were writing theology, not literary criticism. Nevertheless, what they wrote about Virgil's text became, in the Renaissance, part of the scholarly apparatus. Thus, when it is time to explain why souls in Elysium "begin once more to have the will to turn back into bodies" (*Aen.* 6.749), the Jesuit scholar known as Jacobus Pontanus ("Jakob Spanmueller" to his mother) gives a lengthy quotation from Lactantius.[164] Other commentators just summarized Lactantius, as Melanchthon does: "From this passage, Lactantius gathered that the resurrection of the dead was not unheard of (*inauditam*) even by the poets."[165]

Or the name of Lactantius could disappear altogether. Craig Kallendorf has been studying the marginalia in printed editions of Virgil, and in one of them (annotated *c.* 1610) there appears, next to Anchises' first mention of reincarnation, this annotation: "it alludes, apparently, to the resurrection of bodies."[166] Where did this come from? The main source for most of the annotations in this volume is Badius Ascensius; but in this case, Badius is content merely to give a detailed explanation of the Platonic doctrine, pointing out where it differs from *fides nostra*.[167] Perhaps the annotator was also a student of patristic theology.

But one did not actually have to read the Fathers in order to absorb their teaching about Virgil. This particular annotator seems to have been a schoolteacher, and as such he would probably have known, even if he did not use, the Latin textbook *Illustrium poetarum flores* (1512) by Octavianus Mirandula. An anthology of quotations culled from the Latin poets, this little volume was intended for grammar schools, and is where many a

---

[161] Lactantius, *Divinae institutiones* 3.18.
[162] See Courcelle, "Interprétations néo-platonisantes," p. 114.
[163] Augustine, *De civitate dei* 22.26–28; see also 10.30.
[164] Pontanus on *Aen.* 6.749, in *Symbolae*, col. 1510, citing Lactantius, *Divinae institutiones* 3.18 and 7.22.
[165] Melanchthon on *Aen.* 6.749, in *P. Vergilii Maronis poemata* (Zurich: Christoph Froschauer, 1561).
[166] Kallendorf, *Virgil and the Myth of Venice*, p. 59.
[167] Badius on *Aen.* 6.713ff. (Giunta 1544, fol. 353^{r-v}).

schoolboy had his first exposure to the greatest hits and purple passages of Ovid, Virgil, and Terence.[168] It is useful to us, partly because it tells us which lines were most familiar, but also because the quotations are organized thematically (as in *Bartlett's Familiar Quotations*). This, in turn, tells us something of the context in which a passage was interpreted. As it happens, Virgil's description of soul migration is one of the excerpts in Mirandula's anthology. This suggests that the passage was well known. That it appears under the heading "De resurrectione" suggests, furthermore, that the patristic reading of this passage, in which the pagan error was interpreted as a half-way house to Christian truth, was also well known, not merely to the learned, but even to schoolboys.[169]

Scholarship on Ovid was affected in the same way. In the last book of *Metamorphoses*, the philosopher Pythagoras gives a long sermon which is, in fact, a parody of Anchises' speech in the underworld. Nothing is the same for ever, teaches Pythagoras, and after death the souls of men pass into animals; ergo – and this, apparently, is the point of the whole oration – we should all become vegetarians (*Met.* 15.60–478). In the Renaissance, this speech was understood as a summation of the whole poem, but not in its literal meaning. Pontanus, in his 1610 commentary, quotes Lactantius to the effect that this ridiculous doctrine of soul migration should be refuted with laughter rather than argument.[170] And this, as we have said, is how the Elizabethans treated it. But the more serious approach was also in evidence. George Sandys (1578–1644), who translated Ovid and wrote a commentary on him in the decades after Spenser died, gave as a gloss on the sermon, first a quotation from Virgil, to show what the doctrine was, and then a paraphrase of Augustine, to show how it anticipates Christian teaching about the resurrection.[171] Sandys is cautious: Virgil and Ovid (the "Ethnick" or pagan poets) did not grasp the truth wholly, but gathered it by glimpses. But even this is cause for wonder. Harington marvels: "to say trewly of vergill,

---

[168] See Baldwin, *Small Latine*, vol. II, pp. 386–89.

[169] Octavianus Mirandula, *Illustrium poetarum flores, per Octavianum Mirandulam collecta et à studioso quodam summa diligentia in locos communes digesti* (Lyons: Joannes Tornaesius, 1579), pp. 615–17. The section begins with a quotation from the *Eclogues*, where Virgil alludes to the cycles of history (4.31–36). Mirandula explains: "There will be a resurrection of the dead, according to the Platonists when they are understood supernaturally; but when they are understood naturally, their opinion seems false." On *Aen.* 6.744–51 and the longing for new bodies, he comments, "From this we can elicit the truth, that there will be a resurrection of the dead."

[170] Pontanus on *Met.* 15.160, quoting Lactantius, *Divinae institutiones* 7.12, in *Ex P. Ouidii Nasonis metamorphoseon libris xv electorum libri totidem* (Antwerp: Heirs of Martinus Nutius, 1618).

[171] Sandys, *Ovid's Metamorphosis*, p. 697. On the Sandys commentary, see Lyne, *Ovid's Changing Worlds*, ch. 4.

consydering hee had but the lyght of nature, yt ys strawng to see how hee roves at the trewth – though hee hit yt not perfectly."[172]

IMITATION: COMPETITION OR ASSIMILATION?

That phrase "not perfectly" strikes what I take is the right balance in describing Virgil's status in the Renaissance, both as a pagan and as a predecessor. It acknowledges what one scholar has called "the difference that history makes,"[173] in a way that is critical and, at the same time, conciliatory. Both elements need to be emphasized. Today, probably the most influential account of Renaissance poets and their classical predecessors is *The Light in Troy* (1982) by the late Thomas M. Greene. The central figure in Greene's study is Petrarch; and Petrarch was, like Milton, a highly competitive poet. This results, I suspect, in a distortion of emphasis. For Greene, the most important kind of imitation is what he calls heuristic or dialectical imitation, an Oedipal *agon* with the great father-poets of antiquity. Greene is, of course, right when he says that poets were supposed to surpass their predecessors (as when Gabriel Harvey says that Spenser will "ouergo" Ariosto in *The Faerie Queene*).[174] As Quintilian explains, "even those who do not aim for the heights (*summa*) ought rather to compete than follow. For one who strives to be first will perhaps draw even (*aequabit*) with someone, even if he does not pass (*transierit*) him. But no one can equal a man by planning to stand in his footsteps – for the one who follows will always be behind."[175] Spenser, it is clear, does aim for the heights. But, according to Greene, his "sense of historical self-consciousness is sporadic and dim." Unlike Petrarch (and, we might add, Dante), Spenser seems "unconcerned with the exercise of bridging a rupture and playing with the differences between the separated worlds." Although his poems contain numerous allusions to classical poetry, the allusions lack that sense of "etiological firmness" – of where the poet came from and how far he has traveled – which for Greene is the defining feature of Renaissance sensibility.[176]

---

[172] Harington, "Of Paradise and the state of the godly" (ed. Cauchi, p. 77).
[173] Margaret Tudeau-Clayton, *Jonson, Shakespeare and Early Modern Virgil* (Cambridge University Press, 1998), p. 23.
[174] *The Works of Edmund Spenser: A Variorum Edition*, ed. Edwin Greenlaw et al., 11 vols. (Baltimore: Johns Hopkins University Press, 1932–57), vol. x, p. 471.
[175] Quintilian, *Institutio oratoria* 10.2.9–10.
[176] Thomas M. Greene, *The Light in Troy: Imitation and Discovery in Renaissance Poetry* (New Haven: Yale University Press, 1982), pp. 270–74.

We can respond to this by showing that Spenser had more firmness than Greene gives him credit for.[177] Or we can challenge the norm of competition.[178] In an earlier study, which Greene acknowledges, G. W. Pigman III discriminates three versions of imitation, of which the eristic type championed by Greene is only one; the other two he calls transformative and dissimulative.[179] As an example of the non-competitive imitator, Pigman cites Lucretius in his invocation to Epicurus: "I follow [*sequor*] you, glory of the Greeks, and I place my footsteps [*vestigia*] firmly in your footprints, not desiring to compete [*certandi cupidus*], but because my love for you makes me long to imitate you. For why would the swallow contend [*contendat*] with swans?"[180] This is an extreme instance and most poets (one suspects) practiced all three versions of imitation, in combination and in various proportions. In Petrarch, it is safe to say, the element of competition was foremost. Spenser, it seems, was more inclined to dissimulation (which makes light of one's learning as well as one's debts) and especially to transformation.

The Garden of Adonis, which we looked at earlier, is an example. The imagery of the Garden, if not the doctrine, is drawn from Ovid and Virgil. But there is a gap, I have argued, between imagery and tone, which can be accounted for by what the Church Fathers said about reincarnation. Yes, the pagan doctrine was misguided, error-ridden, and absurd; but in that benighted era, it conveyed a profound truth: the soul is meant to live forever, and (what is more) the soul is meant to live forever *in the body*. That Virgil taught this in such a tortured, misleading way was lamentable, but not irremediable. For those who had ears to hear, the poet said more than he knew.

The Garden, though, is not paradise. Time is at large; and while there is no jealousy, quarreling, or playing-hard-to-get – "Franckly each Paramor his leman knowes" (*FQ* 3.6.41) – there is no conversation, either, only babies and sex. It is a good life, for a bunny, but not a human being. Biologically, sex is what perpetuates the various species, but it does not preserve individuals. Spenser's Venus is like Nature in Tennyson:

---

[177] See David Galbraith, *Architectonics of Imitation in Spenser, Daniel, and Drayton* (Toronto: University of Toronto Press, 2000), ch. 3; Colin Burrow, "Spenser and Classical Traditions," in *The Cambridge Companion to Spenser*, ed. Andrew Hadfield (Cambridge University Press, 2001), pp. 217–36; and Lyne, *Ovid's Changing Worlds*, ch. 2, esp. pp. 86–87.
[178] This is rarer, but see Theresa M. Krier, *Gazing on Secret Sights: Spenser, Classical Imitation, and the Decorums of Vision* (Ithaca, NY: Cornell University Press, 1990), p. 79.
[179] G. W. Pigman III, "Versions of Imitation in the Renaissance," *Renaissance Quarterly* 33 (1980), 1–32.
[180] *De rerum natura* 3.3–7, as qtd. in Pigman, "Versions," 19.

> So careful of the type she seems,
> So careless of the single life.

The Garden of Adonis is what Harry Berger has called an "archaic" mode of immortality.[181] It looks forward to resurrection, but stops short at repetition. There is a parallel in the history of ideas. According to Caroline Bynum, "The seed is the oldest Christian metaphor for the resurrection of the body."[182] She goes on, however, to show that the seed metaphor did not end up being used much by the Church, because it was not specific enough. In the resurrection, it is supposed to be the identity of the whole person that revives, including the body; according to most authorities, this is not just going to be formal identity, but particulate, material identity, of individual cells.

In being a cheerful place, the Garden understands more than Virgil, but still less than Spenser, about bodies and immortality. The cheerfulness, though, is not a rebuke to Virgil, but a sublimation, a transvaluation of Virgil's imagery. If he were really competing with Virgil, Spenser ought to be making more noise – as when Milton brags, "dialectically," that his story is

> Not less but more heroic than the wrath
> Of stern Achilles on his foe pursued
> Thrice fugitive about Troy wall; or rage
> Of Turnus for Lavinia disespoused;
> Or Neptune's ire, or Juno's, that so long
> Perplexed the Greek and Cytherea's son. (*Paradise Lost* 9.13–19)

That is not Spenser's way. Nor was it Virgil's, imitating Homer. As a modern poet, and Christian, Spenser's strategy is not to refute Virgil so much as transcend him.

DYNASTIC PROPHECY

This raises a broader question about Renaissance poets and their Roman models. When a poet like Spenser imitates Virgil, what is it, exactly, that he imitates: the words of the poet or his intentions? In the Renaissance, this

---

[181] Harry Berger, *Revisionary Play: Studies in the Spenserian Dynamics* (Berkeley and Los Angeles: University of California Press, 1988), pp. 36–50, 173–83, 195–214, 243–73. See also Fletcher on historical development (*Prophetic Moment*, ch. 4) and Kaske on image sequences (*Biblical Poetics*, ch. 3).
[182] Caroline Bynum, *The Resurrection of the Body in Western Christianity, 200–1336* (New York: Columbia University Press, 1995), p. 5.

was the subject of a great controversy, which was not resolved in Spenser's lifetime.[183] Like the debate over Virgil's name, it turned on the question of whether Latin should be treated as a modern language or a classical one. Erasmus argued, in his famous *Ciceronianus* (1528), that the world has changed since Cicero's time and new ideas (such as Christianity) deserve new words. Of course, we can still learn from Cicero, but what we should imitate are his techniques. This argument was renewed by Peter Ramus in 1557, and by Spenser's friend Gabriel Harvey in 1576. Here is Harvey, quoting Ramus: "The one who would imitate Cicero should contemplate the sources (*principia*) of his eloquence, rather than the surfaces (*extrema*)."[184] In Cicero's case, this is easier, because he composed dialogues on oratorical technique. Virgil, though, left behind no *ars poetica*. How then is one to discover the sources of his eloquence? One way is through commentary.

Let us go back to reincarnation for a moment. There is one more response to reincarnation which we have not considered yet and it comes, as most of these things do, from Servius. Before leaving the underworld through a gate of false dreams, Aeneas views a parade of heroes from Roman history. According to Servius, the purpose of the parade is "to celebrate the Romans and especially Augustus," since many of the worthies are his ancestors. In order to do this, however, Virgil must first solve a technical problem: under what possible circumstances could all of these heroes, from various epochs in Roman history, be gathered in one place and time? The solution is reincarnation: Aeneas sees all of the heroes as unborn souls, who are assembled by Lethe's banks in order to obtain new bodies. And that, according to Servius, is why the speech on reincarnation had to come before the parade, so that the parade would be plausible.[185]

Servius is not trying to wriggle out of reincarnation. Rather, he wants the reader to think about its function in the poem. And, for Servius, reincarnation is both a philosophical doctrine and a literary technique for praising Augustus. The sermon, then, has two purposes: to teach and to celebrate. Virgil, characteristically, combines these functions, and in doing so preserves brevity. But later writers would often separate them. Thus, according

---

[183] For the course of this debate in the sixteenth century, see G. W. Pigman III, "Imitation and the Renaissance Sense of the Past: The Reception of Erasmus' *Ciceronianus*," *Journal of Medieval and Renaissance Studies* 9 (1979), 155–77; prior to Erasmus, see Martin L. McLaughlin, *Literary Imitation in the Italian Renaissance: The Theory and Practice of Literary Imitation in Italy from Dante to Bembo* (Oxford: Clarendon Press, 1995), esp. ch. 12.

[184] *Gabriel Harvey's Ciceronianus*, ed. Harold S. Wilson (Lincoln: University of Nebraska Press, 1945), p. 72.

[185] Servius on *Aen.* 6.752 (Giunta 1544, fol. 355^v).

to Melanchthon, reincarnation is "A wondrous device (*Mira inuentio*) of the Poet, by means of which he digresses to Roman history." And a bit earlier, when the episode begins: "This lays the groundwork for those things which are rehearsed about the posterity of Aeneas and in praise of the Julian household."[186] Melanchthon does not believe in Virgil's doctrine, but he admires his skill as an artist. This assumes that the critic knows what the artist is thinking, what he is trying to accomplish. And Servius thought he did know: at the very beginning of his commentary on the *Aeneid*, he states baldly that Virgil's goal (*Intentio Virgilij*) is "to imitate Homer and to praise Augustus through his ancestors."[187]

Almost all epics in the Renaissance include at least one tableau of dynastic history, and several poets would adopt Virgil's device of a parade in the underworld.[188] Of these imitations, the most faithful was Ronsard's, who in the fourth book of his *Franciade* (1572) makes the hero descend *en enfer* to see his progeny, the kings of France, while they wait around for new bodies. This, explains the *argument en prose*, is "the Pythagorean philosophy which the Greeks called 'metempsychosis.'" For Ronsard, this is a device not a creed. "The Author makes use of this false opinion on purpose, as a plausible way for the spirits of our Kings to come in new bodies: for without such a device, it would not have failed to seem more like history than poetry."[189] Ronsard avoids the fault of Lucan's poem (too many raw facts), but not its fate: like *Pharsalia*, the *Franciade* was never finished.

Most imitations of Virgil are less literal than Ronsard's. The intention is the same ("to praise Augustus") but the device changes. Thus, in Ariosto, Bradamante goes down into Merlin's cave and sees a parade of her ancestors. As in Virgil, these are also the ancestors of the poet's patron. But there is no sermon here on soul migration, for the figures in Merlin's cave are not preexistent souls, but *spirti*, conjured (says Ariosto) "from hell or I know not where," and made up to look like members of the Este clan (*OF* 3.20). Alonso de Ercilla borrows from this scene in Canto 23 of his *Araucana* (1569–89). While in Chile, Ercilla visits Fitón, a magician who lives in a cave, in order to learn about events back in Europe. In Virgil, the entrance to Avernus is guarded by various forms of death: old age, sickness, war; in real life, this is how one "goes" to the underworld. But in Ercilla, the

---

[186] Melanchthon on *Aen.* 6.755, 711, in *P. Vergilii Maronis poemata* (1561 edn.).
[187] Servius, preface to *Aen.* (Giunta 1544, fol. 146ʳ).
[188] See Andrew Fichter, *Poets Historical: Dynastic Epic in the Renaissance* (New Haven: Yale University Press, 1982).
[189] Ronsard, *Œuvres complètes*, ed. Paul Laumonier *et al.*, 20 vols. (Paris: Société des Textes Français Modernes, 1914–75), vol. XVI, p. 18.

entrance to Fitón's cave is crowded with paraphernalia for practicing witchcraft: spittle of rabid dog, heart of griffin, menstrual blood, and so on. Inside there is a crystal ball, animated by demons, in which Ercilla beholds a prophecy of what will happen in 1571, at the battle of Lepanto. In Ercilla's telling, the hero of Lepanto is Don John of Austria, the half-brother of Philip II of Spain. Philip was Ercilla's patron, and Ercilla uses the prophecy to praise his family. Demons are used, but not reincarnation. Spenser uses the same technique in the episode of Merlin's cave that we looked at earlier. Britomart goes into the cave and sees (or hears about, it is not clear which) all of the children and grandchildren she is going to have with her future husband, ending with Spenser's would-be patroness, Queen Elizabeth.

As in Ariosto, the prophecy is a pantomime played by demons. Spenser probably believed in demons, in a way that he did not believe in reincarnation. But that is not, I think, why he separates praise (in Merlin's cave) from reincarnation (in the Garden of Adonis). As a device for praise, reincarnation was dispensable. But as a doctrine, reincarnation had its own use, as a parable about resurrection. There is a lesson here about imitation in general. When, in *Orlando furioso* (which, of course, was Spenser's direct source), the heroine goes down into Merlin's cave, we think of Aeneas going down into Avernus; to complete the parallel, there is even a female guide, named Melissa. But Merlin's cave is not literally the underworld: as we have seen, that is a place where living heroes do not actually go. Instead, the cave performs one of the traditional functions of the underworld, which is to praise one's patron by parading his ancestors. The underworld has other functions, as we have seen: for example, to contemplate vice. But it's the function that poets imitate, not the place.

CHAPTER 6

Virgil's Iliad

> Know'st thou not there is but one theme for ever-enduring bards?
> And that is the theme of War, the fortune of battles,
> The making of perfect soldiers.
> > Walt Whitman, "As I Ponder'd in Silence"

From antiquity onward, the *Aeneid* was divided into two parts: an Odyssean half, of wanderings, and an Iliadic half, of wars. Interpretation of Books 1 through 6 followed the outlines established by ancient commentaries on Homer's *Odyssey*, in which the journey of the hero was allegorized as the soul's progress from sensuality to wisdom. The main difference was that commentaries on the *Aeneid* gave far more attention to the underworld.

Commentary on the second half of the *Aeneid* was less focused, in that no one episode dominated interpretation. There is a contrast here, not only with the first six books, but with much of recent scholarship. More than anything, the episode that has occupied critics in our own time is the death of Turnus in Book 12. In deference to this, we shall begin there, with the ending. But that is a concession: as we shall see, the death of Turnus was important in the Renaissance, but it was not the defining moment of the whole poem.

TURNUS AS TRAGIC HERO

The abruptness of Virgil's ending makes it one of the most provocative in ancient literature.[1] That Aeneas would have to confront Turnus was predictable. The surprise is that Turnus, heretofore fearless, should break down

---

[1] Philip Hardie, "Closure in Latin Epic," in *Classical Closure: Reading the End in Greek and Latin Literature*, ed. Deborah H. Roberts, Francis M. Dunn, and Don Fowler (Princeton: Princeton University Press, 1997), pp. 139–62.

and beg for mercy. What follows is even more astonishing. Aeneas has decided, apparently, to spare Turnus, when his eyes light upon a decorated swordbelt that belonged formerly to his young friend Pallas, dead lately by Turnus' hand. Reminded of his loss, "kindled with rage and grim with anger," Aeneas changes his mind and buries his sword in the suppliant's chest. The limbs of Turnus turn cold, and his spirit goes howling down to Hades. And there the poem breaks off.

Is there a page missing? Did Virgil leave his epic unfinished, as well as unrevised?[2] There is no chorus to tell us what it means, but the concentration of effect – a consequence, perhaps, of Virgil's brevity – recalls the stark and sudden turnings of classical tragedy. As well it might: not only was Virgil well versed in both Greek and Roman drama,[3] but his epic model, Homer's *Iliad*, was also classified in the ancient world as a type of tragedy.[4] Aristotle had said, in the *Poetics*, that an epic might provide material for one or more tragedies, and Minturno, in his *De poeta* (1559), claimed that Virgil's *Aeneid* would furnish the plots or seeds for at least two: a tragedy of Pallas, killed by Turnus, and a tragedy of Turnus, killed by Aeneas.[5]

Does that mean Turnus is a tragic hero? The answer, in the Renaissance, was a qualified *yes*. Or, rather, a double *yes*: yes, Turnus is heroic and, yes, he still needs killing.

Turnus has been called, by critics who defend Aeneas, "a thug."[6] His crimes are grave enough; and yet, historically, the judgment has been more mild. Macrobius, in the *Saturnalia*, refers to the death of Turnus three times and all of them come from the same speech: the plea for clemency. Thus, for Macrobius, *Aen.* 12.933–34 ("And such was your own father, Anchises") illustrates the rhetorical figure *homoiopatheia*, which is the *pathos* that is born from "similarity of feeling."[7] The second half of the same line ("Have pity on the old age of Daunus") is likewise quoted to show how "elegantly" Virgil makes reference to all the stages of maturity – from infancy to old

---

[2] According to Donatus 35, Virgil had only just started to revise the *Aeneid* when he died of sunstroke at Brindisi (Giunta 1544, sig. *ii^v).
[3] See Philip Hardie, "Virgil and Tragedy," in *The Cambridge Companion to Virgil*, ed. Charles Martindale (Cambridge University Press, 1997), pp. 312–26.
[4] Servius on *Aen.* 7.1 (Giunta 1544, fol. 362^r).
[5] Antonio Sebastiano Minturno, *De poeta* (Venice, 1599), Bk. 2 (p. 152).
[6] M. M. Willcock, "Battle Scenes in the *Aeneid*," *Proceedings of the Cambridge Philological Society* 209 (1983), 87–99, at 94; qtd. with approval by Karl Galinsky, "The Anger of Aeneas," *American Journal of Philology* 109 (1988), 321–48, at 323.
[7] Macrobius, *Saturnalia* 4.6.9, in [*Opera*] (Venice: s.n., 1492), fol. lv^v.

age – in order to arouse pity.⁸ Macrobius does not say that Turnus ought to have been spared – or that he ought to have been killed. For modern readers, this is one of the things that makes *Saturnalia* so frustrating: although the main subject of the dialogue is Virgil's poetry, it is not primarily concerned with interpretation, but with rhetorical technique.⁹ We shall return to this theme in our epilogue.

Turnus' technique is superb. He is also courageous. True, he does run away at the end: in this, he is like Hector, running away from Achilles. But there is, says Tasso, this difference between them: whereas Hector fled out of fear, Turnus flees because his sword breaks; his failure, therefore, is one of arms (*arme*) not of courage (*animo*).¹⁰ Tasso is an admirer of Virgil's ending and in the *Liberata* he imitates it at least three times (*GL* 7.93–95, 19.8–26, 20.103–7). The third time comes in Canto 20, when Rinaldo kills Solimano, the Turkish sultan. The emphasis here is on the sultan's sudden paralysis. Like Turnus before him (and Hector before that), Solimano is likened to a man who runs in his sleep: straining his limbs, still he can make no progress (*GL* 20.105; cf. *Aen.* 12.908–12, *Il.* 22.199–201). Before it was published, Tasso predicted that the scene would be controversial: "The death of the sultan in the last canto will not be pleasing to those who are displeased by the death of Turnus: for I believe that Virgil did what he did for many reasons, and some of them I believe I know."¹¹ From his later writings it is clear what Tasso had in mind: the accusation that Turnus was a coward. But Turnus did not, says Tasso, give way to fear out of prudence, much less cravenness, but rather because he was overwhelmed by fate: "It is the gods who make me to know fear, and Jupiter's hostility" (*Aen.* 12.895). Tasso's sultan has the same reaction and the same nobility: when he sees the force of Rinaldo's sword, he trembles and goes pale; before that, however, fear was a stranger to his nature and it is only on account of "eternal decree" (the Christian version of fate) that it takes hold of him now (*GL* 20.104).

---

⁸ Macrobius, *Saturnalia* 4.3.1–5 (1492 edn., fol. liiiiʳ). See also 4.2.11 (fol. liiiiʳ).
⁹ In the work's preface, Macrobius says that everything contained therein is calculated "to make your wit quicker, to prop up your memory, to make your discourse more nimble and your speech more correct" (*Saturnalia* 1.1.11; 1492 edn., sig. eiiᵛ).
¹⁰ Tasso, "Il forno overo della nobiltà," in *Dialoghi*, ed. Ezio Raimondi, 3 vols. in 4 (Florence: Sansoni, 1958), vol. III, p. 57. Other authors who praised Turnus' courage include Pier Candido Decembrio (1392–1497) and Giovanni Pontano (1426–1503); see Craig Kallendorf, *The Other Virgil* (Oxford: Clarendon Press, 2007), pp. 42–44.
¹¹ Tasso, Letter to Scipione Gonzaga (Oct. 4, 1575), in *Lettere poetiche*, ed. Carla Molinari (Parma: Guanda, 1995), p. 246; for Tasso's later writings on this subject, see Molinari's long note on pp. 246–47.

MODERN RELATIVISM

Tasso admires Turnus for his fortitude, and he makes the sultan admirable as well. And yet there is no question but that both men shall have to die.[12] As a genre of oratory, tragedy is a form of sublimation, not of vindication; else we should say (for example) that Macbeth is noble, because he dies bravely. Turnus must be killed, as Tasso explains in his *Discourses on the Heroic Poem* (1594), for "reasons of state," because he is a treaty-breaker and will trouble the peace if he survives; for religion, to provide a human sacrifice; and for revenge. The sacrifice is to appease Pallas' shade in the underworld. It is a barbarous custom, "impious and cruel," but that is a fault (says Tasso) in Virgil's religion, not his art. As for vengeance, Aeneas must be judged according to the standards of his own culture, since, for a pagan knight (*cavaliero gentile*), it was both just and lawful to pursue *la vendetta*.[13]

As a critic, Tasso is working largely from internal evidence: he quotes from Book 11 to show that Aeneas is obligated by Pallas' father to avenge his death, and from Book 10 to explain the custom of human sacrifice. Tasso also compares Virgil with his model, noting (for example) that when Hector kills Patroclus, Achilles does not have as much of an excuse for vengeance, because there was no word from Patroclus' father, and because Hector has broken no treaties. Compared with Homer, then, Virgil is *relatively* civilized.

Tasso is not a complete relativist. Unlike Cinzio, for example, he does not believe there is one law for ancient poetry, another for modern. Mores, though – what Tasso calls the *costumi* of dress, tactics, etiquette, and religion – are subject to alteration, and poets must keep pace. Thus, while it is proper for a Christian poet to adopt the form of classical epic, it would not be proper to invoke the aid of pagan deities. Some things that were right for Homer were wrong for Virgil, and some things that were right for Virgil would be wrong for a modern.

This explains what otherwise looks like an inconsistency between Tasso's criticism and his poetry. In prose, Tasso defends the death of Turnus, but in verse he alters the scene to conform with modern *costumi*. Ariosto had done the same thing in *Orlando furioso*, and so would Spenser in *The Faerie Queene*.

---

[12] As Hotspur must die in Shakespeare; see Martin Mueller, "Turnus and Hotspur: The Political Adversary in the *Aeneid* and *Henry IV*," *Phoenix* 23 (1969), 278–90.
[13] Tasso, *Discorsi del poema eroico* (1594), Bk. 3, in *Prose*, ed. Ettore Mazzali (Milan: Ricciardi, 1959), pp. 610–14.

For all three poets, the problem was the same: Aeneas and Turnus are considered to be engaged in a duel and, in a duel, a Christian knight cannot refuse quarter to a surrendered adversary.[14] The solution was worked out by Ariosto and, once he had shown the way, other poets followed. At the very end of *Orlando furioso* (1516), the Christian knight Ruggiero is attacked at his own wedding by the Saracen knight Rodomonte. Ruggiero gains the advantage, but Rodomonte will not yield, and fights on. It is therefore only in self-defense that Ruggiero kills Rodomonte, whose limbs grow cold and whose spirit goes down howling to the underworld (*OF* 46.140). As a modern version of Virgil's ending, it is complete in every way, except for the mercy plea. With no plea, there can be no rejection, and no offense to modern morality. With no plea, there is also more obvious courage on the part of the Turnus-figure. He must still die, of course – and yet it seems a shame to waste all of that dauntlessness. The result is that Rodomonte becomes less like Virgil's Turnus and more like his Mezentius: savage in battle, even cruel, and then, in death, suddenly tragic. Nothing in his life becomes him like the leaving it.

Tasso borrowed from this solution with both hands. When, in Canto 19 of *Jerusalem Delivered* (1581), the Christian knight Tancredi fights with the pagan knight Argante, the Christian knight gains, once more, the upper hand. Like Ruggiero, he implores his opponent to yield; like Rodomonte, the pagan knight refuses to surrender and fights doggedly on. Tancredi has no choice but to kill his foe, and both their honors are saved: Tancredi's by offering mercy, Argante's by refusing it.[15]

Spenser uses a similar approach in *The Faerie Queene*. In Book 2, Prince Arthur subdues the pagan knight Pyrochles and bids him yield. But Pyrochles, who is an embodiment of stubborn rage, scorns submission.[16] Arthur is "sory" that his foe

> so wilfully refused grace;
> Yet sith his fate so cruelly did fall,
> His shining Helmet he gan soone vnlace,
> And left his headlesse body bleeding all the place. (*FQ* 2.8.52)

---

[14] See Lauren Scancarelli Seem, "The Limits of Chivalry: Tasso and the End of the *Aeneid*," *Comparative Literature* 42 (1990), 116–25. Armies in the Renaissance were more pragmatic: according to J. R. Hale, *War and Society in Renaissance Europe 1450–1620* (New York: St. Martin's Press, 1985), pp. 193–97, the real bar to pillaging a surrendered town was not "Christian charity" but the likelihood that one's troops would have nothing left to live on after the orgy.

[15] See Colin Burrow, *Epic Romance from Homer to Milton* (Oxford: Clarendon Press, 1993), pp. 127–31.

[16] See A. C. Hamilton, *The Structure of Allegory in* The Faerie Queene (Oxford: Clarendon Press, 1961), pp. 112–16; Michael Leslie, *Spenser's "Fierce Warres and Faithfull Loues": Martial and Chivalric Symbolism in* The Faerie Queene (Cambridge: Brewer, 1983), pp. 92–98; Burrow, *Epic Romance*, pp. 128, 130–31.

Who cares? No reader that I know of has ever felt sorry for Pyrochles, or wished that somehow he might have been spared. He is a minor character whose death (as Hamlet would say) comes not near us. Nor, I think, do we much applaud Arthur for his hesitation. His sentiments are correct, but they are expended on such an airy nothing that they hardly matter.

The death of Turnus has been sterilized. Occasionally, there are signs of the ancient flame, but only in parody. In Sidney's *New Arcadia* (1593), the wicked and brutish knight Lycurgus submits to Zelmane in single combat and pleads for mercy. Unfortunately, Lycurgus wears on his arm a bracelet which Zelmane had received from his aunt and given as a love-token to the princess Philoclea. Furious with jealousy, Zelmane cries out, "No villain, die! It is Philoclea that sends thee this token for thy love" and stabs Lycurgus in the heart – though Lycurgus, "wresting his body, and with a countenance prepared to excuse, would fain have delayed the receiving of death's embassadors."[17] Unlike the Aeneas-figures in Ariosto, Tasso, and Spenser, Zelmane is a pagan. Even so, killing Lycurgus is hard to justify, since Philoclea is still alive and also still chaste; Lycurgus has only stolen her bracelet, nothing more. There is mockery here, but of whom? Another parody of the death of Turnus occurs at the end of Spenser's mock epic *Muiopotmos* (1591), when the butterfly Clarion is killed in single combat with the spider Aragnoll. Trapped in Aragnoll's web, Clarion resigned himself "to the mercie of th'auenger" (l. 432), but the spider

> siezed greedelie
> On the resistles pray, and with fell spight,
> Vnder the left wing stroke his weapon slie
> Into his heart, that his deepe groning spright
> In bloodie streames foorth fled into the aire,
> His bodie left the spectacle of care.   (*Muiopotmos* 435–40)

The roles of hero and villain have been reversed: Turnus is the butterfly and Aeneas is the spider, a "greisly tyrant" (l. 433). Our sympathies now are all with Turnus, but the stakes are lower too: the spider is just doing what spiders do, he is not a Christian and, anyway, Clarion is just a bug.

DEFINING *PIETAS*

As poets, Tasso and the rest tried to accommodate Virgil's ending to the *costumi* of their own times. But as a critic, Tasso was determined to employ

---

[17] Sir Philip Sidney, *The Countess of Pembroke's Arcadia* (*New Arcadia*), ed. Victor Skretkowicz (Oxford: Clarendon Press, 1987), p. 462. See Thomas P. Roche, Jr., "Ending the *New Arcadia*: Virgil and Ariosto," *Sidney Newsletter* 10 (1989), 3–12.

historical criteria. This is the method of modern classicists, as well, and yet there is still vigorous debate about which standards are relevant: the rules of war? the reasons of state? the ethics of Philodemus? of Zeno?[18]

The main points of controversy are two. One is the problem of defining *pietas*, a word which means "dutifulness," but which is also related to *pity*.[19] Centuries before Virgil, Aeneas was memorialized in drama, art, and coinage as the hero who rescued his father from Troy by carrying him on his back.[20] Turnus appeals to this reputation for specifically filial piety when he asks to be spared for the sake of his old parent Daunus: "You too had such a father in Anchises."[21] The appeal moves Aeneas, but he kills Turnus anyway. What has become here of Anchises' injunction "to spare the humbled" (*Aen.* 6.853)? Is there a contradiction here, or a compromise?

The problem (again) is an old one and was posed a full century before Servius, by Lactantius (*c.* 240–*c.* 320). According to Lactantius, Aeneas' reputation for *pietas* was based entirely on filial devotion. No man, though, should be called *pius* who, when he is entreated in the name of his father, slays those who do not fight back and who plead for mercy.[22] Lactantius quotes from Virgil extensively, mostly as an authority.[23] But on this one occasion he trains his gun on the poet himself. Why? The title of the work explains everything. *Seven Books of Divine Teachings against the Pagans*, is, like Augustine's *City of God*, simultaneously a defense of Christian teaching and a critique of pagan morality. Hence the attack on Virgil's hero: Aeneas is an example of Roman morality at its finest, and if it can be shown that he is impius, then the morality which he represents is impius as well.

Lactantius finished the *Divine Teachings* in 311, when Christianity was still on the defensive. One year later, the emperor Constantine had his famous vision of the cross and the pace of conversion accelerated. Within a hundred years, the situation was reversed and paganism was in retreat. This is the context in which Servius probably composed his commentary: when he refers, for example, to animal sacrifice, it is always in the past tense, as of

---

[18] See Peter Burnell, "The Death of Turnus and Roman Morality," *Greece & Rome* 2nd ser. 34 (1987), 186–200; and Nicholas Horsfall, *A Companion to the Study of Virgil* (Leiden: Brill, 1995), pp. 192–216.
[19] See James D. Garrison, *Pietas from Vergil to Dryden* (University Park: Pennsylvania State University Press, 1992) and Burrow, *Epic Romance*. For *pietas* in Servius, see Philip North Lockhart, "The Literary Criticism of Servius," diss., Yale University (1959), p. 86 n. 48.
[20] Timothy Gantz, *Early Greek Myth: A Guide to Literary and Artistic Sources* (Baltimore: Johns Hopkins University Press, 1993), pp. 652–53, 713–17.
[21] *Aen.* 12.932–34; Magus (10.524–25) and Liger (10.597–98) make similar pleas, also in vain.
[22] Lactantius, *Divinae institutiones* 5.10.7–9, in *Lactantii Firmiani de divinis institutionibus adversus gentes* (Venice: Simone Bevilaqua, 1497), sig. l ii\u1d63.
[23] See Pierre Courcelle, *Lecteurs païens et lecteurs chrétiens de l'Énéide*, 2 vols. (Paris: Institut de France, 1984), index, s.n. *Lactance*.

something fallen into disuse.²⁴ Along with Macrobius, Servius is one of the last great scholars of pagan, as opposed to Christian, antiquity. And yet it was Servius, not Lactantius, who did most to define the Christian response to Turnus' death.

Servius begins his discussion stating that both motives do credit to Aeneas: he is *pius* for wanting to spare Turnus, and also *pius* for avenging Pallas.²⁵ It is a neat solution and scholars in recent decades have been dismissive: we prefer to savor (or wallow in) tension rather than resolve it. But this preference may be generational. Dante, for example, was undoubtedly the most thoughtful reader of Virgil in the whole of the Middle Ages; and in his *De monarchia* Dante gives what is essentially the Servian explanation of the final scene. The duel with Turnus, says Dante, demonstrates the *clementia* of Aeneas, which was so great that, had it not been for Pallas, Aeneas would have granted Turnus both life and amnesty.²⁶

In the form that Servius gives it, this defense of Aeneas would appear in approximately one third to one half of all editions of Virgil printed in the Renaissance. In many of these, it would also be joined by the remarks of Tiberius Claudius Donatus, whose *Interpretationes virgilianae* are approximately contemporary with Servius and were rediscovered in the late fifteenth century. "Notice," writes Donatus, "how, insofar as he wished to excuse (*ignoscere*) Turnus, the *pietas* of Aeneas' character is conspicuous (*servata*). Also conspicuous is his devotion (*religio*) to Pallas, because his killer did not escape."²⁷ For Donatus, as for Servius and Dante, clemency has a legitimate claim on *pietas*, but not an absolute claim. Like anger, vengeance hath a privilege.

In Renaissance commentaries, this interpretation was elaborated by Landino and Badius Ascensius. According to Landino, Aeneas was

> fierce, but inclining to mercy: he would have spared Turnus if Turnus had spared Pallas. But when, at the prompting of the belt, he bethought himself of Turnus' cruelty, he judged it more pious to give satisfaction to his friend Evander (who had, in fact, lost his own son for his sake) rather than concede life to Turnus, his greatest enemy. Thus he slew him out of *pietas*, rather than cruelty.²⁸

Badius concurs: "In this way Virgil portrays Aeneas as *pius* up to the very end, in that he would have conceded Turnus his life, but that he saw the belt

---

²⁴ C. E. Murgia, "The Dating of Servius Revisited," *Classical Philology* 98 (2003), 45–69.
²⁵ Servius on *Aen.* 12.940 (Giunta 1544, fol. 533ʳ).   ²⁶ Dante, *De monarchia* 2.9.14.
²⁷ T. C. Donatus on *Aen.* 12.947 (Giunta 1544, fol. 533ʳ).
²⁸ Landino on *Aen.* 12.938, in *Publii Virgilii Maronis ... opera cum commentariis* (Venice: Philippus Pincius Mantuanus, 1499), fol. ccciiiʳ.

of slain Pallas, whose death a vow to his father Evander compelled him to avenge."[29] As in Servius, pity and vengeance are both acts of *pietas*, but vengeance (in this case) is more pious than pity itself. The hero does well to pity Turnus, and even better to kill him.

Vengeance has limits, too, but they are limits of custom and context. Thus Tasso: vengeance is permissible, even obligatory, within the historical context of ancient *costumi*. Jacobus Pontanus (1542–1626), whose 1599 commentary on Virgil was used by Ben Jonson and Sir John Harington, makes the same argument. To my knowledge, this is the only printed commentary on Virgil that was available during the Renaissance to even mention Lactantius on the death of Turnus. Printed texts of the *Divine Teachings* were widely available in the Renaissance and, as we saw in the previous chapter, commentators on Virgil sometimes cited Lactantius for his remarks about reincarnation. His comments on the death of Turnus, though, were not picked up by commentators. Pontanus is exceptional, in that he does mention Lactantius, as one of those "who accuse Virgil of cruelty." But he does not actually quote Lactantius or give his argument. Instead, Pontanus moves directly to the defense, noting that it would be unwise, politically, to let Turnus live – also (and at great length) that killing Turnus was required by ancient religion: "Virgil, who died before the birth of God our Savior (by whom truth is revealed to us), followed the customs and religion of his own time when he was writing." Therefore, "those who accuse Virgil as unmerciful, because he showed himself inexorable in the death of Turnus, seem to reproach not so much the death itself, as the false religion of the ancients, in which men were unmerciful, and those who avenged injustices were regarded as pious." These were Tasso's arguments, at once severe and elastic. Admittedly, "Aeneas owes something to Turnus, as man to man." But much more, Pontanus continues, does Aeneas owe to his ally and benefactor, Pallas' father; "and in a case where it is not possible to satisfy both at the same time, he rightly gives preference to the stronger obligation."[30]

WEIGHING ANGER

The second controversy about Virgil's ending, in today's scholarship, concerns anger. When he decides to kill Turnus, Aeneas is *furijs accensus et*

---

[29] Badius on *Aen.* 12.930 (Giunta 1544, fol. 533ᵛ).
[30] Jacobus Pontanus on *Aen.* 12.952, in *Symbolarum libri xvij Virgilij* (Augsburg: Praetorius, 1599), cols. 2348–49.

ira / terribilis (*Aen.* 12.946–47), "kindled with rage and grim with anger." *Furor*, Virgil had said earlier, is *impius* (1.294), and yet here is Aeneas – a man whose badge was *pietas* – kindled with *furia* and consumed with ungoverned, even bestial grief (*sævi . . . doloris*, 12.945). Again, there seems to be a contradiction between what Aeneas does in the final scene and what his father enjoins in the underworld, when he says that passions come from embodiment and must be eradicated (6.730–43).

Is Aeneas compromised by his passions, or humanized? Does he betray his father, or transcend him? According to one school, the anger of Aeneas recapitulates or even institutionalizes the unreasoning hatred of Juno, anatomized by Virgil in the poem's opening sequence, where it takes the shape of a storm.[31] Another school holds that there is a distinction of rages, even a progression: from mindless fury (in the early books) to righteous anger (in the final two).[32]

Restricting ourselves to what was available in the Renaissance, we can find anticipations of both views. In defense of Aeneas, the ancient commentator Tiberius Claudius Donatus distinguishes between the *furia* of Aeneas and the habit of *iracundia*;[33] apparently, Aeneas is wrathful but not wrath-prone. Writing for the opposition is Lactantius again. We have already quoted part of this passage; here is the rest: "How could anyone, therefore, think that Aeneas had anything of virtue in him: one who kindled with fury like straw, forgetful of his father's ghost (in whose name he was entreated) and could not restrain his anger?"[34] Lactantius did not become a Christian until he was about sixty: prior to that, he had received a classical education and to the end of his days he remained, on moral issues, a Stoic. God, he argued, might show anger, but He is not moved by it, much less "enflamed" – and in any case God's anger has nothing to do with vengeance.[35]

---

[31] Michael C. J. Putnam, *The Poetry of the* Aeneid (Ithaca, NY: Cornell University Press, 1965), ch. 4; Putnam, *Virgil's* Aeneid: *Interpretation and Influence* (Chapel Hill: University of North Carolina Press, 1995); and David Quint, *Epic and Empire: Politics and Generic Form from Virgil to Milton* (Princeton: Princeton University Press, 1993), pp. 65–83.

[32] Agathe Thornton, *The Living Universe: Gods and Men in Virgil's* Aeneid (Leiden: Brill, 1976), pp. 159–63; Francis Cairns, *Virgil's Augustan Epic* (Cambridge University Press, 1989), pp. 69–84; Karl Galinsky, "Anger of Aeneas," 343–44; Galinsky, "How to Be Philosophical about the End of the *Aeneid*," *Illinois Classical Studies* 19 (1994), 191–201; and M. R. Wright, "'Ferox uirtus': Anger in Virgil's *Aeneid*," in *The Passions in Roman Thought and Literature*, ed. Susanna Morton Braund and Christopher Gill (Cambridge University Press, 1997), pp. 169–84. For the spectrum of ancient views on anger, see William V. Harris, *Restraining Rage: The Ideology of Anger Control in Classical Antiquity* (Cambridge, MA: Harvard University Press, 2001).

[33] T. C. Donatus on *Aen.* 12.946 (Giunta 1544, fol. 533ʳ).

[34] Lactantius, *Divinae institutiones* 5.10.8–9 (sig. liiʳ).

[35] James R. Averill, *Anger and Aggression: An Essay on Emotion* (New York: Springer-Verlag, 1982), pp. 82–89.

I have said that both views, for and against Aeneas, were available in the Renaissance. But they did not carry equal weight in the scholarship. Lactantius was known in the Renaissance as the "Christian Cicero" and some of his remarks (e.g., on reincarnation) were adopted by commentators on Virgil; again, though, none of the commentators I am aware of quotes, paraphrases, summarizes, or even alludes to his pronouncements about anger. The only commentator who even mentions anger in the final scene is Donatus and his remarks, as we have seen, are exculpatory. For the rest, anger does not seem to be an issue, since they do not comment on it.

There are some notes on anger in places other than commentary. Poliziano, in his essay on "Anger in Boys," claims that the *ira* of Aeneas is the just anger described in Aristotle. On the other side, Francesco Filelfo (1398–1481) denies that there is any such thing as just anger and gives Aeneas as an example of a great man who was diminished by *ira*, when he took revenge for Pallas.[36]

But these are isolated examples. They anticipate the modern debate about anger in the *Aeneid*, but they are not links in a continuous chain. They do not answer one another. They appear in philosophical, not literary, contexts. They do not get excerpted by literary commentators. From this we infer that, where anger is concerned, there is no genealogy of debate in the Renaissance, only intermittent sparks.

This will be surprising to those who have only a superficial knowledge of Christian ethics. Of course, anger is one of the seven deadly sins. And yet John, in his gospel, says that Jesus was consumed with "zeal" when he drove the moneychangers from the temple (2:13–17). This "zeal" was interpreted as anger and used to show that, really, there must be two kinds of anger, righteous and wicked.[37] The righteous kind would have existed even before the Fall and even now prompts us to punish sin. The wicked kind of anger is what Spenser calls "unaduized rashnes"; it is personified, in *The Faerie Queene*, by a man who did not govern his hands

---

[36] Craig Kallendorf discusses both examples in "Historicizing the 'Harvard School': Pessimistic Readings of the *Aeneid* in Italian Renaissance Scholarship," *Harvard Studies in Classical Philology* 99 (1999), 391–403, at 396–97, 401–2 and *Other Virgil*, pp. 37–38; see also Diana Robin, *Filelfo in Milan: Writings, 1451–1477* (Princeton: Princeton University Press, 1991), pp. 75–76.

[37] See Thomas Aquinas, *Summa theologiæ* 2a 2æ 158.8, who also cites Chrysostom; *Luther's Works*, gen. eds. Jaroslov Pelikan and Helmut T. Lehmann, 55 vols. (St. Louis, MO: Concordia, 1958–86), vol. XXI, pp. 78–79, 83 and esp. XXII, p. 233; Pietro Martire Vermigli, *Common Places* 2.2.60, trans. Anthonie Marten (STC 24669; London, 1583), pt. II, p. 293 and 2.9.38 (pt. II, p. 408); John Downame, *Spiritual Physicke to Cure the Diseases of the Soule, Arising from Superfluitie of Choller* (STC 7147; London, 1600), fols. 4^r–4^v, 5^v, 13^r–14^r. Downame's work was reprinted three times (twice in 1609, once in 1613) as *A Treatise of Anger*.

> Ne car'd for blood in his auengement:
> But when the furious fitt was ouerpast,
> His cruell facts he often would repent.   (*FQ* 1.4.34)

The vice of wrath is heedless and hasty; according to most authorities, it is also something that we feel on our own behalf. In contrast, righteous anger – as of a judge, teacher, or parent – is deliberate (not the occasion for remorse later on) and is on behalf of someone else.[38] The anger of Aeneas, which is on behalf of Pallas, might be an example. It is not my intention, though, to show that Christians in the Renaissance *approved* of Aeneas' anger, only that disapproval would not have been automatic.

There was material for controversy, and yet controversy itself did not materialize. The real controversy, such as it was, was over mercy. And even this controversy was limited. Today, it is expected that when we get to Virgil's ending, we will rethink the entire poem. For us, it is the challenge of the ending, rather than its finality, that makes it great. Critics in the Renaissance do not seem to have this horror of closure in the same degree.[39] The ending is shocking and needs to be explained, but it is the climax of the poem, not its crisis. I.e., it does not become a watershed or turning point for interpretation. For most critics in the Renaissance, the death of Turnus is an example of *pietas*, the virtue that has characterized Virgil's hero from beginning to end. A few critics are dissatisfied, but their dissatisfaction is localized and does not lead to radical rethinking.

Filelfo is an example. When he writes about philosophy, the anger of Aeneas is cited as a negative example. But when he writes about the meaning of the *Aeneid*, anger is not even mentioned. According to Filelfo, the purpose of the whole *Aeneid* is praise: praise, in the first six books, of wisdom and prudence; in the last six books, of justice, *pietas*, and especially courage. Over the course of twelve books, the poem also describes the several ages of man: from infancy to adolescence; from youth to adulthood and, in the last book, death. The poem ends fittingly with the death of Turnus, when his life goes "down into shadows" (*sub umbras*). Filelfo interprets this phrase in terms of praise and fame: for Turnus, he writes, "was one who had become enslaved to injustice and sloth, and because of this he died with his name in obscurity forever. But Aeneas is a just man and brave, godlike, even, in all his days, and with each day his glory shines more

---

[38] See Kenneth J. E. Graham, *The Performance of Conviction: Plainness and Rhetoric in the Early English Renaissance* (Ithaca, NY: Cornell University Press, 1994), ch. 4.

[39] See my "Errors about Ovid and Romance," *Spenser Studies* 23 (2008), 215–34.

brightly."⁴⁰ There is nothing here about vengeance or anger. Perhaps that's because Filelfo doesn't start writing about anger until later in his career. When he does, he is puzzled. More than once he marvels (*mirari . . . soleo*) that Virgil would do such a thing.⁴¹ But he doesn't suggest a new interpretation. The death of Turnus is a problem for Filelfo, but it doesn't become the crux of the whole poem.

ORGANIZING INTERPRETATION
I: CLASSROOM TECHNIQUES

Among poets the death of Turnus inspired imitators and among critics it provoked disagreement. But it was a point of contention, not an axis; a finish-line, not a starting-block. The death of Turnus was the climax of Virgil's Iliad, as the underworld was the climax of his Odyssey. Allegorically, Turnus was understood to represent "frenzied feeling" (Fulgentius) or "fleshly desires" (Petrarch).⁴² Killing Turnus, therefore, was the achievement of self-mastery, as the golden bough was the achievement of wisdom. But Turnus' death did not, in the Renaissance, become a magnet for commentary, as the underworld did. On occasion, the death of Turnus was criticized in order to demonstrate Virgil's inferiority – to Homer (by Sperone Speroni) or to Ariosto (by Lionardo Salviati).⁴³ But these critics were snipers; they did not found schools, form a tradition, or contribute to commentaries.

Because it was not organized around the death of Turnus, the mainstream interpretation of the *Aeneid* was both less dark than today's and less focused on the one episode. Instead, the reader's attention was diffused over thousands of separate verses. This was partly a result of educational methods: specifically, the commentary format used in classroom teaching and public lectures, and the use of commonplace books to record examples and memorable sayings under topical headings. To some degree, both methods could divert readers from larger issues.

---

⁴⁰ Filelfo, *Epistolae* 1.12, ed. Vito R. Giustiniani, "Il Filelfo, l'interpretazione allegorica di Virgilio e la tripartizione platonica dell'anima," in *Umanesimo e Rinascimento: Studi offerti a Paul Oskar Kristeller* (Florence: Olschki, 1980), pp. 33–42, at pp. 38–40.
⁴¹ Qtd. in Kallendorf, *Other Virgil*, p. 37.
⁴² Fulgentius, *Opera*, ed. Rudolf Helm (1898; repr. Stuttgart: Teubner, 1970), pp. 105–7; Petrarch, *Seniles* 4.5 in *Operum Francisci Petrarchæ florentini tomi IV* (Basel: Henrichus Petrus, 1554; facsimile repr. Ridgewood, NJ: Gregg, 1965), vol. II, p. 871. Cf. Harington on the death of Rodomonte: allegorically, he is the "vnbridled heat and courage of youth," which is "killed and quite vanquished by marriage." *Orlando Furioso in English Heroical Verse* (STC 746; London: Richard Field, 1591), p. 404.
⁴³ Seem, "Limits of Chivalry," p. 120 n. 10 (Speroni); Kallendorf, "Harvard School," pp. 398–99, 402 (Salviati).

According to one hypothesis, a book in the Renaissance was not the medium for an argument or story, so much as "a space containing textual fragments": fragments which industrious readers copied into their notebooks, arranged under topical headings and later reused, with little regard for context, to ornament or legitimate their own compositions.[44] Another scholar insists that reading in Tudor England was *always* for the purpose of collecting examples – again, with context as a casualty.[45] Robert Bolgar, in his survey of reading programs in Renaissance classrooms, is less dogmatic, but still disheartening. "Hardly any texts," he concludes,

> were studied in their totality, nor were they studied as works of art or as records of human experience. The boys' first aim when reading was always to collect material for their own compositions. They were not taught to pay attention to an author's argument or technique, but simply to collect uncommon idioms, pithy sayings, colourful anecdotes, anything that might one day serve to pad out a limping paragraph of their own. The movement that had promised – and on a different level had in fact achieved – a transformation of European culture, produced an educational discipline which in the event did not rise much above a mechanical and haphazard *bricolage*.[46]

But this picture is too grim.

Students were trained to excerpt quotations, but they were also disciplined to recognize allusions. In Virgil's text, the allusions to other poets, especially Homer, were often remarked by Servius. Servius, though, did not comment on the meaning of those allusions, only on Virgil's fidelity in imitating his model.[47] In the Renaissance, Paulo Manuzio and Eobanus Hessus also recorded Virgil's borrowings, though (again) they did not interpret them. This was perceived as a shortcoming by at least one humanist, Roger Ascham (1514/15–1568). The tutor of Queen Elizabeth, Ascham commended Hessus for collecting Virgil's Greek sources, but complained

---

[44] Mary Thomas Crane, *Framing Authority: Sayings, Self, and Society in Sixteenth-Century England* (Princeton: Princeton University Press, 1993), p. 4.

[45] Eugene R. Kintgen, *Reading in Tudor England* (Pittsburgh, PA: University of Pittsburgh Press, 1996), pp. 15–17, 40–43, 56, 81–82, 182.

[46] Robert Bolgar, "From Humanism to the Humanities," *Twentieth Century Studies* 9 (1973), 8–21, at 11. According to Paul F. Grendler, "Students read more than one work of Vergil but not necessarily complete texts," e.g., several books of the *Aeneid*, but not the whole poem; see *Schooling in Renaissance Italy: Literacy and Learning, 1300–1600* (Baltimore: Johns Hopkins University Press, 1989), pp. 240–41.

[47] Lockhart, "Literary Criticism of Servius," pp. 179–80. Ancient critics recognized the practice of allusion, but formulated no theory. For attempts to fill the resulting gap, see Stephen Hinds, *Allusion and Intertext: Dynamics of Appropriation in Roman Poetry* (New York: Cambridge University Press, 1998); and Joseph Pucci, *The Full-Knowing Reader: Allusion and the Power of the Reader in the Western Literary Tradition* (New Haven: Yale University Press, 1998).

that he did not go far enough: what students needed, Ascham thought, was a commentary that would, first, specify how Virgil altered his sources and then comment on the effect.[48]

This could be remedied, simply by adding more content. The real problem, for teachers and commentators alike, was organization. Printed commentaries were often based on classroom teaching or public lectures, and adopted from them the format of phrase-by-phrase analysis.[49] This was good for teaching rhetoric and style; but, like the commonplace book, it promoted fragmentation and put off both "larger questions" and philosophical challenges.[50]

The danger, however, has been exaggerated. It is true, for example, that sayings recorded in commonplace books were quotations out of context, islanded, unsponsored. In 1531, Melanchthon complained of those who

> think they have collected commonplaces when they have heaped up phrases on a variety of things, excerpted here and there from poets and orators. And because they judge this heap of notable sayings to be the be-all and end-all of learning, they read the authors to no other purpose but to pluck sayings from them, like flowers. Meanwhile, they learn no discipline properly, they understand no piece of writing in its entirety, at no point do they consider the overall character of any piece of discourse.[51]

Philip Melanchthon (b. Philipp Schwarzerd, 1497; d. 1560) was, of course, a devoted follower of Luther and a theologian. He also lectured on Virgil and was an advocate for making commonplace books. But he used them, not as a tool for writing so much as for reading. For Melanchthon, the primary use of a commonplace book was not to store up quotations, but to follow an author's *scopus*, his train of thought. This was done by analyzing the argument into parts, and then classifying the parts under general topics (the so-called *loci communes*, or commonplaces).[52] This encouraged a kind of reading we might call "reading topically."

---

[48] *ECE*, vol. 1, pp. 8–9, 18–20, 347.
[49] Anthony Grafton and Lisa Jardine, *From Humanism to the Humanities: Education and the Liberal Arts in Fifteenth- and Sixteenth-Century Europe* (London: Duckworth, 1986), chs. 1 and 3; and Paul F. Grendler, *Schooling in Renaissance Italy: Literacy and Learning, 1300–1600* (Baltimore: Johns Hopkins University Press, 1989), ch. 9. Dati's lecture, recounted above in ch. 3, is an example.
[50] Grafton and Jardine, *Humanism to the Humanities*, p. 67. See also Karlheinz Stierle, "Les lieux du commentaire," in *Les commentaires et la naissance de la critique littéraire: France/Italie (XIVe–XVIe siècles)*, ed. Gisèle Mathieu-Castellani and Michel Plaisance (Paris: Aux Amateurs de Livres, 1990), pp. 19–29, at p. 22.
[51] Melanchthon, *Elementa rhetorices* (1531), trans. Ann Moss, *Printed Commonplace Books and the Structuring of Renaissance Thought* (Oxford: Clarendon Press, 1996), p. 128.
[52] Moss, *Commonplace Books*, pp. 119–30.

Because the topics in commonplace books were general (e.g., prudence, fortune, war), it was natural to make comparisons with other authors; this made up, in some measure, for the context that was lost by excerpting. But topics could also be used to organize the interpretation of a single author. For example, Craig Kallendorf describes a printed edition of Virgil's works that was owned and annotated by an Italian reader at the beginning of the seventeenth century.[53] At the end of this volume is a handwritten list of "Passages to Inspire a Pious Reader"; there are fifty of them, taken from all three of Virgil's major works, and together they illustrate various aspects of *pietas*, such as compassion, religious obligation, and family devotion. There is nothing here to problematize *pietas*; no reference, for example, to killing Turnus. Still, it shows how the method of topical reading could be used, not just to pulverize a work into free-standing fragments, but to find out how it coheres. As Peter Mack argues, "although the general tendency of the commonplace method is to fragment a text into short reusable segments, it can also encourage readers to explore connections and contrasts of ideas within a text, to discover preoccupations and connections beyond the level of the linear plot."[54]

Another place where connections could be made was in commentaries. True, the format of commentaries was miscellaneous. In addition to geography, history, and whatever literary insight he may have possessed, the commentator was also expected to convey basic information about vocabulary and syntax. But these could be separated. As we saw in Chapter 1, the most widely published of the modern commentators on Virgil was Badius Ascensius. His commentary is long, first, because it repeats material from previous commentators and, second, because it paraphrases every clause. For example, when Aeneas says to Turnus, *Pallas / Immolat, & pœnam scelerato ex sanguine sumit* (*Aen.* 12.948–49), Badius breaks it down as follows: "Pallas (meaning, the son of Evander) 'immolates' you; meaning, with this wound Pallas dedicates you to the shades of the dead. That is, I do this to you on his behalf, and he exacts (through me, you understand) the penalty (meaning the punishment) from (understand 'your') crime-ridden blood (meaning, blood that has been profaned with many crimes)."[55] Badius does this, phrase by phrase, for every book of every poem and that, perhaps, is one reason why he stayed in print so long: he was the best friend of lazy students everywhere; probably of some teachers too.

---

[53] Craig Kallendorf, *Virgil and the Myth of Venice: Books and Readers in the Italian Renaissance* (Oxford: Clarendon Press, 1999), pp. 58–61, 222–24.
[54] Peter Mack, *Elizabethan Rhetoric: Theory and Practice* (Cambridge University Press, 2002), p. 44.
[55] Badius on *Aen.* 12.948–49 (Giunta 1544, fol. 532ᵛ).

This section of the commentary was called the *ordo*. But before he got into the nitty-gritty, Badius always gave an introduction: not just for the poem, or even for each book, but for every block of printed text. This is how Badius introduces the lines that describe the death of Turnus:

> As I have often reminded you (*Vt sæpe admonui*), the poet closes his work in the utmost praise of Aeneas, which consists in conquering Turnus, in casting down his insolent and haughty pride, and in forcing him to get down and beg. And yet, "so that everything will be consistent (*similis*) from beginning to end," as Horace counsels in the *Art of Poetry* [254], Virgil has Turnus say to Aeneas "Take your chance" [*Aen.* 12.932] so that Turnus does not seem to be humbled by lack of courage (*virtute*), but by chance (*forte*). Moreover, when he shows Turnus begging, Virgil does not focus on the one who is begging, but on his father's white hairs, which Turnus hoped would have a great influence on someone who was known to be very *pius* toward his own father. In this way Virgil portrays Aeneas as *pius* up to the very end, in that he would have conceded Turnus his life, but that he saw the belt of slain Pallas, whose death a vow to his father Evander compelled him to avenge. Also, Virgil ended many books with someone's death, and the work as a whole with Turnus' death for this reason: because death is the final limit (*linea*) of things. In this Virgil has imitated Homer, who brought the *Iliad* to a close (*composuit*) by treating of Hector. Now here are some words from Donatus about the final passage: "Turnus is 'low' in the sense that his body is low; he is kneeling and he has cast away his disdainfulness. The victory of Aeneas, which Virgil places at the end of the work, is complete and Virgil has finished the work of heaping up praises for Aeneas, which he has sustained from beginning to end with devices of every kind." Thus Donatus. And now, the *ordo*.[56]

This last phrase, *Ordo autem est*, is the signal for phrase-by-phrase commentary: it marks where Badius would begin to parse Virgil's Latin, in the manner we have seen already.

Badius was no showman: his transitions are abrupt and there is no sense of progression or climax. He does, though, manage to convey a clear sense of the poem's overall shape. Apparently Badius was the kind of teacher who gives the big picture right away and then burrows down into the details, trailing off into technicalities. It is not, shall we say, the most theatrical of lecturing styles: there is no mystery and, therefore, no revelation. Instead, Badius relies on simple repetition: "As I have often reminded you," etc.

From day one, Badius has been telling his students that Aeneas is the ideal man, who unites in his one person the two kinds of life, active and contemplative. In Homer, these were divided: the active life was portrayed in the *Iliad*, the contemplative life in the *Odyssey*; because he combines both

---

[56] Badius on *Aen.* 12.930 (Giunta 1544, fol. 533ᵛ).

kinds of virtue, Virgil's hero is "more glorious" than any of Homer's. But Virgil's hero is also unrealistic. For example, the real Aeneas died by drowning in a river; Virgil's poem omits this and ends instead with the death of Turnus. The purpose of this change, says Badius, is to glorify the hero. Throughout the epic, Virgil is said to portray Aeneas, "not as he was (*fuit*), but as he ought to have been (*fuisse decuit*)." Xenophon, says Badius, did the same thing when he wrote about Cyrus. Why would an author fictionalize his main character? In Virgil's case, it was to make the virtues – of "clemency, prudence, courage, temperance, justice, and the rest" – more attractive. Specifically, Augustus was supposed to read the *Aeneid* and become more like its fictional hero.[57]

ORGANIZING INTERPRETATION
II: THE IDEAL MAN THEORY

This approach was not original or unique to Badius. As other scholars have shown, the same notion of Virgil's hero was held by Petrarch, Boccaccio, Coluccio Salutati, Landino, Scaliger, and Sir Philip Sidney.[58] Sidney, who was familiar with both Scaliger and Landino, argues in his *Apologie for Poetrie* (c. 1583) that the "fained *Cirus* in *Xenophon*" is "more doctrinable ... then the true *Cyrus* in *Iustine*, and the fayned *Aeneas* in *Virgil* then the right *Aeneas* in *Dares Phrigius*." Why? Because the feigned hero has no flaws, just as the feigned villain should have no virtues: "If the Poet doe his part a-right, he will shew you in *Tantalus, Atreus*, and such like, nothing that is not to be shunned; in *Cyrus, Aeneas, Vlisses*, each thing to be followed."[59] Again, as in Badius, Virgil's hero is the ideal man, blameless in all his deeds. So widely held was this belief as to be well nigh universal. A list of its subscribers would be very long indeed; adding to the names already cited, in Germany it would include Melanchthon the Reformer (1530) and Pontanus the Jesuit (1599); in Italy, the Platonist Antonio Maria de' Conti (c. 1560), the Aristotelians Sebastiano Regoli (1563) and Torquato Tasso (1594), and Tasso's defender Camillo Pellegrino (1584); in England, William Webbe

---

[57] Badius, preface to *Aen.* (Giunta 1544, fol. 147ʳ). For Virgil's handling of historical sources, see also Tasso, *Discorsi del poema eroico*, Bk. 3 (*Prose*, p. 565).
[58] See O. B. Hardison, *The Enduring Monument: A Study of the Idea of Praise in Renaissance Literary Theory and Practice* (Chapel Hill: University of North Carolina Press, 1962), pp. 33–34, 80–85 *et passim*; Thomas H. Cain, *Praise in* The Faerie Queene (Lincoln: University of Nebraska Press, 1978), pp. 2–5; Brian Vickers, "Epideictic and Epic in the Renaissance," *New Literary History* 14 (1983), 497–537; and esp. Craig Kallendorf, *In Praise of Aeneas: Virgil and Epideictic Rhetoric in the Early Italian Renaissance* (Hanover: University Press of New England, 1989).
[59] Sir Philip Sidney, *An Apologie for Poetrie* (*ECE*, vol. 1, p. 168).

(1586) and Edmund Spenser (1590).[60] In Spain, it would also include Don Quixote, when he explains the method of Homer and Virgil. In Ulysses, says the Don, "Homer depicts for us a lively picture of a patient and long-suffering man, just as Virgil shows in the person of Aeneas the virtue of a dutiful son and the wisdom of a brave and expert captain. They do not portray them or describe them as they were but as they should have been, to give example by their virtues to the men to come after them."[61]

The ancient spokesman for the ideal man theory was the critic Badius quotes from, Tiberius Claudius Donatus. According to Donatus, Virgil's whole epic is one long panegyric for Aeneas, minimizing his faults and praising his virtues *in such a way that readers will imitate the virtues*; this is both the thesis and the operational premise of Donatus' commentary.[62] After about the ninth century AD, the text of Donatus all but disappeared from European libraries.[63] Now there are some books which vanish and leave behind them a yawning chasm of ignorance; this was not such a book. The connection between poetry and praise was already ancient when Donatus was writing his commentary,[64] and in the twelfth and thirteenth centuries it was revived, independently, by students of Aristotle's *Poetics*. According to Averroës (1126–98) and his Latin translator, Hermann the German (d. 1272), Aristotle divides all poetry, including epic, into praise or satire: praise of what readers should imitate, satire of what they should avoid. For the next four hundred years, this interpretation of Aristotle went practically unchallenged.[65] As a result, when the text of Donatus was rediscovered in the fifteenth century, it was like meeting an old friend.

---

[60] Melanchthon, "Ad lectorem," in *Virgilius Maro Philippi Melanchthonis scholiis doctissimis illvstratus* (Cologne: G. Fabritius, 1563); Pontanus, "Finis Aeneidos" (*Symbolae Virgilij*, vol. 1, p. 5); Bernard Weinberg, *A History of Literary Criticism in the Italian Renaissance*, 2 vols. (Chicago: University of Chicago Press, 1961), vol. 1, p. 269 (for Conti); Don Cameron Allen, *Mysteriously Meant: The Rediscovery of Pagan Symbolism and Allegorical Interpretation in the Renaissance* (Baltimore: Johns Hopkins University Press, 1970), p. 158 (for Regoli); Tasso, *Discorsi del poema eroico*, Bk. 3 (*Prose*, pp. 607–8); Weinberg, *Criticism*, vol. II, p. 1022 (for Pellegrino); Webbe, *Discourse of English Poetrie* (*ECE*, vol. 1, pp. 237–38). For Spenser, see Jerry Leath Mills, "Spenser's Letter to Raleigh and the Averroistic *Poetics*," *English Language Notes* 14 (1977), 246–49.
[61] Cervantes, *Don Quixote* 1.25, trans. Walter Starkie (London: Macmillan, 1964), p. 241.
[62] Preface to Donatus, *Interpretationes virgilianae* (Giunta 1544, fol. 146ᵛ). See Raymond J. Starr, "An Epic of Praise: Tiberius Claudius Donatus and Vergil's *Aeneid*," *Classical Antiquity* 11 (1992), 159–72.
[63] He is mentioned only twice after this in book inventories, once in the tenth century and once in the eleventh; see R. H. Rouse, "Ti. Claudius Donatus," in *Texts and Transmission: A Survey of the Latin Classics*, ed. L. D. Reynolds (Oxford: Clarendon Press, 1983), pp. 157–58.
[64] See Gregory Nagy, "Early Greek Views of Poets and Poetry," in *The Cambridge History of Literary Criticism*, vol. 1: *Classical Criticism*, ed. George A. Kennedy (Cambridge University Press, 1989), pp. 1–77, at pp. 8–18;
[65] See Hardison, *Enduring Monument*, ch. 2; and A. J. Minnis and A. B. Scott, *Medieval Literary Theory and Criticism c. 1100–c. 1375: The Commentary Tradition*, rev. edn. (Oxford: Clarendon Press, 1991), ch. 7.

The idea that all poetry is really a branch of epideictic (ceremonial) rhetoric and that Virgil in his poem is always praising Aeneas was, as Kallendorf puts it, both a "stimulus" to interpretation and a "straitjacket." Kallendorf emphasizes the stimulus, without dismissing the straitjacket. By reducing everything to praise, the ideal man theory "tends to simplify rather than complicate the values it treats, to pass over questions that might divide in favor of assumptions about good and bad around which people can unite."[66]

The ideal man theory was widely held, but it did not stop readers from criticizing Aeneas. We have seen several examples already. Another is given by Kallendorf who, in the conclusion of his most recent book, describes a copy of Landino's edition in which the owner, one Andrea Tordi, has written in the margin, next to the death of Turnus, that his spirit was indignant (*indignata*) because he was not spared, "something which is customarily granted to the conquered – even though he ... was a suppliant, and had been deprived of his wife by Aeneas."[67] Kallendorf calls this "a scathing critique" of Virgil's hero, and so it is. But was it also Virgil's critique, as well as Tordi's?

In the last fifty years, it has been common to say that the critique comes from Virgil himself, that the poet intends us to meditate on Aeneas' downfall as a moral actor. In Virgil's long reception history, there has never been a period when Aeneas did not have detractors. As Richard Thomas has shown, there are fossils of misgiving even in Servius.[68] And, in the Renaissance, Kallendorf has now brought to light several scholars and poets, including Filelfo and John Milton, who seem to anticipate insights from the so-called Harvard school.[69] But there are two important differences between the "pessimism" of classical scholars today and their predecessors in the Renaissance.

First, the early detractors were sporadic and isolated. Seen from above, they form a kind of archipelago. It is tempting to call this a tradition, but there was no *traditio*, "handing over," of ideas from one generation of readers to the next. The islands, as it were, didn't communicate. Filelfo, for example, in his epic *Sphortias* (c. 1455–c. 1477) described an Aeneas-figure who was treacherous, money-minded, and self-absorbed. As Kallendorf notes, this prefigures some of what our own critics have said about Aeneas himself. But *Sphortias* was a dead end. "The poem has never been printed

---

[66] Kallendorf, *Praise of Aeneas*, p. 18.   [67] Kallendorf, *Other Virgil*, p. 221.
[68] Richard F. Thomas, *Virgil and the Augustan Reception* (Cambridge University Press, 2001), ch. 3.
[69] Kallendorf, "Harvard School" and *Other Virgil*.

and survives in only a handful of manuscripts."⁷⁰ There may have been precedents (Kallendorf suggests Petrarch as one), but there were no imitators. It's as if there were Harvard critics but no Harvard school. There was observation, but no conversation, no follow-up, and therefore no development. At most, there was what Eliot calls "the fight to recover what has been lost / And found and lost again and again."

The one episode that does occasion sustained conversation is the death of Turnus. But even on that issue, no one in the Renaissance says that Virgil *intended* to criticize Aeneas or question his mission. This is the second major difference between pessimism *pur et dur* and pessimism *avant la lettre*. What we find instead are readers who criticize Aeneas and adhere to the ideal man theory at the same time. This seems like an impossible contradiction. Petrarch, though, will serve as an example of how it could work in practice. In one letter, which will be looked at later, he says that Aeneas represents *Vir perfectus*, the finished or complete man.⁷¹ Elsewhere, though, he says that Aeneas betrayed Troy (a reference to the historical tradition about Aeneas which Virgil obscured) and that he slaughtered his friends as a sacrifice to demons (an allusion, we suggested in Chapter 5, to the mysterious death of Misenus).⁷² The key to reconciling both passages is context. The first document is an interpretation of the *Aeneid*, using allegory. The second document is a treatise on religious contemplation: here, Petrarch is not trying to explain Virgil, but to show that even the best hero in classical literature is inferior to "Christ, the true father and lord and teacher." Apparently there are two standards of value. When, in the first document, Petrarch describes Aeneas as *Vir perfectus*, he is referring to Virgil's ideal, because he is explaining Virgil's intention. However, as we see from the second document, Petrarch's own ideal is Christian and differs from Virgil's in some particulars.

Of course, betraying one's fatherland (as Aeneas was alleged to have done in Dares Phrygius) is not a virtue in anyone's system. But the way Virgil handles it reveals his intention. In the second document, the one that criticizes Aeneas, Petrarch says that Virgil did everything possible to excuse his hero from the charge of treachery, to the extent that poets and historians since Virgil have accepted his account, even when it does not agree with the supposed eyewitness testimony of Priam's household. That is to say, Virgil used his art, not in order to reveal Aeneas' flaws, but to disguise them. This

---

⁷⁰ Kallendorf, *Other Virgil*, p. 17. ⁷¹ Petrarch, *Seniles* 4.5 (in *Opera*, 1554, vol. II, pp. 867–74).
⁷² Petrarch, *De otio religioso*; Kallendorf gives the Latin text and discusses it in "Harvard School," pp. 394–95.

is the ideal man theory again, but seen now from the perspective of theology and literary history. Virgil had an idea of the complete man, which he tried to express through Aeneas, even to the extent of falsifying history and covering up his defects. Petrarch scoffs now, because the modern ideal, as expressed in Christ, requires no such artistry. Still, Petrarch has a theory of what Virgil was trying to do, and that theory has not changed from the letter where he called Aeneas *Vir perfectus*. Even if, by modern (meaning Christian) standards he falls short, the "fayned" Aeneas of poetry (as Sidney calls him) was intended to be more complete – a "more doctrinable" example of virtue – than the "right" Aeneas of history. The ideal has changed now, with Christianity, but the idealism – the desire to glorify, in poetry, what is ideal – can still be recognized.

ORGANIZING INTERPRETATION III: REPETITION AND REREADING

We have been trying to discover whether, and in what degree, commentaries and classroom lectures on the *Aeneid* were organized by any unifying concept, or were mired hopelessly in miscellaneous detail. As we have just seen, one such concept was praise: Aeneas is the pagan ideal of a perfect man, and by praising him Virgil teaches his readers to be more virtuous.

Another unifying concept was death. In the preface of his commentary, Badius claims that almost every book of the *Aeneid* ends with an *exitus vitæ*.

For example, Virgil ends book one with the death of Priam and Hector, when Dido is described as "asking many things about Priam, many things about Hector" [*Aen.* 1.750]. Book II ends with the death of Creusa; Book III, with that of Anchises; Book IV, with that of Dido; Book V, with that of Palinurus; and Book VI with that of Caieta. And of course, the work as a whole concludes with the death of Turnus.[73]

Committed to repetition, Badius will remind his students of this scheme at least two more times: at the end, when Turnus dies, and also at the poem's midpoint, when Palinurus drowns and Aeneas prepares for his *katabasis* (*Aen.* 5.833–71).[74]

Badius was a schoolteacher before he became a publisher, and this is reflected in his commentaries. He knew what kind of information students need and also how they learn: by repetition. Unlike Poliziano, he was not an

---

[73] Badius, preface to *Aen.* (Giunta 1544, fol. 147ʳ). See also J. C. Scaliger, *Poetices libri septem* 3.25 (Lyon: Antonius Vincentius, 1561), p. 119, where the various death scenes in Virgil are enumerated, book by book, and then compared to show Virgil's variety.
[74] Giunta 1544, fol. 322ʳ.

original scholar. He was, though, a generous teacher and he did not avoid the tedious work (of providing synonyms, for example) which Poliziano shunned. On top of that, Badius was also prolific, a scholar and publisher of seemingly infinite interests and boundless energy.[75]

Paulo Manuzio, who inherited from his father the famous Aldine press, was equally prolific, but not equally conscientious. In 1558, he edited and published an edition of Virgil which was instantly pirated all over Europe. The commentary was a miscellany of marginalia: allusions to Homer and ancient history are indicated, hard constructions were paraphrased, proper nouns glossed, and morals drawn. There was observation, but no survey, no synthesis. In the preface, Manuzio assures us that poetry is worthwhile because it will teach us philosophy. He never says, though, what that philosophy is.

Melanchthon's edition (1530), also popular and also intended for students, has the same problem. Again, the comments are in the form of disconnected marginalia: hard words are glossed, allegories offered, and passages evoking *pathos* labeled. The preface, though, makes a strong argument in favor of synthesis, complaining of those

> who in judging statues inspect only a certain limb, a certain line. Just as laughable are those who, in appraising poems or speeches, follow the common practice of singling out only the "pronouncements," or one or two rare words of no import: a word from one of Cicero's speeches, *velificare* "to make sail," for instance, or a maxim: "That which comes about by woe falls apart woefully." But one must weigh the work as a whole (*uniuersum opus*). And just as, in pictures, we look at the features of bodies as well as their hues (*colores*), so in speech we ought to take into account the content (*res*) as well as the diction (*sermo*).[76]

Here, finally, is unambiguous evidence for the desultory, fragmentary style of reading that scholarship has hypothesized.[77] The practice, according to Melanchthon, is widespread (*vulgò fieri solet*), but not universal: for it is *inepti* who read like this, triflers and dilettantes. In contrast, the true scholar

---

[75] In addition to original works on grammar, morality, history, and theology, Badius also composed commentaries on Terence, Boethius, Juvenal and Persius, Cicero, Horace, Ovid, Sallust, Lucan, Valerius Maximus, Seneca, and Quintilian, as well as modern authors, including Mantuan and Lorenzo Valla; this was on top of running his printing press. See Philippe Renouard, *Bibliographie des impressions et des œuvres de Josse Badius Ascensius, imprimeur et humaniste, 1462–1535*, 3 vols. (Paris: Paul et fils et Guillemin, 1908), esp. the biography in vol. 1; and now Isaac Meir Gewirtz, "The Prefaces of Badius Ascensius: The Humanist Printer as Arbiter of French Humanism and the Medieval Tradition in France," diss., Columbia University (2003).

[76] Melanchthon, "Ad lectorem," *Virgilius Maro Philippi Melanchthonis scholiis doctissimis illvstratus* (1563 edn.), sig. A2ʳ. See also Gabriel Harvey, *Ciceronianus* (1577), trans. Clarence A. Forbes (Lincoln: University of Nebraska, 1945), pp. 86–87.

[77] Mack, *Elizabethan Rhetoric*, pp. 15, 18–19, 45 gives additional examples.

will consider a work in its entirety, and interpret individual sayings according to the intention (*scopus*) of the whole; this is more important for interpreting Scripture, but the same principle applies to poetry.[78] Unfortunately, what the *scopus* of the *Aeneid* is Melanchthon never says, except that Aeneas signifies *vir prudens* and Juno fortune, by which even the wise man is sometimes conquered. This theme, though, is never developed.

Another classic that was supposed to be read *in toto* was Ovid's *Metamorphoses*. Ovid's counter-epic, as it has been called, is notoriously episodic and as such invites browsing. Readers were admonished, though, by Ovid's translators to interpret the tales as a sequence.[79] According to Arthur Golding (1535/6–1606), the theme of that sequence is transformation and its meaning is explained by Pythagoras in the last book: nothing is constant, only the soul is indestructible.[80]

A warning, of course, is not a guarantee of how the book will actually be used. By the same token, we should not assume that any style of reading would be permanent, or was meant to be so. For this we have the testimony of Spenser's schoolmaster, Richard Mulcaster (1531/2–1611). Mulcaster preferred to teach from anthologies, because they promote uniformity and because one medium-size book is usually cheaper than ten small books. True, the longer works will have to be excerpted. But "good writers," argued Mulcaster, are not harmed by this treatment, because their works can be read later, "to their praise which made them, when the student can iudge: to the studentes profit, when he can understand: and the fast retaining of them, when order maintains memorie."[81] Mulcaster didn't worry about chopping the classics up into bits and pieces now because he assumed that grammar school was only the first step of a two-step process, in which basic literacy came first, followed by critical understanding.

One book that we know was read in this way is Virgil's *Aeneid*. "Do we not," asks Sir John Harington (1539/40–1613), "make our children read it commonly before they can understand it, as a testimonie that we do

---

[78] See Timothy J. Wengert, "Philip Melanchthon's 1522 Annotations on Romans and the Lutheran Origins of Rhetorical Criticism," in *Biblical Interpretation in the Era of the Reformation*, ed. Richard A. Muller and John L. Thompson (Grand Rapids, MI: Eerdmans, 1996), pp. 118–40; and Wengert, *Human Freedom, Christian Righteousness: Philip Melanchthon's Exegetical Dispute with Erasmus of Rotterdam* (New York: Oxford University Press, 1998), index, s.v. *scopus*.

[79] See Raphael Lyne, *Ovid's Changing Worlds: English Metamorphoses 1567–1632* (Oxford: Oxford University Press, 2001), pp. 34–46.

[80] Golding, "The Epistle," in *The .xv. Bookes of P. Ouidius Naso, Entytuled Metamorphosis, Translated Oute of Latine into English meeter* (STC 18956; London: Willyam Seres, 1567), sig. aii^r.

[81] Mulcaster, *Positions* (1581), ch. 43, ed. Robert Quick (New York: Longmans, 1881), p. 268. Mulcaster makes an exception for aspiring poets, who may be left to read "the whole bookes and arguments of poetes" at an earlier age than the rest.

generally approue it? And yet we see old men study it, as a proofe that they do specially admire it: so as one writes uery pretily, that children do wade in *Virgill*, and yet strong men do swim in it."[82] Like Mulcaster, Harington seems to anticipate two different stages of reading: the use of Virgil as a basic textbook and, afterwards, the study of Virgil's text by mature adults.

Quintilian envisions the same sequence, but carried on at a faster rate: "it is not enough to scrutinize everything section by section (*per partes*), but rather, once something has been perused (*perlectus*), it should be taken up again from the beginning (*ex integro*)."[83] This second reading, he suggests, should follow the first one immediately. In practice, many of these second readings were no doubt postponed. Books, though, were still expensive (even after the printing press), private libraries were small, and public libraries (in most of Europe) were non-existent. Rereading, in these circumstances, would have been normal.

Where might a second reading occur, and what would be its goals? One place was the university. Judging from probate records, most students at Cambridge seem to have owned a copy of Virgil's works, along with some Ovid, Terence, and Erasmus.[84] What for, since these authors would have been covered already in grammar school? In England, at least, poetry was not part of the university curriculum, but was studied privately, with one's tutor.[85] Poets were also assigned in logic classes, as "empirical data" for dialectical analysis. This seems perverse, but according to Lisa Jardine it did have at least one happy side-effect, that students were compelled, maybe for the first time, to read a poem for its argument, not just for its aphorisms (as they might have done in grammar school).[86]

SIX-BOOK READERS VS. TWELVE-BOOK READERS

Reviewing the evidence, we conclude what should have been obvious all along, that reading styles varied between granular analysis of short passages and wide-ranging, thematic criticism of whole books and poems. An example of the former is Melanchthon's commentary on Virgil, when it points out figures of speech. An example of the latter is the concordantial

---

[82] Harington, "A Brief Apology for Poetry" (1591), in *ECE*, vol. II, p. 212.
[83] Quintilian, *Institutio oratoria* 10.1.20 (Venice: Georgius de Rusconibus, 1572), fol. clxi^v.
[84] Lisa Jardine, "Humanism and the Sixteenth Century Cambridge Arts Course," *History of Education* 4 (1975), 16–31, at 16–17.
[85] Mark H. Curtis, *Oxford and Cambridge in Transition, 1558–1642* (Oxford: Oxford University Press, 1959), pp. 98, 101–7, and esp. 112.
[86] Jardine, "Cambridge Arts Course," pp. 24–25.

study of repeated images, as practiced by commentators on the Bible,[87] and by Badius when he observes that the books of the *Aeneid* are punctuated by death scenes.

How much of this was new? It has been said that commentary in the Renaissance became less allegorical, more linguistic. That may or may not be so in general, but in respect of Virgil it is demonstrably false. There has always been allegorical commentary on the *Aeneid* – witness Servius – and there has always been linguistic commentary – witness Servius again.[88] Perhaps we think of medieval commentary on Virgil as being more allegorical because most of us know only a few commentators, Fulgentius and Silvestris. But these were not the commentators that most readers in the Middle Ages had access to: what they usually had was a digest of Servius.[89]

The style of commentary (and, so far as I can tell, the style of reading) did not change markedly in the Renaissance. In Italy, where most of the commentaries were produced, teaching methods in the 1400s were much the same as they had been in the 1100s.[90]

What did change was not the style of reading but what people read and the style of writing. I shall say more about writing style in the epilogue. As for what people read, the most famous examples of new reading are texts that were lost in the Middle Ages and recovered in the Renaissance: Tacitus, for instance (*c.* 1508), or the complete text of Quintilian (1416). A second kind of new reading is exemplified by Petrarch's Greek manuscript of

---

[87] See Kaske, *Biblical Poetics*, ch. 2.
[88] See Lockhart, "Literary Criticism of Servius"; Robert Andrew Kaster, *Guardians of Language: The Grammarian and Society in Late Antiquity* (Berkeley and Los Angeles: University of California Press, 1988); Gerald Snare, "The Practice of Glossing in Late Antiquity and the Renaissance," *Studies in Philology* 92 (1995), 439–59; and, for allegory, Julian Ward Jones, Jr., "Allegorical Interpretation in Servius," *Classical Journal* 56 (1961), 217–26. Kaster, *Guardians of Language*, p. 170 estimates the ratio of linguistic to other kinds of commentary at six to one.
[89] See Christopher Baswell, *Virgil in Medieval England: Figuring the Aeneid from the Twelfth Century to Chaucer* (Cambridge University Press, 1995), ch. 2 (esp. p. 49). Landino did make use of Silvestris, as did Salutati; see pp. 160–61 n. 54 above. The direct influence of Fulgentius on later commentators, though commonly assumed, seems unlikely. Fulgentius allegorized all twelve books of the *Aeneid* and assigned each one to a stage in human maturity. Subsequent commentators, including Dante, developed a similar approach, but only applied it to the first six books, and did not agree among themselves about which books represented which ages. The source of the whole "ages of man" interpretation was probably Servius, who claims that the nine circles of Virgil's underworld refer to nine stages of life from infancy to old age (*Aen.* 6.426, 705). For the real influence of Fulgentius, we should look at the decades following 1589, when Hieronymus Commelinus published the *editio princeps* of his allegory in Heidelberg. Commelinus reprinted the work twice in fourteen years, once in 1599 and again in 1603. A Parisian edition, by Sebastianus Nivellius, appeared in 1600.
[90] So argues Robert Black, *Humanism and Education in Medieval and Renaissance Italy: Tradition and Innovation in Latin Schools from the Twelfth Century to the Fifteenth Century* (Cambridge University Press, 2001).

Homer, which Petrarch himself could not read but which Boccaccio, his more learned protégé, trained himself to parse, and hired a refugee from Byzantium to translate. So much is well known. But there was also, I would argue, a third kind of new reading, of texts that had always been in plain sight, but were seldom scrutinized. Of these "second-class classics," the chief monument was Virgil's Iliad.

There is a parallel here with the real *Iliad*. As we saw in Chapter 5, stories from Homer's *Odyssey* were remembered by Western readers long after Western scholars stopped reading the *Odyssey* itself – especially stories from the first twelve books. For example, the tale of Odysseus and the Cyclops (from Book 9) was well known in the Middle Ages, but not the test of the bow (Book 21). Stories from Homer's *Iliad* were even less well known. How many writers in the Middle Ages know who Patroclus is? Chaucer never names him; neither does Dante. Lydgate does, but Lydgate names everyone. Again, the relevant question is not merely *What knowledge is available?* but *What knowledge do people actually possess and use?* Even in the 1500s, "everyone is familiar with Homer, but very few have read him."[91]

In the Middle Ages, the text of Virgil's *Aeneid* was widely available, but it was only the Odyssean books that most readers (including most poets) seem to have internalized; the other six books did not go unremarked, but they were discussed in less detail.[92] On this basis we can distinguish two kinds of readers. Dante was a twelve-book reader, but most poets in the Middle Ages were six-book readers. Chaucer, for example, when he summarizes Virgil's epic in the *House of Fame* (c. 1380), devotes 310 lines to Books 1 through 6, but only fifteen lines to Books 7 through 12, a ratio of more than twenty to one. This is typical, and it does not change until the second half of the fifteenth century.

Cristoforo Landino, who began lecturing on Virgil in the early 1460s,[93] illustrates the transition from six-book reading to twelve-book reading. His first major writing on Virgil, *Disputationes camaldulenses* (c. 1473), is a

---

[91] Christiane Deloince-Louette, *Sponde: Commentateur d'Homère* (Paris: Champion, 2001), p. 43. For exceptions, see Philip Ford, "Du Bellay et les mythes homériques," in *Histoire et littérature au siècle de Montaigne*, ed. Françoise Argod-Dutard (Geneva: Droz, 2001), pp. 327–38; and Ford, "What Song the Sirens Sang... : The Representation of Odysseus in Ronsard's Poetry," in *Ronsard, figure de la variété: En mémoire d'Isidore Silver*, ed. Colette H. Winne (Geneva: Droz, 2002), pp. 99–114.

[92] See my "Lavinia and Beatrice: The Second Half of the *Aeneid* in the Middle Ages," *Dante Studies* 119 (2001), 103–24, at 106–9.

[93] See Landino's *Scritti critici e theorici*, ed. Roberto Cardini, 2 vols. (Rome: Bulzoni, 1974), vol. 1, pp. 20–28; Arthur Field, "A Manuscript of Cristoforo Landino's First Lectures on Virgil, 1462–63," *Renaissance Quarterly* 31 (1978), 17–20; and Field, "An Inaugural Oration by Cristoforo Landino in Praise of Virgil (From Codex «2», Casa Cavalli, Ravenna)," *Rinascimento* 2nd ser. 21 (1981), 235–45.

dialogue on the active and contemplative life, as illustrated by Virgil's *Aeneid*. For Landino, the journey from Troy to Italy signifies the progress of the soul, from sensuality (in youth) to contemplation (in adulthood). As we have seen, this reading was traditional. Landino's main innovation was to make Carthage represent the active life rather than sex.[94] While he stays with Dido, Virgil's hero is engrossed in politics. But his true home is Italy, where he finds wisdom in the Sibyl's cave and settles down to a life of contemplation. After he arrives, though, there is really nothing left for Aeneas to learn, or Landino to say. Perhaps, offers Landino, the wars in Italy signify the memories of active life that tempt a man away from contemplation and back into politics; or they may represent turbulence that arises in the soul when it reattaches itself to temporal objects.[95] But Landino does not elaborate: whereas there were 150 pages on Books 1 through 6, there are only two pages on Books 7 through 12, and only a sentence or two on Turnus' death.

Landino's dialogue was published in 1482, and is well known to scholars. However, as I argued in Chapter 1, this dialogue was probably less influential than the full-length commentary on Virgil that Landino published six years later. Whereas the dialogue was reprinted only eight times before 1600,[96] Landino's commentary was reprinted more than thirty times in the same period. The chief difference is one of scope: whereas the dialogue peters out after six books, a commentary must cover all twelve.

There was, of course, some overlap: in his *Aeneid* commentary, Landino mentions the dialogue several times and refers us there for details.[97] Where there is a connection between the first and second halves, he draws it.[98] For example, the forest (*sylva*) is always an image of matter (*hyle*). In Carthage, says Landino, the forest was inhabited by creatures of the earth, bears and such, which represent the material concerns that attend civic life, and the vices these concerns give rise to. In Italy, there are still forests, but they are populated by creatures of the air, songbirds which signify the harmony of

---

[94] Before and after Landino, most commentators interpret Dido as *libido*; see Marilynn Desmond, *Reading Dido: Gender, Textuality, and the Medieval* Aeneid (Minneapolis: University of Minnesota Press, 1994), ch. 2; and John Watkins, *The Specter of Dido: Spenser and Virgilian Epic* (New Haven: Yale University Press, 1995), pp. 49–50.

[95] Landino, *Disputationes camaldulenses*, Bk. 4, ed. Peter Lohe (Florence: Sansoni, 1980), pp. 209–11.

[96] See Lohe's edn., pp. xvi, xxiv–xxv. In addition to the Latin editions, there was apparently an Italian translation by one of Landino's students, Andrea Cambini; Landino mentions this in his Dante commentary (*Inf*. 1.63), but there is no other record of it.

[97] Kallendorf, *Praise of Aeneas*, pp. 137–64.

[98] Michael Murrin, *The Allegorical Epic: Essays in Its Rise and Decline* (Chicago: University of Chicago Press, 1980), p. 216 n. 30.

the soul when reason holds sway, even when it is still in the body.⁹⁹ This sounds like a promising topic, but Landino is not equipped to explore it. As a Christian, he knows the body is not *per se* a source of wickedness, but as a Platonist he has a deeply engrained suspicion of the body, which hinders him from saying anything positive. The result is that, allegorically, Books 7 through 12 are static, if not redundant. Like oriel windows, they amplify and elaborate the existing architecture, rather than form a new wing.

What animates the second half of Landino's commentary is the idea of praise. In Book 7, after the forests of Italy, Virgil commends her people. Why does he praise them, if in subsequent books they will become Aeneas' enemies? Erasmus would pose a similar question at the end of his *De ratione studii* (1511), when he proposed that a well-trained student reading Cicero and Virgil will ask himself, "Why did Cicero pretend fear in his defense of Milo? And why did Virgil, in depicting Turnus, heap so much praise on Aeneas's foe?"¹⁰⁰ Erasmus never gives an answer, but Landino suggests one. The beauty of his new Italian bride, the courage of his enemies, even the animus of Juno: all these are magnified so that, by overcoming them, Virgil's hero will seem glorious.¹⁰¹ For Servius, praise of Aeneas was praise of Augustus, "by way of his ancestors."¹⁰² But for Landino, praise of Aeneas is really praise of his virtues. As he explains in a preface, Virgil's hero is the complete man (*perfectum uirum*), who teaches people of every age, sex, calling, and condition to perform their proper duties (*sua officia*).¹⁰³

This is the ideal man theory again. Landino had used it before, when in his 1462–63 lectures on Virgil he derived the name *Aeneas* from Greek *ainos*, "praise."¹⁰⁴ The method, then, was not new, even to Landino. What was new was its range of exercise. In the *Camaldulensian Dialogues*, Landino had been limited by his theme, whether action is better than contemplation. The main speaker in the dialogue, Leon Battista Alberti, comes out in favor of contemplation and illustrates his thesis using Virgil's epic. But only the first, Odyssean half of the *Aeneid* is really suitable for this treatment, because that is the part describing contemplation.

As we have seen, critics from Servius onward classified the books of the *Aeneid* according to their primary models in Homer. According to the traditional division, the Odyssean books were supposed to describe the

---

[99] Landino on *Aen*. 7.32–34 (1499 edn., fol. ccxlviʳ).
[100] Erasmus, *Opera omnia* (Amsterdam: North-Holland, 1969–), ord. I, vol. II, p. 145.
[101] Landino on *Aen*. 7.47ff. (1499 edn., fol. ccxlviᵛ).
[102] Servius, preface to *Aen*. (Giunta 1544, fol. 146ʳ).
[103] Landino on *Aen*., "In P. Virgilii interpretationes prohœmium" (1499 edn., sig. aiiᵛ).
[104] Kallendorf, *Praise of Aeneas*, p. 137.

private, contemplative ideal of the philosopher; the Iliadic books, the political ideal of the statesman or general.[105] Landino, in his *Dialogues*, had nothing to say about the public virtues, because he was concerned there to extol the private ones. Hence, the discussion of Books 7 through 12 is only a few pages long. That would do for a conversation, but not for a commentary. But Landino had painted himself into a corner. The solution, in his commentary, was praise and the ideal man theory, which he outlines in his preface. Unlike the ages of man allegory, or the allegory of spiritual development (which Landino did not abandon), the ideal man theory does not require any kind of sequence. Never mind that, in Book 6, Aeneas had already obtained the *summum bonum*. In Books 7 through 12, he would be the very model of a modern major general – brave and wise, judicious and self-controlled – whose example readers would imitate.

THE RENAISSANCE OF VIRGIL'S ILIAD

Between 1488 and 1536, Landino's commentary was printed and reprinted more than thirty times: first in Florence, then in Lyon, Milan, Naples, Nuremberg, Paris, Strasbourg, and especially Venice. Not quite the first, it was initially the most successful of the new, print-age commentaries (surpassed among the moderns only by Badius).[106] Prior to Landino, and in Landino's own early writings, the focus of readers and poets was almost exclusively on Virgil's Odyssey.[107] After Landino, commentary on all twelve books became the norm.[108]

Poets, too, began to imitate the scenes and characters from Virgil's Iliad. For instance, Virgil's Turnus (*Aen.* 7–12) and Mezentius (*Aen.* 10) stand behind Ariosto's Rodomonte and Tasso's Argante; as Camilla (*Aen.* 11) stands behind Boiardo's Marfisa, Boiardo and Ariosto's Bradamante,

---

[105] James Nohrnberg, *The Analogy of* The Faerie Queene (Princeton: Princeton University Press, 1976), pp. 60–63 cites examples from Spenser, Tasso, pseudo-Plutarch's *Life of Homer*, Portus's preface to Homer, Cooper's *Dictionary*, Chapman's translation of Homer, Antonio Maria de' Conti's *Orationes et præfationes*, "the Homeric Allegorist 'Heraclides Ponticus,'" Servius, Macrobius, Fulgentius, Petrarch, Badius Ascensius, Filelfo, Landino, and Webbe.

[106] Another commentary on the *Aeneid*, probably by Giulio Pomponio Leto (1428–97), was published in Brescia the year before Landino's, but was reprinted only two or three times.

[107] Dante was one exception; see my "Lavinia and Beatrice." Petrarch was another (pp. 225–26 below).

[108] Again, there were exceptions: the commentaries of Agostino Dati (1507), Sulpitius Verulanus (1511), Caesar Delphinus (1523), and Nascimbaenus Nascimbaenius (1570). Only Dati, though, had any popularity, and his was a special case, since he only commented on the first lines of Book 1. In the vernacular commentaries of Johannes Fabrinus and Filippus Venutus, the labor of commentary was divided between two authors: the former on *Aen.* 1–7, the latter on *Aen.* 8–12. But since their commentaries were always printed together (beginning in 1575–76), there was never a gap in coverage.

Tasso's Clorinda, and Spenser's Britomart; as the night raid of Nisus and Euryalus (*Aen.* 9) stands behind the nocturnal sorties of Ariosto's Cloridano and Medoro (*OF* 18, 19) and Tasso's Argante and Clorinda (*GL* 12).[109] Tasso's Altamoro (who tries, unsuccessfully, to bribe Goffredo with gold in *GL* 20) recalls Virgil's Magus (who tries, unsuccessfully, to bribe Aeneas with gold in *Aen.* 10). The description of Rinaldo's shield in *GL* 17 is ostentatiously modeled on the description of Aeneas' shield in *Aen.* 8; Boiardo's catalogue of North African ships in *OI* 2.29 and Tasso's catalogue of Egyptian armies in *GL* 17 are both patterned after the catalogue of Etruscan armies in *Aen.* 7; Tasso's Aletto (*GL* 8 and 9) has the same name, pedigree, and function as the demonic agent of disorder in *Aen.* 7; Spenser's House of Care (*FQ* 4.5) is loud with echoes from Vulcan's smithy (*Aen.* 8); and so on. Images recur as well: the fire-breathing chimera on Solimano's helmet (*GL* 9.25; cf. *Aen.* 7.785), arrows that fall like snowflakes (*FQ* 2.11.18; cf. *Aen.* 11.610–11), and, in a popular woodcut, living captives fastened to rotting corpses (*Aen.* 8.485–88). This last, a torture invented by Mezentius, was used by Alciato as an emblem for venereal disease (*Gallica scabies*), to describe the cruel union of faithful wife with infected husband.[110]

A reviving interest in the Iliadic portion of the *Aeneid* can also be traced in the critical writings of the period. Ronsard, when he wants to describe the elaborate tropes and heightened diction that epic verse requires, cites nine examples, all of them from Virgil's *Aeneid*, eight of them from his Iliad.[111] Vida, in discussing the works that a young man should read first, suggests poetry about young people and lists examples from Books 7 through 12 of the *Aeneid*: the trials of young Ascanius in Book 8, the death of Pallas in Book 10, of Lausus (also in Book 10), of Euryalus in Book 9.[112] But these are mere anecdotes. A bigger and more useful sample can be obtained from Book 3 of Tasso's *Discorsi del poema eroico* (1594), which quotes from Virgil's epic fifty-one times. Analyzing the quotations book by book (Table 3), we see, first, that there was no section of the poem from which Tasso could not quote fluently and, second, that quotations from the last six books actually outnumber those from the first.

Subject matter accounts for some of this: Tasso was writing a war poem, and for war Virgil's Iliad was an obvious source. But Ronsard's epic, what he wrote

---

[109] On the night raid, see Chapter 4, above.
[110] Andrea Alciato, *Emblemata* (Lyon: G. Rouilius, 1550), p. 212 ("Nupta contagioso").
[111] Ronsard, *Les œuvres de Pierre de Ronsard*, ed. Isidore Silver, 6 vols. (Chicago: University of Chicago Press, 1966–68), vol. IV, p. 12.
[112] Vida, *De arte poetica* (1527), 1.110–22, trans. Ralph G. Williams (New York: Columbia University Press, 1976), p. 11.

Table 3 *Citations from Virgil's* Aeneid *in Book 3 of Tasso's* Discorsi del poema eroico

Book of the Aeneid	Number of citations	
1	6	
2	2	
3	8	Total 22
4	3	
5	2	
6	1	
7	9	
8	5	
9	2	
10	2	Total 29
11	5	
12	6	

of it, is largely from Virgil's Odyssey. And yet, when he quotes Virgil in his preface, it is mostly from the last six books. My point here is not that Ronsard and Tasso liked the second half of Virgil's epic better than the first: that would be hard to prove and is probably not true. But something has changed, between Chaucer's time and Spenser's, whereby critics and poets are now reading the last six books with renewed attention. This, more than any difference in interpretation (which did not alter greatly between the Middle Ages and the Renaissance), is what distinguishes Renaissance views of the *Aeneid* from medieval: not what the poem means, but how much of it people read.

How could reading more books of the *Aeneid* not change what the poem means? It depends on the method used to interpret the "new" books. Where that method was the ideal man theory, Virgil's hero was always virtuous, albeit in different ways, no matter which half you were reading. The experience of reading all twelve books was richer but not qualitatively different from reading six.

Why did scholars begin studying the second half? One of the important themes in Books 7 through 12 is the colonization of Italy. But Dido, in Books 1 and 4, is a colonist too;[113] and Buthrotum, which Aeneas visits in Book 3, was a colony founded by Augustus.

As readers and scholars, we sometimes lose sight of this, because Dido was already in Libya when Aeneas arrived. But the real native in Virgil's

---

[113] See my "Virgilian Models of Colonization in Shakespeare's *Tempest*," *ELH* 70 (2003), 709–37.

story is Iarbas, the African prince who wooed Dido and was rejected in favor of Aeneas. In a play which Christopher Marlowe probably wrote as a student, *Dido Queen of Carthage* (c. 1585), Iarbas is characterized as lovesick and jealous. He complains that the newcomer, Dido, has accepted the benefits of hospitality, but rejected its obligations; this was a motif of colonization narratives. Like Caliban in Shakespeare's *Tempest*, Iarbas makes an offer of marriage (or, in Caliban's case, just sex); when the offer is rejected, he is indignant rather than bashful. Marlowe amplifies the role of Iarbas to the extent that Dido's sister, Anna, falls in love with him and together they commit suicide. His voice is silenced, but before that happens we hear an echo, maybe for the first time, of what might have been: a Virgilian critique of colonization.[114]

Where Marlowe found the inspiration for this is unclear, but it was not from any of the major commentaries. There is a woodcut, in some editions of Badius, that shows what seem to be the famous caravels of Columbus.[115] But there is no mention of it in Badius himself.

This is surprising, but not inexplicable. For one thing, the places that, in this period, produced most of the commentaries on Virgil – Italy, France, and Germany – were not active yet in overseas colonization.[116] And although many of Europe's ruling families traced their genealogy from Aeneas or at least Troy, their notion of empire was often limited. Some of these fictional genealogies (such as Charles V's) made sweeping claims to universal lordship.[117] But others were primarily dynastic: the genealogies, for example, of France's kings or Ferrara's dukes. These record the *translatio* of Trojan empire, not the expansion; and the *imperium* they celebrate is not that of ultramarine conquest, but of national sovereignty.[118]

A second reason why colonization is so pitifully under-represented in the commentaries is inertia. As we have seen in this chapter and the last,

---

[114] Wilson-Okamura, "Virgilian Models," 726–28; Emily C. Bartels, *Spectacles of Strangeness: Imperialism, Alienation, and Marlowe* (Philadelphia: University of Pennsylvania Press, 1993), ch. 2.
[115] Wilson-Okamura, "Virgilian Models," 710–11.
[116] See Chapter 1, Figure 3. The countries that were active in colonization, Spain and Portugal, did contribute to classical scholarship, but their focus (as my colleague Charles Fantazzi explains) was often on Iberian authors, such as Martial and Seneca.
[117] See Frances A. Yates, *Astraea: The Imperial Theme in the Sixteenth Century* (1975; repr. Harmondsworth: Peregrine-Penguin, 1977), pt. 1 and esp. Mary Tanner, *The Last Descendant of Aeneas: The Hapsburgs and the Mythic Image of the Emperor* (New Haven: Yale University Press, 1993).
[118] See Andrew Fichter, *Poets Historical: Dynastic Epic in the Renaissance* (New Haven: Yale University Press, 1982); Peter Marinelli, *Ariosto and Boiardo: The Origins of* Orlando Furioso (Columbia: University of Missouri Press, 1987), chs. 2–3; Sylvia Federico, *New Troy: Fantasies of Empire in the Late Middle Ages* (Minneapolis: University of Minnesota Press, 2003); Alan Shepard and Stephen D. Powell, eds., *Fantasies of Troy: Classical Tales and the Social Imaginary in Medieval and Early Modern Europe* (Toronto: Centre for Reformation and Renaissance Studies, 2004).

commentary on Virgil – even in the Renaissance, a period of great dynamism in classical scholarship – was essentially conservative. Like a coral reef, it developed through accretion and elaboration. Real innovation was not prohibited, but it was unusual. Servius, if he could have read the modern commentaries on Virgil, would have found in them much that he did not anticipate, but almost nothing that he could not assimilate. Assuming he was pagan, he might have objected to Virgil being Christianized. But even this was not new: before Servius was born (c. AD 380), Virgil's fourth, messianic eclogue was already being characterized by Lactantius (c. AD 240–c. 320) as a prophecy about Christ and attributed by the emperor Constantine (c. AD 272/3–337) to the direct inspiration of the Holy Ghost.[119]

What was new, I am arguing, was not how the *Aeneid* was studied, but how much. In the Middle Ages, most readers stopped after Book 6; in the Renaissance, more of an effort was made to comment on and even imitate the whole poem, all twelve books of it. But we have still to account for the change: if colonization did not cause it, what did?

The boring (but probably correct) answer is the Renaissance of classical scholarship that began in the middle of the thirteenth century and was Christianized by Petrarch in the fourteenth.[120] That is, the renaissance of Virgil's Iliad was an aspect of *the* Renaissance that we learn about in grammar school (and learn to be skeptical of in graduate school). There has, of course, been much controversy over what the Renaissance was and even whether it happened. Still, the word *renascentia* was used in the fourteen- and fifteen-hundreds and there are some features of the movement that are too obvious to ignore: a devotion to the *studia humanitatis* (i.e., grammar, rhetoric, history, poetry, and ethics); a determination, both to establish through scholarship and then to enforce through education and especially criticism, standards of linguistic purity; and a new enthusiasm for hunting up and comparing old manuscripts. To be sure, for all of these goals one can identify medieval precedents. The Latin, moreover, of the early humanists is far from being purely classical. Initially, then, the difference was one of degree – which became amplified, over time and through competition, to a difference in kind.

Nowhere was this difference more marked than in the search for manuscripts. In this field, the great age of discovery was the fifteenth

---

[119] See Pierre Courcelle, "Les exégèses chrétiennes de la quatrième Églogue," *Revue des études anciennes* 59 (1957), 294–319 and Sabine MacCormack, *The Shadows of Poetry: Vergil in the Mind of Augustine* (Berkeley and Los Angeles: University of California Press, 1998), pp. 21–31.
[120] For this chronology, see Ronald G. Witt, *In the Footsteps of the Ancients: The Origins of Humanism from Lovato to Bruni* (Leiden: Brill, 2000).

century.¹²¹ The Magellan of that era, energetic and well organized, was Poggio Bracciolini (1380–1489). But before there can be a Magellan, there has to be a Columbus, and the Columbus of manuscript-discovery was Petrarch (1304–74). It was Petrarch who assembled the text of Livy's history (all but the last five books, which were discovered in 1527), Petrarch who exhumed Propertius, Petrarch who recognized the significance of and put back into circulation Cicero's letters to Atticus. In doing so, Petrarch not only expanded our knowledge of classical literature, revealing (*inter alia*) a new side of Cicero's personality: by making copies of and imitating Cicero's letters, Petrarch also changed the style (and even content) of letter-writing between friends for the next five hundred years.¹²²

What does this have to do with Virgil's Iliad? Petrarch did not discover a new text by Virgil. In his personal copy of Virgil (a valuable codex which was stolen from Petrarch in 1326 and restored to him in 1337, and which he seems to have used as a kind of family Bible, recording important dates, such as Laura's death and the death of his son, on the flyleaf), he annotated the first six books of the *Aeneid* more heavily than the last, mostly with excerpts from Servius and Macrobius.¹²³ This is not surprising: in many things (his Latin, for example), Petrarch was still a man of his time, which is to say, of the late Middle Ages. If he also outlived his age, it was partly through simple longevity. If he wrote and discovered more than most, it was partly because he had more time. For when he died, Petrarch was only one day short of his seventieth birthday, and in the last decade of his drawn-out life Petrarch published something that was new in scholarship on Virgil, an allegory of the *Aeneid* which gives full weight to the last six books.

For Petrarch, Aeneas is the ideal man, a combination of active and contemplative virtues. The reward of these virtues is glory, which in the

---

¹²¹ There is a first-hand account in *Two Renaissance Book Hunters: The Letters of Poggio Bracciolini to Nicolaus de Nicolis*, trans. P. W. G. Gordan (New York: Columbia University Press, 1974). For a survey of accomplishments, see L. D. Reynolds and N. G. Wilson, *Scribes and Scholars: A Guide to the Transmission of Greek and Latin Literature*, 2nd edn. (Oxford: Clarendon Press, 1974), ch. 4. For the history of individual texts, see Remigio Sabbadini, *Le scoperte dei codici latini e greci ne' secoli XIV e XV*, rev. Eugenio Garin, 2 vols. (Florence: Sansoni, 1967); Sabbadini, *Storia e critica di testi latini*, 2nd edn. (Padua: Antenore, 1971); and L. D. Reynolds, ed., *Texts and Transmission: A Survey of the Latin Classics*, rev. edn. (Oxford: Clarendon Press, 1986).
¹²² See Marc Fumaroli, *L'âge de l'éloquence* (1980; repr. Paris: Michel, 1994), pp. 172–74; Andrew Burnstein, "Jefferson and the Familiar Letter," *Journal of the Early Republic* 14 (1994), 195–220, at 199–202; and Marc Bizer, "Letters from Home: The Epistolary Aspects of Joachim Du Bellay's Les Regrets," *Renaissance Quarterly* 52 (1999), 140–79, at 145–52, 157–59.
¹²³ Mary Louise Lord, "The Use of Macrobius and Boethius in Some Fourteenth-Century Commentaries on Virgil," *International Journal of the Classical Tradition* 3.1 (1996), 3–22, at 4.

epic is personified by Lavinia. The main obstacles are Amata, who represents the flesh, and Turnus, who represents the desires of the flesh. The distinction is important. When it is unrestrained, the flesh feeds upon itself (Amata commits suicide). But to achieve glory (Lavinia), Aeneas must also conquer the desires of the flesh (Turnus). That is, he must learn to *enjoy* saying no – and this is why Venus arrives at the end, to show that virtue is fun when it becomes a habit.[124]

Petrarch's allegory of the *Aeneid* appears in a letter to a young poet, Federigo Aretino. In his own lifetime Petrarch issued collections of his letters, which were eventually printed. But, so far as I can find, the allegory which he proposed in this letter was not widely adopted. (Neither, we recall, was Landino's allegory of Dido, as political ambition.) Its importance lies, rather, in the mere fact of its existence. Written *c.* 1365, Petrarch's letter predates the discovery and colonization of the New World by more than a century. (So does Landino's twelve-book commentary, though not by as many years.) Why, when Petrarch had focused his annotations on the first six books, did he suddenly, at the end of his life, stretch himself to cover all twelve? For the same reason, I would suggest, that he raided old libraries in search of new manuscripts by his idol Cicero: because his appetite for all things classical was more keen than most of his peers'. He read more of Virgil, because he wanted more.

Also, Petrarch was competitive. Like Aeneas, Petrarch wanted glory and in scholarship glory derives from discovery. A hundred years later, when Landino was giving lectures in Florence and writing his commentaries, the rivalry between scholars was, if possible, even fiercer.[125] Some, like Poliziano or Filippo Beroaldo (1453–1505), distinguished themselves by eccentricity, giving lectures on books that were still outside the scholarly mainstream, such as Apuleius or the Greek Anthology. The other way to establish a reputation was by being exhaustive: for example, to publish as Landino did a commentary on all of Horace's poems (not just the satires), all three parts of the *Divine Comedy* (not just the *Inferno*), and all twelve books of Virgil's *Aeneid*. As we have seen, his approach to these books was traditional

---

[124] Petrarch, *Seniles* 4.5 (in 1544 edn. of *Opera*, vol. II, pp. 867–74). On the importance of this letter, see J. Christopher Warner, *The Augustinian Epic, Petrarch to Milton* (Ann Arbor: University of Michigan Press, 2005), pp. 33–37. There is a translation by Aldo S. Bernardo *et al.*, *Letters of Old Age*, 2 vols. (Baltimore: Johns Hopkins University Press, 1992), vol. I, pp. 139–51.

[125] For lively images of scholarly competition, see Grafton and Jardine, *Humanism to the Humanities*, pp. 94, 97; Julia Haig Gaisser, "Teaching Classics in the Renaissance: Two Case Histories," *Transactions of the American Philological Association* 131 (2001), 1–21; and Christopher S. Celenza, *The Lost Italian Renaissance: Humanists, Historians, and Latin's Legacy* (Baltimore: Johns Hopkins University Press, 2004), ch. 5.

(allegory and the ideal man). Those had been Petrarch's methods as well. And yet it was Petrarch and Landino, with their old-fashioned methods, not Poliziano and Beroaldo, with their new-found texts, who initiated the next phase in Virgil scholarship. For the new phase this time was not a revolution so much as a revival; a renaissance, in the most basic sense, of reading all twelve books.

CAMILLA

What did this new generation of readers remember from Virgil's Iliad? We have already mentioned, in this and previous chapters, several popular episodes: the night raid of Nisus and Euryalus; the lovemaking of Venus and Vulcan; the death of Turnus; and Camilla. Camilla was hardly the first woman warrior in classical poetry (Virgil himself compares her with the Amazons Penthesilea and Hippolyte, *Aen.* 11.659–62). But in a literary culture that was still Latin-based, as the Renaissance most certainly was, Camilla was more accessible than her Greek sources.[126]

Like most figures from Virgil's Iliad, Camilla leads only a shadowy existence in the Middle Ages. Dante salutes her (*Inf.* 1.107) and locates her in limbo, with Aeneas and the other virtuous pagans (*Inf.* 4.124–26). It is not until the Renaissance, however, that Camilla becomes a recognizable type in vernacular culture. This is one of the more tangible results of the revival we have been sketching. In the 1500s, for example, Camilla becomes a social model, for the learned and literary gentlewoman (the forerunner of the eighteenth-century bluestocking).[127] Her main influence, though, is on epic. Except for Camões's *Lusíados* (1572), the great epics of this period all include at least one version of Camilla.[128] These can be classified into three

---

[126] Thomas P. Roche, Jr., "Ariosto's Marfisa: Or, Camilla Domesticated," *Modern Language Notes* 103 (1988), 113–33, at 113.

[127] See Lisa Jardine, "'O decus italiae virgo,' or The Myth of the Learned Lady in the Renaissance," *Historical Journal* 28 (1985), 799–819, at 804–7.

[128] See Albert S. Cook, "The Amazonian Type in Poetry," *Modern Language Notes* 5 (1890), 161–64; Phillip Elliott Parotti, "The Female Warrior in Renaissance Epic," diss., University of New Mexico (1972); Margaret Tomalin, *The Fortunes of the Warrior Heroine in Italian Literature: An Index of Emancipation* (Ravenna: Longo, 1982); Lillian S. Robinson, *Monstrous Regiment: The Lady Knight in Sixteenth-Century Epic* (New York: Garland, 1985); Roche, "Camilla Domesticated"; Kathryn Schwarz, *Tough Love: Amazon Encounters in the English Renaissance* (Durham, NC: Duke University Press, 2000); Frédérique Verrier, *Le miroir des amazones: Amazones, viragos et guerrières dans la littérature italienne des XVe et XVIe siècles* (Paris: Harmattan, 2003). After 1600, see Simon Shepherd, *Amazons and Warrior Women: Varieties of Feminism in Seventeenth-Century Drama* (Brighton, Sussex: Harvester, 1981); Diane Dugaw, *Warrior Women and Popular Balladry, 1650–1850* (Cambridge University Press, 1989); and Daniel E. Freeman, "'La guerriera amante': Representations of Amazons and Warrior Queens in Venetian Baroque Opera," *Musical Quarterly* 80 (1996), 431–60.

subtypes: tragic, comic, and romantic. The tragic Camillas, like Tasso's Clorinda, die as virgins. The comic Camillas, of whom Ariosto's Marfisa is the best and perhaps only example, are sexually neutral: Marfisa facilitates her brother's marriage, but she herself seems destined to live out her days as an aunt, rather than mother. This is in contrast with the romantic Camilla, who has no vocation for celibacy, but wields arms in order to find – and then rescue – her future husband. Examples of this third type include Boiardo's Bradamante (and Ariosto's), Tasso's Erminia, and Spenser's Britomart.

This third subtype is the most common and, in the sense that she represents something distinctive about Renaissance epic, the most important too. By the same token, of all the character-types that were spawned by Virgil's poem, the romantic Camilla is one of the least Virgilian. In Virgil, the Amazon is always tragic: like Turnus, she fights courageously, but on the wrong side.[129] What is more, the real Camilla is a virgin. Virginity in Camilla is not an accident of biography, a consequence of her premature death; it is part of her identity, in the same way that sternness is part of her personality. She is not a freemartin, though; say, rather, that the energy which other women fritter away as sex Camilla forms or transposes – I am deliberately avoiding *sublimates* – into autonomy. This compound intensity, of tragedy and isolation, is dramatically powerful and poetically rare; so rare that, in Renaissance epic, the two elements are seldom combined. In Tasso's Clorinda, we have Camilla's tragedy, but not her same standoffishness (since, just before she dies, she becomes aware that she is really in love with Tancredi). In Spenser's Belphoebe, we have Camilla's stern singleness (she never falls in love with anyone), but not her tragedy.[130]

Clorinda and Belphoebe, though, are secondary to the main action. More central to their respective plot-lines – and more representative of the poems in which they appear – are the romantic Camilla-types, such as Bradamante and Britomart. These are the women whose stories we follow from canto to canto and book to book, whose characters (and I use the word here advisedly) develop and unfold. Insofar as they are virgins and warriors, they are versions of Camilla. But their virginity is a stage, not an identity, since both women are eager for love and marriage.

Camilla illustrates, then, two features of the new scholarship and the new poetry: the revival of reading Virgil's Iliad, and the centrality of love in

---

[129] See also Penthesilea, who dies fighting the Trojans and then is juxtaposed with Dido-as-Diana (*Aen.* 1.490–502).
[130] See my "Belphoebe and Gloriana," *English Literary Renaissance* 39 (2009), 47–73.

Renaissance epic. This last is something that every reader has noticed: the question is where it comes from, and what relation it has to classical epic. In our period, the most common term for epic was "heroic poem" (*poema eroico*), and the Greek word *hērōs*, "hero," was routinely derived from *eros*, "love."[131] The etymology comes from Plato, but the type of love is not platonic. In the epics, love is active and practical, not speculative or contemplative. There is no suggestion, for example, that being in love will help Britomart comprehend the mystery of the Trinity or the paradox of Incarnation (as Dante is helped at the end of *Paradiso*); it will make the heroine chaste and courageous, but it will not make her a theologian.[132]

The contrast with Dante is striking, but in comparison with Virgil the Christian poets are like Dante's white pearl on a white forehead, distinguishable not by doctrine so much as emphasis and tone. As we saw in the last chapter, there is in Virgil a profound mistrust of embodiment, and even of matter, which was at odds with Christian teaching about the Incarnation, and which did not escape the notice of commentators or poets. In Virgil, this suspicion of the body also extends to physical love and desire. It was not always thus: in Virgil's early poetry, *amor vincit omnia* (*Ecl.* 10.69). But in his later poetry, physical *amor* is usually distracting or destructive.

If the leit-motif of Virgil's plot was renunciation, the modern epics are about reconciliation. So far from being an enemy of empire, physical love unites noble blood-lines and establishes dynasties.[133] So much has been written about Virgil's fear of sex that we suspect an exaggeration. And yet, as we saw in Chapter 4, that was Virgil's reputation: virginal in person and, in his descriptions of sex, chaste even to the point of being too cold. This may be a distortion but it is not, for the Renaissance, an anachronism.

The question that remains, and it is the last of the major problems addressed in this book, is why – in the very period when Virgil's authority

---

[131] Thomas P. Roche, Jr., *Petrarch and the English Sonnet Sequences* (New York: AMS, 1989), pp. 107–12.
[132] Cf. Murrin on Tasso: "A poet who neglects to tell us that Jerusalem fell on a Friday at the ninth hour is not encouraging a theological perspective" (*Allegorical Epic*, p. 126).
[133] The point has been made in various ways: see Fichter, *Poets Historical*; Barbara J. Bono, *Literary Transvaluation: From Vergilian Epic to Shakespearean Tragicomedy* (Berkeley and Los Angeles: University of California Press, 1984), pp. 61–79, 81–82; Mihoko Suzuki, *Metamorphoses of Helen: Authority, Difference, and the Epic* (Ithaca, NY: Cornell University Press, 1989), pp. 92–150; Barbara Pavlock, *Eros, Imitation, and the Epic Tradition* (Ithaca, NY: Cornell University Press, 1990); Burrow, *Epic Romance*; Watkins, *Specter of Dido*, chs. 1 and 5; Jane E. Everson, *The Italian Romance Epic in the Age of Humanism: The Matter of Italy and the World of Rome* (Oxford: Oxford University Press, 2001), ch. 6; Jo Ann Cavallo, *The Romance Epics of Boiardo, Ariosto, and Tasso: From Public Duty to Private Pleasure* (Toronto: University of Toronto Press, 2004); Helen Cooper, *The English Romance in Time: Transforming Motifs from Geoffrey of Monmouth to the Death of Shakespeare* (Oxford: Oxford University Press, 2004), ch. 5; and Warner, *Augustinian Epic*.

as a model for epic poetry was at its maximum – did epic become so un-Virgilian as to be erotic? In concrete terms, how is it that Camilla, when she finally reenters vernacular literature after centuries of neglect, so often sheds her tragic aspect and trades virginity for marriage and motherhood?

THE MODERNITY OF ROMANCE

Generically, we might explain this as "the rise of romance." In the Renaissance, complicated stories about love and chivalry were popular with readers of every class, all nations, and both sexes. But what was romance, and how was it different from epic?[134] Spenser, we notice, does not actually use either term. When, in his letter to Raleigh, Spenser mentions his predecessors, he does not distinguish between Virgil and Ariosto, except to say that Virgil is "antique": they are both "Poets historicall" and they both follow the same method, of combining all the knightly virtues into one character. A contemporary of Spenser, George Puttenham (1529–90/91), says that the chronicler John Hardying (1378–1465) was "a Poet Epick or Historicall," as if *epic poet* and *historical poet* were synonyms.[135] In his discussion of the various genres, there is no mention of epic *per se*, but there is a long chapter on "Poesie historicall," of which romance is a subspecies: what Puttenham calls the "historicall ditty."[136] The difference is one of meter rather than content.

In Italy, the difference between *epopeia* and *romanzo* is a subject of controversy. The theorists of romance, Cinzio and Pigna, argue that romance is a new genre, distinct from epic, which did not exist in Aristotle's time and has its own rules. Tasso denies this. Romance, he argues, is not a separate genre at all and the rules of Aristotle still apply. But Tasso does allow for changes in taste. Thus, while he does not condone or employ the term *romance*, he does distinguish between two kinds of epic, ancient and modern. For Tasso, the modern epic differs from the ancient in four important ways: its divine machinery is Christian; its style is sweeter; it has more variety (because modern audiences are easily bored); and it has more love stories.[137]

---

[134] For a review of scholarship and problems, see my "Errors about Ovid and Romance," *Spenser Studies* 23 (2008), 215–34.
[135] George Puttenham, *The Arte of English Poesie* (1589) 1.31, ed. Gladys Doidge Willcock and Alice Walker (Cambridge University Press, 1936), p. 62.
[136] Puttenham, *Arte* 1.19 (ed. Willcock and Walker, pp. 39–42).
[137] Tasso, *Discorsi del poema eroico*, Bk. 2 (love and religion, in *Prose*, pp. 545–52), Bk. 3 (variety, pp. 577–91), and Bk. 4 (style, pp. 657–58).

This last item confirms something we remarked earlier, that the Camilla-figures of Renaissance poetry are prone, in a very un-Virgilian way, to falling in love and getting married. This was new, and the newness of it was noticed by contemporaries. Tasso is tolerably well read in classical epic and he perceives that, while ancient literature does have some love stories (e.g., the *Argonautica* of Apollonius Rhodius), the theme of love is relatively underdeveloped, especially in Virgil. True, there is the story of Dido and Aeneas. "And yet it seems that Virgil is more restrained and sparing than some of us would be, for he might have said many things about the love of Aeneas, about the love of Iarbas, about the love of Turnus and Lavinia – matters on which Virgil was silent, or which he only hinted at."[138] A modern epic, he thinks, will have more love stories, and the love stories will be more central.

How this shift came about Tasso does not say. Not believing in romance as a separate genre, he cannot invoke it as an explanation. He acknowledges, though, that the shift is real. An example is his own character Armida. For most of *Jerusalem Delivered*, Armida is Dido-as-temptress and then, when Rinaldo abandons her, Dido-as-vengeful-psychopath.[139] But in the last canto, Armida echoes the Magnificat of the Virgin Mary (*Ecce ancilla domini*), converts to Christianity, and exchanges vows with Rinaldo to become one another's "servant" (*servo*, *GL* 20.134) and "handmaiden" (*Ecco l'ancilla tua*, 136). In earlier romances, the conversion of one partner usually cleared the way for the pair to get married – in which case Armida will become, with Rinaldo, a co-founder of the Este dynasty.[140]

Another example of the shift that Tasso registers but does not explain comes from Ronsard's *Franciade* (1572), a poem that was going to be the great epic of France, until the author abandoned it after only four books. The hero of the tale is Francus, the wandering son of Trojan Hector. In Book 2 Francus sails to Crete where he meets two princesses, Clymene and Hyante. Both sisters fall in love with Francus, but he will not marry them because his destiny is in Gaul. In Book 3 Clymene becomes jealous and drowns herself; this makes the father suspicious.[141] But the surviving sister, Hyante, is still in love. A sorceress, she takes Francus to the underworld in

---

[138] Tasso, *Discorsi del poema eroico*, Bk. 2 (*Prose*, p. 547).
[139] Cf. Armida's curse (*GL* 16.57–60) with Dido's (*Aen.* 4.365–67, 382–87).
[140] Jo Ann Cavallo, "Tasso's Armida and the Victory of Romance," in *Renaissance Transactions: Ariosto and Tasso*, ed. Valeria Finucci (Durham, NC: Duke University Press, 1999), pp. 77–111.
[141] Cf. the love story which Marlowe invents for Dido's sister, Anna, in *Dido Queen of Carthage* (c. 1585). In Marlowe's version, Anna falls in love with Iarbas, the rejected suitor of Dido, and all three of them commit suicide on Dido's pyre. Varro's version, preserved in Servius, is given below, n. 155.

Book 4 and shows him the future kings of France up to Charlemagne and Pepin, who will be his descendants.

Here the fragment breaks off. It is a mélange of various episodes from classical epic: the Medea story as told by Apollonius; the Dido story, which was modeled on Apollonius; and the parade of unborn descendants, which Virgil invented and we discussed in Chapter 5. What has not, to my knowledge, been commented on is Ronsard's handling of Dido, the way he divides up her qualities between two sisters. The one sister, Clymene, inherits Dido's impulsiveness and commits suicide. The other sister, Hyante, inherits Dido's knowledge of magic and becomes, in effect, a sibyl.[142]

It is tempting here to invoke the familiar dichotomy of virgin and whore. But that is too easy. For one thing, Clymene and Hyante are both virgins. More importantly, both sisters are in love. The impulsive love of Clymene differs from the prophetic love of Hyante, not in being physical, but in being ungoverned.[143]

Love, in most of the Virgilian epics that were produced during the Renaissance, is good, much better than in Virgil himself. If we take the long view, the embrace of love as a subject for epic probably goes back to the Hellenistic poet Apollonius of Rhodes (3rd century BC).[144] Virgil makes use of Apollonius' subject matter and adopts also the subjective style of Hellenistic poetry.[145] Love itself, though, he subordinates: to an episode in the first half and a theme in the second.

In both halves, love is usually tragic. Taking the long view again, we can see this as part of Virgil's Hellenistic inheritance.[146] As we noted in Chapter 1, though, the term *Hellenistic* was not used by critics until after our period: scholars in the Renaissance were familiar with some Hellenistic texts, but they didn't group or comment on them as a category. Thus, for Tasso, Apollonius and his *Argonautica* are not representatives of a school or movement in ancient literature – indeed, Tasso has no notion of the movement's existence. Instead, they are forerunners of something modern, the epic about love.

---

[142] Cf. Suzuki, *Metamorphoses* on the division of Helen-characters into victims and temptresses.
[143] It is the same in Tasso's first epic, *Rinaldo* (1559); see Cavallo, "Tasso's Armida," p. 84.
[144] Pavlock, *Eros, Imitation*, ch. 1.
[145] See Brooks Otis, *Virgil: A Study in Civilized Poetry* (Oxford: Oxford University Press, 1964), chs. 2–3 and Wendell Clausen, *Virgil's* Aeneid *and the Tradition of Hellenistic Poetry* (Berkeley and Los Angeles: University of California Press, 1987). Virgil's use of Apollonius was well known, even to those who had not actually read the *Argonautica*, because it was mentioned by Servius at the beginning of his commentary on Book 4 (Giunta 1544, fol. 266ᵛ).
[146] Pavlock, *Eros, Imitation*, ch. 2.

DIDO AND LAVINIA: THE IMPORTANCE OF *ENEAS*

Why love became so important was more than Tasso could say, or we need to speculate.[147] We can specify, though, with some precision, how and when married (rather than tragic) love became part of the Western tradition – not as an episode or theme, but as a subject and even the climax of an epic poem. The key document is the anonymous *Roman d'Eneas*, produced at the court of Anjou *c.* 1160. Composed, like its near-contemporaries the *Roman de Thèbes* (*c.* 1150) and the *Roman de Troie* (1165), in a deliberately archaic French, it is one of the earliest and best examples of *roman antique*. Like the other *romans antiques*, the *Eneas* is a story from classical literature, with classical deities and classical rituals, but told in a modern language, using modern prosody (octosyllabic couplets instead of dactylic hexameter), and with modern (i.e., medieval) motivations for its characters. In length, it is about 10,000 lines depending on the version (cf. 9,896 for the *Aeneid*) and follows closely the order of events established by Virgil, with some differences.[148]

First, the sympathy with Dido that was latent in Virgil's original is here overt and ostentatious: a conflation of Virgil's Dido with Ovid's in *Heroides* 7, she is a tragic queen, more sinned against than sinning.[149] Second, the role of Turnus is reduced. Politically, he seems to represent "the danger of decentralized, early feudal rule and the chaos of private war."[150] His death scene, though, is passed over quickly and is no longer the climax of the narrative. Instead (and this third change is the most important), the poem ends with the courtship and marriage of Aeneas and Lavinia.

This is hard to accept because, compared with Dido, Lavinia seems bland. John Watkins makes the point forcefully:

---

[147] Douglas Kelly thinks it has something to do with ecclesiastical reforms in the twelfth century which redefined marriage and placed a new emphasis on consent and mutuality; see *The Conspiracy of Allusion: Description, Rewriting, and Authorship from Macrobius to Medieval Romance* (Leiden: Brill, 1999), pp. 171–94.

[148] The standard critical edition (based on the A manuscript) is by J. J. Salverda de Grave, *Enéas, roman du xiie siècle*, 2 vols. (Paris: Champion, 1925 and 1929). For secondary works, see Aimé Petit and Jean Dufournet, "Bibliographie de l'*Enéas*," in *Relire le* Roman d'Enéas, ed. Jean Dufournet (Paris: Champion, 1985), pp. 189–99, which lists editions, translations, critical studies (both of the Old French *Eneas* and of its Middle High German adaptation, the *Eneit* by Heinrich van Veldekeits), and general studies of the *roman antique*. English readers are well served by John A. Yunck's translation, *Eneas: A Twelfth-Century French Romance* (New York: Columbia University Press, 1974), which includes a long introduction and annotated bibliography.

[149] See Raymond Cormier, *One Heart One Mind: The Rebirth of Virgil's Hero in Medieval French Romance* (University, MS: University Monographs, 1973), pp. 131, 136.

[150] Baswell, *Virgil in Medieval England*, p. 206.

[A]s an embodiment of Augustan restraint who hardly speaks, Lavinia pales beside Dido. Her most memorable act is blushing when her mother begs Turnus not to confront the Trojans. Her blush is so inscrutable that classicists still debate whether it reveals her love for Turnus or her embarrassment over her mother's hysterics. Her *pudor* makes her an appropriate ancestor for Augustus, but it can never be as engaging as Dido's passionate intensity.[151]

What Lavinia lacks is not conviction so much as substance. Turnus, we know, loves her madly, but there is not enough of her in Virgil's poem for us to share his excitement. For the reader, and perhaps for Aeneas too, Lavinia is a trophy, a token; Lillian Robinson calls her "the consolation prize."[152] Dido, in comparison, has a whole book to herself (*Aeneid* 4) and makes big appearances in two more books that everyone remembers (Books 1 and 6); this explains, even justifies, what one critic calls the "Didocentricism" of current scholarship.[153]

There is almost no one who has not shed tears for Dido, from Ovid and Augustine to the present day.[154] In her madness, perhaps, she is less attractive (at least to my male students). But Dido is febrile, not fragile; indeed, Virgil has endowed Dido with an iron will: to flee her homeland, to found a city and give laws, to curse her lover when he sneaks away, to follow through on a secret plan for suicide, and in the underworld to maintain her Ajax-like silence when Aeneas desires to explain himself. Compared with Virgil's Dido, Ovid's Dido (in *Heroides* 7) is a simplification. A mere victim, she is sad, but somehow not tragic – not tragic because not strong. We pity her more, and care about her less. The result, historically, was that Ovid's Dido remained a filter, instead of a character in her own right. Chaucer, when he summarizes Dido's career in the *House of Fame*, borrows details from Ovid, but integrates them back into

---

[151] Watkins, *Specter of Dido*, p. 27. The description of Lavinia's blush (*Aen.* 12.64–71; cf. *Il.* 4.141) was a favorite one for later poets to imitate: *The Works of Edmund Spenser: A Variorum Edition*, ed. Edwin Greenlaw *et al.*, 11 vols. (Baltimore: Johns Hopkins University Press, 1932–57), vol. 11, pp. 120, 296 gives examples from Spenser, Ovid, Statius, Claudian, and Ariosto.

[152] Robinson, *Monstrous Regiment*, p. 58.

[153] Colin Burrow, review of John Watkins, *The Specter of Dido* (1995), in *Modern Philology* 95 (1997), 103–6, at 103, 105–6.

[154] There are excellent surveys of Dido's reputation through the ages, of which the most complete is Paola Bono and M. Vittoria Tessitore, *Il mito di Didone: Avventure di una regina tra secoli e culture* (Milan: Mondadori, 1998). See also D. C. Allen, "Marlowe's *Dido* and the Tradition," in *Essays on Shakespeare and Elizabethan Drama in Honor of Hardin Craig*, ed. Richard Hosley (Columbia: University of Missouri Press, 1962), pp. 55–68; N. M. Horsfall, "Dido in the Light of History," *Proceedings of the Virgil Society* 13 (1973–74), 1–13; Desmond, *Reading Dido*; and Watkins, *Specter of Dido*, ch. 2.

the Virgilian story. In this way, Ovid colors the reading of Virgil, but does not actually replace him.

Another filter between Virgil's text and the reader was the knowledge, widespread in the ancient world and never lost in the Middle Ages, that Virgil distorts the historical record about Dido: that in north Africa there really was a fugitive queen from Lebanon, but that she lived three hundred years after the fall of Troy; that her name was Elissa; and that when her first husband, Sicharbas, died, she chose suicide on a funeral pyre rather than submit to a forced marriage with one of the local potentates. This story was available from multiple sources – including Servius, Macrobius, and the Church Fathers – and in letters and sermons Dido was cited repeatedly as an example of conjugal chastity.[155]

There were two Didos, then: the historical Dido who died for loyalty and the fictional Dido who died for love. Poets knew about both and used both in their fiction. In Petrarch's *Africa*, which he began in 1338 but never published, the historical Dido appears under her own name, as the woman who dies rather than remarry. But there is also a second Dido-figure, Sophonisba, who waylays her Roman conqueror, kills herself when he breaks off the affair, and is damned to hell then as a suicide.[156] Boccaccio, in his earlier works, created several female characters who were based on Virgil's fictional queen. But after his meeting with Petrarch, in 1350, his major works were written in Latin and featured the Dido of history.[157] Spenser, too, included both versions of Dido in his *Faerie Queene*. On one side are the temptresses, such as Duessa, Phaedria, and Acrasia, who lure men away from the quest; on the other side is Amavia, who is loyal to her husband and resembles the historical Dido in committing suicide after his death.[158]

---

[155] Servius notes the chronological gap of 300 years in his commentary on *Aen.* 1.267. In Book 4 he records that Dido's real name was *Elissa*; she was called *Dido*, he speculates, from the Punic word for *virago*, "heroine," because she jumped into the fire to avoid a second marriage (36, 674). In Book 5, he cites the opinion of Marcus Terentius Varro (116–27 BC), the great Roman antiquarian, that it was not Dido who fell in love with Aeneas, but her sister, Anna (4). According to Macrobius, *Sat.* 5.17.4–6, everyone knows that the story of Dido and Aeneas is fiction; we acquiesce, though, on account of its *pulchritudo* (Venice 1492, fol. lxviii'). Tertullian mentions the historical Dido four times, as do Jerome (twice), Timaeus of Tauromenium, Justin, Florus, Orosius, Otto of Freising, Servius, Macrobius, the Planudean Appendix, Priscian, Petrarch (twice), Boccaccio (four times), Benvenuto da Imola, John Lydgate, Giorgio Merula, Cristóbal de Virues, Gabriel Lobo Lasso de la Vega, George Buchanan, George Turberville, Jan Kochanowski (twice), Thomas Heywood, George Rivers, and Hans Sach; see Mary Louise Lord, "Dido as an Example of Chastity: The Influence of Example Literature," *Harvard Library Bulletin* 17 (1969), 22–44, 216–32.

[156] See Kallendorf, *Praise of Aeneas*, ch. 2 and Warner, *Augustinian Epic*, ch. 1.

[157] See Kallendorf, *Praise of Aeneas*, ch. 3.   [158] See Watkins, *Specter of Dido*, ch. 5.

For some of us, Dido would be too much; for others, more than we could hope for. For Aeneas, however, Dido is not enough. No woman is. This may be a flaw in his character, and yet many readers have felt sorry for Aeneas. Whether he deserves it or not, they want him to found Rome *and* find love. Virgil makes no promises. "Learn virtue from me," says Aeneas, "and the real nature of labor; let others teach you about happiness (*fortunam*)" (*Aen.* 12.435–36). At the end of the *Aeneid*, we know that Aeneas and Lavinia are going to be married. We know also from Anchises' prophecy that they will conceive a child together, Silvius (*Aen.* 6.761–66). But there is nothing about love.

On the other hand, there is nothing in the poem to say they *won't* be happy. This is why the *Eneas* romance was so important. What Virgil left out, *Eneas* puts back in: the wonderment of Lavinia when she saw Aeneas for the first time; how she made the first move (one critic says she is even more "aggressive" about love than Dido);[159] the theory of love and the conduct of lovers; advice from Lavinia's mother (who did not commit suicide after all); how Lavinia worried about Aeneas while he was on the battlefield; how he apologized for not coming right back to her when Turnus was dead.

Much of this, especially the falling in love and the doctrine of love, comes from Ovid.[160] And this is where, in my view, we should locate Ovid's real contribution to the development of romance, properly understood.[161] For the *Eneas*-poet, Ovid was not a rival to Virgil so much as an alloy or quarry. Whatever his intentions might have been, Ovid provided the materials – the images and topoi – for making the *Aeneid* into a conventional love story. At the very moment – almost in the very poem – when medieval romance was coming into being, epic itself was being transformed, if not distorted. The story was ending with marriage and the warrior was turning into a lover. No longer just *pius Aeneas*, in the French text he was now "Eneas, li cortois, li fins amis, li douz amis, gentilz Eneas"; he was burning "de fine amor toz tens estable."[162] The final redaction of the poem, made in the late fourteenth century, intensified the love interest even further.[163]

---

[159] Cooper, *English Romance*, pp. 231–32.
[160] See Edmond Faral, "Ovide et quelques autres sources du *Roman d'Enéas*," *Romania* 40 (1911), 161–234; and Erich Auerbach, *Literary Language and Its Public in Late Latin Antiquity and in the Middle Ages* (1958), trans. Ralph Manheim (Princeton: Princeton University Press, 1965), pp. 208–15.
[161] See my "Errors about Ovid and Romance."
[162] Annie Triaud, "Survie de l'*Enéas* dans une version tardive," in *Relire le* Roman d'Enéas, ed. Jean Dufournet (Paris: Champion, 1985), pp. 169–87, at 180.
[163] See Triaud, "Survie de l'*Enéas*," pp. 177–80.

VEGIO'S SEQUEL: THE MISSING LINK WITH THE MIDDLE AGES

By the early thirteenth century, *Eneas* was being referred to as the "roman d'Eneas *e da Laivine*."[164] The change is significant. There have been maybe four big events (I do not say ideas) in the reception history of Virgil's poem, and one of these is the filling out of Lavinia's character and making her an adequate replacement for Dido. What sets this apart from the other big events – let us say, the compilation by Servius of other ancient commentators, the discovery of Donatus' *Vita* in the fifteenth century, and the renaissance of Virgil's Iliad a hundred years later – is that Lavinia's flowering had almost nothing to do with the scholarly tradition of commentary and literary criticism. There had been hints, in Fulgentius (fifth century AD), John of Salisbury (*c.* 1115–80), and Bernardus Silvestris (fl. 1136), that Lavinia was supposed to replace Dido.[165] But it was a poet who developed the hints and turned Lavinia into a real character.

We can begin now to answer the question we posed earlier. How, when Virgil was such a cold fish, did love become so important in Renaissance epics like *Orlando furioso* and *The Faerie Queene*? Where, for example, did married heroines like Britomart come from? Let us start with the second question. Britomart and her literary sisters are a combination of Camilla, the woman warrior, and Lavinia, the desiring wife. Of the two components, Camilla is more familiar to us, but in fact the older and more established type was Lavinia. Camilla was the innovation, the Renaissance contribution to epic storytelling. Why are Renaissance epics so much more positive about love than Virgil was? I have no final answer for this, except to push the question back another four hundred years, to the High Middle Ages: as long as there have been vernacular adaptations of the *Aeneid*, from *Eneas* onward, love has been one of the grand themes and marriage has been the climax.

The success of *Eneas* was international. Originally composed at the French court of Anjou, it was translated almost immediately into Middle High German by Heinrich van Veldeke (fl. 1175). Today, the French text is extant in nine manuscripts, including three from Italy and one, possibly two, from England.[166] Five or six copies survive from the early to late fourteenth century, which gives an idea of how long the poem was

---

[164] See G. Raynaud de Lage, "Les 'romans antiques' dans l'*Histoire ancienne jusqu'à César*," *Le moyen âge*, 4th ser., 12 (1957), 267–309, at 297 (emphasis mine).
[165] See my "Lavinia and Beatrice," pp. 108–12.
[166] For provenance and dates, see Cormier, "Gleanings on the Manuscript Tradition of the *Roman d'Eneas*," *Manuscripta* 18 (1974), 42–47.

popular.¹⁶⁷ It wasn't until 1891, though, that the romance made the jump to print.¹⁶⁸ In what form, then, would it have influenced Renaissance epic? If there really is a connection between Lavinia in the Middle Ages and Britomart in the Renaissance, we need to fill in some missing links.

One link is tapestry. For generations, the Hapsburg emperors traced their lineage back to Troy, by way of Aeneas and Lavinia. Images of their wedding were made in tapestry and served as icons of imperial authority. Philip II of Spain owned one, as did someone at Hampton Court (perhaps Cardinal Wolsey).¹⁶⁹

Another link is Boccaccio's *Teseida* or *Teseide*, which today is famous chiefly as the source for Chaucer's Knight's Tale. The poem has twelve books, each with as many lines as the corresponding book of the *Aeneid*. Its main source, other than Virgil, is Virgil's most faithful imitator, Statius. Virgil ends with death, Statius with a funeral. Boccaccio, though, ends with a marriage; hence the poem's full title, *The Theseid of Emily's Nuptials*. This is where Boccaccio breaks from his classical sources and shows himself a modern. Boccaccio's epic was finished in 1340; it does not allude directly to the *Eneas* romance, but it was written during a period when the French text was still being copied by Italian scribes and caters to a similar taste: a taste for vernacular stories based on classical models, with marriage as the climax rather than death. The *Theseid* was printed in 1475 and remained in print until at least 1579. Castelvetro credited Boccaccio with inventing ottava rima, as a vernacular substitute for the heroic meter of Homer and Virgil.¹⁷⁰ Tasso accepted this account and proclaimed Boccaccio as the founder of modern epic, "the first to write about love and arms in our language."¹⁷¹

Eneas had an influence on English authors, as well. As Helen Cooper explains,

There is no Middle English version of the *Eneas* itself, but it was a text known in the Angevin court of Henry II, and its treatment of love was rapidly transmitted into the English romance tradition through the mediation of French and Anglo-Norman authors who knew it and whose influence can be directly traced in

---

¹⁶⁷ In "Lavinia and Beatrice," I mistakenly cited Baswell, *Virgil in Medieval England*, pp. 178 and 379 n. 42 for the existence of a fifteenth-century MS.; Baswell, though, was referring to another poem.
¹⁶⁸ *Enéas: texte critique*, ed. Jean-Jacques Salverda de Grave (Halle: Niemeyer, 1891). Selections were published earlier by Alexandre Peŷ in 1856.
¹⁶⁹ See Tanner, *Last Descendant*, ch. 5; Philip's tapestry is reproduced on p. 137. For the Hampton Court tapestry, see W. A. Sessions, *Henry Howard, the Poet Earl of Surrey: A Life* (Oxford: Oxford University Press, 1999), p. 238.
¹⁷⁰ Lodovico Castelvetro, *Poetica d'Aristotele vulgarizzata e sposta*, ed. Werther Romani, 2 vols. (Rome: Laterza, 1978–79), vol. II, pp. 157–58.
¹⁷¹ Tasso, *Discorsi del poema eroico* (1594), Bk. 6 (*Prose*, p. 724).

England. The centrality of its representation of desiring women was passed directly forwards into early printed romances, along with their Petrarch-like language of desire.[172]

Cooper gives the examples of *William of Palerne* (*c.* 1200, printed *c.* 1515) and Hue of Rhuddlan's *Ipomydon* (*c.* 1190, printed 1522 and 1527).

A fourth link between *Eneas* and the Renaissance is Maffeo Vegio (1407–58)'s supplement to the *Aeneid*, also known as Book 13.[173] This was not the first sequel to the *Aeneid*, nor would it be the last.[174] But unlike the other Book 13s, Vegio's was wildly popular. It was finished in 1428; after an interval of more than five hundred years, there are still almost fifty surviving manuscripts, some of them made after printed copies were also available. Not that printed copies were rare, either. The first was made in 1471, only two years after the *editio princeps* of Virgil himself. After that it was reprinted scores of times, usually with Virgil's own *opera*. In the fifteenth century, Vegio and his supplement were praised by Lorenzo Valla and Francesco Filelfo; in the sixteenth century, his similes were praised by Julius Caesar Scaliger.[175] A Scots translation, by Bishop Gavin Douglas (*c.* 1476–1522), was composed in 1513 and published in 1553 (STC 24797). An English translation, by the physician Thomas Twyne (1543–1613), appeared in 1573 (STC 24801) and was reprinted five times (1584, 1596, 1600, 1607, 1620). Again and in both cases, the translation of Vegio was published with a translation of Virgil's own text; Twyne even titled his translation *The .xiii. Bookes of Æneidos*.

---

[172] Cooper, *English Romance*, p. 234.
[173] For Vegio's supplement there is now a critical edition and a new English translation; see *Das Aeneissupplement des Maffeo Vegio* (with a German translation), ed. Bernd Schneider (Weinheim: Acta Humaniora, 1985) and *Short Epics*, trans. Michael C. J. Putnam (Cambridge, MA: Harvard University Press, 2004), reviewed by me in *Classical Bulletin* 81 (2006), 240–42. The best introduction is Kallendorf, *Praise of Aeneas*, ch. 5; see also A. C. Brinton, *Maphaeus Vegius and His Thirteenth Book of the Aeneid: A Chapter on Virgil in the Renaissance* (Stanford: Stanford University Press, 1930), which includes an old-spelling text of the Twyne translation; Charles S. Ross, "Maffeo Vegio's 'short Cristyn wark,' with a Note on the Thirteenth Book in Early Editions of Vergil," *Modern Philology* 78 (1981), 215–26; and Margaret Tudeau-Clayton, "Supplementing the *Aeneid* in Early Modern England: Translation, Imitation, Commentary," *International Journal of the Classical Tradition* 4 (1998), 507–25. Putnam lists additional studies in his introduction and bibliography.
[174] A correspondent of Vegio, Pier Candido Decembrio, began to write one in 1419 but only completed eighty-nine verses; he playfully accused Vegio of plagiarism. For even less famous sequels, see Hans Kern, *Supplemente zur Äneis aus dem 15 und 17 Jahrhunderdt* (Nuremberg: Stich, 1896) and Paul Gerhard Schmidt, "Neulateinische Supplemente zur Aeneis. Mit einer Edition der *Exsequiae Turni* von Jan van Foreest," in *Acta conventus neo-latini lovaniensis*, ed. Jozeph Ijsewijn and Eckhard Kessler (Louvain: Leuven University Press, 1973), pp. 517–55.
[175] For Valla and Scaliger, see Brinton, *Maphaeus Vegius*, 4–5. Filelfo is quoted in the opening section of Badius's commentary on the supplement (Giunta 1544, fol. 533ᵛ).

Vegio was becoming, like Servius, a classic in his own right. As with Servius, there was even a commentary. Two commentaries, in fact: one by Badius Ascensius (1501), whose commentary on Virgil we have already quoted many times, and one by Nicolaus Erythraeus (1538/9), whose edition of Virgil was used by Tasso and Montaigne. Of the two, Badius's commentary was reprinted much more frequently and in what follows I shall try to read Vegio through it. Mostly it is concerned with pointing out images and phrases that Vegio has borrowed from Virgil, so I shall use the same method.

Vegio's sequel is short, only 630 verses. It narrates the exsequies of Turnus, the nuptials of Lavinia, and the death of Aeneas, mostly in the form of speeches. The death of Aeneas comes from *Metamorphoses* 14.566–608, which tells how Aeneas drowned in the river Numicius and was transformed into a god. The language, though, comes from Virgil and, where possible, the material as well. Vegio almost never invents anything out of whole cloth. Whenever he needs to say something, he searches his text (or his memory) of the *Aeneid* in order to find the proper Virgilian way of saying it; then he uses that form.

This method has two main effects. First, by using Virgil's own language, Vegio makes his sequel sound Virgilian.[176] The second effect is more complicated. Not only does Vegio reuse Virgil's language, he also recycles Virgil's images. This tends to make the whole story – not just Vegio's, but Virgil's story – more symmetrical. An example is the wedding banquet of Aeneas and Lavinia. First, Aeneas tells his companion, the faithful Achates, to fetch gifts from the treasures they have brought from Troy (*Supp.* 478–89). As Badius notes in his commentary, this little episode comes from *Aen.* 1.643–56, where Aeneas sends Achates to fetch gifts for Dido from what remains of the Trojan treasury. The description of the dinner proper (*Supp.* 490–509) follows the same pattern. As Badius puts it, "All the trappings (*Totus . . . apparatus*) of the banquet are drawn from *Aeneid* 1, where the banquet of Dido is described thus," at which point he cites the appropriate parallels from *Aen.* 1.637–41 and 701–02: purple couches, water to wash the hands, "Ceres" (i.e., grain products), choice meats, and an army of waiters to serve them.[177]

There are differences and these, too, elicit commentary. When Vegio says that King Latinus spent the night admiring the face and manners of the

---

[176] George Duckworth, "Maphaeus Vegius and Vergil's *Aeneid*: A Metrical Comparison," *Classical Philology* 64 (1969), 1–6; Kallendorf, *Praise of Aeneas*, pp. 106–26.
[177] Badius on *Supp.* 487 (Giunta 1544, fol. 538ᵛ).

young Ascanius, until finally he took him into his lap (*Supp.* 501–08), Badius notes that this, too, is taken from the description of Dido's dinner banquet, where Dido takes an *imago* of Ascanius into her lap (it is really Cupid in disguise) and admires his appearance (*Aen.* 1.712–19). But in contrast with Dido, Badius says that Latinus behaves "decorously" (*decenter*) and "with more propriety" (*magis ... congrue*). For whereas Dido only took notice of the boy's *forma*, the old king marvels at his words and his face (*vultus*), which Badius calls the "index of the mind."[178] This is parallel for the sake of comparison. There is continuity with the past, and also progress. Italy is like Carthage, but does not repeat Carthage; rather it overgoes Carthage and completes – supplements – what was lacking: in Dido's case, propriety and decorum.

In the sequel, however, propriety and pleasure are not mutually exclusive. Again, the wedding banquet will serve as an example. Vegio records that the guests ate until their hunger was satisfied. Does this mean that the banquet was sparing and did not encourage gluttony?[179] Or, on the contrary, that its fare was inexhaustible? The setting provides a clue: according to Vegio, the guests were waited on by countless servants (*ministri innumeri*), a thronging crowd (*Turba frequens*).[180] As for hunger being satisfied (*compressa fames*), Badius derives the phrase from one in Virgil, *exempta fames*, a formula that is used once after the Trojans have a picnic on the beach (*Aen.* 1.216), and a second time after Aeneas has dinner with the Etruscan king, Evander (*Aen.* 8.184).[181] In ancient and medieval commentary, there was a tradition of contrasting both meals, which are frugal, with the luxurious fare served at Dido's court.[182] And it is possible that Vegio wanted a similar contrast here. But if so, the point was lost on Badius, who complains that "luxury of this sort seems to befit the opulence of Tyre more than the parsimony of Italy."[183] In other words, Vegio has not sufficiently distinguished the corrected pleasures of Latium from their counterparts in Carthage. That correction was intended by Vegio is clear to Badius, from his comments on Latinus and Ascanius. But Vegio does not carry the point farther than he has to: for him, pleasure can be purified without being purged out of existence.

---

[178] Badius on *Supp.* 501 (Giunta 1544, fol. 538ᵛ). [179] Watkins, *Specter of Dido*, p. 110.
[180] *Supp.* 496–97, 500 (Giunta 1544, fol. 538ᵛ).
[181] Badius on *Supp.* 509 (Giunta 1544, fol. 538ᵛ). Cf. also *Aen.* 8.184: "Postquam exempta fames, & amor compressus edendi" (Giunta 1544, fol. 400ᵛ).
[182] Macrobius, *Saturnalia* 2.1.1 and John of Salisbury, *Policraticus* 8.6.730b, cited by Watkins, *Specter of Dido*, p. 128.
[183] Badius on *Supp.* 493 (Giunta 1544, fol. 538ᵛ).

We notice the same pattern in his description of Aeneas when he sees Lavinia for the first time:

> Hæc inter matrum innumera, nur[u]umque caterua
> In medium comitata venit Lauinia virgo
> Sydereos deiecta oculos, quam Troius heros
> Virtute & forma ingentem, mirabile dictu,
> Vt vidit, primo aspectu stupefactus inhæsit,
> Et secum Turni casus miseratus acerbos,
> Qui haud parua spe ductus, ouans in prælia tantos
> Ciuisset motus, durisque arsisset in armis.[184]

[Meanwhile, the maiden Lavinia came into their midst, her starry eyes downcast, accompanied by a numberless throng of matrons and young married women. When the Trojan hero saw her, so virtuous, as well as beautiful – wonderful to tell – he clove to the sight at once, stunned, and in his heart he pitied the bitter fate of Turnus, whose motivation was not slight, driven in his exultation to stir up great battles, to rage in fierce arms.]

As with the banquet scene, the phrasing comes from Virgil himself. The first three lines (*Hæc ... oculos*) are, as Badius points out, drawn from Virgil's description of Lavinia and her mother going to sacrifice at the temple:

> Subuehitur magna matrum regina caterua,
> Dona ferens, iuxtaque comes Lauinia uirgo,
> Causa mali tanti, atque oculos deiecta decoros.[185]

[The queen goes up with a long train of matrons, bearing gifts, with the maiden Lavinia at her side, the cause of so much woe, her lovely eyes cast down.]

How do we interpret those eyes? The ancient commentator T. C. Donatus (who had not been discovered yet when Vegio was writing) gives two options: "Lavinia casts her eyes down, perhaps on account of her current unpopularity [as the source of her country's ills], perhaps from virginal modesty."[186] Vegio blames Turnus for the war, not Lavinia, so the first option is not relevant. But he still makes Lavinia observe the proprieties by keeping her head down: this is how Aeneas can tell that she is "virtuous, as well as beautiful." And yet Lavinia's virtue in no way eclipses her physical attractiveness. Compare Virgil's description of Turnus when he sees Lavinia blush:

> Illum turbat amor, figitque in virgine vultus;
> Ardet in arma magis.[187]

---

[184] Vegio, *Supp.* 466–73 (Giunta 1544, fol. 538ʳ⁻ᵛ).   [185] *Aen.* 11.478–80 (Giunta 1544, fol. 493ᵛ).
[186] T. C. Donatus on *Aen.* 11.480 (Giunta 1544, fol. 494ʳ).   [187] *Aen.* 12.70–71 (Giunta 1544, fol. 510ʳ).

[He is overwhelmed by love and fixes his gaze on the virgin; more than ever he burns for battle.]

Vegio omits the blush, but keeps the pattern of stimulus and response: Aeneas reacts to Lavinia's starry eyes in the same way (*aspectu inhæsit*) that Turnus reacted to her blushing (*figitque in virgine vultus*). Indeed, says Vegio, now Aeneas can understand why Turnus went to war! To be sure, Aeneas is overwhelmed by love and we might say, therefore, that Aeneas corrects something that was defective in Turnus. But he is still recognizable as a lover.

There are more echoes to analyze. The image that links them – and the link is there in Virgil, not just Vegio – is the train (*caterua*) of followers. When, in Vegio, Lavinia leads in her *caterua* of matrons and young married women, he is (as we have seen) echoing Virgil's description of her mother, leading a long *caterua* of matrons (*Aen.* 11.478–79). Behind both scenes, though, stands the description of a third *caterua*, that of Dido:

> Regina ad templum, forma pulcherrima Dido,
> Incessit, magna iuuenum stipante caterua.
> Qualis in Eurotæ ripis, aut per iuga Cynthi
> Exercet Diana choros, quam mille secutæ
> Hinc atque hinc glomerantur Oreades: illa pharetram
> Fert umero, gradiensque deas supereminet omneis.
> Latonæ tacitum pertentant gaudia pectus.
> Talis erat Dido, talem se læta ferebat
> Per medios, instans operi, regnisque futuris.
> Tum foribus diuæ, media testudine templi
> Septa armis, solioque alte subnixa resedit.
> Iura dabat, legesque uiris: operumque laborem
> Partibus æquabat iustis, aut sorte trahebat.[188]

[The queen strode to the temple, lovely-bodied Dido
with a great company of youths thronging about.
Just as, on the shores of Eurotas or over the peaks of Cynthus,
Diana directs her dancing bands, followed by a thousand
Oreads, who gather on every side – she carries a quiver
on her shoulder, when she walks she towers over all the goddesses,
and gladness plies the silent heart of Latona –
such was Dido, thus did she bear herself in gladness
through their midst, spurring on the task, the kingdom to be.
Then at the door of the goddess, in the center of the temple vault,
girt with arms, enthroned on high, she took her seat,
gave men orders and laws, and distributed their tasks
evenly, or assigned them by lot.]

---

[188] *Aen.* 1.496–508 (Giunta 1544, fol. 185ᵛ).

Figure 4. Prompted by Venus (viz., beauty), Aeneas woos Lavinia. Detail of woodcut illustration in *Publij Uirgilii Maronis opera*, ed. Sebastian Brant (Strasbourg: Grüninger, 1502). Reproduced in A. C. Brinton, *Maphaeus Vegius and His Thirteenth Book of the Aeneid* (Stanford: Stanford University Press, 1930), p. ii.

This is the first time that Aeneas has seen Dido, and so it is fitting that Vegio recalls this particular moment when he wants to describe the hero's first impressions of Lavinia. The implication is that Aeneas is now seeing Lavinia as he once saw Dido: not as a mænad, crazed by love and threatening vengeance, but as a queen, regal in her bearing, rendering judgments; a law-giver, an empire-builder even. It is a picture of Dido at her best, and now it is become a picture of Lavinia, as if to say that she will be what Dido could have been, had it seemed otherwise to the gods.

Again, this is a way of presenting Lavinia as a corrected version of Dido, and as such, there is always the danger that it will drain both parties of the very qualities that made Dido attractive in the first place. But in comparing Lavinia to Dido as she seemed to Aeneas in her prelapsarian state, Vegio is careful to avoid the impression that Aeneas is just looking for a capable administrator (see Figure 4). He does this in part by eliminating any reference to Lavinia's role in the government of Latium and in part by emphasizing Lavinia's physical beauty (as Virgil had emphasized Dido's).

Vegio also tells us how Aeneas responded to that beauty:

> Vt vidit, primo aspectu stupefactus inhæsit.
> [As soon as he saw her, he clove to the sight, stunned.]

This is a composite of two lines from Virgil, Turnus looking at Lavinia and Dido looking at Aeneas:

> Obstupuit primo aspectu Sidonia Dido.[189]
> [Dido from Sidon was stunned at first sight.]

Again the echo is flagged by Badius.[190] We have noticed already that Aeneas looks at Lavinia the way Turnus once looked at her, and as he himself once looked at Dido. Now Vegio reverses the perspective once again, and shows us Aeneas looking at Lavinia as Dido once looked at him. Again, Vegio alludes to a point in Dido's career that precedes her fatal love-madness: she is falling in love, but she has not yet been degraded by love. Aeneas, therefore, loses nothing by the comparison. And yet, love retains its power to "stun" (literally, to stupefy). By comparing Aeneas to Dido, Vegio attributes to Lavinia the power to compel an erotic response: Aeneas' reaction to her suggests that she has become, not just a consolation

---

[189] *Aen.* 1.613 (Giunta 1544, fol. 192^r).
[190] Badius on *Supp.* 470 (Giunta 1544, fol. 538^r). Vegio may also be recalling moments from vernacular literature, Dante's meeting with Beatrice and Boccaccio's with Fiametta; see Vladimiro Zabughin, *Vergilio nel rinascimento italiano da Dante a Torquato Tasso*, 2 vols. (Bologna: Zanichelli, 1921, 1923), vol. 1, pp. 282–83.

Figure 5. Lavinia's wooing and wedding feast. Detail of woodcut illustration to Maphaeus Vegius, *Supplementum*, in *P. Vergilii Maronis opera* (Zurich: Froschauer, 1564), p. 460. From the copy in the Rare Book Collection, The University of North Carolina at Chapel Hill. This series of woodcuts first appeared in 1559, at Frankfurt am Main, and was copied several times over the next fifty years; see Theodore K. Rabb, "Sebastien Brant and the First Illustrated Edition of Vergil," *Princeton University Library Chronicle* 21 (1960), 187–99, at 198.

prize, but a real alternative to the woman he was forced to leave behind in Carthage. Aeneas also seems to be recovering something that we might have thought he had lost: the capacity to fall in love (Figure 5).

Vegio was only twenty-one when he wrote the *Supplement*. The year was 1428, and many of the great discoveries that we associate with classical scholarship in the Renaissance were still in the future. Humanism was still young and the medieval tradition of *roman antique* was not yet dead. There were, so far as we know, no new manuscripts of the *Eneas* being copied, but the old ones were only half a century old. Whether Vegio ever held one we don't know. What he wrote, though, shows that he was working under its influence: the influence, by this time, not just of one poem, but a tradition of poems (including Boccaccio's *Theseid*) in which love and marriage were the natural conclusion of a story based on Virgil. Vegio was an heir to that tradition, and preserved it for another two hundred years.

VEGIO'S INFLUENCE

How could anyone read the *Aeneid* and see Lavinia as a plausible substitute for Dido? What Vegio did to Virgil was maybe perverse. It is an example, though, of something that had been going on since the Middle Ages. This is a paradox that will be familiar to everyone who has studied Renaissance epic, "that precisely the period which saw the birth, development, and flowering of humanist ideas and of literature based on those ideas is the very same period in which the 'medieval' genre of the romance epic saw its major flowering in Italy, culminating in the work of Ariosto."[191] Ariosto was, like Vegio, a synthesizer of the old and the new. Bradamante is an example. She is a warrior, like Camilla, and in this respect she is new. But at the end of the poem she gets married to Ruggiero, and in this respect she is old. It is the same with Spenser's Britomart.

Both aspects of this character, the warrior and the wife, come (in a sense) from Virgil. But if we go back and read the *Aeneid*, they are hard to recognize, especially the wife. But Spenser and Ariosto did not read Virgil in the pristine isolation of an OCT or Teubner. Between 1469, when it first appeared, and 1599, when Spenser died, the *Aeneid* was printed and reprinted at least 439 times. No fewer than 137 of those reprintings, or just under one-third, were accompanied by Vegio's sequel. This made the sequel more popular (or at least more available) than any of the actual commentaries on Virgil. Authoritative though he was, not even Servius (printed 125 times over the same period) circulated this widely.

The *Supplement* was a work of fiction, not a commentary. But it functioned like a commentary in the way it channeled interpretation. To be sure, no paratext, whether it be sequel or commentary, has the power to *define* a text for any reader. That is one of the beautiful things about reading, that we can skip or ignore anything we choose: headnotes, commentaries, introductions, our own marginal notations, anything. But people did read Vegio and, until the second half of the seventeenth century, publishers kept printing him. While they did, it was Vegio's privilege to demonstrate, for the world and for other poets, how Aeneas could fall in love again and Virgil could be modern.

---

[191] Everson, *Italian Romance Epic*, p. 3.

Epilogue

> If you take from Virgil his language and metre, what do you leave him?
> S. T. Coleridge, *Table Talk* (May 8, 1824)

One of the themes of this book has been continuity: with ancient commentators, especially Macrobius and Servius; with medieval commentators; and with the medieval conception of Virgil as a love poet. The other has been modernity. The Renaissance was conscious of itself as something new, and sometimes the claims were true. They did learn to read Greek again, their Latin did sound more like the language of Cicero, and they did discover manuscripts that were not widely available in the Middle Ages (such as Donatus' life of Virgil). To be modern in this sense is to be post-medieval. Other times, modern means Christian or post-classical. Vegio's supplement was modern in both senses. The story it tells is a medieval one and is modern, therefore, in the sense of being post-classical. There were differences, of course. Compared with *Eneas*, Vegio's poem places more emphasis on the marriage ceremony and the banquet afterward.[1] Also, the love story in Vegio is told primarily from Aeneas' point of view, rather than Lavinia's. But this is not what made Vegio a Renaissance author. Rather, what made Vegio modern in the sense of being post-medieval was his Latin.

Ruskin mocked the Renaissance for "its worldliness, inconsistency, pride, hypocrisy, ignorance of itself, love of art, of luxury, and of good Latin."[2] He was right about the Latin. Today, the Renaissance is understood to have begun as an attempt to write, first, Latin verse and, later, Latin prose in a purer, more classical style: i.e., in the style of Cicero and Virgil rather than,

---

[1] The ceremony is a mixture of classical and modern, wherein the religious elements are suppressed but the civil elements are preserved; see Vladimiro Zabughin, *Vergilio nel rinascimento italiano da Dante a Torquato Tasso*, 2 vols. (Bologna: Zanichelli, 1921, 1923), vol. 1, pp. 282–83.
[2] John Ruskin, *Modern Painters*, 2nd edn. (London: Smith, Elder, 1873), 4.20.34. Cf. C. S. Lewis, *English Literature in the Sixteenth Century Excluding Drama* (Oxford: Oxford University Press, 1954), pp. 18–31.

say, Duns Scotus and Hrabanus Maurus.³ We don't like to call it this, but it was a kind of secular fundamentalism, where *fundamentalism* does not necessarily mean "anti-modern ignorance" but "a return to first principles through careful study of original source-texts." Vegio was part of this movement. The Latin of his *Aeneid* sequel is not perfectly classical, but it is more classical than, say, Dante's eclogues, or even Petrarch's.

Classical Latin style: that is what made Vegio modern, it is what preserved the love story of Aeneas and Lavinia for another two hundred years, and it is also what saved Vegio from his detractors. For critics in the Renaissance, the main complaint about Vegio's sequel was not that he had misunderstood or distorted Virgil, but that what Vegio "added" to the *Aeneid* was so obvious as not to need saying. Vegio's excuse was that Virgil had died prematurely, before the *Aeneid* was finished. But would the poem have ended differently if Virgil had lived? Badius argued it would not. "Such as feel sorry for the poet and dream (*somniant*) that he would have gone farther are mistaken. Nor was Virgil thwarted by death, for although he did not achieve the correction (*castigationem*) of his work, he did achieve its conclusion (*finem*)." This, thinks Badius, is evident from the design of the book as a whole: the first six books are modeled on the wanderings of Odysseus and signify *vita contemplativa*; the last six books are based on Homer's *Iliad* and signify *vita activa*.⁴ The *Aeneid* is complete as it stands and therefore Vegio's "completion" is unnecessary. In his commentary on the supplement, Badius compares it with a fifth wheel on a four-wheel cart. That Aeneas would become a god we already knew from Jupiter's prophecy in Book 1. That he would subdue the Rutulians, marry Lavinia, and perform sacrifices to the gods was also self-evident, and not worth spelling out. What redeems the sequel is its style. The way it's put together, says Badius, is cold and stiff, but the vocabulary is worth studying and the figures of speech.⁵

---

³ See Hannah H. Gray, "Renaissance Humanism: The Pursuit of Eloquence," *Journal of the History of Ideas* 24 (1963), 497–514; Paul Oskar Kristeller, "Renaissance Humanism and Classical Antiquity," in *Renaissance Humanism: Foundations, Forms, and Legacy*, ed. Albert Rabil, Jr., 3 vols. (Philadelphia: University of Pennsylvania Press, 1988), vol. 1, pp. 5–16; and esp. Ronald G. Witt, *In the Footsteps of the Ancients: The Origins of Humanism from Lovato to Bruni* (Leiden: Brill, 2000).
⁴ Badius, preface to *Aeneid* (Giunta 1544, fol. 147ʳ). Badius continues: what Homer does in forty-eight books, Virgil accomplishes in only twelve; this is "more glorious" and contributes to Virgil's reputation for brevity.
⁵ Badius on the argument of *Supp.* (Giunta 1544, fol. 533ᵛ). For Vegio's redundancy, see also Angelo Decembrio, *De politia litteraria* (1462) 1.11, qtd. in Jacobus Pontanus, *Symbolarum libri XVIJ Virgilij* (Augsburg: Praetorius, 1599), p. 10. Thomas Twyne explains that he translated Vegio into English because he was "mooued with the worthines of the worke, and the neerenes of the argument, verse, and stile vnto *Virgil*, wherin as I iudge, the writer hath declared himself an happie imitatour" ("To the gentle and courteous *Readers*," *The .xiii. Bookes of Æneidos* [STC 24802; London: William How, for Abraham Veale, 1584], unsigned).

This is not how any of us would introduce a poem that we liked, or wanted our students to find interesting. And yet this is what most commentary in the Renaissance is like, not just about Vegio, but also about Virgil and other poets. For scholars writing today, literary criticism equals interpretation. There is plenty of that in Renaissance commentaries, especially about the underworld, but not as much as we would like or expect. I began reading the old commentaries on Virgil because I wanted to know what his text *meant* in the Renaissance, especially to poets. But the old commentators are not always interested in meaning. They will provide allegory, but more often they will offer information: information about science, about history, geography, and especially information about language.[6] Much of this is extremely basic. For example, in his commentary on the opening lines of the *Aeneid* Servius informs us (among other things) that Troy is a province of Asia, Italy is part of Europe, *altum,* "deep," means *mare,* "sea," and when Virgil says *Italiam venit,* "to Italy he came," he is using artistic license to omit the conjunction *ad,* "to." Another favorite topic is figures of speech, as when Servius explains that *arma* (in the phrase *arma virumque*) is the trope of metonymy.[7]

Most of the later commentaries are based on Servius and follow his example. In studying them, it is easy to become frustrated, or to blame them for writing about the wrong things, or to imagine ourselves as Virgil, picking through dung for nuggets of gold. But that would be a mistake. As we saw in Chapter 4, the one thing about Virgil that everyone in the Renaissance could agree to praise, critics and worshipers alike, was his style. That is the main reason why students read him in school, and why there was so much about Virgil's language in the commentaries.

If we want, we can ignore this and focus exclusively on interpretation. But that kind of reading is an anachronism. Virgil in the Renaissance was a style as much as an idea. If we want to understand the *Aeneid* historically – not only as a product of its time, but as a poem in time – if we want to read the epic that inspired Spenser and Tasso and Ariosto the way the poets read it, we must learn how to listen for sound as well as sense, for style as well

---

[6] See Robert A. Kaster, "The Grammarian's Authority," *Classical Philology* 75 (1980), 216–41; Anthony Grafton, "Renaissance Readers and Ancient Texts: Comments on Some Commentaries," *Renaissance Quarterly* 38 (1985), 615–49; and Gerald Snare, "The Practice of Glossing in Late Antiquity and the Renaissance," *Studies in Philology* 92 (1995), 439–59.

[7] Why the emphasis on tropes and schemes? See Gisèle Mathieu-Castellani, "Le commentaire de la poésie (1550–1630): l'écriture du genre," in *Les commentaires et la naissance de la critique littéraire: France/Italie (XIVe–XVIe siècles),* ed. Gisèle Mathieu-Castellani and Michel Plaisance (Paris: Aux Amateurs des Livres, 1990), pp. 41–50, at 47–48.

meaning. The commentaries can help us with this; indeed, that is one of the main things they were designed for.

When we do this, of course, there will be new questions. For example, if (as I argued in Chapter 3) the *Georgics* was primarily important as an example of the middle style, what are the elements of that style? For that matter, if Virgil's style was so important, why don't the Renaissance poets who imitate Virgil sound more like him? These are the problems I will address in my next book.

APPENDIX A

*Virgil commentaries in Latin editions,
1469–1599*

EXCLUDING POEMS, PREFATORY LETTERS, AND
DEDICATIONS

Notation: 40+3* = 40 printings + 3 printings whose existence or contents are unconfirmed in the available catalogues (see p. 21, above). An exhaustive, two-volume bibliography by Craig Kallendorf is now in preparation.

Author	Title	Total	1470s	1480s	1490s	1500s	1510s	1520s	1530s	1540s	1550s	1560s	1570s	1580s	1590s
Aelius-Antonius Nebrissensis	Ecphrases admodum familiares	1								1					
Anemoecius, Wolphgangus	Scholia ex graecis et latinis auctoribus in Bucolica	3							2		1				
Appendix Commentator	[Commentum]	1			1										
Badaluchus, Scipio	In elegiam De rosa expositio	1											1		
Badius Ascensius, Iodocus	[Commentarii]	40+3*				6+1*	9	5	3+1*	4+1*	5	2	3	3	
Badius Ascensius, Iodocus	In priapi lusum	2						2							
Barlandus, Adrianus	Annotationes in IV priores Aeneidos libros	3+2*								1		1	1*	1*	
Baroltanus, Nicolaus Scelsius Michael	Foscarilegia	1							1						
Barth, Michael	Commentarii	1+1*											1+1*		
Becchius, Philippus	Annotationes	2+4*								1	1+2*	1*	1*	1*	1*
Bellofilius, Johannes	Virgilii Tityrus, Ecloga, allegorica interpretatione illustrata	1									1				

Author	Title	Total	1470s	1480s	1490s	1500s	1510s	1520s	1530s	1540s	1550s	1560s	1570s	1580s	1590s
Bembus, Petrus	De Virgilii Culice et Tarentii fabulis liber	2													
Benvenutus, Johannes	[Vita]	1					1								
Beroaldus, Philippus (Maior)	[Hypotheses, seu argumenta, et Annotatiunculae]	2				2									
Beroaldus, Philippus (Maior)	Annotationes in commentarios Servii	23+15*		2	4+6*	8+2*	4	2+4*	1	1+1*	1	1*	1*	
Bersmanus, Gregorius	Enarratio in Georgica	2											2	
Bersmanus, Gregorius	Scholia	3											2	1
Bolzanus, Valerius	[Commentary]	1						1						
Bonfinis, Matthaeus	Annotationes super locum Aeneidos libri IV ubi IN et ET incuria quadam sibi positum videtur	2+2*									1	1	1*	1*	
Buschius, Hermannus	Commentum in Aeneida	1								1					
Calderinus, Domitius	Commentarii in opuscula quaedam vergiliana	43+7*	4+4*	11+1*	9+1*	9	5	2+1*		1	2				
Calphurnius, Johannes	Liminary letter	1	1												
Camerarius, Joachim	Explicatio	2									2				

Author	Title	Total	1470s	1480s	1490s	1500s	1510s	1520s	1530s	1540s	1550s	1560s	1570s	1580s	1590s
Caminadus, Augustinus Vincentius	Argumenta et annotamenta	1				1									
Campanus Colensis, Franciscus	Lucubrationes	17					1			3	3	4	3	3	
Campanus, Constantius	[Unknown]	1+2*										1	1*	1*	
Carpensis, Virgilius	[Textual variants]	1											1		
Cerutus Veronensis, Federicus	Enarrationes in libros IIII Georgicorum Virgilii	1													1
Chytraeus, Nathanael	In Virgilium Prolegomena et in eiusdem Eclogam primam collectanea	1													1
Constantius Fanensis, Iacobus	[Commentarii]	12									1	3	2	3	3
Corradus, Sebastianus	Commentarius	2										1			1
Crinitus, Petrus	[Vita]	1											1		
Crucius Bononiensis, Iacobus	[Annotationes]	15+1*						2			1	3	3	3	3+1*
Crusius, Martinus	Scholia in I. II. et III. Virgilii eclogam	1										1			
Culmanus, Leonhardus	Scholia	7+2*							3	2+1*	1	1	1*		

Author	Title	Total	1470s	1480s	1490s	1500s	1510s	1520s	1530s	1540s	1550s	1560s	1570s	1580s	1590s
Datus, Augustinus	Commentary on *Aeneid*	17				1	6	4	3		1	2			
Delphinus, Caesar	In carmina sexti Aeneidos libri digressio	1						1							
Doletus, Stephanus	Annotatiunculae de lingua latina	8+6*								1			3+1*	1+3*	1+1*	1
Donatus, Aelius	Vita Vergilii	108+4*	12	17	21	11	6	4	7	7	5+3*	2	4	6+1*	7	1
Donatus, Tiberius Claudius	Interpretationes vergilianae	51+4*		2+2*	11	11	7	6	3+1*	6	3		1	1*	1	
Eclogues Commentator	Commentum familiare	28+3*		1*	19+2*		4	3	2							
Erythraeus, Nicolaus	[Marginal commentary]	10							1	1	1	2		4	2	
Erythraeus, Nicolaus	[Metrical treatises]	8							1	1	1	2		3	1	
Erythraeus, Nicolaus	Index	12							1		2	2		4	3	
Fabricius Chemnicensis, Georgius	[Servius emendatus]	3+2*								1	1	1	1*	1*		
Fabricius Chemnicensis, Georgius	[T. C. Donatus emendatus]	3+3*									1 1+1*	1	1*	1*		
Fabricius Chemnicensis, Georgius	Indices (2)	2+2*										1	1	1*	1*	
Fabricius Chemnicensis, Georgius	Observationes virgilianae lectionis	15+9*										1	3+1*	3+1*	6+3*	2+4*

Author	Title	Total	1470s	1480s	1490s	1500s	1510s	1520s	1530s	1540s	1550s	1560s	1570s	1580s	1590s
Fabrinus, Johannes	[Commentary on *Aen.* 1–7]	5											2	2	1
Foresi, Bastiano	[Commentary on *Georgics*]	1		1											
Franciscus Nigro	Diversorum carminum ex Francisco Nigro numeri	1				1									
Frischlinus Alemmanus, Nicodemus	Bucolica et Georgica paraphrasi exposita	3												2	1
Frisius Tigurinus, Io.	Annotationes	1												1	
Fulgentius, Fabius Planciades	Expositio virgilianae continentiae	2+1*												1+1*	
Gabianus, Paulus	Varia lectio in Virgilium	1										1			
Georgics Commentator	Commentum familiare	9+1*			9+1*										
Gogrevius, M. Mento	Bucolicorum Virgilii simplex et dilucida metaphrasis	1											1		
Gorius, Baldassar Theodorus	Res virgiliana	1												1	
Gorraeus, Richardus	Commentarium	1										1			
Grimoaldus, Nicolaus	[In Georgica paraphrasis elegantissima]	1													1

Author	Title	Total	1470s	1480s	1490s	1500s	1510s	1520s	1530s	1540s	1550s	1560s	1570s	1580s	1590s
Guellius Germanus, Valens	Commentationes et paralipomena	1												1	
Hartungus, Joannes	Annotationes in libros Maronis Aeneidos diligenti cura ab ipso auctore collectae	2+2*									1	1	1*	1*	
Hegendorphus, Christophorus	Scholia in Georgica	7+6*					1					3+1*	1+4*	1+1*	
Heldelinus, Gaspar	Paraphrasis in XVI. orationes Vergilii, quae quidem primo Aeneidos libro continentur	1							1						
Helias, Jacobus	[Commentarii in Aen. 4]	1											1		
Hessus, Helius Eobanus	Adnotationes	15+2*					1		4	6+1*	3	1	1*		
Hortensius Montfortius, D. Lambertus	Enarrationes in XII libros Aeneidos	4									1		2		1
Humbertus Montismoretanus	[Argumenta et annotationes]	1						1							
Iohannes a Meyen Landinus, Christophorus	[Marginal commentary] [Commentarii]	30+4*	2+3*	12	7+1*	3	3	3						1	2
Landinus, Christophorus	De laude Vergilii	1		1											

Author	Title	Total	1470s	1480s	1490s	1500s	1510s	1520s	1530s	1540s	1550s	1560s	1570s	1580s	1590s
Landinus, Christophorus	Disputationes camaldulenses	8		2	3		1						1		1
Leonberger, Georgius	Ad Virgilii opera Loci aliquot	1								1					
Lucienburgius, Jo.	Inclyta Aeneis ... in regiam Tragicomoediam ... redacta	1											1		
Malatesta, Carolus	[Commentary on *Eclogues*]	2												1	1
Malatesta, Carolus	Trattato dell' artificio poetico	2												1	1
Mancinellus, Antonius	[Commentarii]	45+4*			8	10+2*	9	8	7+1*	1+1*	2				
Manutius Minor, Aldus	Testimonia of Virgil	4												2	2
Manutius, Paulus (Venutus)	Adnotationes in libri margine	30+7*										1	8	8 11+3*	2+4*
Marcellus, Nonius	Vocum virgilianarum expositiones	2						1		1					
Melanchthon, Philippus	Argumenta seu dispositiones rhetoricae in Eclogas Virgilii	2											2		
Melanchthon, Philippus	Scholia	35+7*							12	6	5	5+1*	2+4*	4+2*	1

Author	Title	Total	1470s	1480s	1490s	1500s	1510s	1520s	1530s	1540s	1550s	1560s	1570s	1580s	1590s
Melanchthon, Philippus	Scholia in Georgica (from lecture notes)	2								2					
Michel de Tours, Guillaume	[Les Georgiques … moralement exposées]	1					1								
Modicius Monteferratensis, Gulielmus	Virgilius a calumniis vindicatus	1												1	
Musonius, Johannes	Lucubrationes	1+1*								1+1*					
Nannius Alcmarianus, Petrus	Deuterologiae sive spicilegia in quartum librum Aeneidos Virgilii	1								1					
Nannius Alcmarianus, Petrus	In P. Virgilii Mar. Bucolica commentaria docta et accurata	1										1			
Nascimbaenus Nascimbaenius	Explanatio in sex primos Aeneidos libros	3+1*											2		1+1*
Orsinus, Fulvius	Notae ad Servium in Bucolica et Georgica	3+2*								1*				2+1*	1
Orsinus, Fulvius	Virgilius collatione scriptorum graecorum illustratus	2											2		
Parrhasius, Janus	Commentaria	1						1							

260

Author	Title	Total	1470s	1480s	1490s	1500s	1510s	1520s	1530s	1540s	1550s	1560s	1570s	1580s	1590s
Paulinus, Fabius	Hebdomades, sive septem de septenario libri, habiti in unius Virgilii versus explicatione: "Obloquitur numeris septem discrimina vocum"	1												1	
Philargyrius, Junius	Scholia in Bucolica et Georgica	3+1*												2+1*	
Pierius Valerianus, Iohannes	Castigationes et varietates virgilianae lectionis	30+3*						6	6+1*	5+2*	5	2	3	3	
Politianus, Angelus	[Annotationes]	1*									1*				
Pomponius	Interpretatio, commentarii	4+2*		1					1	1		1	1*	1*	
Pomponius Laetus	Pomponius Laetus Lectori	1			1										
Pontanus, Jacobus	Symbolarum libri XVII	1													1
Probus	Commentariolus	40+3*				2	8	7	7	2+1*	5	3	3+1*	3+1*	
Probus	Vita Vergilii	1	1												
Pulci, Bernardo	Prefatione nella bucolica di Virgilio	2		1	1										
Ramus, Petrus	Praelectiones	16+6*									4	3+1*	3+4*	5+1*	1
Regulus, Sebastianus	In I Aeneidos librum Virgilii ex Aristotelis De arte poetica et rhetoricis praeceptis explicationes	2										2			

Author	Title	Total	1470s	1480s	1490s	1500s	1510s	1520s	1530s	1540s	1550s	1560s	1570s	1580s	1590s
Rhodiginus, Ludovicus Caelius	[Commentarii]	15+2*						1		1	3	3	3+1*	3+1*	1
Riccardinus Philologus, Benedictus	In Virgilium annotationes	3					2	1							
Riccius, Stephanus	Paraphrases et succinctae quaestiones in Eclogas Virgilii	4										3	1		
Richardus le Blanc?	[Notae]	1									1				
Ruellus, Io.	In Virgilii Moretum scholia	1							1						
Sanctius Brocensis, Franciscus	Scholia	1													1
Scaliger, Joseph	In Appendicem commentarii et castigationes	4											2		2
Schott Argentinensis, Johannes	Enchiridion poeticum: haec habet epitheta Vergilij ac aliorum	1					1								
Schott Argentinensis, Johannes	Preface to *Aeneid*	1				1									
Scoppa, Lucius Iohannes	[Commentarii]	14+2*								2		3	3+1*	3+1*	
Servius Maurus Honoratus	Commentarii	121+8*	8	18	19 17+4*	14	9	11+1*	9+2*	5	3	3+1*	3+1*	5
Servius Maurus Honoratus	Vita	2	1				1								

Author	Title	Total	1470s	1480s	1490s	1500s	1510s	1520s	1530s	1540s	1550s	1560s	1570s	1580s	1590s
Servius, Donatus, et al.	Vita Vergilii	3	1		1				1						
Stephanus, Henricus	De criticis veteribus graecis et latinis, eorumque variis apud poetas potissimum reprehensionibus	1												1	
Stephanus, Henricus	Schediasma de dilectu in diversis apud Virgilium lectionibus adhibendo	3											1	1	1
Stephanus, Henricus	Scholia	4											1	1	2
Stigelius, Jo.	Commentarii docti, breves ac succincti in P. Virgilii Maronis quatuor libros Georgicorum	1											1		
Sturmius, Johannes	In priores tres Eclogas commentariolus	2										2			
Sylburgius, Frid.	Epistolae [on restoration of Erythraeus]	2												1	1
Titius, Robertus	Ad Georgica Virgilii praelectiones quatuor	1													1
Torrentinus, Hermannus	Commentum	49+9*			5+5*	17+2*	18+2*		4	1	2	1	1		
Tuccius, Marianus	Monitum	1						1							

Author	Title	Total	1470s	1480s	1490s	1500s	1510s	1520s	1530s	1540s	1550s	1560s	1570s	1580s	1590s
Unknown	[Annotationes in opera, breves sed non contemnendae]	2+1*													1*
Unknown	[Difficilium vocabulorum interpretatio Germanica]	3+6*										2+1*	1+3*	2*	
Unknown	[*Eclogues* commentary]	5						2		1	1		1		
Unknown	[Marginal commentary on Appendix]	1												1	
Unknown	[Marginal commentary on *Eclogues*, *Georgics*, and *Aeneid*]	16				1				3	2	3	1	5	1
Unknown	[Marginal commentary on *Supplementum*]	1											1		
Unknown	[Notes on *Aen.* 4 (Italian)]	1									1				
Unknown	[Scansion of opera and *Supp.*]	1										1			
Unknown	[Virgil's imitations from the Greek poets]	1													
Unknown	Albani comantis	1												1	
Unknown	Annotatiunculae in librum primum	1												1	

264

Author	Title	Total	1470s	1480s	1490s	1500s	1510s	1520s	1530s	1540s	1550s	1560s	1570s	1580s	1590s
Unknown	Elucidatio pro tyrunculorum in arte poetices institutione insigni	1				1									
Unknown	Familiaris expositio [opusculorum]	1					1								
Unknown	In eglogam Solini	1													
Unknown	Index moralitatum in enchiridion virgilianum	1				1									
Unknown	Italian Vita Virgilii	2												1	1
Unknown	Preface to *Georgics*	2												2	
Various	Annotations to Virgil	1												1	
Vasio, Giovanni Paolo	La vita di Virgiliio	1								1					
Venutus, Filippus	[Commentary on *Aen.* 8–12]	5											2	2	1
Venutus, Filippus	[Commentary on *Geo.*]	2												1	1
Verulanus, Sulpitius	Annotationes	1						1							
Vives, Iohannes Ludovicus	Io. Lodovici Vivis in Bucolica Vergilii interpretatio, potissimum allegorica. [= Allegoriae]	20+2*								4	3	3	3	3+1*	3+1*	1
Willichius, Iodocus	Chronologia in Aeneida Virgilii	1									1				

265

Author	Title	Total	1470s	1480s	1490s	1500s	1510s	1520s	1530s	1540s	1550s	1560s	1570s	1580s	1590s
Willichius, Iodocus	Commentarii in Virgilii Opuscula	3									2	1			
Willichius, Iodocus	De consilio et scopo Aeneidos	1										1			
Willichius, Iodocus	Dialysis quatuor libros in Georgicorum Virgilii	8+3*							1	2	3	2+1*	1*	1*	1*
Willichius, Iodocus	Scholia in Bucolica	5+3*							1	4			1*	1*	1*

APPENDIX B
Virgil commentaries ranked by number of printings

EXCLUDING POEMS, PREFATORY LETTERS, AND DEDICATIONS

Notation: 119+5* = 119 printings + 5 printings whose existence or contents are unconfirmed in the available catalogues (see p. 21, above). An exhaustive, two-volume bibliography by Craig Kallendorf is now in preparation.

ECLOGUES

Total	Author	Title	1470s	1480s	1490s	1500s	1510s	1520s	1530s	1540s	1550s	1560s	1570s	1580s	1590s
119+5*	Servius Maurus Honoratus	Commentarii	8	18	19	16+1*	14	9	11+1*	9+2*	5	2	3+1*	5	
107+4*	Donatus, Aelius	Vita Vergilii	12	17	21	11	6	4	7	7	5+3*	3	6+1*	7	1
45+4*	Mancinellus, Antonius	[Commentarii]			8	10+2*	9	8	7+1*	1+1*	2				
39+3*	Probus	Commentariolus				2	8	7	7	2+1*	5	2	3+1*	3+1*	
38+3*	Badius Ascensius, Iodocus	[Commentarii]				4+1*	9	5	3+1*	4+1*	5	2	3	3	
33+7*	Melanchthon, Philippus	Scholia							12	6	4	5+1*	1+4*	4+2*	1
29+8*	Torrentinus, Hermannus	Commentum			2+4*	8+2*	11+2*	3	1	2	1	1			
29+7*	Manutius, Paulus (Venutus)	Adnotationes in libri margine											7	8	11+3*	2+4*
30+4*	Landinus, Christophorus	[Commentarii]		2+3*	12	7+1*	3	3	3		1				
21+12*	Beroaldus, Philippus (Maior)	Annotationes in commentarios Servii		2		3+3*	8+2*	4	2+4*	1	1+1*		1*	1*	
30+3*	Pierius Valerianus, Iohannes	Castigationes et varietates virgilianae lectionis						6	6+1*	5+2*	5	2	3	3	
28+3*	Eclogues Commentator	Commentum familiare		1*	19+2*		4	3	2						

268

Total	Author	Title	1470s	1480s	1490s	1500s	1510s	1520s	1530s	1540s	1550s	1560s	1570s	1580s	1590s
19+2*	Vives, Iohannes Ludovicus	Io. Lodovici Vivis in Bucolica Vergilii interpretatio, potissimum allegorica. [= Allegoriae]							4	3	3	2	3+1*	3+1*	1
10+6*	Ramus, Petrus	Praelectiones									3	2+1*	2+4*	2+1*	
14+2*	Rhodiginus, Ludovicus Caelius	[Commentarii]					1			1	3	2	3+1*	3+1*	1
13+2*	Scoppa, Lucius Iohannes	[Commentarii]								2	3	2	3+1*	3+1*	
8+6*	Doletus, Stephanus	Annotatiunculae de lingua latina							1	1+1*		3+1*	1+3*	1+1*	1
11+2*	Hessus, Helius Eobanus	Adnotationes						1	3	3+1*	3	1	1*		
12	Constantius Fanensis, Iacobus	[Commentarii]								1	3	2	3	3	
10	Erythraeus, Nicolaus	[Marginal commentary]							1		1	2		4	2
7+2*	Culmanus, Leonhardus	Scholia							3	2+1*	1	1	1*		
5+2*	Willichius, Iodocus	Scholia in Bucolica							1	4			1*	1*	
3+2*	Orsinus, Fulvius	Notae ad Servium in Bucolica et Georgica								1*				2+1*	1
3+2*	Pomponius	Interpretatio, commentarii		1					1	1			1*	1*	

269

Total	Author	Title	1470s	1480s	1490s	1500s	1510s	1520s	1530s	1540s	1550s	1560s	1570s	1580s	1590s
5	Unknown	[*Eclogues* commentary]						2		1			1		1
4	Iohannes a Meyen	[Marginal commentary]											1	2	1
3+1*	Philargyrius, Junius	Scholia in Bucolica et Georgica												2+1*	
4	Riccius, Stephanus	Paraphrases et succinctae quaestiones in Eclogas Virgilii										3	1		
3	Anemoecius, Wolphgangus	Scholia ex graecis et latinis auctoribus in Bucolica							2		1				
3	Bersmanus, Gregorius	Scholia												2	1
3	Frischlinus Alemmanus, Nicodemus	Bucolica et Georgica paraphrasi exposita												2	1
2+1*	Unknown	[Annotationes in opera, breves sed non contemnendae]											2		1*
1+1*	Barth, Michael	Commentarii											1+1*		
2	Camerarius, Joachim	Explicatio									2				
2	Malatesta, Carolus	[Commentary on *Ecl.*]								1				1	
2	Marcellus, Nonius	Vocum virgilianarum expositiones						1							1

270

Total	Author	Title	1470s	1480s	1490s	1500s	1510s	1520s	1530s	1540s	1550s	1560s	1570s	1580s	1590s
2	Melanchthon, Philippus	Argumenta seu dispositiones rhetoricae in Eclogas Virgilii											2		
2	Pulci, Bernardo	Prefatione nella bucolica di Virgilio		1	1										
2	Sturmius, Johannes	In priores tres Eclogas commentariolus										2			
1	Bellofilius, Johannes	Virgilii Tityrus, Ecloga, allegorica interpretatione illustrata								1					
1	Caminadus, Augustinus Vincentius	Argumenta et annotamenta					1								
1	Chytraeus, Nathanael	In Virgilium Prolegomena et in eiusdem Eclogam primam collectanea												1	
1	Crusius, Martinus	Scholia in I. II. et III. Virgilii eclogam										1			
1	Gogrevius, M. Mento	Bucolicorum Virgilii simplex et dilucida metaphrasis											1		
1	Gorraeus, Richardus	Commentarium										1			

271

Total	Author	Title	1470s	1480s	1490s	1500s	1510s	1520s	1530s	1540s	1550s	1560s	1570s	1580s	1590s
1	Humbertus Montismoretanus	[Argumenta et annotationes]						1							
1	Nannius Alcmarianus, Petrus	In P. Virgilii Mar. Bucolica commentaria docta et accurata										1			
1	Pontanus, Jacobus	Symbolarum libri XVII												1	
1	Richardus le Blanc ?	[Notae]									1				
1	Sanctius Brocensis, Franciscus	Scholia												1	
1	Unknown	[Scansion of opera and *Supp.*]								1					
1	Unknown	[Virgil's imitations from the Greek poets]										1			
1	Unknown	In eglogam Solini				1									
1	Unknown	Index moralitatum in enchiridion virgilianum												1	

GEORGICS

Total	Author	Title	1470s	1480s	1490s	1500s	1510s	1520s	1530s	1540s	1550s	1560s	1570s	1580s	1590s
119+5*	Servius Maurus Honoratus	Commentarii	8	18	19	16+1*	14	9	11+1*	9+2*	5	2	3+1*	5	
44+4*	Mancinellus, Antonius	[Commentarii]			8	10+2*	9	8	6+1*	1+1*	2				
39+3*	Probus	Commentariolus				2	8	7	7	2+1*	5	2	3+1*	3+1*	
37+3*	Badius Ascensius, Iodocus	[Commentarii]				4+1*	8	5	3+1*	4+1*	5	2	3	3	
30+7*	Melanchthon, Philippus	Scholia							12	5	4	3+1*	2+4*	3+2*	1
28+7*	Manutius, Paulus (Venutus)	Adnotationes in libri margine									1	7	8	10+3*	2+4*
21+12*	Beroaldus, Philippus (Maior)	Annotationes in commentarios Servii		2		3+3*	8+2*	4	2+4*	1	1+1*		1*	1*	
30+3*	Pierius Valerianus, Iohannes	Castigationes et varietates virgilianae lectionis				7+1*	2	6	6+1*	5+2*	5	2	3	3	
29+4*	Landinus, Christophorus	[Commentarii]		2+3*	12			3	3						
21+3*	Torrentinus, Hermannus	Commentum			3+3*	9	8	1							
14+2*	Rhodiginus, Ludovicus Caelius	[Commentarii]							1		1	3	2	3+1*	3+1*	1

273

Total	Author	Title	1470s	1480s	1490s	1500s	1510s	1520s	1530s	1540s	1550s	1560s	1570s	1580s	1590s
10+6*	Ramus, Petrus	Praelectiones									1	3+1*	2+4*	4+1*	
13+2*	Scoppa, Lucius Iohannes	[Commentarii]								2	3	2	3+1*	3+1*	
8+6*	Doletus, Stephanus	Annotatiunculae de lingua latina						1		1+1*		3+1*	1+3*	1+1*	1
7+6*	Hegendorphus, Christophorus	Scholia in Georgica								1	1	3+1*	1+4*	1+1*	
10	Erythraeus, Nicolaus	[Marginal commentary]								1	1	2		4	2
8+2*	Willichius, Iodocus	Dialysis quatuor libros in Georgicorum Virgilii								1	3	2	1*		
9+1*	Georgics Commentator	Commentum familiare		9+1*											
6+1*	Hessus, Helius Eobanus	Adnotationes					1		2	3+1*					
3+2*	Orsinus, Fulvius	Notae ad Servium in Bucolica et Georgica								1*				2+1*	1
3+2*	Pomponius	Interpretatio, commentarii							1	1			1*	1*	
4	Iohannes a Meyen	[Marginal commentary]											1	2	1
3+1*	Philargyrius, Junius	Scholia in Bucolica et Georgica												2+1*	1
2+1*	Unknown	[Annotationes in opera, breves sed non contemnendae]										2			1*

Total	Author	Title	1470s	1480s	1490s	1500s	1510s	1520s	1530s	1540s	1550s	1560s	1570s	1580s	1590s
3	Frischlinus Alemmanus, Nicodemus	Bucolica et Georgica paraphrasi exposita												2	1
3	Bersmanus, Gregorius	Scholia												2	1
2	Bersmanus, Gregorius	Enarratio in Georgica												2	
2	Melanchthon, Philippus	Scholia in Georgica (from lecture notes)								2					
2	Venutus, Filippus	[Commentary on *Geo.*]												1	1
2	Unknown	Preface to *Georgics*												1	
2	Marcellus, Nonius	Vocum virgilianarum expositiones						1		1					
1	Titius, Robertus	Ad Georgica Virgilii praelectiones quatuor												1	
1	Unknown	Annotatiunculae in librum primum												1	
1	Unknown	[Virgil's imitations from the Greek poets]										1			
1	Caminadus, Augustinus Vincentius	Argumenta et annotamenta				1									

275

Total	Author	Title	1470s	1480s	1490s	1500s	1510s	1520s	1530s	1540s	1550s	1560s	1570s	1580s	1590s
1	Cerutus Veronensis, Federicus	Enarrationes in libros IIII Georgicorum Virgilii													1
1	Unknown	[Scansion of opera and *Supp.*]								1					
1	Foresi, Bastiano	[Commentary on *Georgics*]		1											
1	Stigelius, Jo.	Commentarii docti, breves ac succincti in P. Virgilii Maronis quatuor libros Georgicorum											1		
1	Pontanus, Jacobus	Symbolarum libri XVII													1
1	Grimoaldus, Nicolaus	[In Georgica paraphrasis elegantissima]					1								
1	Michel de Tours, Guillaume	[Les Georgiques … moralement exposées]								1					
1	Culmanus, Leonhardus	Scholia													

AENEID

Total	Author	Title	1470s	1480s	1490s	1500s	1510s	1520s	1530s	1540s	1550s	1560s	1570s	1580s	1590s
119+6*	Servius Maurus Honoratus	Commentarii	8	18	19	16+3*	13	9	11+1*	9+1*	5	3	3+1*	5	
51+4*	Donatus, Tiberius Claudius	Interpretationes Vergilianae		2+2*	11	11	7	6	3+1*	6	3	1	1*	1	
23+15*	Beroaldus, Philippus (Maior)	Annotationes in commentarios Servii		2		4+6*	8+2*	4	2+4*	1	1+1*	1	1*	1*	
36+1*	Badius Ascensius, Iodocus	[Commentarii]				4	7		5	3+1*	4	5	2	3	3
28+7*	Melanchthon, Philippus	Scholia								12	5	3	3+1*	1+4*	3+2*	1
27+7*	Manutius, Paulus (Venutus)	Adnotationes in libri margine										1	6	8	10+3*	2+4*
29+4*	Landinus, Christophorus	[Commentarii]		2+3*	12	7+1*	2	3	3						
30+2*	Pierius Valerianus, Iohannes	Castigationes et varietates virgilianae lectionis						6	6+1*	5+1*	5	2	3	3	
17	Campanus Colensis, Franciscus	Lucubrationes						1		3	3	4	3	3	
17	Datus, Augustinus	Commentary on Aeneid				1	6	4	3	1	2				

Total	Author	Title	1470s	1480s	1490s	1500s	1510s	1520s	1530s	1540s	1550s	1560s	1570s	1580s	1590s
15+2*	Rhodiginus, Ludovicus Caelius	[Commentarii]						1		1	3	3	3+1*	3+1*	1
14+2*	Scoppa, Lucius Iohannes	[Commentarii]								2	3	3	3+1*	3+1*	
8+6*	Doletus, Stephanus	Annotatiunculae de lingua latina							1	1+1*		3+1*	1+3*	1+1*	1
12	Constantius Fanensis, Iacobus	[Commentarii]									1	3	2	3	3
10	Erythraeus, Nicolaus	[Marginal commentary]							1		1	1	2	4	2
8	Landinus, Christophorus	Disputationes camaldulenses		2	3	1							1		1
4+2*	Pomponius	Interpretatio, commentarii [Commentary on *Aen.* 1–7]		1					1	1			1	1*	
5	Fabrinus, Johannes	Annotationes in IV priores Aeneidos libros											2	2	1
3+2*	Barlandus, Adrianus	[Commentary on *Aen.* 8–12]							1	1			1	1*	
5	Venutus, Filippus	Explanatio in sex primos Aeneidos libros											2	2	1
3+1*	Nascimbaenius Nascimbaenius	Annotationes super locum Aeneidos libri IV ubi IN et ET incuria quadam sibi positum videtur											2		1+1*
2+2*	Bonfinis, Matthaeus											1	1*	1*	
4	Iohannes a Meyen	[Marginal commentary]											1	2	1

Total	Author	Title	1470s	1480s	1490s	1500s	1510s	1520s	1530s	1540s	1550s	1560s	1570s	1580s	1590s
4	Hortensius Montfortius, D. Lambertus	Enarrationes in XII libros Aeneidos										1	2		1
2+2*	Hartungus, Joannes	Annotationes in libros Maronis Aeneidos diligenti cura ab ipso auctore collectae									1	1	1*	1*	
3	Bersmanus, Gregorius	Scholia												2	1
2+1*	Unknown	[Annotationes in opera, breves sed non contemnendae]											2		1*
2+1*	Fulgentius, Fabius Planciades	Expositio virgilianae continentiae												1+1*	1
2	Corradus, Sebastianus	Commentarius									1			1	
2	Beroaldus, Philippus (Maior)	[Hypotheses, seu argumenta, et Annotatiunculae]				2									
2	Regulus, Sebastianus	In I Aeneidos librum Virgilii ex Aristotelis De arte poetica et rhetoricis praeceptis explicationes											2		
2	Marcellus, Nonius	Vocum virgilianarum expositiones						1		1					
1	Willichius, Iodocus	Chronologia in Aeneida Virgilii									1				

Total	Author	Title	1470s	1480s	1490s	1500s	1510s	1520s	1530s	1540s	1550s	1560s	1570s	1580s	1590s
1	Nannius Alcmarianus, Petrus	Deuterologiae sive spicilegia in quartum librum Aeneidos Virgilii								1					
1	Verulanus, Sulpitius	Annotationes					1								
1	Pontanus, Jacobus	Symbolarum libri XVII													1
1	Buschius, Hermannus	Commentum in Aeneida								1					
1	Caminadus, Augustinus Vincentius	Argumenta et annotamenta				1									
1	Schort Argentinensis, Johannes	Preface to *Aeneid*				1									
1	Unknown	[Virgil's imitations from the Greek poets]										1			
1	Heldelinus, Gaspar	Paraphrasis in XVI. orationes Vergilii, quae quidem primo Aeneidos libro continentur							1						
1	Unknown	[Scansion of opera and *Supp.*]									1				
1	Delphinus, Caesar	In carmina sexti Aeneidos libri digressio											1		
1	Unknown	[Notes on *Aen.* 4 (Italian)]						1							

Total	Author	Title	1470s	1480s	1490s	1500s	1510s	1520s	1530s	1540s	1550s	1560s	1570s	1580s	1590s
1	Willichius, Iodocus	De consilio et scopo Aeneidos										1			
1	Paulinus, Fabius	Hebdomades, sive septem de septenario libri, habiti in unius Virgilii versus explicatione: "Obloquitur numeris septem discrimina vocum"													1
1	Helias, Jacobus	[Commentarii in Aen. 4]												1	
1	Lucienburgius, Jo.	Inclyta Aeneis … in regiam Tragicomoediam … redacta												1	

281

Index

Characters, places, and episodes in Homer and Virgil are indexed under the work (*Appendix virgiliana, Eclogues, Georgics, Aeneid, Iliad, Odyssey*) in which they appear. Characters and episodes in Ariosto, Boiardo, Ronsard, Shakespeare, Sidney, Spenser, and Tasso are indexed under the author's name. Literary characteristics, such as decorum and brevity, are indexed under "Virgil, critical reputation." Renaissance printers are indexed under "printers, Renaissance," with the towns where they were active. The appendices are not indexed, but the list of commentators in Appendix A is alphabetized.

Actium, battle of 51–52, 58
Adams, H. M. 21 n. 18
Aeneas 151
   as ancestor of modern princes 223, 238
   as Augustus 57, 59–60, 219
   as ideal man 59–60, 100, 152, 202, 207–12, 214, 219–20, 222, 225, 227
   as lover 106–7, 231, 233, 236, 242–46, 248–49
   death and apotheosis 240, 249
   historical 59–60, 208–9, 211–12
   unfavorable judgments 5, 158–62, 197–98, 199–203, 210–12
Aeneid 63, 77, 83, 86, 134
   closure, completeness 191–92, 202, 207, 238, 249
   commentators, principal 31–38, 91, 220
   composition of 79, 101–3, 125, 131, 134, 140, 192, 249
   episodes, most popular 6–7, 11, 145–47, 149–53, 183–84, 203, 227
   intention, authorial 57, 59, 189, 202
   six-book vs. twelve-book readers 148 n. 10, 150, 215–27
   structure 130, 134, 146, 147, 150, 191, 202–3, 207–20, 249
   style 87, 89, 91–93, 134, 136–37, 138, 139, 174, 251
   characters, places, episodes
      Achates 240
      Acheron 156 n. 37
      Age/Sickness/War 189
      Allecto 221
      Amata 226, 236, 242
      Anchises 146, 147, 154, 155, 162, 174–85, 188–90, 197, 200, 207, 212, 236
      Anna 223, 231 n. 141, 235 n. 155
      "Arma virumque cano" 63, 85–86, 92, 153, 250
      Ascanius 221, 240–41
      Avernus 156 n. 37, 170
      burials 95, 158–61, 177 n. 133, 240
      Buthrotum 222
      Caieta 212
      Camilla 112, 220, 227–30, 237, 247
      Carthage 218, 240–41
      catalogue of Etruscan armies 221
      Cerberus 152, 154, 169
      Creusa 212
      Cupid 241
      Daunus 192, 197
      death scenes 95, 207, 212, 216, 238, 240; see also *Aeneid*, characters: Turnus
      Diana 243
      Dis 168–69, 170–72
      Elysium 164, 174, 177 n. 133, 183
      Evander 194, 198–99, 206, 207, 241
      Fama, "Rumor" 131
      forest 218–19
      Gates of Dis 170–72, 180
      Gates of Sleep 153–57
      golden bough 158, 160, 166–69, 203
      Hector 212
      Hippolyte 227
      Iarbas 223, 231, 231 n. 141
      "Ille ego qui quondam" (spurious opening) 85–87, 88, 91–92
      Italy 147, 149, 218–19, 222, 241
      Ixion 165
      Juno 147, 187, 200, 214, 219

Jupiter 80, 170, 173, 193, 249
Latinus 156 n. 37, 240–41
Lausus 221
Lavinia 7, 187, 210, 219, 226, 231, 233–47, 248–49
Liger 197 n. 21
Magus 197 n. 21, 221
Marcellus 53, 72
Mars 92
Mezentius 195, 220, 221
Minerva 147
Misenus 158–61, 166, 177 n. 133, 211
monsters 156
Nisus and Euryalus 109–13, 221, 227
Palinurus 176, 212
Pallas 191–203, 206–7, 221
parade of Roman worthies 162, 188–90
Penthesilea 227, 228 n. 129
Polydorus 166, 169
Priam 212
Proserpina/Persephone 158, 160, 168
Pygmalion 169
sex scenes 106–8, 116, 229
shield of Aeneas 59 n. 52, 221
ships transformed into nymphs 145–46, 166
Silvius 236
Sisyphus 154, 164, 165
storms 95, 200
Styx 173
Tantalus 165, 208
Tartarus 168, 171
Thrace 169
Tityos 165–66
Tree of False Dreams 156
Troy 135, 146–47, 149, 211, 218
Turnus 6–7, 11, 29 n. 49, 150, 187, 191–203, 206–7, 210, 211, 212, 218, 219, 220, 226, 227, 228, 231, 233–34, 236, 238, 240, 242–43
Venus 107, 117, 147, 173, 187, 226, 227
Vulcan 107, 221, 227
see also Aeneas; Cumae, Cumaean sibyl; Dido; epic (genre); and underworld
Aeschylus 10
ages of civilization 89, 99
ages of man 202, 216 n. 89, 218, 220
Agrippa, Marcus 55
Alain de Lille 60 n. 56
Alamanni, Luigi 84
Alberti, Leon Battista 219
Alciato, Andrea 221
Alcibiades 117–18
Alexander (Maecenas or Pollio's slave) 63, 109, 113–14

Alighieri, Dante 10, 71, 119, 127, 128, 136, 142, 149, 153, 157–58, 160, 165–66, 168, 185, 198, 216 n. 89, 217, 220 n. 107, 227, 229, 245 n. 190, 249
Alighieri, Pietro 157–58
allegory 19, 35–37, 71, 79 n. 11, 81 n. 22, 82, 92, 166, 179 n. 145, 216, 250
   biographical 51–53, 56, 63, 69, 74, 87, 113–15
   moral 66, 114–15, 161, 163–72, 179, 203, 211, 213, 218–19, 225–26, 227
   see also *Odyssey*: allegorical interpretation; science; *and* underworld, descent: types of
Allen, Don Cameron 25 n. 33, 35 n. 72, 79 n. 8, 81 n. 21, 127 n. 116, 148 n. 10, 209 n. 60, 234 n. 154
Alpers, Paul 70 n. 91
allusions, treatment of in commentaries 68–69, 110–11, 204–5
Amazons see *Aeneid*, characters, places, episodes: Camilla
America 226
anachronism 4–6, 43, 90, 124, 229, 247, 250–51
Anacreon 28, 118
anger 6, 161, 187, 198, 199–203
Annaeus Cornutus, L. 107
Anser 52
anthologies 183–84, 205, 214
Antony, Lucius 52
Antony, Mark 51–52, 60
Apollonius of Rhodes 41, 231, 232
Appendix virgiliana 63 n. 68, 80 n. 18
   Catalepta 72, 80 n. 18
   Culex 26, 63, 89
   "Experientiae virgilianae" (Virgil's epigrams) 47 n. 1
   "On the Letter Y" 167
   Priapea 55 n. 29, 80 n. 18, 108–9, 118
Apuleius 114 n. 56, 226
Aquinas, Thomas 201 n. 37
Aretino, Federigo 226
Aratus 23
Arbaleste, Christophe 122 n. 91
archaeology, in Renaissance 17, 27, 37, 119
archaisms 74, 94, 124, 136, 233
Ariosto, Ludovico 5, 7, 9, 92–93, 107–8, 128, 162, 185, 203, 230, 234 n. 151, 237, 247, 250
   as critic of Virgil 57, 60
   and patrons 56, 57, 59, 60, 163, 189
   Orlando furioso characters and episodes
      Angelica 88, 111, 112
      Bradamante 189–90, 220, 228, 247
      Cloridano and Medoro 111, 112, 221
      Ferraù and Olimpio 112–13
      Marfisa 228
      Merlin's cave 163, 189–90

Ariosto, Ludovico (cont.)
  Rodomonte 163, 194–95, 203 n. 42, 220
  Ruggiero 194–95, 247
Aristarchus 19 n. 11, 150
Aristotle 4, 23 n. 27, 82, 103, 128, 134, 171 n. 108, 192, 201, 208, 209, 230
Armstrong, Elizabeth 30 n. 59
art, Virgil in 2 n. 4, 7, 56, 223, 238
Ascham, Roger 68, 120, 204–5
Ascensius *see* Badius Ascensius, Jodocus
astronomy and astrology 17, 78, 79, 81, 92, 105, 152, 170, 172–73
Auerbach, Erich 74 n. 107, 138 n. 173, 236 n. 160
Augustine, St. 17, 47, 175–78, 181–84, 197, 234
Augustus 51–53, 115
  as friend or classmate 56
  as patron 51–53, 55–60, 71, 71 n. 92, 72, 75, 89, 114, 125, 134, 160, 188–90, 208, 222, 234
  unfavorable judgments of 60, 64–66, 154–55
Ausonius 107
Averill, James R. 200 n. 35
Averroës 209

Bacon, Sir Francis 118, 142
Badius Ascensius, Jodocus xii, 28, 30, 35, 42, 55 n. 29, 63 n. 68, 66, 90, 109 n. 38, 117, 167, 223
  influence 32, 33, 36, 37, 42, 77–78, 183, 212–13
  as teacher 37, 206–8, 212–13
  on *Aen.* 59, 111, 146 n. 3, 155, 159, 163, 165 n. 78, 166, 167, 168, 169 n. 99, 170, 172, 177, 181, 183, 198, 206–8, 212, 216, 220 n. 105, 249
  on *Ecl.* 51 n. 15, 53 n. 22, 56 n. 38, 57, 58, 62 n. 66, 65, 67, 69, 71 n. 92, 72, 73, 74
  on *Geo.* 77–78, 90
  on Vegio's *Supplementum* 240–45, 249
Balavoine, Claudie 66 n. 75, 69 n. 88
Baldwin, T. W. 113 n. 52, 146, 178 n. 136, 184 n. 168
Baldwin, William 164–65
Bandino, Domenico di 60 n. 57, 116 n. 64
Barbaro, Ermolao 141 n. 184
Barkan, Leonard 107 n. 30, 109 n. 40
Barnfield, Richard 113
Bartels, Emily C. 223 n. 114
Barzun, Jacques 9
Baswell, Christopher 22 n. 23, 31 n. 63, 86 n. 40, 164 n. 70, 176 n. 128, 216 n. 89, 233 n. 150, 238 n. 167
Bausi, Francesco 97 n. 79
Bavius 52
Bembo, Pietro 104 n. 18, 118
Bennett, Josephine Waters 180 n. 149
Benvenuto da Imola 33 n. 67, 235 n. 155

Beranek, Bernard Francis 151 n. 20, 157 n. 42
Berger, Harry, Jr. 187
Bernardus Silvestris *see* Silvestris, Bernardus
Beroaldo, Filippo, the Elder 33, 226
Bible xii, 28, 95, 169, 214, 216
  episodes, quotations from 73, 117, 162, 169, 170, 171, 176, 177, 178, 181, 182, 201
Binns, J. W. 24 n. 31, 30
Biow, Douglas 169 n. 98
Bizer, Marc 225 n. 122
Black, Robert 216 n. 90
Blyth, Charles R. 177 n. 131
Boccaccio, Giovanni 127, 168–69, 208, 217, 235, 238, 245 n. 190, 246
body, human 79, 80, 155, 165, 166, 218–19; *see also under* underworld
Boethius 179 n. 144, 213 n. 75
Boiardo, Matteo Maria 9, 56
  characters and episodes
    Bradamante 220, 228
    catalogue of ships 221
    Fata Morgana 167
    Marfisa 220
Bolgar, Robert 204
Bolisani, Ettore 38 n. 81, 40 n. 84
Bologna 35
Bolsena 16
Bono, Barbara J. 229 n. 133
Bono, Paola 6 n. 12, 234 n. 154
books, availability of *see* libraries *and* printed editions of Virgil
Borges, Jorge Luis 101
Bowditch, Phebe Lowell 58 n. 44
Bracciolini, Poggio 4, 32, 126, 225
Bradley, A. C. 179 n. 143
Brand, C. P. 88 n. 53
Brant, Sebastian 244
Braund, Susanna Morton 81 n. 20
Brescia 22, 220 n. 106
Brinton, A. C. 239 nn. 173, 175, 244
British Library 21 n. 18
British Museum 21 n. 18
Brown, Virginia 21 n. 16, 49 n. 8
Brutus, Marcus 51
Brugnoli, Giorgio 49 n. 8, 54 n. 26, 116 n. 68
Buchanan, George 235 n. 155
Bucolics see Eclogues
Burnell, Peter 197 n. 18
Burnstein, Andrew 225 n. 122
Burrow, Colin 111, 180 n. 150, 186 n. 177, 195 nn. 15, 16, 197 n. 19, 229 n. 133, 234 n. 153
Bussi, Giovanni Andrea 33, 38 n. 81
Bynum, Caroline Walker 187
Byzantium 127, 148, 217

Caesar, Julius *see* Julius Caesar, C.
Cain, Thomas 208 n. 58
Cairns, Francis 200 n. 32
Calderinus, Domitius 63 n. 68, 104 n. 15
Caldwell, Tanya M. 138 n. 175
Caligula 138
Callimachus 41, 126 n. 110, 141
Calvin, John 175, 178 n. 138, 179 n. 142
Cambini, Andrea 36 n. 75, 218 n. 96
Cambridge University 26 n. 41, 27 n. 42, 30, 48, 68, 215
Camões, Luis Vaz de 227
Cantor, Norman 9
Capriano, Giovanni Pietro 141 n. 183
Cassiodorus, Magnus Aurelius 123
Cassius Longinus, C. 51
Cassius Dio 55
Castelvetro, Lodovico 133–36, 146, 238
Castiglione, Baldassarre 74, 118, 119, 128 n. 120
Castravilla, Ridolfo or Anselmo 153, 157
Catalepta see under Appendix virgiliana
Catholicism *see* religion: Catholic and Protestant
Catullus 4, 20 n. 12, 33, 37, 41, 104, 110–11, 117
Cauchi, Simon 25 n. 38, 178 n. 135
Cavallo, Jo Ann 229 n. 133, 231 n. 140, 232 n. 143
Cave, Terence 78 n. 6
Cebes 109
Celenza, Christopher S. 226 n. 125
censorship *see* Index of Prohibited Books
Ceres 168
Cervantes, Miguel de 209
Chalcidius 173 n. 117, 179 n. 144
Chapman, George 139, 220 n. 105
Charles V, Emperor 223
Chaucer, Geoffrey 26, 217, 222, 234, 238
Chaudhuri, Sukanta 70 n. 91
Cheney, Patrick 88 n. 52
Chile 189
chronology *see* history, knowledge of Roman
Chrysostom 201 n. 37
Cicero, Marcus Tullius 23 n. 27, 27, 29, 30, 49, 54, 66, 71, 87, 93, 96, 97, 121 n. 83, 126 n. 111, 128, 135, 154, 155, 168, 172, 187–88, 213, 219, 225, 226, 248
Cinzio, Giovambattista Giraldi 37, 100 n. 86, 102, 103 n. 9, 107, 125 n. 104, 128, 132, 136 n. 164, 137 n. 169, 194, 230
civil wars (Roman) 51, 60
Clarke, Howard 79 n. 8, 127 n. 116, 147 n. 10
Claudianus 39, 234 n. 151
Clausen, Wendell 232 n. 145
Cleopatra 51
Cobb, Samuel 124
Cockayne, Sir Aston 124 n. 102
codex (Mediceus, Palatinus, Romanus) *see* manuscripts: of Virgil
Coleman, Dorothy Gabe 25 n. 36
Coleridge, Samuel Taylor 142, 248
Colie, Rosalie 83 n. 32
colonization 222–24
Columbus, Christopher 223
Columella 17
Commelinus, Hieronymus 26 n. 42, 216 n. 89
commentaries
    classroom origins 19, 37, 203, 212–16, 250
    contents and organization, typical 18–19, 20, 24, 37, 42, 91, 203, 205, 206–7, 250
    ranking their influence 6, 10, 31–37, 41, 42, 64–66, 68, 145, 220, 247
    see also Grammaticus, characteristics of; *and* printed editions of Virgil
commonplace books 203–6
Comparetti, Domenico 1, 55 n. 32
concordance (of Virgil's poetry) 25
Congleton, J. E. 70 n. 91
Conrad of Hirsau 71 n. 92
Constance 32
Constantine I, Emperor 71, 197, 224
Conte, Gian Biagio 121 n. 84
Conti, Antonio Maria de' 125 n. 103, 141 n. 183, 208, 220 n. 105
Conti, Natale 147, 165, 168 n. 91, 169
continuity, of ancient and medieval traditions 8, 10, 32, 36, 41, 60, 71, 78–81, 90, 93, 101–3, 125–26, 130, 131, 139, 146, 150, 152, 153–63, 162 n. 64, 164, 172, 173–78, 181–85, 209, 210–12, 213 n. 75, 216, 217, 219, 222, 223–24, 226–27, 232–33, 232 n. 145, 235, 237, 246–47, 248; *see also* Servius Honoratus, Maurus: authority and influence
Cook, Albert S. 227 n. 128
Cooper, Helen 70, 75 n. 113, 229 n. 133, 236 n. 159, 238–39
Cooper, Thomas 60, 124 n. 101, 220 n. 105
Cormier, Raymond 233 n. 149, 237 n. 166
Corrado, Sebastiano 54
cosmology, cosmography 73, 75, 82, 152, 172–73, 176
costumi, "customs" 128, 194, 199
Courcelle, Pierre 71 n. 93, 167 n. 86, 175 n. 121, 176 n. 124, 182 n. 159, 183 n. 162, 197 n. 23, 224 n. 119
Courcelles, Dominique 78 n. 6
court (royal), as hell 171
Courtney, Edward 122 n. 91
Cowley, Abraham 141 n. 185
Crane, Mark L. 66 n. 77
Crane, Mary Thomas 204 n. 44
Cremona 51

Crocetti, Camillo Guerrieri 37 n. 78, 100 n. 86
Culex see under *Appendix virgiliana*
Cumae, Cumaean sibyl 72, 150, 154, 158, 160, 162, 164, 170, 190, 218, 231–32
Cummings, R. M. 124 n. 102
Curtis, Mark H. 26 n. 41, 215 n. 85
Cyrus the Younger 59, 208

Daniel, Pierre 22 n. 23, 54
Dante *see* Alighieri, Dante
Dati, Agostino xii, 91–92, 205 n. 49, 220 n. 108
Dares Phrygius 60, 208, 211
Davies, Martin 21 n. 17, 22 nn. 23, 24, 53 n. 24
Davies, Percival Vaughan 93 n. 63, 98 n. 81
Decembrio, Angelo 96–98, 132, 193 n. 10, 239 n. 174, 249 n. 5
De Hamel, C. F. R. 25 n. 33
Deitz, Luc 78 n. 6
Deloince-Louette, Christiane 127 n. 116, 217 n. 91
Delphinus, Caesar 220 n. 108
Demeter 168
ps.-Demetrius Phalereus 136 n. 163, 137 n. 166
demons 5, 153, 158–61, 169, 189–90, 211
Demosthenes 27, 29, 120, 135
Descartes, René 9
Desmond, Marilynn 6 n. 12, 172 n. 112, 218 n. 94, 234 n. 154
Di Cesare, Mario 21 n. 16, 97 n. 78, 141 n. 184
dictionaries (Renaissance) 28, 61
Dido 6–7, 80, 106–7, 125 n. 105, 146, 153, 169, 212, 231–32
  as colonist 222–23, 234
  as political ambition 36–37, 218, 226
  as responsible monarch 234, 243–45
  as sexual temptation 36, 149, 218, 231
  compared with Lavinia 233–47
  "Didocentricism" 6–7, 234
  historical 235
  in Ovid 233, 234–35
Dolet, Étienne 104 n. 18
Dolven, Jeff Andrew 164 n. 74
Domitius Afer, Cn. 125
Donatus, Aelius 19
  biography of Virgil xii, 4, 15 n. 1, 50–55, 56, 72, 79, 86, 89–90, 102, 106 n. 23, 109, 113, 114 n. 59, 116, 117, 118, 124, 125, 107, 134, 192 n. 2
  influence and availability 48, 49–50, 53, 131, 237, 248
  commentary on *Ecl.* 56, 57, 62, 69, 73, 75
Donatus auctus 50 n. 12, 52 n. 21, 53 n. 25, 54–55, 79–80, 89 n. 55, 116–17, 118, 123, 124
Donatus, Tiberius Claudius xii, 16, 19, 31–32, 41, 42, 49, 111, 163, 169 n. 99, 198, 200, 201, 207, 209, 242

Donne, John 179
Donnelly, M. L. 49 n. 9, 56 n. 34
Dorne, John 23 n. 27
Douglas, Gavin 176–77, 178 n. 135, 239
Downame, John 201 n. 37
dreams *see under* underworld
Dryden, John 10, 124 n. 102
Du Bellay, Joachim 61, 67 n. 82, 120, 140 n. 178, 217 n. 91
Dubois, François 42–44
Duckworth, George 240 n. 176
Dudley, Robert, earl of Leicester 63
Dufournet, Jean 233 n. 148
Dugaw, Diane 227 n. 128
Duffy, Eamon 175 n. 122
Dymoke, Tailboys 140 n. 179

Eclogues 47–76, 77, 83 n. 30, 85, 86, 89, 105
  bookishness 57, 66–69, 70–71
  commentators, principal 26 nn. 42, 43, 31, 33, 36, 56–57, 68
  genre 69–70, 73, 75–76
  historical background 50–53
  intention, authorial 56–59, 65–66, 67, 71 n. 92, 89–90
  non-pastoral themes 67, 69, 70–71, 75
  origin of pastoral 69–70, 73
  popularity 54, 67, 77
  style 64, 73–76, 89, 91–93
  I ("Tityrus") 56, 58, 62, 64–66, 70, 71, 73, 74, 75, 91
  II ("Alexis") 56, 65 n. 73, 66, 69, 72, 75, 109, 113–15, 125 n. 104
  III ("Palaemon") 52, 69, 74, 75
  IV ("Pollio") 56, 66, 71–72, 73, 75, 76, 184 n. 169, 224
  V ("Daphnis") 56, 66
  VI ("Varus/Silenus") 53 n. 22, 54 n. 27, 72–73, 75, 76
  VII ("Corydon") 52, 66 n. 79, 68
  VIII ("Damon/Sorceress") 53 n. 22, 56, 57, 66, 69, 72
  IX ("Moeris") 52, 56, 58, 64–66
  X ("Gallus") 51, 69, 75, 115
  see also allegory, biographical; homosexuality; *and* patronage
Eco, Umberto 66
editing, editions *see* printed editions of Virgil *and* textual criticism in Renaissance
education
  classroom practices 18–19, 33, 103 n. 13, 113–15, 203–8, 206–7, 212–16, 250
  Virgil as textbook 23, 37, 67, 77, 103, 113, 125, 140, 163, 206–7, 250
Egypt 51, 52

Eliot, John 62 n. 64
Eliot, T. S. 1, 124, 151, 211
Elizabeth I, Queen (of England) 25, 62, 68, 162, 190, 204
Ellrodt, Robert 181 n. 156
El-Rouayheb, Khaled 112 n. 50
Elyot, Sir Thomas 95, 163–64
empire *see* history, knowledge of Roman
Empson, William 70 n. 91
Eneas see Roman d'Eneas
England *see* printed editions of Virgil: countries where produced
Ennius, Quintus 119–24
epic (genre) *see Aeneid*; Homer; Iliad; Odyssey; romance (genre); *and* Virgil, critical reputation: compared with Homer
Epicureanism 71, 72–73, 80, 152, 165–66, 186, 197
epideictic rhetoric *see* praise
Epidius 56
epigrams, Virgil's *see under Appendix virgiliana*
epigraphy *see* inscriptions
epistles 3, 17 n. 5, 24, 41, 42, 56, 68, 72, 92, 225, 226, 235
Erasmus, Desiderius 68, 98 n. 81, 114–15, 128, 135, 188, 215, 219
Ercilla, Alonso de 189–90
Erickson, Wayne 151 n. 21
Erythraeus, Nicolaus 25, 240
Este 56, 59, 60, 163, 189, 223, 231
Estienne, Henri 28–29, 55 n. 29
Estienne, Robert 28
Ettin, Andrew V. 83 n. 29
Euphuism 140
Everson, Jane E. 229 n. 133, 247 n. 191
evidentia, "vividness" 95, 128, 133–34, 136, 138
examples, use of 163–66, 203–6, 207–12
Experientiae virgilianae see under Appendix virgiliana

Fabricius, Georgius 27, 86 n. 45
Fabrinus, Johannes 220 n. 108
Fall of Man 172, 181
Fantazzi, Charles 223 n. 116
Faral, Edmond 90 n. 57, 236 n. 160
Farnaby, Thomas 29 n. 51
Fata, Frank J. 35 n. 72
Fate 181, 193
Faustus, Perellius 125
Febvre, Lucien 24 n. 29
Federico, Sylvia 223 n. 118
Fehrenbach, R. J. 26 n. 41
Feinstein, Wiley 111 n. 48
Fera, Vincenzo 38 n. 81
Ferrara 59, 223
Ferraro, Salvatore 125 n. 108

Fichter, Andrew 189 n. 188, 223 n. 118, 229 n. 133
Ficino, Marsilio 117 n. 70
Field, Arthur 94 n. 66, 217 n. 93
Fike, Matthew 151 n. 20, 157 n. 42
Filelfo, Francesco 92, 201, 202–3, 210–11, 220, 239
Fitzgeoffrey, Charles 124 n. 102
Fitzherbert, John 83
Fletcher, Angus 151 n. 21, 187 n. 181
Florence 15, 16, 35, 40, 152, 220, 226
florilegia *see* anthologies
Florus 235 n. 155
Foerster, Donald M. 138 n. 175
Ford, Andrew 148 n. 10
Ford, Margaret Lane 30 n. 60
Ford, Philip 127 n. 116, 217 n. 91
fortune, chance 214
Fournel, Jean-Louis 134 n. 155
Fowler, Alastair 82 n. 29
France *see* printed editions of Virgil: countries where produced
Francis I, King (of France) 56
Freeman, Daniel E. 227 n. 128
Freeman, Thomas 102 n. 7
friendship 50, 51, 111, 114–15
Fulgentius 36, 168 n. 92, 203, 216, 220 n. 105, 237
Fumaroli, Marc 104 n. 18, 126 n. 111, 142 n. 188, 225 n. 122
fundamentalism, Renaissance as secular 249
Fundius, Petrus 91–92
furor see anger

Gaisser, Julia Haig 4 n. 7, 20 n. 12, 24 n. 30, 33 n. 66, 33, 37 n. 80, 41 n. 86, 226 n. 125
Galand-Hallyn, Perrine 78 n. 6, 98 n. 83
Galbraith, David 186 n. 177
Galinsky, Karl 192 n. 6, 200 n. 32
Gallus, Cornelius 51, 52, 105, 115
Gambara, Lorenzo 103
Gantz, Timothy 197 n. 20
Garrison, James D. 197 n. 19
Gaskell, Philip 24 n. 29
gates *see under Aeneid*: characters, places, episodes
Gellius, Aulus 53, 79, 82, 101–2, 107, 121, 125 n. 106, 131, 134
  influence 20, 48
Genette, Gérard 7
Geneva 26 n. 42, 28, 29
genre *see under Eclogues and Georgics*; epic (genre); *and* Wheel of Virgil
geography 18, 250
Georgics 29, 63, 77–100, 179 n. 145
  commentators, principal 26 n. 42, 33, 36, 77–78
  criticized as unpoetical 82
  division of books 78, 83

Georgics (cont.)
  episodes, most popular 83
  genre 77, 82–83
  imitations of 77, 82–85
  intention, authorial 57
  labor 63, 77–78, 82
  style 89, 91–93, 251
  variety, defined by 78, 82–83, 98–99
  episodes
    laus Italiae (2.136–76) 63, 83
    Orpheus and Eurydice (4.453–527) 51–53, 83
    parts of the plow (1.160–75) 83
    plague (4.470–532) 83, 84
    sphragis/colophon (4.563–66) 38–39, 42
    universal dominion of Eros (3.242–44) 83, 99
Germany *see* printed editions of Virgil: countries where produced
Gewirtz, Isaac Meir 213 n. 75
Geymonat, Mario 38 n. 81, 71 n. 95, 86 n. 42
Giocondo, Fra Giovanni 17
Giustiniani, Vito R. 203 n. 40
Giustulo da Spoleto, Pierfrancesco 85
gluttony 162, 165, 241
gold 122, 166–70, 221
Goldfinch, John 21 n. 17, 22 nn. 23,24, 53 n. 24
Golding, Arthur 178, 179 n. 144, 214
Goldschmidt, Georg *see* Fabricius, Georgius
Gonzaga, Cesare 118
Gonzaga, Scipione 137 n. 170, 193 n. 11
Googe, Barnabe 84, 122, 167 n. 87
Gordan, P. W. G. 225 n. 121
Grafton, Anthony 2, 8, 16 n. 2, 18 n. 6, 19 n. 8, 20, 33 n. 68, 38 n. 81, 41 n. 85, 52 n. 19, 67 n. 81, 103 n. 13, 114 n. 60, 205 n. 49, 226 n. 125, 250 n. 6
Graham, Kenneth J. E. 202 n. 38
Grammaticus, characteristics of 19, 38, 39 n. 83, 90, 149, 152, 153, 206
Grant, W. Leonard 70 n. 91
Gray, Hannah H. 249 n. 3
greed 147, 164, 165, 166–70, 171
Greek language and literature, knowledge of 10, 15, 26 n. 42, 28, 30, 67–69, 73, 77, 92, 97, 117, 126–27, 132–33, 140–41, 148–49, 167, 168, 173 n. 117, 204–5, 216, 219, 226, 227, 229, 232 n. 145, 248
Gregory the Great, Pope 152
Greek Anthology, The 226
Greenblatt, Stephen 175 n. 122
Greene, Robert 140
Greene, Thomas M. 97 n. 80, 185–86
Greenlaw, Edwin A. 180 n. 150
Grendler, Paul F. 19 n. 8, 23 n. 27, 103 n. 13, 204 n. 46, 205 n. 49
Griffo, Francesco 23

Grimoald, Nicholas 29 n. 50
Guellius Germanus, Valens 73 n. 103
Guy-Bray, Stephen 113 n. 54

habit 145, 157, 158, 163, 170–72, 226
Haebler, Konrad 25 n. 33
Hagen, Hermann 22 n. 23
Hale, David G. 127 n. 116
Hale, J. R. 195 n. 14
Hallyn, Fernand 79 n. 8, 82 n. 28
Hamilton, A. C. 195 n. 16
Hampton Court 238
Hankins, James 92 n. 60, 180 n. 147
Hankins, John E. 178 n. 136, 181 nn. 151, 153, 156
Hardie, Philip 79 n. 9, 148 n. 12, 191 n. 1
Hardison, O. B. 57 n. 43, 81 n. 24, 208 n. 58, 209 n. 65
Hardyng, John 230
Harington, Sir John 57, 95 n. 69, 107–8, 161–62, 164, 177–78, 177 n. 133, 178 n. 139, 184, 203 n. 42, 214
  his copy of Virgil 25, 30, 108
Harris, William V. 200 n. 32
Harvard School *see* pessimistic readings
Harvey, Gabriel 28, 48, 137, 185, 188, 213 n. 76
Hathaway, Baxter 133 n. 152
Hebrew, knowledge of 92
Heidelberg 25, 38 n. 81, 216 n. 89
Helfer, Rebeca 87 n. 48
Hellenistic poetry, awareness of 6, 16, 41, 232
Hellinga, Lotte 30 n. 57
Henry II, King (of England) 238
Henry, Prince of Wales 162
Hepp, Noémie 127 n. 116, 132 nn. 146, 147, 133 n. 151, 140 n. 181
Heraclides Ponticus 220 n. 105
Hercules 125, 151–52, 170
Heresbachius, Conradus 84
Hermann the German 209
Hermogenes 78 n. 6
Herren, Michael W. 52 n. 21
Herrick, Marvin T. 49 n. 7
Hesiod 26 n. 42, 67 n. 82, 68, 80 n. 17, 98, 124–25, 137 n. 169, 141 n. 183, 204–05
Hessus, Helius Eobanus 26, 38, 67–69, 204
Heyne, Christian Gottlob 21 n. 18, 26 n. 42, 28 n. 47
Heywood, Thomas 60 n. 58, 235 n. 155
Hieatt, A. Kent 26 n. 39
Hinds, Stephen 204 n. 47
Hirsch, Rudolf 24 n. 29
history, knowledge of Roman 18, 33, 51–52, 54, 55, 60, 213, 250
Holford-Strevens, Leofranc 48 n. 4, 168 n. 93
Homer 78 n. 6, 103, 122
  Batrachomyomachia and *Arachnomachia* 89

knowledge of in Middle Ages and Renaissance 10, 91–91, 126–27, 147–49, 216
prolixity and flowery language 97, 129–38
see also *Iliad*; *Odyssey*; translations, translators: of Homer; and Virgil, critical reputation: compared with Homer
Homerulus 127
homosexuality 108–18
Horace v, 21, 23 n. 27, 35 n. 72, 61, 66, 94, 101, 102 n. 5, 103, 104, 118, 119, 120, 122, 123, 130 n. 133, 165, 207, 213 n. 75, 226
Horsfall, Nicholas 48 n. 2, 55 n. 29, 80 n. 18, 125 n. 108, 197 n. 18, 234 n. 154
Hough, Graham 35 n. 72
Houliston, Victor 85 n. 39
Hubaux, Jean 109 n. 39
Hughes, Merritt Y. 35
Hulubei, Alice 23 n. 26, 28 n. 47, 37 n. 79, 54 n. 28, 70 n. 91, 146 n. 5
humanism *see* Renaissance, characteristics of the
Hunt, Maurice 83 n. 29

ideal man *see under* Aeneas
Iliad 15, 68, 89, 134, 146, 147, 148, 191, 192, 207, 217, 219–20, 249
    characters and descriptions
        Achilles 65, 131, 187, 193, 194
        Ajax 91
        Ajax like donkey (11.558–62) 128–29, 136
        Greeks like flies (2.469–73) 128–29, 136
        Hera's chariot (5.720–32) 137
        Hector 91, 161, 193–94, 207, 231
        Patroclus 194, 217
        Thersites 137
Ilias latina 127
"Ille ego qui" verses *see under* Aeneid
illustrations *see* art, Virgil in
imitation 77, 120, 146
    classroom exercises 29, 67–68
    not always competitive 185–87
    of episode's function 153, 187–90
    as intention of Virgil's works 57, 65, 67, 71 n. 92, 72, 89–90, 189, 204
    as interpretation 3–4
    as *sine qua non* of poetry 78, 82, 133–34, 159, 189
    see also under Georgics *and* Virgil, critical reputation
imperialism *see* colonization *and* Augustus: unfavorable judgments of
Index of Prohibited Books 27, 84
influence, distinct from innovation 10, 20, 35–37, 40–41, 47–48, 201, 210–11, 212–13, 217, 218, 226
inscriptions 16–18, 39–40

intention, authorial 3, 205, 214; *see also under Aeneid, Eclogues, and Georgics*
Irvine, Martin 19 n. 10
Iser, Wolfgang 7
Islam 112–13
Italy *see* printed editions of Virgil: countries where produced; *and under* Aeneid

James I, King (of England) 162
Jardine, Lisa 18 n. 6, 19 n. 8, 103 n. 13, 205 n. 49, 215, 226 n. 125, 227 n. 127
Jarry, Louis 22 n. 23
Jauss, Hans Robert 7
Javitch, Daniel 5 n. 8, 93 n. 62, 111 n. 48, 128 n. 118
Jed, Stephanie H. 106 n. 22
Jerome, St. 49, 167, 183
John of Austria, Don 190
John of Garland 90–91
John of Salisbury 156 n. 39, 237, 241 n. 182
Johnson, A. F. 21 n. 20
Johnson, Samuel 103 n. 9, 132, 138 n. 174
Jones, Howard 22 n. 25, 30 n. 58
Jones, Julian Ward, Jr. 79 n. 11, 148 n. 13, 157 n. 43, 160, 162 n. 64, 216 n. 88
Jones, Richard Foster 120 n. 82, 142 n. 187
Jonson, Ben 10, 74, 95, 102, 104–6, 118, 123–24, 140, 179, 179 n. 142
    his copy of Virgil 25, 30
Julius Caesar, C. 51, 56, 58, 59, 189
Justin (epitomator) 235 n. 155
Justin Martyr 73
Justinian's Digest 16
Juvenal 64, 109 n. 39, 125 n. 105, 213 n. 75

Kallendorf, Craig 2, 5, 19 n. 7, 21, 23 n. 27, 25 n. 35, 33 n. 69, 35 n. 72, 36 n. 76, 50 n. 10, 53 n. 24, 57 n. 43, 103 n. 13, 109 n. 37, 118 n. 75, 141 n. 184, 146, 147 nn. 8, 9, 149 nn. 14, 17, 161 n. 55, 167 n. 85, 177 n. 132, 183, 193, 201 n. 36, 203 nn. 41, 43, 206, 208 n. 58, 210–11, 218 n. 97, 219 n. 104, 235 nn. 156, 157, 239 n. 173
Kaske, Carol V. 164 n. 74, 187 n. 181, 216 n. 87
Kaster, Robert 19 n. 10, 66 n. 76, 216 n. 88, 250 n. 6
katabasis see underworld
Kelly, Douglas 233 n. 147
Kennedy, William J. 24
Ker, W. P. 2
Kern, Hans 239 n. 174
King, John N. 83 n. 29
Kintgen, Eugene R. 204 n. 45
Koch, Eoban *see* Hessus, Helius Eobanus
Kochanowski, Jan 235 n. 155
Kreider, Alan 175 n. 122

Krier, Theresa M. 186 n. 178
Kristeller, Paul Oskar 249 n. 3
Kronenberg, M. E. 31 n. 61

Lactantius 47, 71, 152, 167, 182–84, 197–98, 199–203, 224
Lage, G. Raynaud de 237 n. 164
Lamberton, Robert 79 n. 8, 147 n. 10
Landino, Cristoforo xii, 17–18, 32, 35, 208, 226–27
   Disputationes camaldulenses (c. 1480) 35–37, 80 n. 17, 94, 146, 149, 150, 160, 161, 163, 171, 217–20, 220 n. 105, 226
   commentary on Dante (1481) 35 n. 72, 36 n. 75, 119, 120–21, 149, 160, 177 n. 132, 218 n. 96, 226
   commentary on Virgil (1488) 31 n. 62, 32, 36–37, 65 n. 74, 74, 98, 111 n. 43, 147, 149, 150, 155, 156, 159, 160, 163, 167, 169 n. 100, 171, 175 n. 121, 179 n. 144, 181, 198, 210, 216 n. 89, 218–20, 226
Latin language 17, 42–44, 49, 119–24, 128, 152, 187–88, 204, 206–8, 213, 216, 224, 240, 248–51
   orthography 10, 15–18, 38–44
Lazzarelli, Lodovico 85
laurel 15, 17
Lecointe, Jean 78
Leedham-Green, E. S. 26 nn. 41, 42, 68 n. 85
Leibniz, Gottfried Wilhelm 101
Leipzig 27
Leo X, Pope 40
Lepanto, battle of 190
Leslie, Michael 195 n. 16
Leto, Giulio Pomponio 38 n. 81, 220 n. 106
letters *see* epistles
Lewis, C. S. 9, 67, 126 n. 111, 132 n. 146, 142, 145, 248 n. 2
Le Goff, Jacques 175
limbo 177 n. 133, 227
libraries 10, 16, 21 n. 18, 26, 32, 36, 38 n. 81, 126, 152, 215
Liburnio, Niccolò 94
Lilly, Marie Loretto 84 n. 35, 85 n. 38
Livius Andronicus, L. 119, 121
Livy, Titus 225
Lockhart, Philip North 81 n. 20, 197 n. 19, 204 n. 47, 216 n. 88
Lodge, Thomas 62
Loewenstein, Joseph 88 n. 49
Lohe, Peter 35 n. 74, 218 n. 96
London 27, 30
Lord, George de Forest 127 n. 116, 148 n. 10
Lord, Mary Louise 33 n. 67, 80 n. 19, 179 n. 144, 225 n. 123, 235 n. 155

Lorimer, H. L. 138 n. 175
Lorsch 38 n. 81
Lotspeich, Henry Gibbons 26, 169 n. 96
Louvain 35
love, as epic subject 8, 227–47
Low, Anthony 83 n. 29
Lowry, Martin 27 n. 44
Lucan 82, 151, 158–59, 163, 173, 189, 213 n. 75
Lucian and ps.-Lucian 117–18
Lucretius 73, 82, 119, 120, 165, 180 n. 150, 182, 186
lust 36, 83, 109, 115, 157, 165, 166, 203
Luther, Martin 175, 176 n. 127, 177, 178 nn. 137, 138, 201 n. 37
Lydgate, John 217, 235 n. 155
Lyly, John 140
Lyne, Raphael 87 n. 48, 180 n. 150, 184 n. 171, 186 n. 177, 214 n. 79
Lyon 34, 40, 220
Lytle, Guy Fitch 58 n. 44

MacCormack, Sabine 71 n. 93, 176 n. 124, 181 n. 157, 224 n. 119
Mack, Peter 48 n. 3, 62 n. 66, 213 n. 77
Macrinus, Salmonius 56
Macrobius Ambrosius Theodosius 25, 56, 79, 93, 96, 125, 130, 135, 156, 165 n. 78, 172–73, 179 n. 144, 192–93, 220 n. 105, 235, 241 n. 182
   influence 48–49, 97–98, 148, 172, 225, 248
Maecenas, C. 52, 55, 60–64
Maevius 52
magic *see* witchcraft
magician, Virgil as 55–56, 116
Maioragio, Marcantonio *see* Conti, Antonio Maria de'
Malaman, Alessandra 38 n. 81
Mambelli, Giuliano 21 n. 18, 22 n. 23, 24 n. 28, 29 n. 51
Mancinelli, Antonio xii, 38 n. 81, 42, 51 n. 15, 52 n. 19, 53 n. 22, 56 n. 38, 57, 58, 62 n. 66, 65, 66 n. 79, 67, 68–69, 72, 73, 74, 77–78
Mandelbaum, Allen 142 n. 189
Manilius, Marcus 78
Mantua 51, 58, 65, 119
Mantuanus, Baptista Spagnuoli 10, 40 n. 84, 62, 67, 213 n. 75
manuscripts 19, 160
   classified by script 16–17, 38 n. 81
   of texts not available in Middle Ages 32, 41, 48, 78, 116–17, 118, 121 n. 83, 126–27, 209, 216, 224–25, 226, 248
   of Virgil 16–18, 33, 38 n. 81, 39, 42, 86
Manuzio, Paulo 27–29, 32, 52 n. 19, 65 n. 74, 114, 155, 204, 213

Maranta, Bartolomeo 96, 132
Maresca, Thomas E. 151 n. 20
marginalia 3, 7, 20 n. 12, 36, 179 n. 144, 183, 210, 247
Marinelli, Peter 223 n. 118
Marlowe, Christopher 10, 113, 223, 231 n. 141
Marot, Clément 56
marriage *see* love, as epic subject
Marshall, Peter K. 32 n. 64, 33 n. 65
Martial 48, 61–64, 86, 104, 109 n. 39, 223 n. 116
Martín, Adrienne L. 112 n. 51
Martin, Henri-Jean 24 n. 29
Martindale, Charles 3 n. 6
Martini, Giuseppe Sergio 20 n. 14, 41 n. 87
Martyr, Peter *see* Vermigli, Pietro Martire
Mary, the Virgin 231
Matsuda, Takami 175 n. 123
matter *see under* underworld
Mathieu-Castellani, Gisèle 250 n. 7
May, Steven W. 23 n. 27
Mazzola, Elizabeth 175 n. 122
McKenzie, D. F. 24 n. 29
McKitterick, David 30 n. 57
McLaughlin, Martin L. 43, 97 n. 80, 104 n. 18, 188 n. 183
McPherson, David C. 25 n. 37
McRae, Andrew 84 n. 33
Medea 232
Medici (dynasty and family members) 15, 17, 32, 40
medicine *see* body, human
medieval interpretations 31, 36, 41, 55–56, 60, 90, 150, 152, 156, 157–63, 162 n. 64, 164, 172, 176, 213 n. 75, 216, 217, 222, 227, 235, 237, 241, 248
medieval romance *see* romance (medieval)
Meerhoff, Kees 119 n. 79
Mercury 39
Meres, Francis 53
Melanchthon, Philip 26, 32, 35, 111 n. 47, 161, 183, 189, 205, 208, 213–14, 215
Merula, Giorgio 235 n. 155
metempsychosis *see* reincarnation
meter *see under* Virgil, critical reputation
Micheloctius, Nicolaus 17
Milan 49
Mills, Jerry Leath 209 n. 60
Milo 219
Milton, John 10, 104, 185, 187, 210
Minnis, A. J. 3 n. 5, 209 n. 65
Minturno, Antonio Sebastiano 94, 95–96, 103, 192
Mirandula, Octavianus 183–84
Mirror for Magistrates 164–65
Miskimin, Alice S. 26 n. 39
mock-epic 89

modernity 8, 17, 42–43, 127–28, 130 n. 133, 187, 194–96, 199, 228–32, 248–50; *see also* Renaissance, The: characteristics of
Modicius, Gulielmus 70 n. 90
Moffet, Thomas 85, 89
Molinari, Carla 193 n. 11
Momigliano, Arnaldo 2
money *see* gold
Monferran, Jean-Charles 141 n. 185
Montaigne, Michel de 25, 108, 146, 240
Montrose, Louis 171 n. 107
Mortet, Charles 21 n. 21
Moss, Ann 22, 44 n. 93, 205 nn. 51, 52
Mountford, J. F. 81 n. 22, 125 n. 106
Mueller, Martin 194 n. 12
Mulcaster, Richard 214–15
Muret, Marc-Antoine 154
Murgia, C. E 198 n. 24
Murrin, Michael 35 n. 72, 79 n. 9, 81 n. 22, 148 n. 12, 166, 167 n. 85, 168 n. 88, 218 n. 98, 229 n. 132
Musaeus 80 n. 17
Musicò, Livia Castano 20 n. 12

Naevius 121
Nagy, Gregory 57 n. 43, 209 n. 64
Naples 55 n. 32, 106, 117
Nascimbaenius, Nascimbaenus 161, 220 n. 108
Nashe, Thomas 61, 67 n. 82, 139
Nature *see under* Virgil, critical reputation
Naumann, Heinrich 49 n. 8
necromancy *see* witchcraft
Nero 121
Netherlands *see* printed editions of Virgil: countries where produced
Neuse, Richard T. 88 n. 50
New World 226
Nichols, Fred J. 70 n. 91
Nicole, Pierre 141 n. 185
Nisbet, R. G. M. 81 n. 20
Nitchie, Elizabeth 23 n. 27, 118 n. 73
Nitzsche, Jane Chance 158 n. 44, 172 n. 112
Nohrnberg, James 170 n. 101, 181 n. 156, 220 n. 105
Nolhac, Pierre de 25 n. 34
Norwich commentator 176
Nuremberg 68

Oates, J. C. T. 26 n. 41
obscenity *see Appendix virgiliana: Priapea*; Index of Prohibited Books; *and* Virgil, critical reputation: praised for chaste diction
O'Connell, Michael 59 n. 50
Octavia 53
Octavius Avitus, Q. 125

Odyssey 134, 146, 217
  allegorical interpretation 37, 79, 126, 147–49, 151, 191, 207, 219–20, 249
  characters, episodes, places
    Calypso 148, 149
    Circe 148, 149
    Cyclops 217
    Helen 232 n. 142
    Ithaca 148–49, 150
    Odysseus 148, 208, 209, 217
    test of the bow 150, 217
    underworld 150, 154, 158, 159
oral formulaic style 130
ordo 206–07
Orgel, Stephen 58 n. 44
Orosius, Paulus 235 n. 155
Orpheus 80 n. 17, 152
Orsinus, Fulvius 26 n. 42
orthography *see under* Latin language
Otis, Brooks 232 n. 145
Otto of Freising 235 n. 155
Ovid 21–23, 68, 86 n. 42, 87, 88, 104, 109, 122, 126 n. 110, 139, 170 n. 103, 184, 213 n. 75, 215, 233, 234–35, 236
  Metamorphoses 78 n. 6, 129, 170 n. 103, 178, 179 n. 144, 180, 181 n. 157, 184–85, 186, 214, 234 n. 151, 240
Oxford 23 n. 27, 30, 215 n. 85

Pace, Richard 39 n. 83
Padoan, Giorgio 160 n. 53
pagan ritual, ethics *see under* religion
paleography *see* manuscripts: classified by script
Palingenius Stellatus, Marcellus 167 n. 87
pantheism 175
Panzer, Georg Wolfgang 41 n. 87
paraphrase 29, 206–7, 213
paratexts 7, 24, 247
Paris (city) 29, 35, 40, 42
Paris (Trojan prince) 147
Parker, Deborah 35 n. 72
Parker, Patricia 147 n. 6, 171 n. 107
Parotti, Phillip Elliott 227 n. 128
Parrasio, Aulo Giano 94
Parry, Graham 58 n. 44
Pascal, Blaise 77
Pasquier, Bernadette 2 n. 4
pastoral *see Eclogues*
Patterson, Annabel M. 66 n. 75, 77 n. 1
patristic interpretation 175 n. 121, 176 n. 124, 182, 235; *see also* Augustine, St.; Jerome, St.; *and* Lactantius
patronage 50–66, 113–14, 187–90; *see also* Augustus: as patron *and* Este
Paulinus, Fabius 96

Paul, St. 72, 176
Pavlock, Barbara 111 n. 48, 229 n. 133, 232 nn. 144, 146
Pedemonte, Francesco Filippi 94
Penkethman, John 47 n. 1, 87 n. 47, 167 n. 87
Pellegrino, Camillo 208
Pelletier, Jacques 127 n. 117, 130, 132
Periochae vaticanae 116
Perithous 152
Perosa, Alessandro 20 n. 12
Persius 86, 213 n. 75
Pertusi, Agostino 127 n. 114
pessimistic readings 2, 64–66, 210–12; *see also* Aeneas: unfavorable judgments
Petit, Aimé 233 n. 148
Petrarch, Francesco 4, 9, 80 n. 19, 88, 121, 123, 136, 147, 167, 170, 203, 208, 216, 220 n. 105, 224–27, 235 n. 155, 249
  Africa 235
  commentaries used by 25
  competitiveness 185–86, 226
  his copy of Virgil 25, 179 n. 144, 225
  critical sometimes of Aeneas 6, 161, 211–12
  as twelve-book reader 220 n. 107, 225–27
Peŷ, Alexandre 238 n. 168
Pfeiffer, Rudolf 28 n. 46, 40 n. 85
Phaer, Thomas 50 n. 11, 81, 86 n. 41
Philargyrius I 116 n. 64
Philip II, King (of Spain) 190, 238
Philippi, battle of 51
philosophy *see* Epicureanism, Platonism, Stoicism, *and under* Virgil, biography
physici and *res physica* 81, 92, 165; *see also* science
Pierius Valerianus *see* Valeriano, Pierio
pietas 111, 113, 196–200, 206, 207, 236
Pigman, G. W., III 43 n. 92, 186, 188 n. 183
Pilato, Leonzio 127
Pilohette 25 n. 37
Pindar 68
pity *see pietas*
Plant, Marjorie 30 n. 60
Planudean Appendix 235 n. 155
Plato, Platonism 28, 35, 73, 80, 117, 117 n. 70, 118, 152, 156, 172–74, 179–80, 181, 182–83, 208, 219, 229
Plautus 119, 120, 123
Pléiade, the 140–41
Pliny the Younger 108
Plotia Hieria 109
Plotinus 147
Plouton/Ploutos 168–69
Plutarch and ps.-Plutarch 126, 139, 220 n. 105
Pluto 168–69
Poggio *see* Bracciolini, Poggio
Polenton, Sicco 54 n. 28, 95, 116 n. 64

political interpretations *see* Augustus *and* history, knowledge of Roman
Pollard, A. W. 21 n. 18
Pollard, Graham 30 n. 60
Pollio, Asinius 52, 57, 71–72, 109, 113
Poliziano, Angelo 15–20, 32, 33 n. 67, 38 n. 81, 38–40, 41–43, 48, 68, 84, 106, 109, 132, 201, 212, 226
Polyclitus, Bed of 107
Pompey 173
Pomponius Atticus, Titus 225
Pontano, Giovanni 84, 95, 96, 141 n. 185, 193 n. 10
Pontanus, Jacobus 25, 37, 47 n. 1, 52 n. 20, 65 n. 74, 73 n. 103, 96 nn. 74, 77, 108, 125 n. 103, 130 n. 129, 154 n. 30, 161 n. 57, 183, 184, 199, 208, 249 n. 5
Popes, as patrons of scholarship 27, 40; *see also* Vatican
pornography *see Appendix virgiliana: Priapea*; Index of Prohibited Books; *and* Virgil, critical reputation: praised for chaste diction
Portugal *see* printed editions of Virgil: countries where produced
Portus, Aemilius 220 n. 105
Powell, Stephen D. 223 n. 118
Porphyry 183
praise 56–60, 65–66, 161, 187–90, 202, 207–12, 219–20
Pratensis, Jacobus 17
Praxiteles 117
Prescott, Anne Lake 88 n. 51
pride 164, 171, 207
printed editions of Virgil xii, 83, 239
    compared with other classics 21–23
    cost 19, 25, 27–28, 37, 50, 215
    countries where produced 9, 21–23, 27–30, 35, 223
    format and typography 23, 24, 25, 29, 37, 86 nn. 40, 41
    markets for 20–24, 27–28, 29–30, 37
    ownership 25–26, 30–31
    proofreading 4–5
    reprints 23, 25, 29, 31, 36, 40, 41–42, 63 n. 68, 68, 84–85, 91, 239, 247
    statistics 10, 20–25
printers, Renaissance
    Allde, J. (London) 122 n. 91
    Allott, Robert (London) 62 n. 64
    Alvisius, Johannes (Venice) 101 n. 1
    Berthelet, Thomas (London) 95 n. 70
    Bevilaqua de Gabis/Papiensis/Ticinensis, Simone (Venice, Vicenza) 64 n. 69, 78 n. 6, 125 n. 105, 168 n. 92, 197 n. 22
    Bishop, George (London) 29 n. 50

Brome, Henry (London) 62 n. 64
Bynneman, Henry (London) 27 n. 43
Choris Cremonensis, Bernardinus de (Venice) 117 n. 70
Creede, Thomas (London) 140 n. 179
Denham, Henry (London) 61 n. 59, 124 n. 101, 162 n. 63
de Worde, Wynander (London) 27 n. 43
Doesborcke, Iohan (Antwerp) 56 n. 33
Fabritius, G. (Cologne) 209 n. 60
Field, Richard (London) 111 n. 47, 203 n. 42
Froschauer, Christoph (Zurich) 183 n. 165, 246
Giunta da Firenze, Luca Antonio, Heirs of (Venice) xii et passim
Grüniger, Joannes (Strasbourg) 244
Gryphius, Sebastianus (Lyon) 23, 104 n. 15, 122 n. 88
Jaggard, William (London) 60 n. 58
Jenson, Nicholas (Venice) 176 n. 125
How, William (London) 82 n. 25
Kerver, Thielman (Paris) 55 n. 29
Kyngston, Felix (London) 29 n. 51
Kyngston, John (London) 26 n. 39
Manuzio, Aldo (Venice) 17 n. 5, 23, 27, 34, 109 n. 38
Middleton, Henry (London) 52 n. 19, 86 n. 45, 114 n. 59, 156 n. 35, 162 n. 63
Moseley, Humphrey (London) 141 n. 185
Newbery, Radulph (London) 29 n. 50, 167 n. 87
Nivellius, Sebastianus (Paris) 123 n. 92, 216 n. 89
Okes, Nicholas (London) 102 n. 7
Orwin, Thomas, Widow of (London) 28, 29 n. 48
Nutius, Martinus, Heirs of (Antwerp) 184 n. 170
Pannartz, Arnold (Rome) 21
Pates, John (Leiden) 86 n. 41
Petrus, Henrichus (Basel) 203 n. 42
Pincius Mantuanus, Philippus (Venice) 155 n. 33, 198 n. 28
Praetorius, J. (Augsburg) 47 n. 1, 96 n. 74, 108 n. 33, 154 n. 30, 199 n. 30
Purslowe, George (London) 47 n. 1, 87 n. 47, 167 n. 87
Richardus de Luero, Simon (Venice) 117 n. 70
Roigny, Johannes (Paris) 117 n. 72
Rouilius, G. (Lyon) 221 n. 110
Rusconibus, Georgius de (Venice) 101 n. 2, 215 n. 83
Seres, Willyam (London) 214 n. 80
Sessa, Giovambatista Marchio (Venice) 119 n. 77, 160 n. 54
Soardus de Saviliano, Lazarus (Venice) 104 n. 15
Sweynheym, Conrad (Rome) 21
Tornaesius, Joannes (Paris) 102 n. 3, 184 n. 169
Torrentinus, Laurentius (Florence) 55 n. 29
Tortis, Baptista de (Venice) 104 n. 15

printers, Renaissance (cont.)
    Valgrisi, Vincenzo (Venice) 93 n. 62
    Vascosanus, Michaël (Paris) 117 n. 72
    Veale, Abraham (London) 82 n. 25, 122 n. 91
    Vincentius, Antonius (Lyon) 67 n. 82, 95 n. 71, 111 n. 45, 174 n. 119, 212 n. 73
    see also Badius Ascensius, Jodocus (Paris); Estienne, Henri (Paris); Estienne, Robert (Paris); and Manuzio, Paolo (Venice, Rome)
Priscian 122 n. 91, 235 n. 155
Probus, Marcus Valerius 32, 42, 52, 56, 62 n. 66, 65, 77–78
Propertius Aurelius, Sextus 122, 125, 225
prophecy
    dynastic 59, 187–90, 236
    messianic 71–72, 75, 224
Prudentius 167
Pucci, Joseph 204 n. 47
pudor, "modesty" 234, 242
Pugh, Syrithe 87 n. 48
purgatory 173–78
Putnam, Michael C. J. xiii, 200 n. 31, 239 n. 173
Puttenham, George 53, 56, 74 n. 108, 75 n. 115, 230
Pythagoras 166–67, 179 n. 143, 184, 189, 214

Quint, David 60 n. 55, 98 n. 81, 168 n. 89, 200 n. 31
Quintilian, M. Fabius 4, 48, 101 n. 2, 104, 121, 125–26, 129, 131, 134 n. 156, 135 n. 158, 139, 140, 185, 213 n. 75, 215, 216
Quitslund, Jon A. 35 n. 72, 175 n. 121, 180 n. 148, 181 n. 156

Rabb, Theodore K. 246
Rabelais, François 156
Rabuse, Georg 149 n. 16
Raimondi, Ezio 135 n. 158, 136 n. 163, 138 n. 171
raison d'état 194
Ramos, María José Vega 141 n. 185
Ramus, Peter 27 n. 42, 29, 54, 62 n. 66, 68–69, 119, 140, 188
Rand, Edward Kennard 149 n. 16
Rathborne, Isabel E. 151 n. 21
Raya, Gino 84 n. 37
Read, David 168 n. 90
reading, types of 203–8, 212–16
reception history, approaches to 1–10, 40–41, 124, 250–51
Redgrave, G. R. 21 n. 18
Reformation see religion: Catholic and Protestant
Regius, Raphael 78 n. 6, 134 n. 156
Regoli, Sebastiano 208
reincarnation 173, 176, 178–85, 186–87, 188–90, 214

religion
    early Roman, knowledge of 19, 33, 79, 94, 249
    pagan and Christian 41, 71–72, 73, 74, 75, 109 n. 38, 128, 164, 165, 175–85, 186–87, 189, 194–203, 211–12, 219, 223–24, 230, 248
    Catholic and Protestant 27–30, 175–78, 208
Renaissance, The
    characteristics of 8, 32, 37, 41, 67, 103, 116–17, 119, 126 n. 111, 152, 185, 216–17, 224–27, 248–50
    as period term v, 8, 119, 224
Renouard, Philippe 213 n. 75
Republic, fall of Roman 147
resurrection 181–85, 186–87, 190
revenge 194, 198–99, 200, 201
Reynolds, L. D. 16 n. 3, 225 n. 121
rhetoric see style
Rho, Antonia da 49
Rhu, Lawrence F. 136 n. 161
Richthofen, Erich von 149 n. 16
Rigolot, François 140 n. 180
ritual see religion: early Roman; and witchcraft
Rivers, George 235 n. 155
Roberts, Julian 30 n. 55
Robin, Diana 201 n. 36
Robinson, Lillian S. 227 n. 128
Roche, Thomas P., Jr. 196 n. 17, 227 n. 126, 229 n. 131
Roman d'Eeneas (c. 1160) 233–39, 248
Roman history and religion see history, knowledge of Roman; and religion: early Roman, knowledge of
romance (genre) 194, 229, 230–31, 236, 247
romance (medieval) 233–39
    Middle English 238–39
Romano, Antonino 62 n. 66, 69 n. 88
Rome (city), 17, 20, 22, 23, 27, 39, 40 n. 84
Ronsard, Pierre de 9, 140–41, 217 n. 91, 221–22
    Franciade characters and episodes
        Clymene and Hyante 231–32
        Francus 231–32
        parade of French kings 189
        prefaces 107, 222
Ross, Charles S. 168 n. 88, 239 n. 173
Ross, David O. 79 n. 9
Rossi, Niccolò see Erythraeus, Nicolaus
Rota Virgilii see Wheel of Virgil
Rouse, R. H. 32 n. 64, 209 n. 63
Rubinstein, Alice Levine 127 n. 116, 132 n. 147
Rucellai, Giovanni 85
Rufus, Mutianus 68
Ruscelli, Girolamo 92–93
Ruskin, John 248

Sabbadini, Remigio 32 n. 64, 225 n. 121
Saccone, Eduardo 111 n. 48
Sach, Hans 235 n. 155
Sackville, Sir Thomas 164
sacrifice, human 5, 158–61, 166, 194, 211
Saint-Gelais, Mellin de 56
Sallust 213 n. 75
Saloninus, Asinius 71
Salutati, Coluccio 118, 122 n. 89, 141 n. 184, 147, 151–52, 159, 160 n. 54, 161, 167, 172 n. 114, 208, 216 n. 89
Salverda de Grave, J. J. 233 n. 148, 238 n. 168
Salviati, Lionardo 203
Samuel (biblical prophet) 162
Sandys, George 181 n. 157, 184
Saul (biblical king) 162
Sayles, R. T. D. 26 n. 41
Scaglione, Aldo 19 n. 11
Scala, Bartolomeo della 17 n. 5, 43–44, 84
Scaliger, Joseph 22 n. 23, 48, 63 n. 68, 130
Scaliger, Julius Caesar 47, 67 n. 82, 69–70, 73 n. 104, 95, 99–100, 100 n. 87, 111, 125 n. 103, 129–33, 174, 208, 212 n. 73, 239
Schiebe, Marianne Wifstrand 62 n. 66, 69 n. 88
Schiller, Friedrich 140
Schlunk, Robin R. 79 n. 9, 148 n. 12
Schmidt, Paul Gerhard 239 n. 174
Schultz, J. T. 81 n. 22, 125 n. 106
Schwarz, Kathryn 227 n. 128
science 78–82, 126, 152, 155, 165, 166, 168–69, 172–73, 250; *see also* astronomy and astrology; *and* cosmology, cosmography
Scipio, Dream of 172
Scodel, Joshua 83 n. 29
Scopus 205, 214
Scott, A. B. 209 n. 65
Sedulius 167
Seem, Lauren Scancarelli 195 n. 14, 203 n. 43
seminal reasons (*logoi spermatakoi*) 181 n. 156
Seneca (the Younger) 17, 104 n. 17, 121, 138, 213 n. 75, 223 n. 116
sequels to the *Aeneid* 239, 247
Servius Danielis (Servius auctus) 22 n. 23, 111 n. 44
Servius Honoratus, Marius 49, 49 n. 8, 115–16, 179, 210
  authority and influence 25, 26 n. 42, 28 n. 47, 29, 31–33, 36, 41, 48, 56 n. 38, 59, 65, 77–78, 115, 118, 148, 150, 151, 154–55, 156, 165, 167, 197–99, 216, 223–24, 225, 237, 240, 247, 248, 250
  characteristics of his commentary 19, 33, 66, 80–81, 90, 153, 167, 188–90, 204, 216 n. 88
  and Christianity 41, 197–98, 223–24

  errors in 26 n. 42, 33
  printed editions xii, 31–33, 42, 198
  on *Aen.* 57, 59, 79, 80–81, 86, 111 n. 43, 115, 146 nn. 1, 3, 154–55, 156, 158–59, 165–67, 168, 169 n. 99, 170, 173, 179 n. 145, 181, 188–90, 192 n. 4, 197–99, 219, 220 n. 105, 232 n. 145, 235, 250
  on *Ecl.* 19, 51 n. 15, 51–53, 54 n. 27, 56, 57, 58, 62 n. 66, 65–66, 67, 69, 71, 72–74, 75–76, 107 n. 28, 109 n. 39, 113–15, 125 n. 104
  on *Geo.* 51–53, 67 n. 82, 77–78, 179 n. 145
Sessions, W. A. 83 n. 29, 238 n. 169
sex *see Aeneid*: sex scenes; *Eclogues*: origin of pastoral; homosexuality; *and* Virgil, biography: sex life
Shaw, David 30 n. 55
Shakespeare, William 10, 102, 139, 140
  episodes, favorite in Virgil 146
  hell and purgatory, descriptions of 178
  reincarnation in 179
  characters
    Caliban 223
    Claudio 178
    Hamlet 178, 182
    Hotspur 194 n. 12
    Shylock 179
Shepard, Alan 223 n. 118
Shepherd, Simon 128
Shuger, Debora 106 n. 22
Sibyl *see* Cumae, Cumaean sibyl
Sidney, Mary, Countess of Pembroke 53
Sidney, Sir Philip 53, 63, 139, 164
  Arcadia 196
  on *Aen.* 59, 100, 111, 208, 212
  on *Ecl.* 64–65, 66, 74
silkworms 85
Silvestris, Bernardus 36, 149 n. 16, 157–58, 159–61, 179 n. 144, 216, 237
similes 128–29, 136, 139, 221, 239, 243
Simonsuuri, Kirsti 138 n. 175
Singleton, C. S. 153
Siro 72, 80
Skelton, John 157
skepticism *see under* underworld
Skutsch, Otto 121 n. 85
Smith, G. Gregory xii
Snare, Gerald 19 n. 10, 103 n. 13, 216 n. 88, 250 n. 6
Socrates 117–18, 148; *see also* Plato, Platonism
Solerti, Angelo 25 n. 35
Sophocles 10, 57
Sowerby, Robin 132 n. 148
Spain *see* printed editions of Virgil: countries where produced
Spargo, John Webster 55 n. 32, 72 n. 96, 116 n. 66

Spencer, T. J. B. 132 n. 149
Spenser, Edmund 10, 35 n. 72, 48, 49 n. 9, 139, 185–88, 209, 222
  allusions to *Ecl.* 11 ("Alexis") 113
  compared with Ennius and Chaucer 124
  his copy of Virgil 26, 30–31
  and *Geo.* 85–93
  patronage 61–64, 190
  three styles 62–63, 87, 93
  Colin Clouts Come Home Again 171 n. 106
  Fowre Hymnes 147
  FQ 7, 9, 62, 82, 93, 124, 185, 194, 220 n. 105, 230, 234 n. 151, 250
    source of underworld examples 9, 150–51
  Muiopotmos 89, 196
  Shepheardes Calender 62–63, 64, 82, 85, 87, 93, 113 n. 55, 117
  Virgils Gnat 26, 63, 89
  characters and episodes in *FQ*
    Acrasia 235
    arrow simile (*FQ* 2.11.18) 221
    Amavia 235
    Archimago 150
    Arthur 195–96
    Ate 150, 171 n. 110
    Belphoebe 111, 171, 228
    Bower of Bliss 150, 157, 171
    Britomart 190, 221, 228, 229, 237, 247
    Busirane 150
    Calidore 150
    Corydon 113 n. 55
    Cymochles 163
    dedicatory sonnets 7, 63–64
    Despair 150
    Duessa 150, 235
    Florimell 150
    Forest of Error 150
    Garden of Adonis 150, 180–87
    Gulfe of Greedinesse 171
    House of Care 221
    House of Pride 150, 171
    Malengin 150, 171 n. 110
    Mammon 150, 168–69, 170
    Merlin's Cave 150, 162, 190
    Morpheus 150
    Night 150
    Orgoglio 150
    Pastorella 150
    Phaedria 235
    Philotime 169
    proem (Book 1) 85–87, 93
    Pyrochles 195–96
    Seven Deadly Sins 171, 201–2
    Timias 111
    Venus 186
  Wrath 201–2
Speroni, Sperone 133–36, 138, 141, 203
Stahel, Thomas H. 35 n. 74, 94 n. 66, 160 n. 54
Stanyhurst, Richard 81, 86 n. 41, 123
Starr, Raymond J. 62 n. 66, 69 n. 88, 209 n. 62
Statius 48, 111 n. 48, 234 n. 151, 238
Stierle, Karlheinz 205 n. 50
Stillman, Robert E. 66 n. 78
Stirling, Brents 180 n. 150
Stok, Fabio 54, 116 nn. 67, 68
Stoicism 80–81, 115, 152, 181, 197
Storer, Walter Henry 140 n. 180
Strier, Richard 5
Stuart, Duane Reed 54 n. 28, 55 n. 29
style 56
  as character 103–6, 108, 117, 130
  importance of 19, 37, 48, 49, 73–76, 104 n. 18, 141–42, 192–93, 205, 213, 215, 216, 230, 248–51
  see also Wheel of Virgil *and under Aeneid*; *Eclogues*; *Georgics*; *and* Virgil, critical reputation
Suerbaum, Werner 2 n. 4
Suetonius Tranquillus, C. 55 n. 29
Sulpicius Apollinaris, C. 53
Summers, Claude J. 109 n. 40
Supplementum, Libri XII Aeneidos see Vegio, Maffeo
Sutri 16
Suzuki, Mihoko 229 n. 133, 232 n. 142
Switzerland 36
syncretism 81 n. 20, 149; *see also* Grammaticus, characteristics of; *and* religion: pagan and Christian
syphillis 221

Tacitus 56, 216
Talon, Omer 141 n. 185
Tanner, Mary 223 n. 117, 238 n. 169
Tansillo, Luigi 84
Tarrant, R. J. 48 n. 2
Tasso, Torquato 229 n. 132, 250
  his copy of Virgil 25, 240
  as literary critic 59, 60 n. 54, 94 n. 64, 119 n. 76, 132, 134–39, 141 n. 185, 142, 164, 193–94, 196, 199, 208, 220 n. 105, 221–22, 230, 232–33, 238
  and patrons 59, 231
  quotations from *Aen.*, distribution of 221
  Rinaldo 232 n. 143
  Gerusalemme liberata characters and episodes
    Aletto 221
    Altamoro 221
    Argante 111, 195, 220

Armida 231
catalogue of Egyptian armies 221
Clorinda 111, 221, 228
Erminia 228
Goffredo 221
Lesbino 112–13
Rinaldo 59, 193, 231
shield of Rinaldo 59 n. 52, 221
Solimano 112, 193–94, 221
Tancredi 195, 228
Terence 21, 23 n. 27, 49, 66, 119, 184, 213 n. 75, 215
Tertullian 235 n. 155
Tesauro, Alessandro 85
Tessitore, M. Vittoria 6 n. 12, 234 n. 154
textual criticism in Renaissance 4–5, 16–18, 19, 20, 106, 121, 123, 124, 224–25
  of Virgil 27, 33, 37–40, 42, 86, 92, 101, 109, 247
Theocritus 26 n. 42, 57, 65, 66–69, 71 n. 92, 72, 75, 89–90, 124–25, 204–05
Theodontius 152
Theseus 152, 164, 170
Thomas, Richard F. 48 n. 2, 210
Thompson, David 149 n. 16
Thornton, Agathe 200 n. 32
Thornton, Bruce 83 n. 29
Thucydides 66
Thynne, William 26 n. 39
Tiberianus 167
Timaeus 173
Timaeus of Tauromenium 235 n. 155
Tomalin, Margaret 227 n. 128
Tordi, Andrea 210
Torrentinus, Hermannus 27 n. 43, 31
tragedy 57, 192, 195, 228, 230, 232, 234
translatio imperii 223
translations, translators 68, 122, 162, 173 n. 117, 178, 184, 209, 214, 237, 239, 249 n. 5
  of Homer 15, 68, 127, 132, 217, 220 n. 105
  of Virgil 24, 63, 81, 86 n. 41, 87 n. 47, 123, 146, 167 n. 87, 176–77
Triaud, Annie 236 nn. 162, 163
Tuchman, Barbara 9
Tudeau-Clayton, Margaret 23 n. 27, 25 n. 37, 82 n. 26, 103 n. 13, 185 n. 173, 239 n. 173
Tunison, J. S. 55 n. 32
Turberville, George 235 n. 155
Tusser, Thomas 84
Tuve, Rosemond 5
Twyne, Thomas 50 n. 11, 86 n. 41, 239, 249 n. 5
Tylus, Jane 83 n. 29
typography *see under* printed editions of Virgil

underworld 6–7, 9, 146, 212, 250
  as body or matter 147, 152, 158, 163, 172–73, 181–83, 186–87, 200, 229
  as climax and epitome 11, 36, 149–53, 169, 191, 203, 220
  as damnation 154, 163, 164, 165–66, 176
  as device to celebrate patrons 187–90
  as greed 166–70, 171
  as habit 145, 157, 158, 163, 170–72
  as moral example 158, 163–66, 208
  as royal court 171
  as setting for choice, temptation 166–68
  descent
    skepticism about physical 151–52, 153–63, 159–62, 163, 170, 190
    types of 145, 152, 157–58, 159–61, 163, 170, 172, 189–90
    undertaken in dream 153–57, 159, 161–62
    for Cerberus, Gates of Sleep, golden bough, etc., *see under Aeneid*
Upson, Hollis Ritchie 49 n. 8
usury 165

Valeriano, Pierio xii, 8, 31 n. 62, 32, 37–40, 41, 42, 86–87, 106, 111 n. 43
Valerius Maximus 123, 213 n. 75
Valla, Lorenzo 55 n. 29, 213 n. 75, 239
Van Doren, Mark 142 n. 189
Van Dorsten, J. A. 29 n. 52
Varchi, Benedetto 137 n. 169
Varius Rufus 92, 101, 109
Varro, Marcus Terentius 22 n. 23, 39, 183, 235 n. 155
Varus, Alfenus 72 n. 99
Varus, P. Quinctilius 72
Vasari, Giorgio 119
Vatican 16–18, 38 n. 81, 44
Vega, Gabriel Lobo Lasso de la 235 n. 155
Vega, Lope de 88
Vegio, Maffeo xii, 11, 239–50
Van Veldeke, Heinrich 237
Vélez-Sainz, Julio 58 n. 44
Velleius Paterculus 47
Veneratio (daughter of Pluto) 169
Venice 25, 27, 30, 37, 50, 220
Venier, Matteo 22 n. 22, 33 n. 71, 38 n. 81
Venutus, Filippus 220 n. 108
Vermigli, Pietro Martire 162 n. 63, 178 nn. 137, 138, 139, 201 n. 37
Verrier, Frédérique 227 n. 128
Verulanus, Sulpitius 220 n. 108
Vettori, Piero 136 n. 163
Vickers, Brian 57 n. 43, 208 n. 58
Vida, Marco Girolamo 85, 89, 98–99, 106–7, 120, 128, 132, 137, 141 n. 185, 221

Virgil
  biography
    ancient sources 47–50, 54–55
    appearance, physical 114
    birth stories 15, 17
    counselor to princes 50, 52, 54–56
    death 53, 101–02, 105, 133, 192, 249
    education, erudition 49, 55, 56, 72–73, 78–82, 94, 95–96, 99, 137 n. 169, 141 n. 183, 150
    epitaph 87
    name, meaning of 15, 17
    Parthenias, "the virgin" 15, 106, 109, 115, 117, 118, 124, 130, 229
    patrons 50–66
    philosophy, student of 72–73, 78–81, 152, 213
    as proto-Catholic 173–78
    as proto-Christian 71–72, 75, 128, 149, 152, 166, 171, 181–85
    provincial origins and speech 50–51, 115, 119
    sex life 106–18; *see also* Parthenias, "the virgin"
    vernacular legends 55–56, 72, 116
    wealth, lands 50–53, 89, 114
  critical reputation
    ancient sources 47–50
    compared with Homer 29, 40, 57, 80 n. 17, 96–97, 107, 120, 124–41, 189, 194, 203, 204, 207, 213, 249
    compared with other poets 26 n. 42, 52, 66–69, 67, 67 n. 82, 75, 80 n. 17, 82, 119–25, 126, 137 n. 169, 141 n. 183, 158–59, 163, 203, 206
    criticized 203
      as flatterer 57–58, 59–60, 65, 72
      as mere imitator 124–25, 133, 139–41
      as mere technician 132–34, 138–42, 248
    praised
      as apt for all ages 95, 214–15, 219
      as laborious reviser 79, 101–3, 104–06, 122, 123, 124, 125–26, 129–33, 139–40, 192, 249
      as master of all styles 89–99
      as model imitator 26 n. 42, 67, 99–100, 124–25, 127–28
      as perfector of Latin language 119–24
      as second Nature 96–100, 101, 127–28, 129
      as supreme stylist 79, 137, 138–42, 248–51
      for ambiguity/mystery 137–38
      for brevity 67, 93, 94, 96, 97, 98, 107, 129–38, 141, 192, 249 n. 4
      for chaste diction 103–08, 116, 117, 123, 124, 125 n. 104, 129–32, 134, 229
      for *copia* 93, 94, 96, 98, 135
      for decorum 74–75, 91, 98, 107, 124, 128–29, 131
      for elegance/selectivity 96, 131, 192–93
      for gravity/magnificence 124, 136–37, 138, 139
      for plain diction 94, 107–8, 133
      for refinement, polish 53, 101–8, 122–42
      for variety 75–76, 77–100, 105–06, 134, 230
      for metrical virtuosity/onomatopoeia 95, 137, 141–42, 248
      testimonials, panegyrics 47, 99, 131
virginity 228–30, 232, 242; *see also* Virgil, biography: *Parthenias*
Virues, Cristóbal de 235 n. 155
vitae *see* Virgil, biography: ancient sources
Vives, Juan Luis 65, 67 n. 82, 96, 114–15, 129, 132, 134, 137 n. 169, 156 n. 38
Volumnia Cytheris 51
Vredeveld, Harry 68 n. 83
Vulcacius Sedigitus 121

Wallace, Andrew 82 n. 26
Walsingham, Sir Francis 63–64
war, as epic subject 8, 63, 89, 92, 134, 146, 147, 191, 218, 220, 221
  see also civil wars (Roman)
Warner, J. Christopher 226 n. 124, 229 n. 133, 235 n. 156
Watkins, John 6 n. 12, 175 n. 120, 176 n. 129, 218 n. 94, 229 n. 133, 234 n. 154, 235 n. 158, 241 nn. 179, 182
Webbe, William 67 n. 82, 74 n. 108, 84, 108–9, 117 n. 71, 120 n. 82, 121 n. 83, 123, 125 n. 103, 137 n. 169, 141 n. 185, 208, 220 n. 105
Weinberg, Bernard 78 n. 6, 94, 96 n. 75, 103 n. 12, 128 n. 118, 133, 136 n. 165, 141 n. 182, 209 n. 60
Wengert, Timothy J. 214 n. 78
Wesley, Samuel 102 n. 7
Wheel of Virgil 51, 62–63, 87–91, 93
White, Peter 58 n. 44
Whitman, Walt 15, 191
Wilde, Oscar 100 n. 87, 104
Wilkinson, L. P. 83
Willcock, M. M. 192 n. 6
Willichius, Jodocus 31
Wilson, Harold S. 28 n. 45
Wilson, N. G. 16 n. 3, 225 n. 121

Wilson-Okamura, David Scott 2 n. 3, 54 n. 26, 150 n. 19, 202 n. 39, 217 n. 92, 220 n. 107, 222 n. 113, 223 n. 114, 228 n. 130, 230 n. 134, 236 n. 161, 237 n. 165, 238 n. 167, 239 n. 173
Winterbottom, Michael 126 n. 112
witchcraft 153, 157–63, 166, 170, 189–90, 211, 231–32
Wither, George 62 n. 64
Witt, Ronald G. 103 n. 14, 224 n. 120, 249 n. 3
Wolsey, Thomas 238
Wright, M. R. 200 n. 32

Xenophon 59, 208

Y (letter) 166–67
Yarnall, Judith 147 n. 10
Yates, Frances A. 223 n. 117
Yeats, William Butler 47, 104
Yunck, John A. 233 n. 148

Zabughin, Vladimiro 2, 38 n. 81, 54 nn. 26, 28, 245 n. 190, 248 n. 1
Zenodotus 19 n. 11
Zetzel, James E. G. 52 n. 16
Ziolkowski, Jan M. xiii, 2 n. 1